EDUCATIONAL RESEARCH PRACTICE IN SOUTHERN CONTEXTS

Bringing together a unique collection of 18 insightful and innovative internationally focused articles, *Educational Research Practice in Southern Contexts* offers reflections, case studies, and critically, research methods and processes which decentre, reframe, and reimagine conventional educational research strategies and operationalise the tenets of decolonising theory.

This anthology represents a valuable teaching resource. It provides readers with the chance to read high-quality examples of research that critique current ways of doing research and to reflect on how research methods can contribute to the project of decolonising knowledge production in and about education in, for example, Africa, South Asia, Asia, and Latin America. It grapples with everyday dilemmas and tricky ethical questions about protection, consent, voice, cultural sensitivity, and validation, by engaging with real-world situations and increasing the potential for innovation and new collaborations.

Educational Research Practice in Southern Contexts will be essential reading for anyone teaching educational research methods and will encourage novice and experienced researchers to rethink their research approaches, disentangle the local and global, and challenge those research rituals, codes, and fieldwork practices which are often unproblematically assumed to be universally relevant.

Sharlene Swartz is Head of the Equitable Education and Economies research division at the Human Sciences Research Council, South Africa.

Nidhi Singal is Professor of Disability and Inclusive Education at the Faculty of Education, University of Cambridge, UK.

Madeleine Arnot is Emerita Professor in Sociology of Education in the Faculty of Education at the University of Cambridge, UK.

"Researching research itself – how knowledge is produced, what methodologies are deployed, what research practices are at play – in the context of resurgent and insurgent decolonisation of the 21st century is urgent and very necessary. This well-curated volume does just this very well from diverse vantage points, covering various aspects of ethics, gender, responsibility, reflexivity, spirituality, sovereignty, visuality, polyvocality, and inequality as they impinge on research itself. The field of education is the departure point in the agenda to critique hegemonic knowledge paradigms and articulation of submerged Southern epistemologies".

Sabelo J. Ndlovu-Gatsheni, *Professor/Chair of Epistemologies of the Global South and Vice-Dean of Research in the Africa Multiple Cluster of Excellence, University of Bayreuth, Germany*

"There's much talk now of decolonizing knowledge. What does that mean for education, and specifically for research in education? Sharlene Swartz, Nidhi Singal and Madeleine Arnot have put together a unique and wide-ranging collection, across continents and cultures. This book gives us distinctive perspectives on conceptual debates, hands-on research experience, and a remarkable range of research methods, from statistics to poetry, all considered from Global South positions".

Raewyn Connell, *Professor Emerita, University of Sydney, Australia*

"Many universities are now exploring how to decolonise their curricula. But how can we transform the North-South hierarchies often taken as 'given' within educational research? This book brings together a stimulating collection of methodological and theoretical reflections by educational researchers working in diverse contexts in the Global South. Moving beyond the familiar 'insider-outsider' debates in educational research, these writers engage with the political, cultural and institutional aspects of knowledge construction. This exciting collection will prove invaluable to educational researchers committed to addressing inequalities in cultural values, voice, identities and knowledges".

Anna Robinson-Pant, *Professor/UNESCO Chair in Adult Literacy and Learning for Social Transformation, School of Education and Lifelong Learning, University of East Anglia, UK*

EDUCATIONAL RESEARCH PRACTICE IN SOUTHERN CONTEXTS

Recentring, Reframing and Reimagining Methodological Canons

Edited by Sharlene Swartz, Nidhi Singal and Madeleine Arnot

Foreword by Linda Tuhiwai Smith

Designed cover image: © Getty Images

First published 2024
by Routledge
4 Park Square, Milton Park, Abingdon, Oxon OX14 4RN

and by Routledge
605 Third Avenue, New York, NY 10158

Routledge is an imprint of the Taylor & Francis Group, an informa business

© 2024 selection and editorial matter, Sharlene Swartz, Nidhi Singal and Madeleine Arnot; individual chapters, the contributors

The right of Sharlene Swartz, Nidhi Singal and Madeleine Arnot to be identified as the authors of the editorial material, and of the authors for their individual chapters, has been asserted in accordance with sections 77 and 78 of the Copyright, Designs and Patents Act 1988.

With the exception of the Foreword by Linda Tuhiwai Smith, Chapter 1 and Chapter 17, no part of this book may be reprinted or reproduced or utilised in any form or by any electronic, mechanical, or other means, now known or hereafter invented, including photocopying and recording, or in any information storage or retrieval system, without permission in writing from the publishers.

The Foreword by Linda Tuhiwai Smith, Chapter 1 and Chapter 17 of this book are freely available as a downloadable Open Access PDF at http://www.taylorfrancis.com under a Creative Commons Attribution-Non Commercial-No Derivatives (CC-BY-NC-ND) 4.0 license.

Funding for open access and permissions provided by the by Human Sciences Research Council (HSRC).

Trademark notice: Product or corporate names may be trademarks or registered trademarks, and are used only for identification and explanation without intent to infringe.

British Library Cataloguing-in-Publication Data
A catalogue record for this book is available from the British Library

Library of Congress Cataloging-in-Publication Data
Names: Swartz, Sharlene, editor. | Singal, Nidhi, editor. |
Arnot, Madeleine, editor.
Title: Educational research practice in southern contexts : recentring, reframing and reimagining methodological canons / Edited by Sharlene Swartz,
Nidhi Singal and Madeleine Arnot ; Foreword by Professor Linda Tuhiwai Smith.
Description: Abingdon, Oxon ; New York, NY : Routledge, 2024. |
Includes bibliographical references and index. |
Identifiers: LCCN 2023025812 (print) | LCCN 2023025813 (ebook) |
ISBN 9781032409337 (hardback) | ISBN 9781032409306 (paperback) |
ISBN 9781003355397 (ebook)
Subjects: LCSH: Education--Research--Developing countries. |
Education--Research--Methodology--Developing countries. |
Decolonization--Developing countries. | Multicultural education--Developing countries.
Classification: LCC LB1028.25.D44 E38 2024 (print) |
LCC LB1028.25.D44 (ebook) | DDC 370.7209172/4--dc23/eng/20230804
LC record available at https://lccn.loc.gov/2023025812
LC ebook record available at https://lccn.loc.gov/2023025813

ISBN: 978-1-032-40933-7 (hbk)
ISBN: 978-1-032-40930-6 (pbk)
ISBN: 978-1-003-35539-7 (ebk)

DOI: 10.4324/9781003355397

Typeset in ITC Galliard Pro
by KnowledgeWorks Global Ltd.

CONTENTS

List of Figures   *viii*
List of Tables   *ix*
Foreword: Reimagining Education Research Practices – from the South to North   *x*
Linda Tuhiwai Smith
Permissions   *xv*

1. Recentring, Reframing and Reimagining the Canons of Educational Research   1
   Sharlene Swartz, Nidhi Singal and Madeleine Arnot

PART I
Centring Southern Experiences of Education, Knowledge and Power   19

2. Towards a Postcolonial Research Ethics in Comparative and International Education   21
   Leon Tikly and Tim Bond

3. Researching Disability and Education: Rigour, Respect and Responsibility   42
   Nidhi Singal

4. Decentring Hegemonic Gender Theory: The Implications for Educational Research   60
   Shailaja Fennell and Madeleine Arnot

vi Contents

5 Indigenous Anti-Colonial Knowledge as 'Heritage Knowledge' for Promoting Black/African Education in Diasporic Contexts 78
George Sefa Dei

6 Postcolonial Models, Cultural Transfers and Transnational Perspectives in Latin America: A Research Agenda 96
Gabriela Ossenbach Sauter and María del Mar del Pozo

PART II
Reframing the Codes, Rules and Rituals of Educational Research Practice 113

7 Reflexivity and the Politics of Knowledge: Researchers as 'Brokers' and 'Translators' of Educational Development 115
Arathi Sriprakash and Rahul Mukhopadhyay

8 Non-Chinese Researchers Conducting Research in Chinese Cultures: Critical Reflections 134
Kokila Roy Katyal and Mark Edward King

9 (Re)Centring the Spirit: A Spiritual Black Feminist Take on Cultivating Right Relationships in Qualitative Research 151
Christina S. Morton

10 Fieldwork for Language Education Research in Rural Bangladesh: Ethical Issues and Dilemmas 172
M. Obaidul Hamid

11 Informed Consent in Educational Research in the South: Tensions and Accommodations 187
Fauzia Shamim and Rashida Qureshi

PART III
Reimagining Educational Research Approaches for Emancipation 205

12 Indigenous Data, Indigenous Methodologies and Indigenous Data Sovereignty 207
Maggie Walter and Michele Suina

13 Focus Groups and Methodological Rigour Outside
    the Minority World: Making the Method Work to Its
    Strengths in Tanzania   221
    Hilde Jakobsen

14 Social Network Interviewing as an Emancipatory
    Southern Methodological Innovation   243
    Sharlene Swartz and Alude Mahali

15 Getting the Picture and Changing the Picture: Visual
    Methodologies and Educational Research in South Africa   265
    Claudia Mitchell

16 Entering an Ambiguous Space: Evoking Polyvocality in
    Educational Research through Collective Poetic Inquiry   281
    *Kathleen Pithouse-Morgan, Inbanathan Naicker,
    Vitallis Chikoko, Daisy Pillay, Pholoho Morojele
    and Teboho Hlao*

17 Researching Family Lives, Schooling and Structural
    Inequality in Rural Punjab: The Power of a *Habitus
    Listening Guide*   300
    Arif Naveed

18 Pedagogy of Absence, Conflict and Emergence:
    Contributions to the Decolonisation of Education
    from the Native American, Afro-Portuguese
    and Romani Experiences   319
    *Miye Nadya Tom, Julia Suárez-Krabbe and
    Trinidad Caballero Castro*

List of Contributors   *336*
Index   *345*

FIGURES

9.1	Data collection process	157
14.1	The eight stages of Social Network Interviewing	254
15.1	Dividing fence	270

TABLES

14.1	A summary of the three research studies through which Social Network Interviewing was developed	249
14.2	Stage 1 of Social Network Interviewing – selecting appropriate people to interview	256
14.3	Stage 2 of Social Network Interviewing – introducing the topic through a problem-based declarative statement	257
14.4	Stage 3 of Social Network Interviewing – discussing community norms and social attitudes	257
14.5	Stage 4 of Social Network Interviewing – evaluating how contexts affects the issue	258
14.6	Stage 5 of Social Network Interviewing – critiquing current behaviour	258
14.7	Stage 6 of Social Network Interviewing – differentiating between individual and collective agency	259
14.8	Stage 7 of Social Network Interviewing – differentiating between individual and collective agency – developing strategies for change	260
14.9	Stage 8 of Social Network Interviewing – enlarging networks to embed change	261
17.1	Listenings, methods, and objectives	302

FOREWORD

Reimagining education research practices – from the South to North

Linda Tuhiwai Smith

My first encounters and experiences in learning the theories and methods of education research were challenging, intellectually traumatic in the sense that the world of knowledge I knew and wanted 'to research' was so far away from what the literature, what education experts, and what politicians and leading thinkers in New Zealand suggested I ought to be doing that I felt for a while I was swimming in a deep pool of 'double consciousness' (Du Bois, 1903). Initially, I began my research journey wanting to bring to the foreground the history of Māori education and the history of Māori in colonial education. But then I ran into the 'small' problem of the terms 'History' and 'History of Education'. My scope fell outside where History, as the story of the victors, was said to begin and where the History of New Zealand education officially started with the arrival and actions of British missionaries and a colonial settler government. I loved researching the archives but spent most of my energy being excited by how bold and resistant my people were in the face of colonial policies (Simon & Smith, 2001). I then moved to the curriculum and then to pedagogies, to teachers and language revitalisation, constantly trying to engage with what we were taught was 'the international literature' which in fact was literature from the North. I ran into a similar 'small' problem trying to develop my doctoral proposal on 'cultural literacy' where I was totally off the page in terms of how that term was being used in the literature (Simon & Smith, 2001).

With each change of focus I fell out of scope and felt out of place. It was that sense of epistemic dissonance coupled with a determination to find my own way that led me to the work of decolonising methodologies. It all came to a head when my Head of Department rejected my PhD proposal, fairly brutally but with humour and compassion so I didn't burst into tears, by telling me to do something I loved and wanted to spend the rest of my life thinking

DOI: 10.4324/9781003355397-0

This chapter has been made available under an open access CC-BY-NC-ND 4.0 license.

about. At last, I was given permission to pursue my path, a path not yet known and a path I would need to step forward upon carefully and critically. Those early research experiences helped me think about education and social science research practices more deeply and critically, more philosophically, and yet more focussed on research practice, on methods, ethics, researcher insight, and thought processes. The decolonising methodologies I identified were ones I observed Indigenous communities, leaders, and activists practising in their discourses, actions, strategies, and mobilisations.

Researcher practices, the practices of education research are where I started my journey as a decolonising and Indigenous researcher and where, in the beginning, I fell out of scope and felt out of place. Being out of place was and is about orientation to place, to the direction a researcher faces as well as being about context. In simple terms, "With whose lens do we see and hear? With what frame do we foreground and centre our focus?" "What do we try hard not to see, hear, or accept because the literature told us those things do not exist?", and "How can we reframe, recentre, and reimagine research methods?" It is my real excitement to foreground or foreword the chapters and writers in this book. I am especially pleased to see a diverse range of researchers who are thinking and writing about actual practices from the Global South.

The chapters in this book address many of the fundamental dimensions and knowledge practices that researchers need, such as ethics, Indigenous data sovereignty, cultural and social practices that mediate researcher practices, methods that work in communities, and ways to theorise education research practices. The chapters are deeply grounded in the debates raised by anti-colonial and decolonial scholars, scholars from the Global South about education, schooling, knowledge, pedagogy, and power. This book will provide a richness of ideas and practices that should inform education research in the Global North as well as the South. It will provide an entry point to critiques from Southern theory of many of the canons of research methodology that have been entrenched by the Global North as being somehow 'universal'. When I was a graduate student most education research methods books to which I had access were heavy volumes, literally and figuratively, laden with assumptions about how these methods would apply in the Global South. It was not just methods' books either as texts that highlighted theory were similarly grand in their assumptions and claims about educational contexts across the globe. This book will be enormously useful to education graduate students and established education researchers as it brings together in one volume a depth of intellectual discussion and examples of research practices informed by Southern theory.

The first part of *Educational Research Practice in Southern Contexts* introduces us to a theoretical context for decolonising education research and for critically questioning the philosophical and moral tenets of research. These chapters provide an ease of introduction to Southern theoretical approaches which are grounded in intersectional theories of settler colonial theory, postcolonial and decolonial theory, critical Indigenous theory, and theories of imperialism in relation to gender, race, caste, and class. These first chapters critique the knowledge canon of Northern theory and the hegemony of language categories and classification systems for understanding gender, learning abilities, and communities. This section of the book is an important introduction to the key theoretical debates and challenges that educate researchers about their practices, the framing of their questions, the assessment of the significance of their research, and their understanding of ethics and approaches to methods. Many of the concepts discussed in these early chapters are raised again in later chapters as examples of why the concept is so critical. Just as one example alone the absence and/or abuse of codes of ethics has been a source of contention across Indigenous communities whose colonial histories are steeped in examples of inhumane, exploitative, and harmful research or what Eve Tuck (2009, p. 409) refers to as "'damage-centred' research". Indigenous concern about researcher ethics has led to the development of a number of Indigenous protocols and ethical standards for researchers to meet before they enter communities. The kinds of decolonising scholarship that has deeply engaged researchers from the South are not necessarily well known to researchers in the North although many Southern researchers are trained in Northern institutions and many institutions of the South reproduce the canons of the North. The South-North binary is a very fluid idea in terms of how knowledge travels in the age of the internet. The first section of the book is a great introduction, what I would call 'Greetings and Invitations to the North from the South'.

The second section of the book contains research practice examples from very diverse non-Western contexts including examples of communities from the South who study in the North. These chapters talk directly to the practice of becoming an education researcher and being and knowing as an education researcher. For those researchers who have grown up in or identify with ethnic or tribal or marginalised communities, returning from higher education to carry out research is often fraught with tensions, challenges, and surprises as researchers navigate their way through the requirements of institutional ethics and the expectations of communities, the negotiation around language and meaning, trust and distrust, and identity and responsibilities. As these chapters argue, a reimagination and reframing process develops, or sometimes erupts, that engage participants in research in new ways as they begin to redefine themselves into active and engaged research participation. Over my career, I have witnessed the transformation that has occurred in my communities from once being suspicious of research to now wanting our own community members to be trained in research and in some cases to establish our own community-based research institutes. Indigenous community engagement in knowledge agenda setting, the framing of questions, and designing of methods alongside genuine capacity building has been exciting to observe in my tribal communities. I have become a research elder in my communities, advising, mentoring, training, and guiding but not necessarily doing interviews or analysing data. The shift in the relations of power between researcher and researched opens up a whole new dimension of knowledge creation and ethical research. This section of the book raises the nuances and possibilities of decolonising research practices across multiple contexts and through the lens of different researchers and methods. Every method and tool in a researcher's toolbox gets reimagined in a decolonising frame and re-negotiated in terms of matters as important (to researchers) as who gets their name on a journal article, who attends conferences, who makes decisions, and who gets to ask the questions of an elder in an interview. It becomes possible to grasp the implications and changes that emancipatory research can release when power and control in research gets redistributed or shifts from the researcher community towards the researched community. It is not a fixed position but a fluid and constantly renegotiated positionality that researchers come to know.

The final section of the book moves into the new terrain, novel methodologies, and new practices for researchers working in decolonising frameworks. Transforming the power relations of research shifts everything, some things radically, and others more subtly. It reframes agendas and priorities, changes expectations of researcher knowledge and practices, changes education and research training, changes questions, and shifts the emphasis away from colonising and deficit framing of problems. In the New Zealand context, for example, every application for research funding requires researchers to show how their research addresses Te Tiriti o Waitangi, the Treaty of Waitangi and supports mātauranga Māori or Indigenous knowledge and methodologies. It has been a 30-year process of change that has transformed the national expectations of all researchers. In the field of Indigenous Studies, other long-held projects are still being pursued especially in the areas of data sovereignty, intellectual and cultural property rights, and the role of states, governments, and institutions in holding Indigenous data, artifacts, and human remains. Those legacies of colonialism are still being litigated but in a changed world where Museums have returned human remains and cultural items and are hyper-sensitive to questions of provenance and ownership. In a future world of artificial intelligence, for example, protocols over data sovereignty, decolonising algorithms, and protecting the diversity and integrity of Indigenous knowledge systems become highly relevant. In a world of climate change where impacts will not fall equitably on all groups in society the need for further innovative questions and methods becomes more urgent.

This book puts into scope many of the issues that researchers from the South have been working on for decades. It provides opportunities for North-South dialogue, for grappling with research practices and developing a critical education research praxis for all education researchers. I think that graduate students and their teachers, researchers, and institutions will find this volume of work challenging, inspiring, helpful, and supportive. I hope they use this book in the curriculum and in the formal training of researchers in research ethics, theory, and practice.

References

Du Bois, W. E. B. (1903). *The souls of black folks*. Chicago, IL: A.C. McClurg.
Simon, J. A., & Smith, L. T. (2001). *A civilising mission? The making of the new Zealand's native schools system 1867–1969*. Auckland, New Zealand: Auckland University Press.
Tuck, E. (2009). Suspending damage: A letter to communities. *Harvard Educational Review, 79*(3), 409–428.

PERMISSIONS

The editors would like to thank all authors for their contributions. The following chapters have been used with permission of the copyright holder:

Chapter 2 Leon Tikly and Tim Bond. (2013). Towards a postcolonial research ethics in comparative and international education. *Compare: A Journal of Comparative and International Education*, 43(4), 422–442.

Chapter 3 Nidhi Singal. (2019). Researching disability and education: Rigour, respect, and responsibility. In N. Singal, P. Lynch, & S. T. Johansson (Eds.), *Education and disability in the Global South: New perspectives from Africa and Asia* (pp. 41–58). London, England: Bloomsbury Publishing.

Chapter 4 Shailaja Fennell and Madeleine Arnot. (2008). Decentring hegemonic gender theory: The implications for educational research. *Compare: A Journal of Comparative and International Education*, 38(5), 525–538.

Chapter 5 George Sefa Dei. (2012). Indigenous anti-colonial knowledge as 'heritage knowledge' for promoting Black/African education in diasporic contexts. *Decolonization: Indigeneity, Education & Society*, 1(1), 102–119.

Chapter 6 (edited for length) Gabriela Ossenbach and María del Mar del Pozo. (2011). Postcolonial models, cultural transfers and transnational perspectives in Latin America: A research agenda. *Paedagogica Historica*, 47(5), 579–600.

Chapter 7 Arathi Sriprakash and Rahul Mukhopadhyay. (2015). Reflexivity and the politics of knowledge: Researchers as 'brokers' and 'translators' of educational development. *Comparative Education*, 51(2), 231–246.

Chapter 8 (edited for length) Kokila Roy Katyal and Mark Edward King. (2014). Non-Chinese researchers conducting research in Chinese cultures: Critical reflections. *International Journal of Research & Method in Education*, 37(1), 44–62.

Chapter 9 Christina S. Morton. (2020). (Re)centering the spirit: A spiritual black feminist take on cultivating right relationships in qualitative research. *Journal of College Student Development, 61*(6), 765–780.

Chapter 10 M. Obaidul Hamid. (2010). Fieldwork for language education research in rural Bangladesh: Ethical issues and dilemmas. *International Journal of Research & Method in Education, 33*(3), 259–271.

Chapter 11 Fauzia Shamim and Rashida Qureshi. (2013). Informed consent in educational research in the South: Tensions and accommodations. *Compare: A Journal of Comparative and International Education, 43*(4), 464–462.

Chapter 12 Maggie Walter and Michele Suina. (2019). Indigenous data, indigenous methodologies and indigenous data sovereignty. *International Journal of Social Research Methodology, 22*(3), 233–243.

Chapter 13 Hilde Jakobsen. (2012). Focus groups and methodological rigour outside the minority world: Making the method work to its strengths in Tanzania. *Qualitative Research, 12*(2), 111–130.

Chapter 14 Sharlene Swartz and Alude Mahali. (2021). Social network interviewing as an emancipatory southern methodological innovation. In S. Swartz, A. Cooper, C. M. Batan, & L. Kropff Causa (Eds.), *The Oxford handbook of global south youth studies* (pp. 553–573). New York, NY: Oxford University Press.

Chapter 15 (edited for length) Claudia Mitchell. (2008). Getting the picture and changing the picture: Visual methodologies and educational research in South Africa. *South African Journal of Education, 28*(3), 365–383.

Chapter 16 Kathleen Pithouse-Morgan, Imbanathan Naicker, Vitallis Chikoko, Daisy Pillay, Pholoho Morojele and Teboho Hlao. (2014). Entering an ambiguous space: Evoking polyvocality in educational research through collective poetic inquiry. *Perspectives in Education, 32*(4), 149–170.

Chapter 18 (edited for length) Miye Nadya Tom, Julia Suárez-Krabbe and Trinidad Caballero Castro. (2017). Pedagogy of absence, conflict, and emergence: Contributions to the decolonization of education from the Native American, Afro-Portuguese, and Romani experiences. *Comparative Education Review, 61*(51), 121–145.

Authors names have been updated at their request in the Contributors section.

1
RECENTRING, REFRAMING AND REIMAGINING THE CANONS OF EDUCATIONAL RESEARCH

Sharlene Swartz, Nidhi Singal and Madeleine Arnot

Educational research has long been in the academic spotlight, affected as it has been by egalitarian movements which explore the implications of the ownership and control of knowledge for social justice (see, for example, Arnot, 2002; Brown & Wisby, 2020; Husen, 1988). However, over the last 10 years, the activist and scholarly gaze has focused on the ways in which knowledge about education in Southern contexts is produced, especially in light of coloniality (see Takayama, Sriprakash, & Connell, 2017), and whether it can be uncoupled from hegemonic knowledge paradigms, which privilege Northern contexts. The movement to decolonise metropolitan knowledge draws attention to *how* practically this uncoupling could be done and what should replace it in terms of new approaches to research practice (Matias, 2021). Such debates demand that attention be given to recentring intellectual endeavour and reframing empirical research practice. They reimagine embedded orthodoxies about *what* and *how* to research such that the framing and the process enable rather than disempower marginalised Southern cultures and communities.

Educational Research Practice in Southern Contexts addresses these pressing concerns by bringing together key theoretical critiques and examples of novel methodological perspectives and research practices. Our purpose is to open up the debate about 'what works' when researching Southern contexts, first at the ontological (being) and epistemological (knowing) level and second by learning about first-hand experience of conducting research in such contexts. What unites those in this debate is a concern to recognise different cultural ways of *being, knowing*, and *doing* and the heterogeneous relational worlds of Southern contexts. There has been a tendency to stereotype, label, or misrepresent Southern worlds, especially when their historical and cultural determinants are ignored or deflected as irrelevant to research objectives.

The focus of this book, therefore, is to bring to the fore new approaches and new ways of doing educational research. Whilst not comprehensive of the richness of decolonising theory in the social sciences, it offers important opportunities to grapple with the theoretical and methodological critiques of mainstream research paradigms used in a range of education disciplines, and exemplifies, through the experiences of both experienced and novice researchers, ways of rethinking research questions, and reconsidering the relevance of the rituals, codes of practice, and the methods of knowledge production. Such examples challenge the reader to consider tricky ethical questions about, for example, cultural sensitivity and recognition of Indigenous cultures, counterstrategies to deal with issues such as informed consent, protection, and voice. It provides researchers with reflections on how to engage with real-world situations and demonstrates the potential for innovation in, for example, reading history, using audio-visual tools and poetry, investigating educational movements, or finding new ways to collaborate with those being researched. Above all, the book demonstrates that there is an emergent cadre of both experienced and early career researchers from a wide range of countries who are developing new ways of designing, collecting, and analysing data across different Southern contexts.

The advantage of an anthology drawing together previously published and new articles is to be found in reshaping research training in education. Our first-hand experience of teaching university research methods courses to students from the Global South has shown us that, on the whole, they have had little opportunity to read into the scholarship from their own country – having been largely taught the value of 'Northern ways'. They are encouraged to use the protocols and methods of research that, on first sight, have taken little account of very different material and cultural factors in, for example, low-income economies, in societies with very different stratification systems, or in communities experiencing conflict. Students often struggle to make their research designs feasible knowing, or finding out once in the field, that such designs cannot easily cope with the different hierarchical age, gender/sexuality, and religious power relations within their communities.

Researchers' anxiety, which results from being pressured to meet the criteria of originality and validity, can distort what they are able to achieve in the field, despite their considerable courage and tenacity to get at 'the truth'. Young researchers who are keen to have their work published in English language international peer-reviewed journals might find that they focus less on where research might make a difference *in situ* and more on what is 'acceptable' to a Western audience's concerns. In effect, many Southern scholars who learnt their craft in Northern universities are helping shape the public image of their own countries through the lens of Northern cultures – contributing to what Santos (2014) called 'epistemicide'. Aware of this danger, they urge standard education research training programmes and researchers to reflect on their appropriateness for such Southern contexts and to make every effort to 'buy into' the burgeoning research by national or local scholars.

With this challenge in mind, we have brought together key publications that contribute new approaches to educational research methods training, purposively focusing on addressing the realities of Southern contexts. Of central concern here is the desire to create what can be called 'a just research practice' and what Cooper, Swartz, Batan, and Kropff Causa (2021, p. 14) term 'epistepraxis' – "aligning theory, method and knowledge creation with an intentional justice objective" in practice. Below we consider how the decolonisation debate has worked up this agenda.

'A just research practice': decolonising education research

In the social sciences and humanities, since the mid-20th century, postcolonial scholars such as Frantz Fanon (1959), Edward Said (1978), Homi Bhabha (1994), Gayatri Spivak (1988), and bell hooks (1984) have foregrounded the effects of colonialism and the representations of the colonised that keep domination in place. They drew attention to the struggles by those who experience domination to carve out new intellectual paths. Their research endeavours rejected their silencing and the marginalisation of the diverse cultural identities, experiences, and worldviews of the 'Othered' – the invisible and the oppressed.

Today, those who identify with and use decolonising theory have expanded the work of these foundational scholars, offering ways in which colonisation and its cultural, political, and economic effects are experienced in the Academy and how they might be mitigated with just systems of power and the inclusion of Indigenous knowledge (Mihesuah & Wilson, 2004) and epistemologies of the South (Santos, 2018; Santos & Meneses, 2020). Critical awareness is now being associated with decolonising practices that use empowering, rather than disempowering, methods for collecting and interpreting knowledge, shifting its forms of authorship, widening the modes of dissemination, and rethinking the outcomes of knowledge production in the context of unequal power relations and social inequalities.

This process of decolonising knowledge production in all its aspects is of particular importance to educational researchers. Decolonial scholars from multiple locations in the Global South have written extensively about social exclusion in colonised or ex-colonial systems of education, discriminating between children and youth, for example, on the basis of cultural difference (Wiredu, 2006), language (wa Thiong'o, 1987), religion (Ahmed, 1992), gender and sexuality (Lorde, 1984; Lugones, 2003), ethnicity/race (Rollock, 2013; Strong et al., 2023), and disability (Singal, 2013). The pervasiveness of colonial systems of power (Grosfoguel, 2007; Mignolo, 2013) continues within colonial forms of pedagogy (Freire, 1970), often shaped by cultural essentialism and its deprecatory effects (Hountondji, 1990; Mamdani, 1996). Southern scholars counter such legacies with the need for democratic processes in education (Mbembe, 2001), valuing the centrality of education for social transformation (Mugo, 2004). Demands for decolonising knowledge range from "de-imperialization, de-Westernization, de-patriarchization, de-racialization, de-corporatization, de-canonization, and de-secularization" (Ndlovu-Gatsheni, 2020, p. 369). These demands have been taken up globally where students, faculty, and community activists put pressure on universities to promote 'cognitive' and 'epistemic' justice, as de Sousa Santos (2014) so aptly describes it. At the centre of this contemporary struggle has been the need to re-examine not only "the biography and geography of authoritative knowledge" (Swartz, Nyamnjoh, & Mahali, 2020, p. 166) but also the canons and orthodoxies of educational research methodologies.

Educational researchers have only sporadically engaged with these debates and perhaps, even less actively, addressed the wealth of writing and research emanating from Southern countries. Halai and Wiliam's (2011) valuable collection *Research Methodologies in the 'South'* and *The Handbook of Critical Theoretical Research Methods in Education* (Matias, 2021) are exceptions in this regard. As Arnot and Fennell (Chapter 4) argue, the direction of influence has largely been one way – from North to South, dependent often on the source of Northern or international funding for economic development, and the dominance of the English publishing industry and its connections to higher education in the Global North. In terms of research style, education research which is located primarily within the social sciences and humanities has worked with a diversity of methodological and epistemological paradigms – from positivism to constructivism and from experimental designs to action research – and has recently embraced multiple contemporary approaches borrowed from allied disciplines such as ethnography, autoethnography, visual methods, hermeneutics, and poetical enquiry. Quantitative researchers have complemented this with the results of surveys, experimental designs, evaluation schemes, and high-level mathematical modelling. Yet, with this diversity of methodology, the underlying conventions (or 'canons') are driven by the expectations of institutions in the Global North (mainly Western Europe and North America). This has meant a centring of methodological concerns which are perceived to hold 'scientific rigour' such as reliability, validity, and replicability, and on ensuring that social scientific methods are institutionalised and thus passed down as a toolbox of research to new generations of scholars. However, as critical schools of thinking have emerged, these canons are being called into question because of their underlying social assumptions and the unequal research relations they generate or rely upon. The perceived gap between the concerns and the hegemonic modes of production of Northern knowledge and the lived experience of those living in peripheralised Global South societies, especially in formerly colonised countries, has fuelled demands for what is often referred to as 'Southern theory' (Comaroff & Comaroff, 2012; Santos, 2014) – a new-world social science that engages with the scholarly theories, knowledge, and the creative work of the South (Connell, 2007).

Southern theory represents the growing critical awareness (and some discontent) in the field of education and development that researching Southern contexts has been directed and even conducted by scholars from the Global North, often using Northern funding agendas and employing generally unacknowledged Southern research staff. Part of the problem is the extractive (monetisation and marketisation) nature of Northern research. Northern canons of research practice have served important potentially benevolent purposes – aiming to build theory, ensuring rigour, and protecting those amongst whom (or more often *on* whom) research is conducted – yet there are many adverse sequelae of internationally rather than locally funded research. Such research has tended to ignore or bypass the colonial histories of educational systems that helped create the inequalities of access, quality, and outcomes that are now the concern of international policy-makers and to ignore the role that Indigenous cultures have played in encouraging learning and which continue to provide important lessons on how best, in context, ever greater learning can be achieved. Southern/Indigenous scholarship appears to have played little part in shaping educational agendas (Connell, 2007; Dei, 2011; Tuhiwai Smith, 2012), yet localised, informal, and community-based initiatives and national educational reform movements could play an important part in international modelling of educational reform strategies. Recentring the canons of research implies therefore the reorganisation of funding and research leadership, greater visibility, and stronger validation of Southern scholars (one of the principles that shaped the selection of this collection).

Recentring Southern experiences of education, knowledge and power

The emergence of 'Southern theory' has stimulated a wide range of debates about postcolonial, critical race and Indigenous theory that are relevant to education research. In the two decades since the 1999 publication of Tuhiwai Smith's ground-breaking volume, *Decolonizing Methodologies: Research and Indigenous Peoples* (revised in 2012 and 2021), which aimed to centre Indigenous Māori knowledge in the process of research, and thus reclaim control over the activity of research itself, much attention has been paid, particularly by Southern scholars, to decentre knowledge ownership and centre marginalised voices and to respect cultural norms. Other publications have contributed towards these aims. For example, *Indigenous Research Methodologies* (Chilisa, 2012) is a textbook that situates research in a larger, historical, cultural, and global context and focusses on the importance of partnerships in research from an Afrocentric perspective. The *Handbook of Critical and Indigenous*

Methodologies (Denzin, Lincoln, & Tuhiwai Smith, 2008) draws on multiple disciplinary lenses to redefine inquiry and pedagogies. It engages with critical constructs such as race/diversity, gender representation (queer theory, feminism), and culture and shows how critical and Indigenous theory helps to define and guide the field.

Yet, as persuasive and as welcome as these developments are, to date limited attention has been given to cultivating a decolonising research praxis. Such a praxis would take seriously research partnership and reciprocity, power relations within empirical studies, recognition of historical context, and local Southern cultures and agendas. Some of these issues have been written about specifically in educational research relationships (Halai & Wiliam, 2011; McGregor & Marker, 2018; Ndimande, 2012; Swartz & Nyamnjoh, 2018). *Cross-Cultural Perspectives in Educational Research* (Robinson-Pant, 2005), for example, reveals the dilemmas faced by international graduate students studying education in the United Kingdom when defining a research question, choosing appropriate methods, collecting data, deciding which language to use, and writing their theses whilst addressing cultural differences.

The canons of educational methodologies, whilst valuable, are now being challenged for the assumptions they make about their applicability to Southern contexts. The contexts in which research problems are conceptualised and designed need interrogating. Questions such as who sets the educational research agenda, what is framed as an educational 'problem', and the assumptions underpinning such thinking need to be examined closely. Another recurring (and more recently emerging) theme focuses on dissemination – who is the audience of the research? (Robinson-Pant & Singal, 2020). Said (1982, p. 7) asked the questions: "Who writes? For whom is the writing being done? In what circumstances?" This is particularly important in the field of international education and development if it uses largely homogenised and deficit-driven representations of the Global South.

In terms of the ethics of research, a consistent conceptual ignorance, or 'presence of absence', pervades research studies. A familiarity is assumed when relating to Southern education systems because of their colonial foundations, but the religious, political, and financial diversity of such systems requires researchers to be cautious about their research designs and generalisations. Most concerning is the asymmetry of ignorance, where Northern ignorance of Southern contexts goes unchallenged whilst Southern ignorance of Northern contexts is met with derision (Chakrabarty, 2009). Prominent in these absences are the exclusion of cultural practices, religious or spiritual engagement, the ways of doing and knowing, the informal community modes of teaching and learning, hierarchies of cultural respect and honour, and an ethics of mutuality or reciprocity amongst people in marginal and Southern contexts (Walsh, 2007). A further absence is the elision of people's *history* in research (Bhambra, 2014). This often leads to a deficit view of Southern contexts and different groups within them – a view arrived at by ignoring or contracting the histories of enslavement, continued contemporary global practices of domination, and exclusion from resources that led to current circumstances faced by educational institutions, communities, and people.

Scholars have pointed to assumptions about the universality of method and the imperialism involved in such assumptions (Ake, 1982; Alatas, 2006; Amin, 2011; Chakrabarty, 2009). Educational research textbooks speak of research participants as if they were universal – for example, 'the child', 'the student', 'the teacher', 'the girl' – rather than local or particular (Cooper, Swartz, & Mahali, 2018). Educational research methods handbooks emanating from the North tended in the past to draw on the experiences mainly of young people in North America or Western Europe, predominantly in urban rather than rural environments. Consequently, assumptions have had to be continuously challenged about, for example, linearity in youth transitions through schooling and into work (Arnot, Jeffery, Casely-Hayford, & Noronha, 2012), the homogeneity of female educational experiences (Unterhalter & North, 2019), expectations about teachers' work (Moon, 2012; Sayed, 2018), the power of English language as a progressive force (for example, Kalyanpur, Boruah, Molina, & Shenoy, 2022), and about parents', especially mothers' educational aspirations and expectations (Lukalo, 2021) in Southern contexts.

In Part I of this book, we bring together five key contributions that engage with the process of decolonising dominant educational theory and its problematics. These five chapters represent some of the major challenges demanded by a decolonial perspective of the dominant epistemologies, ontologies, and theories in education. The authors explore, in different ways, the politics of knowledge embedded in colonial theory, by identifying exclusions, categorisations, and paradigms, which do not easily transfer or are damaging when used in Southern contexts. A common thread unites these analyses – that of aiming to achieve an ethical approach in research that acknowledges, understands, and investigates key distortions of Southern cultures. These distortions may be a result of sometimes very simplistic conceptualisations of development, or the use of Northern gender binaries, or an assumed homogenisation of experiences of children with disabilities, or the failure to engage with Indigenous knowledge or heritage. The chapters challenge hegemonic models of research to conduct research with a strong moral basis – an agenda that is carried through to the reframing of educational research methods.

Reframing the codes, rules and rituals of educational research practice

Enhanced visibility of the Southern experience is powerful in disrupting the Northern hegemonic lens in current educational research practice. Giwa's (2015, p. 2) assertion that "if the South is worth knowing and exploring, voices from the South should be heard in 'knowing' the South" is very pertinent. The chapters in Part I indicate the importance of using culture-specific paradigms, cultural engagement, bi-cultural working, and situated dialogue. A common thread in these critical reflections is the centrality of what Santos (2004) refers to as an "ecology of knowledges" (p. 168) which call for "the promotion of non-relativistic dialogues among knowledges, granting 'equality of opportunities' to the different kinds of knowledge to build a more democratic and just society, and the decolonising knowledge and power" (Santos, Nunes, & Meneses, 2008, p. xx). These ambitions beg the question about how Southern cultures can be captured empirically and how people's voices can be elicited and heard.

Southern theory considers research in its broadest sense as an organised scholarly activity that is deeply connected to power (Tuhiwai Smith, 2021), a site of contestation. Research as a set of human activities produces/reproduces particular social relations of power, which makes it far more political than simply a moral and civilised search for knowledge. Thus, decolonising research practice is not simply about challenging or making refinements, it is also about challenging the taken-for-granted ways of 'performing' research – for example, its design, the methods of data collection, interactions between Northern and Southern researchers, and between researchers and participants during fieldwork, and the analysis of data.

Research as a 'performance' involves rapport-building and trust, navigation, confidentiality, and anonymity; it involves ethics approval. Each of these can involve (frequently) misconceived notions of homogeneity across spaces. But when reframed through a decolonial lens, the research process has the potential to reclaim language, histories, and knowledge and disrupt power dynamics. Recent writings by various scholars are beginning to capture this shift and make visible the need to disrupt Northern hegemonic ways of *doing* research and doing it ethically (Robinson-Pant & Singal, 2013). Questions are raised about how this is done: Who is involved in knowledge creation? Whose voice counts? Who represents whom?

The recentring of power relations within research is increasingly focused on the role and position of 'Southern researchers' whether they be from the Global South or from the North learning to research Southern contexts. Some have addressed the notion of *who* is the researcher by referring to the insider-outsider continuum and arguing for the need for researchers and researched to share certain characteristics (for instance, in the case of disability research). A critical engagement with the insider/outsider duality, and by extension the politics of identity, emphasises the fluidity and 'in-between-ness' of membership roles and the identities of researchers vis-à-vis the researched (Sultana, 2007). However, McFarlane (2006) argues that this divide again reflects the notion within the Western academy that the South is a space that "knowledge travels to rather than from" (p. 1418).

Breakey, Nyamnjoh, and Swartz (2021) note that one way of challenging Northern hegemony is to reconfigure researchers' relationships with the context and communities in which they carry out research. This reconfiguration can be posited in an emancipatory light, where emphasis is placed on the co-creation and co-dissemination of knowledge in order to give voice to realities otherwise marginalised by the extraverted gaze of Southern scholarship (Moletsane, 2015). However, Qureshi's (2011) poignant reflection suggests that Southern researchers are vulnerable because of the academic culture's lack of confidence in the South's ability to produce authentic knowledge. This perceived or real weak academic culture undermines the trustworthiness of the knowledge generated by Southern scholars.

Indeed, many Southern scholars have received training in educational research in Northern institutions; some with strong diasporic identities have highlighted the challenges of 'returning' to the field to undertake research with a strong Northern lens and finding themselves faced with having to think, amongst other things, about the limits of positionality. Acker (2000, p. 153) argued that the tensions of being on either side "cannot be fully resolved", suggesting that discourses around the insider-outsider dichotomy move to include creative ways of dealing with the challenges of representation. Pardhan (2011), reflecting on her ethnographic research which explored the experiences of female pre-primary teachers in Karachi, noted:

> [I] often found myself on a lonely journey, uncertainly navigating predicaments in diverse aspects of the research design that I encountered in the lived world of the rural and urban research sites of a Southern context. Added to this challenge were the limited accounts of other researchers, who may have encountered similar quandaries, and from which I could draw both comfort and a sense of certainty to negotiate various dimensions of the fieldwork process.
>
> *Pardhan (2011, p. 118)*

Globally, this means that researchers who are described by Sriprakash in Chapter 6 as 'brokers' or 'translators' of knowledge production need to develop not just a conscious and continuous situated reflexivity (McFarlane, 2006) but new forms of 'knowing'. This requires researchers to confront the fluidity of their identities within discourses of global knowledge production. It is also about making visible the ruptures with taken-for-granted knowledge and contributing to the growing knowledge base that chronicles the experiences of researchers from the Global South. Acknowledging and confronting these identities create permeable spaces, which allow researchers to be inside, outside, and somewhere in between (Dwyer & Buckle, 2022) and knowledge creation to be more malleable to these different experiences.

One often ignored tension between the 'accepted' ways of doing research and a more contextually sensitive approach that comes to the forefront in the field is when researchers are faced with the question about who has the right to be named? A common assumption in the dominant paradigm is to protect confidentiality, with most institutional frameworks assuming that disguising names is the standard ethical practice. Yet as Guenther (2009, p. 412) acknowledges, "the decision to name or not to name is rife with overlapping ethical, political, methodological, and personal dilemmas", which are not discussed enough in the literature. This argument is developed in Gordon's (2019) work with women in Bihar who challenged her efforts to make them 'invisible'. As one of the participant's stated: "Mentioning my name is positive not only for us but for village and country too (Pratibha Kumari)" (p. 546). In contrast, Qureshi (2011) raises the issues of 'vulnerability' and what the notion of informed consent by research participants means when working in a context where "the majority of people are illiterate and the research culture is weak, the meaning of research itself is hard to explain" (p. 97).

The chapters in Part II of this book describe other ethical issues for researchers who, even if not outsiders in the normal sense, are nevertheless 'outsiders' by having been trained abroad. Our selection of previously published work exemplifies the excellent work that both experienced and novice researchers have done reflecting on their positionality in relation to the insider-outsider debate, how being culturally sensitive challenges notions of informed consent and anonymity, and the link between language and translation. Research relationships highlighted in this section involve ethical questions about the requirement to properly understand cultural context, an endarkened feminist approach that embraces love, compassion, reciprocity, and ritual (Chapter 9). The section draws on examples of research from India, Hong Kong, Bangladesh, and Africa by students in the United States and the South generally. These examples show the ways in which normative ethical and practical approaches to collecting data can become of value for non-Western societies and marginalised communities within Western societies if the usual rules and rituals of research are reimagined.

Re-imagining research approaches for emancipation

Fully recentring and reframing educational praxis such that it becomes emancipatory for participants entails making explicit and preferably flattening the gradient of power and control at key stages in the research process, from determining the research agenda and design to interpretation, analysis, and dissemination (Lenette, 2022; Singal, 2018; Swartz, 2011). Participants ought to benefit from research and researchers have a responsibility to give back (Chilisa, 2012; Denzin et al., 2008; Tuhiwai Smith, 2021).

Genuine inclusivity implies an emphasis on co-production and ultimately co-ownership by research participants. As Tuhiwai Smith (2021, p. 250) observes, "the activity of research is transformed when the researched become the researchers, changing how questions are framed, priorities ranked, problems are defined, and even the very terms of participation". At a minimum, as Swartz and Nyamnjoh (2018) argue, research should be interactive and engaging, going beyond mere talk or survey completion. Participants should be afforded multiple opportunities to state their opinions or describe their experiences so that research contains 'polyphonic voices' and 'parallax perspectives' rather than poor representations hastily caught on paper or in once-off speech moments.

These themes of agency, engagement, and empowerment need to be expanded to include a focus on change as the study proceeds – what is usually termed participatory action research (Boog, 2003). Swartz and Nyamnjoh (2018) caution that research methods such as photo-elicitation, photo-voice, community mapping, and social network interviews may only be interactive, rather than participatory, if they lack the intent of "gains in ownership and empowerment … [placing] participants at the centre of transforming their marginality" (p. 10). Emancipatory research, involving a far more radical level of inclusion, invites participants to set their own research agendas and understand and change their situation through the research process as self-emancipation. Research moves from interactive to emancipatory when the traditional researcher retains only the role of facilitator:

> Interactive research is owned by the researcher, whilst participatory research is owned by both researcher and the researched. In emancipatory research, the research belongs to the researched. Put simply and from the perspective of the traditional researcher, ownership or power along this continuum transitions from *mine* to *ours* to *theirs*.
>
> *Swartz and Nyamnjoh (2018, p. 1)*

In short, emancipatory research is 'research as freedom', research that changes people's lives. Those who pursue research as freedom will need to explain to funders (and institutional review boards) the rationale for iterative research that metamorphoses to better serve the interests of the researched as the study progresses.

> Furthermore, research participants themselves might need to be helped to see the potential of emancipatory research and aided to develop skills to begin to set their own research agendas and to be able to resist having research imposed upon them.
>
> *Swartz and Nyamnjoh (2018, p. 10)*

The chapters in Part III of this book demonstrate not only some of these aspirations but also the tensions between concepts of research as 'socially just', as 'participatory' or action-oriented, and as potentially emancipatory. Tuhiwai Smith (2012) reminds us that these reimagined strategies do not reject "all theory or research or Western knowledge. Rather, it is about centring our concerns and world views and then coming to know and understand theory and research from our own perspectives and for our own purposes" (p. 41).

Part III proposes innovative methods of data collection and analysis. This includes exploring the analysis of Indigenous data sovereignty, how to employ focus groups in a cross-cultural setting, and a description of social network interviewing as an emancipatory practice that offers something back to research participants. Other chapters demonstrate how to employ visual methodologies such as drawings, photo-voice and photo-elicitation, visual productions, and material culture. Working with notions of plural identities and polyvocality, researchers show how to use collective poetic inquiry, to analyse polyvocal identities with a *Habitus Listening Guide*, and how best to approach research of counter-hegemonic social movements in North America. The chapters draw on diverse contexts from Pakistan, South Africa, New Zealand, Tanzania and Native American, Afro-Portuguese, and Romani educational experiences. The imaginative work of these researchers encourages further innovations in research methodologies in the future.

Conclusion

McKeever (2000, p. 101) has very aptly pointed out that "conducting research in a post-colonial context can be like a game of snakes and ladders. The only way to proceed is to cling to the ladders of the oppressed while trying to avoid the snakes of the colonial past". Lorde (1984, p. 112) memorably argued that:

> Those of us who stand outside the circle of this society's definition of acceptable ... [those] forged in the crucibles of difference – those of us who are poor, who are lesbians, who are Black, who are older – know ... *the master's tools will never dismantle the master's house*. They may allow us temporarily to beat him at his own game, but they will never enable us to bring about genuine change. And this fact is only threatening to those ... who still define the master's house as their only source of support.

Clinging to 'the ladders of the oppressed' or using 'the master's tools' "means that only the narrowest perimeters of change are possible and allowable" (Lorde, 1984, p. 111). The authors of the chapters in this book are in precisely this quandary, but, through their efforts both theoretically and methodologically, we can consider the viability of using those tools in Southern contexts. Their critical insights proffer novel or adapted research tools of data collection/analysis, challenging us to be more sensitive, courageous, and innovative when researching unfamiliar cultures.

Education researchers who are concerned with the power, culture, and practices associated with institutionalised education, to social movements concerned with education, and to those involved in education, whether children, youth, teachers, parents, or youth workers in Southern contexts, are arguably still at an early stage in recognising the depth of impact of colonial legacies that frame their projects from initiation to completion. We are a long way from saying that solutions have been found to this history of dominance, for example of Anglophone or Hispanic empires, or to the social scientific research approaches we use to study education in other cultures. International education and comparative education have set agendas which assume to know what education is for and how educational institutions work.

In contrast, this collection offers scholars and students a bridge to move further into the current postcolonial and transnational debates in relation to which research methods need to be rethought or relinquished. It allows readers to consider how, in practice, they can reframe, recentre, and reimagine current research methods and, in doing so, offers an opportunity for Southern scholars to develop confidence to publish their methodological insights and fieldwork expertise and to advocate "for a wider range of experiences as constitutive of the human condition" (Cooper et al., 2018, p. 15). This search for more appropriate methods has to be active, forceful, imaginative, and different. It is this ambition that holds the authors together in a loose community of innovators.

We hope that the much-needed dialogue between Northern researchers and those from Southern contexts, especially within educational research training programmes, will be started or further invigorated by the powerful insights, epistemologies, and practices found here. Such dialogue has the potential to assist those already trained in Western social science research methodology and those in national and international evidence-led organisations and policy-making agencies to rethink their research and address concerns about Northern hegemony in the production of knowledge. It will encourage a new research culture that reflects and acts upon cultural difference and results in a more humane ethical practice attuned to postcolonial settings.

References

Acker, S. (2000). In/out/side: Positioning the researcher in feminist qualitative research. *Resources for Feminist Research, 28*(3–4), 153–172.
Ahmed, L. (1992). *Women and gender in Islam: Historical roots of a modern debate.* New Haven, CT: Yale University Press.

Ake, C. (1982). *Social science as imperialism: A theory of political development* (2nd ed.). Ibadan, Nigeria: Ibadan University Press.
Alatas, S. F. (2006). *Alternative discourses in Asian social science: Responses to Eurocentrism*. New Delhi, India: Sage.
Amin, S. (2011). *Eurocentrism: Modernity, religion, and democracy: A critique of eurocentrism and culturalism* (2nd ed.). Cape Town, South Africa: Pambazuka Press.
Arnot, M. (2002). *Reproducing gender? Essays on educational theory and feminist politics*. London, England: Routledge.
Arnot, M., Jeffery, R., Casely-Hayford, L., & Noronha, C. (2012). Schooling and domestic transitions: Shifting gender relations and female agency in rural Ghana and India. *Comparative Education, 48*(2), 181–194.
Bhabha, H. K. (1994). *The location of culture*. London, England: Routledge.
Bhambra, G. (2014). *Connected sociologies* (1st ed.). London, England: Bloomsbury.
Boog, B. W. (2003). The emancipatory character of action research, its history and the present state of the art. *Journal of Community & Applied Social Psychology, 13*(6), 426–438.
Breakey, J., Nyamnjoh, A., & Swartz, S. (2021). Researching the South on its own terms as a matter of justice. In S. Swartz, A. Cooper, C. M. Batan, & L. K. Causa (Eds.), *The Oxford handbook of Global South youth studies* (pp. 539–551). New York, NY: Oxford University Press.
Brown, A., & Wisby, E. (Eds.). (2020). *Knowledge, policy and practice in education and the struggle for social justice: Essays inspired by the work of Geoff Whitty*. London, England: UCL Press.
Chakrabarty, D. (2009). *Provincializing Europe: Postcolonial thought and historical difference*. Princeton, NJ: Princeton University Press.
Chilisa, B. (2012). *Indigenous research methodologies*. Los Angeles, CA: Sage.
Comaroff, J., & Comaroff, J. (2012). *Theory from the South, or how Europe is evolving toward Africa*. Boulder, CO: Paradigm.
Connell, R. (2007). *Southern theory: The global dynamics of knowledge in social science*. Cambridge, England: Polity Press.
Cooper, A., Swartz, S., Batan, C. M., & Kropff Causa, L. (2021). Realigning theory, practice, and justice in Global South youth studies. In S. Swartz, A. Cooper, C. M. Batan, & L. K. Causa (Eds.), *The Oxford handbook of Global South youth studies* (pp. 3–18). New York, NY: Oxford University Press.
Cooper, A., Swartz, S., & Mahali, A. (2018). Disentangled, decentred, and democratised: Youth studies for the Global South. *Journal of Youth Studies, 22*(1), 29–45.
Dei, G. (Ed.). (2011). *Indigenous philosophies and critical education: A reader*. New York, NY: Peter Lang.
Denzin, N. K., Lincoln, Y., & Tuhiwai Smith, L. (Eds.). (2008). *Handbook of critical and indigenous methodologies*. Thousand Oaks, CA: Sage.
Dwyer, S. C., & Buckle, J. L. (2022). Cultural insider-outsider: Reflecting on positionality in shared and differing identities. In P. Liamputtong (Ed.), *Handbook of qualitative cross-cultural research methods: A social science perspective* (pp. 85–99). Northampton, PA: Edward Elgar Publishing.
Fanon, F. (1959). *Black skin, white masks*. New York, NY: Grove Press.
Freire, P. (1970). *Pedagogy of the oppressed*. New York, NY: Continuum.
Giwa, A. (2015). Insider/outsider issues for development researchers from the Global South. *Geography Compass, 9*(6), 316–326.

Gordon, R. (2019). 'Why would I want to be anonymous?' Questioning ethical principles of anonymity in cross-cultural feminist research. *Gender & Development, 27*(3), 541–554.

Grosfoguel, R. (2007). The epistemic decolonial turn. *Cultural Studies, 21*(2–3), 211–223.

Guenther, K. M. (2009). The politics of names: Rethinking the methodological and ethical significance of naming people, organizations, and places. *Qualitative Research, 9*(4), 411–421.

Halai, A., & Wiliam, D. (Eds.). (2011). *Research methodologies in the South*. Karachi, Pakistan: Oxford University Press.

hooks, b. (1984). *Feminist theory: From margin to center*. Boston, MA: South End Press.

Hountondji, J. (1990). Scientific dependence in Africa today. *Research in African Literatures, 21*(3), 5–15.

Husen, T. (1988). Research paradigms in education. *Interchange, 19*(1), 2–13.

Kalyanpur, M., Boruah, P. B., Molina, S. C., & Shenoy, S. (2022). *The politics of English language education and social inequality: Global pressures, national priorities and schooling in India*. London, England: Routledge.

Lenette, C. (2022). *Participatory action research: Ethics and decolonization*. London, England: Oxford University Press.

Lorde, A. (1984). The master's tools will never dismantle the master's house. In A. Lorde (Ed.), *Sister outsider: Essays and speeches* (pp. 110–114). Berkeley, CA: Crossing Press.

Lugones, M. (2003). *Pilgrimages: Theorizing coalition against women of color*. Lanham, MD: Rowman & Littlefield.

Lukalo, F. (2021). *Mothers and schooling poverty, gender and educational decision-making in rural Kenya*. London, England: Routledge.

Mamdani, M. (1996). *Citizen and subject: Contemporary Africa and the legacy of late colonialism*. Princeton, NJ: Princeton University Press.

Matias, C. E. (Ed.). (2021). *The handbook of critical theoretical research methods in education*. London, England: Routledge.

Mbembe, A. (2001). *On the postcolony*. Berkeley, CA: University of California Press.

McFarlane, C. (2006). Crossing borders: Development, learning and the North–South divide. *Third World Quarterly, 27*(8), 1413–1437.

McGregor, H. E., & Marker, M. (2018). Reciprocity in Indigenous educational research: Beyond compensation, towards decolonizing. *Anthropology & Education Quarterly, 49*(3), 318–328.

McKeever, K. (2000). Snakes and ladders: Ethical issues in conducting educational research in a postcolonial context. In H. Simons & R. Usher (Eds.), *Situated ethics in educational research* (pp. 101–115). London, England: Routledge.

Mignolo, W. (2013). Geopolitics of sensing and knowing: On (de)coloniality, border thinking, and epistemic disobedience. *Confero, 1*(1), 129–150.

Mihesuah, D. A., & Wilson, A. C. (Eds.). (2004). *Indigenizing the academy: Transforming scholarship and empowering communities*. Lincoln, NE: University of Nebraska Press.

Moletsane, R. (2015). Whose knowledge is it? Towards reordering knowledge production and dissemination in the Global South. *Educational Research for Social Change, 4*(2), 35–47.

Moon, B. (Ed.). (2012). *Teacher education and the challenge of development: A global analysis*. London, England: Routledge.

Mugo, M. (2004). *Education and liberation in Africa: An analysis of the role of education in the struggle for social transformation*. Nairobi, Kenya: Africa Educational Publishers.

Ndimande, B. S. (2012). Decolonizing research in postapartheid South Africa: The politics of methodology. *Qualitative Inquiry*, *18*(3), 215–226.

Ndlovu-Gatsheni, S. J. (2020). Geopolitics of power and knowledge in the COVID-19 pandemic: Decolonial reflections on a global crisis. *Journal of Developing Societies*, *36*(4), 366–389.

Pardhan, A. (2011). Ethnographic field methods in research with women: Field experiences from Pakistan. In A. Halai & D. Wiliam (Eds.), *Research methodologies in the 'South'* (pp. 117–145). Karachi, Pakistan: Oxford University Press.

Qureshi, R. (2011). Who pays the price? The ethics of vulnerability in research. In A. Halai & D. Wiliam (Eds.), *Research methodologies in the 'South'* (pp. 90–116). Karachi, Pakistan: Oxford University Press.

Robinson-Pant, A. (2005). *Cross-cultural perspectives on educational research*. New York, NY: McGraw-Hill Education.

Robinson-Pant, A., & Singal, N. (2013). Researching ethically across cultures: Issues of knowledge, power and voice. *Compare*, *43*(4), 417–421.

Robinson-Pant, A., & Singal, N. (2020). Beyond authorship and accountability? The ethics of doctoral research dissemination in a changing world. *British Educational Research Journal*, *46*(4), 859–877.

Rollock, N. (2013). A political investment: Revisiting race and racism in the research process. *Discourse: Studies in the Cultural Politics of Education*, *34*(4), 492–509.

Said, E. (1978). *Orientalism*. New York, NY: Pantheon Books.

Said, E. (1982). Opponents, audiences, constituents and community. *Critical Inquiry*, *9*(1), 1–26.

Santos, B. (2004). A critique of lazy reason: Against the waste of experience. In I. Wallerstein (Ed.), *The modern world-system in the longue durée* (pp. 157–197). Boulder, CO: Paradigm.

Santos, B. (2014). *Epistemologies of the South: Justice against epistemicide*. Boulder, CO: Paradigm.

Santos, B. (2018). *The end of the cognitive empire: The coming of age of epistemologies of the South*. Durham, NC: Duke University Press.

Santos, B., & Meneses, M. P. (2020). *Knowledges born in the struggle: Constructing the epistemologies of the Global South*. New York, NY: Routledge.

Santos, B., Nunes, J. A., & Meneses, M. P. (2008). Introduction: Opening up the canon of knowledge and recognition of difference. In B. de Sousa Santos (Ed.), *Another knowledge is possible: Beyond Northern epistemologies* (pp. x–xii). London, England: Verso.

Sayed, Y. (2018). *Continuing professional teacher development in Sub-Saharan Africa: Improving teaching and learning*. London, England: Bloomsbury.

Singal, N. (2013). *Disability, poverty and education*. London, England: Routledge.

Singal, N. (2018). Researching disability and education: Rigour, respect and responsibility. In N. Singal, P. Lynch, & S. T. Johansson (Eds.), *Education and disability in the Global South: New perspectives from Africa and Asia* (pp. 41–58). London, England: Bloomsbury.

Spivak, G. C. (1988). Can the subaltern speak? In C. Nelson, & L. Grossberg (Eds.), *Marxism and the interpretation of culture* (pp. 271–313). Urbana, IL: University of Illinois Press.

Strong, K., Walker, S., Wallace, D., Sriprakash, A., Tikly, L., & Soudien, C. (2023). Black lives matter and global struggles for racial justice in education. *Comparative Education Review, 67*(S1), S1–S198.

Sultana, F. (2007). Reflexivity, positionality and participatory ethics: Negotiating fieldwork dilemmas in international research. *ACME: An International Journal for Critical Geographies, 6*(3), 374–385.

Swartz, S. (2011). "Going deep" and "giving back": Strategies for exceeding ethical expectations when researching amongst vulnerable youth. *Qualitative Research, 11*(1), 47–68.

Swartz, S., & Nyamnjoh, A. (2018). Research as freedom: A continuum of interactive, participatory, and emancipatory methods to understand youth marginality. *HTS Theological Studies, 74*(3), 1–11.

Swartz, S., Nyamnjoh, A., & Mahali, A. (2020). Decolonising the social sciences curriculum in the university classroom: A pragmatic-realism approach. *Alternation, 36,* 165–187.

Takayama, K., Sriprakash, A., & Connell, R. (Eds.) (2017). Contesting coloniality: Rethinking knowledge production and circulation in Comparative and International Education. *Comparative Education Review, 61*(S1), S1–S24.

Tuhiwai Smith, L. (2012). *Decolonizing methodologies: Research and indigenous people* (2nd ed.). London, England: Zed Books.

Tuhiwai Smith, L. (2021). *Decolonizing methodologies: Research and indigenous peoples* (3rd ed.). London, England: Zed Books.

Unterhalter, E., & North, A. (2019). *Education, poverty and global goals for gender equality: How people make policy happen.* London, England: Routledge.

Walsh, C. (2007). Shifting the geopolitics of critical knowledge: Decolonial thought and cultural studies 'others' in the Andes. *Cultural Studies, 21*(2–3), 224–239.

wa Thiong'o, N. (1987). *Decolonising the mind: The politics of language in African literature.* London, England: James Currey.

Wiredu, K. (2006). *The search for an African enlightenment: A philosophy of Ubuntu.* New York, NY: Continuum.

PART I
Centring Southern experiences of education, knowledge and power

2
TOWARDS A POSTCOLONIAL RESEARCH ETHICS IN COMPARATIVE AND INTERNATIONAL EDUCATION

Leon Tikly and Tim Bond

Although there has been a proliferation of critical literature on research ethics in educational and social research, only limited attention has been given to a consideration of the place of research ethics in comparative and international education (CIE). For example, recent influential texts on research in CIE (Cowan & Kazamias, 2009; Crossley, Watson, & Bray, 2003; Phillips & Schweisfurth, 2007) barely refers to research ethics. This is surprising given the attention that has traditionally been given to issues of researching across cultures within CIE, the complex ethical issues that this raises and the deep-seated nature of power and inequality implicit in researching in postcolonial settings. Further, there has been only a limited attempt to apply insights from postcolonial theory to research ethics in education (Chilisa, 2009; Tuhiwai Smith, 1999).[1] This is despite the growth in literature that has applied postcolonial theory to a broader understanding of education in the postcolonial world (Coloma, 2009; Crossley & Tikly, 2004; Hickling-Hudson, Matthews, & Woods, 2004; Tikly, 1999).

The aim of this chapter is to critically consider the possibilities of postcolonial theory for understanding research ethics in CIE and to outline the basis for a postcolonial approach to research ethics. The chapter starts by outlining a view of postcolonial theory and of the postcolonial condition as the basis for deconstructing dominant approaches to research ethics, whilst the second part of the chapter explores in more depth the implications of postcolonialism for research ethics.

Postcolonial theory, ethics and social justice

This section provides a broad view of postcolonial theory by summarising key ideas elaborated elsewhere (Tikly, 1999, 2001, 2004, 2011a). However, postcolonial theory is not singular or coherent. This account is therefore

DOI: 10.4324/9781003355397-3

necessarily partial, by presenting a particular 'take' on postcolonial theory and on the postcolonial condition in order to advance an understanding of research ethics later in the chapter.

Postcolonial theory emerged in its current form in the cultural turn of the social sciences, although it draws on a longer tradition of critical, anti-colonial writing and theorising (Young, 2001). Developed in the disciplines of literary and cultural studies, it operates as a 'critical idiom' (Loomba, 2004) for interrogating the discursive basis of Western rule. The value of postcolonial scholarship for CIE is that through focusing on the discursive basis of education in former colonising and colonised countries, it allows the cultural effects of a Western education on non-Western cultures to be analysed in depth.

However, this focus on the cultural and discursive level does not imply that the material (including the economic and political) dimensions of the postcolonial condition are insignificant or lack ethical implications. Nor is it being implied that there is nothing 'outside of the text', as some forms of poststructuralism suggest. Rather, as argued elsewhere (Tikly, 2001, 2004, 2011b), education in the postcolonial world is shaped by a range of economic and political forces at a number of scales, including the local, national, regional, and global, alongside other characteristics of contemporary globalisation, including climate change and the spread of global diseases such as HIV/AIDS. These more material aspects provide a powerful rationale for a consideration of research ethics as they 'articulate' with the cultural/discursive level (Morley & Chen, 1996). It is through discourse that the material world is interpreted and understood and unequal power relationships are legitimated. Thus, ethical discourses are more than simply words or language. They legitimise social practices that have material effects.

Much postcolonial theory has elaborated the 'postcolonial condition', that is, a global shift in the cultural, political, and economic arrangements that arise from the experiences of European colonialism, both in former colonised and in colonising countries. There has been much debate about the meaning of the term and particularly the use of the suffix 'post' given that some countries continue to be colonised and that many formerly colonised countries retain large inequalities between postcolonial elites and the majority of the population. It is also important not to present a homogenous and essentialised understanding of the postcolonial condition as it includes a plurality of development paths and dynamic cultural contexts. Crucially, colonised and formerly colonised groups continue to struggle against its effects. Furthermore, the postcolonial condition is also characterised by the emergence of a 'new imperialism' (Harvey, 2003; Tikly, 2004) by which is meant the economic, political, military, and cultural hegemony of the United States and its Western allies within contemporary globalisation.[2] For all of these reasons, it is more helpful to consider postcolonialism as a general *process* of disengagement of formerly colonised countries from European colonialism and classical imperialism and their reinsertion into the flows and networks that characterise contemporary globalisation.³

The view of postcolonialism as a process has implications for the way that colonialism is *understood* and narrativised. In keeping with postmodern and, in particular, poststructuralist emphases, postcolonial theory provides a critique of the 'metanarratives' of the European enlightenment. Writers such as Foucault and Derrida have proved particularly influential. This re-narrativisation reconceptualises colonialism, not as a sub-plot of some 'grander' (European) narrative, but as a violent process central to the development of globalisation.

This decentring of European thought is highly significant to any consideration of ethics. Western ethics comprise different ethical imperatives, including those arising from religious and more secular humanist traditions with differential influence in colonial and postcolonial settings. However, within the European enlightenment a particular universalist view of ethics has predominated and has subordinated other Western and, especially, non-Western ethical traditions. This has been linked to a trajectory of Western humanist thought, which has taken as its normative point of reference the white, affluent European male subject. Although claiming to be 'universal', key writers in the field of moral philosophy were influenced by notions of biological and cultural difference and hierarchy such that non-Western cultures were assumed to lack sufficient capacity for reason for inclusion within a universal ethic (Goldberg, 1993; Manzo, 1997). Moral philosophy and Western humanism have also been premised on a notion of ethical rationalism (Christians, 2007) that separates reason from emotion and means from ends. It is through the coupling of an instrumentalist view of science and progress to a process of *othering* of non-Western cultures that Western humanism has been complicit not only in colonialism but in other barbarisms of the modernist era, including slavery, war, and genocide, all in the cause of 'progress'. The incisive critique of enlightenment ethics by postcolonial, poststructuralist, and feminist scholars raises the question as to whether any post-enlightenment universal ethic is possible.

Foucault and his followers argue that there have been significant shifts in Western humanist influence in the development of globalisation in the post-World War II period, linked to the development of a new neo-liberal governmentality (the overall art or rationality of government in Western liberal democracies). This shift has seen a growing emphasis on *homo economicus* as the subject of ethical discourse, that is, the individual economic agent unfettered by the state, free to pursue his or her own economic interests. This individualistic model contrasts with the models of economic/social actors posited in many non-Western traditions. In this way, development economics with their associated ethics show a distinct cultural bias from their inception (Escobar, 1995; Tikly, 2003a, 2004).

Writing within a postcolonial perspective, the ideas of the sociologist Boaventura de Sousa Santos are particularly helpful for framing a discussion about research ethics and are therefore considered in some detail. Santos has identified mechanisms by which Western knowledge claims the power to exclude other approaches to understanding the world as though they were 'non-existent'. These include: the assertion of modern science and high culture as the sole criteria for truth and aesthetic quality; a Western, linear view of time, development, and progress; the classification and naturalisation of differences that are used to legitimise hierarchies; universalising assumptions of Western knowledge and ethics that exclude local contexts and realities; and a 'logic of productivity' in which economic growth becomes the sole criterion through which development and progress are evaluated. These logics combine in a production of absence or non-existence as ignorant, backward, inferior, local or particular, and unproductive or sterile (Santos, 2012, pp. 52–53), each imbued with ethical deficit.

Linked to the decentring of modernist metanarratives has been an 'epistemic shift'. This involved going beyond the old 'binary oppositions' of 'coloniser' and 'colonised', 'First' and 'Third' world and 'Black' and 'White' and the development of more contingent and complex views of colonial culture, politics and identities, achieved, for example, by: focusing on the 'unstable', 'hybrid', and 'fractured' nature of colonial and postcolonial identities (Bhabha, 1984, 1996); the complex interplay of colonialism, patriarchy, and caste in the formation of different subject positions amongst the colonised (Spivak, 1988); and processes of transcultural 'mixing' and exchange, alongside the complexities of diasporic identification (Gilroy, 1993). The formation of exiled and refugee communities has contributed to this process. The fluidity and historicity of cultures and of cultural relations are paramount in this approach, thus challenging views of cultures as hermetically sealed, essentialised, and static entities. This is important for our purposes because it complicates and liquefies the relationship between ethics and any particular cultural or intellectual tradition. It requires ethics to open to the influence of other ethical traditions and how different views on ethics, even within one cultural tradition, may draw on traditional as well as modern's and postmodern ethical values and outlooks.

This mixture of ethical sources and influences has underpinned the struggle against Western colonialism and imperialism and inspired contemporary postcolonial thought. Young (2001) provides a detailed account of the development of anti-colonial thought that highlights the interplay between Indigenous intellectual traditions and aspects of Western thought in anti-colonial writing (see also Ashcroft, Griffiths, & Tiffin's, [1989] collection of essays, *The Empire Writes Back*).

Gandhi (1910), for example, criticised Western modernity with its reliance on violence as inherently 'evil' and counter-posed it with ancient Indian civilisation and the non-violent tradition, which he characterised as 'holy'. He combined Indian ethics with aspects of Western thought from the ideas of Tolstoy, Ruskin, Thoreau, and Emerson. Steve Biko's conception of black consciousness contrasted an African humanism based on collectivity and a spirit of *Ubuntu* (togetherness) with the individualism of 'White' (European) civilisation. Black consciousness was also influenced by Christian ethics (as reinterpreted by Black theologians). Similarly, ideas of African socialism (*Nkrumah, Kaunda, Diop*) and of self-reliance (*Nyerere*) combined an inherently communal African ethic with a reading of Western Marxism and an analysis of the class-based nature of African societies. These combinations of different traditions not only challenge the colonised/coloniser binary but also generate the richness and diversity of ethics in anti-colonial thought.

This early wave of postcolonial literature, written in national struggles for liberation, contains a nascent alternative view of humanism, often developed in antithesis to Western humanism. This has provided a point of departure for some postcolonialists from Eurocentric postmodernist and poststructuralist thought (Parry, 1995) that seeks only to deconstruct the effects of knowledge/power and involves self-consciously building on previous anti-colonial discourses to conceptualise alternatives based on emancipatory visions of social justice. We will argue that this shift provides a starting point for reconceptualising a postcolonial research ethics.

There remains a tension, however, within postcolonial theory between the deconstructive aspect, which focuses on a deep suspicion of Western humanism, and the more 'reconstructive' aspects, which focus on developing alternatives to colonial rule and elaborating visions of social justice. Some of these tensions are evoked by the reality that many attempts at 'reconstruction' in the post-independence periods have not only served to perpetuate inequality but, in some instances, have been associated with acts of cruelty, war, and genocide in the name of 'progress' that echo excesses committed under colonialism. These tensions may be amplified by the continuing hegemony of Western forms of knowledge and views of ethics as part of a new global discourse of 'development' (Escobar, 1995). The persistence of these tensions raises important philosophical questions about whether it is possible to conceive of any epistemological basis on which a postcolonial and emancipatory ethics can be based.

One possible starting point is Santos' view of developing an *epistemology of the South*. For Santos (2012), this involves several moves. Firstly, it involves replacing a sociology of absences (above) with a "sociology of emergences' so that the 'emptiness of the future according to linear time (an emptiness that may be all or nothing) becomes a future of plural and concrete possibilities, utopian and realist at one time, and constructed in the present by means of activities of care" (p. 54). Drawing on the work of Ernst Bloch, Santos describes the sociology of emergences as the inquiry into alternatives that are contained in the horizon of concrete possibilities. It acts both on possibilities (potentiality) and on capacities (potency). It has an ethical core that is linked to a vision of what *ought to be*. As it involves an anticipatory consciousness, it must – unlike Western rationalist thought – also necessarily involve a theory of emotions.

Linked to this is a concept of the *ecology of knowledges* (Santos, 2007). This starts with the assumption that all practices and human relations not only imply more than one form of knowledge but also concomitantly imply ignorance. Santos notes the excessive over-reliance on practices based on scientific knowledge in modern capitalist society but without pressing for outright rejection of scientific 'rationalist' knowledge. Santos sees the 'remedy' to the supposed superiority of scientific discourse as lying in greater cognitive justice in which the majority of the population are granted access to hegemonic, scientific knowledge and then using this in counter-hegemonic ways. This also involves recognising alternative forms of knowledge and promoting interdependence between scientific and non-scientific knowledges.

For Santos (2012), the development of an ecology of knowledge rests on the possibility of inter-cultural *translation* that allows for, "mutual intelligibility among the experiences of the world, both available and possible" (p. 58). This translation of knowledges is presented as *diatopical hermeneutics* making the ecology of knowledges possible. Translation between two or more cultures involves identifying their isomorphic (distinctive) concerns and the different answers they provide. Diatopical hermeneutics stem from the idea that all cultures are incomplete and may, therefore, be enriched by engaging in dialogue with or confronting other cultures. As Panikkar (n.d.), the originator of the concept, explains, diatopical hermeneutics stands for the thematic consideration of understanding the other *without assuming that the other has the same basic self-understanding*.

However, Santos (2012) argues that recognising the relativity of cultures does not require adopting relativism as a philosophical stance. It does imply, however, "conceiving of universalism as a Western particularity whose supremacy as an idea does not reside in itself, but rather in the supremacy of the interests that support it" (p. 23). Diatopical hermeneutics presupposes a 'negative universalism': the impossibility of cultural completeness.

International treaties on human rights are an example of a universalising Western discourse. This is significant because human rights are often considered as underpinning research ethics by scholars in CIE. Santos (2002) contends that, "as long as human rights are conceived of as universal, they will operate as a globalized localism, a form of globalization from above" (p. 44). This matters because, arguably, human rights policies have for the most part been at the service of the economic and geopolitical interests of the hegemonic capitalist states, the same states that have legitimated "unspeakable atrocities" revealing "revolting double standards" (p. 45). The distinctive Western liberal mark in human rights discourses was established in the universal declaration of 1948:

> which was drafted without the participation of the majority of the peoples of the world; in the exclusive recognition of individual rights, with the only

exception of the collective right to self-determination which, however, was restricted to the peoples subjected to European colonialism; in the priority given to civil and political rights over economic, social and cultural rights; and in the recognition of the right to property as the first and, for many years, the sole economic right. (p. 45)

Crucially, Santos also recognises what he describes as the emancipatory potential of human rights discourses, but realising this potential involves a process of translation.

This process of translation needs to start from the recognition that all cultures have distinctive conceptions of human dignity that effectively legitimise different forms of equality and inequality. Expanding on the work of translation, Santos offers an example of developing a common understanding of human dignity by bringing together the Western concept of human rights, the Islamic concept of *umma* and the Hindu concept of *dharma* (one could add to this the African concept of *ubuntu*). He identifies a common concern across different cultural traditions for productive life, even if expressed in different ways: for example, in the modern capitalist conceptions of 'development', in Gandhi's conception of *swadeshi* or the Indigenous peoples' conception of *sumak kawsa*. Whereas the capitalist conceptions of development are based on conventional economics and on the idea of infinite growth resulting from gradually subjecting practices and knowledges to the logic of the market, *swadeshi* and *sumak kawsay* are based on the idea of sustainability and reciprocity, respectively. This process of translation is enabled by a dynamic view of culture that envisages reiterative processes of cross-cultural translation in response to each encounter with diversity. It is possible to envisage processes of translation taking place at different scales from the global through the regional, national, local and, pertinent to this chapter, in inter-cultural research partnerships. Thus, in CIE research, it is not only the subject of the research that is under ethical scrutiny but the ethics that inform the research process.

Santos' ideas are significant for the model of situated and dialogic ethics we develop in the second part of the chapter. Also, significant here is the work of the economist and philosopher Amartya Sen. Although situated outside of the broader postcolonial literature we argue that Amartya Sen's ideas about human capabilities (Sen, 1999), on identity (Sen, 2006) and on justice (Sen, 2009) address key issues identified by postcolonial critics. For Sen, the usual objective of development, namely economic growth, is replaced by the realisation of human freedom. Consequently, 'development' ought to be principally concerned with the nurturing of capabilities (opportunities) that individuals and groups require to realise their valued 'functionings' (beings and doings). These necessarily differ according to cultural context but might include being well-nourished, mobile, well-educated, autonomous and independent, safe, respected, having paid work and taking part in democratic debate, etc. Central to Sen's ideas is the realisation of human capabilities through processes of informed public dialogue at a number of levels. This, in turn, relies on a comparative rather than a universal view of ethics in arbitrating between different justice claims that may rest on different assumptions.

Of particular interest for our discussion is the possibility that Sen's view of reason as the basis for moral judgment. Sen demonstrates that, far from being a 'Western' concept, the use of reasoned judgment has been central to Eastern intellectual traditions and integral to ideas about justice.[4] Sen (2009) also highlights that there need be no conflict between the use of emotions and reason in making value judgments. Thus:

> there is no particular ground for denying the far-reaching role of instinctive psychology and spontaneous responses. They can supplement each other, and in many cases an understanding of the broadening and liberating role of our feelings can constitute good subject matter for reasoning itself. (p. 128)

Like Santos' work on translation, this view of justice supports the desirability of a dialogical view of ethics.

Implicit in both Santos' and Sen's ideas about the possibility for cross-cultural dialogue on ethical issues, but not elaborated in detail, is the question of humanism. Humanism is important in any discussion of ethics (including research ethics) because it speaks to the agency of the ethical subject (what it is to be and to act ethically). As we have seen, much poststructuralist thought is not only highly critical of Western humanism but is also deeply suspicious of the whole idea of humanism. The influence of Foucault's work on many poststructuralist and postcolonial writers concerning how human subjectivity is constituted through disciplinary institutions and discourses has been particularly significant in this regard.[5] Many postcolonial scholars have, however, attempted to set out what can be defined as a new or 'critical humanism' that protects the possibility of emancipatory agency.

For Edward Said (2004), a new humanism must "excavate the silences, the world of memory, of itinerant, barely surviving groups, the places of exclusion and invisibility, the kind of testimony that doesn't make it onto the reports" (p. 81–82). Similarly, Paul Gilroy (2006) sets out a vision of a 'new cosmopolitanism' based on a planetary humanism. As he explains:

> The planetary consciousness I am invoking was a precious result of anticolonial conflict. It is now a stimulus to multi-culture and a support for anti-racist solidarity. It was linked to a change of scale, a wholesale reimagining of the world which had moral and political dimensions. (p. 289)

Building on Gilroy's ideas of a new cosmopolitanism, and in keeping with Santos' ideas about translation, Mbembe and Posel (2005) argue that:

> This new humanism is underpinned, too, by the insistence that debates about democracy should move beyond simply the idea of rights (important as these are), to engage the question of obligation. In a politics of hope, which revives our commitment to human dignity for all, we need to grapple with the question: what are the obligations and responsibilities which a democracy requires of its citizens, as much as of its state. (p. 284)

The view of critical humanism is important for our purposes because it provides the possibility of moral and ethical agency linked to social justice and inter-cultural dialogue as the basis for the development of research ethics.

Towards a postcolonial research ethics in education

In this section, we critically apply our reading of postcolonial theory to research ethics in CIE. In particular, we consider how postcolonial theory contributes to a critique of Western research ethics; provides a context for understanding research ethics as an aspect of the postcolonial condition; and provides a basis for developing an emancipatory, situated and dialogical view of research ethics appropriate for the postcolonial era.

Kitchener and Kitchener (2009) present a five-level model of ethics in social research. This involves consideration of ethics from the point of view of individual action, ethical rules that govern decision-making (including, for example, the ethical guidelines that govern educational research), ethical principles that underpin rules, ethical theory that provides a framework for interpreting and explaining guidelines and rules and meta-ethics that explores the meaning of ethics itself. The current discussion is largely at the level of ethical theory. We will continue at this level as we consider how postcolonial scholarship contributes to a critique of Western research ethics in favour of situated and dialogic approaches to research ethics. We draw extensively on critical (emancipatory) literature on research ethics, whilst rejecting some of the underlying assumptions. In particular, much of this literature presents too homogenous a view of culture and does not take sufficient account of the more global and transversal ethical issues that are so important for CIE research.

Postcolonial theory and the critique of dominant approaches to research ethics

We have argued in the previous section that postcolonial theory provides the basis for a distinctive critique of dominant approaches to research ethics in CIE. Although much CIE research does not make explicit its ethical basis, it is possible to identify two distinctive approaches. Each has different underlying assumptions about the ethical basis of education and about the research process. We present each approach as an 'ideal type' for heuristic reasons. In reality, they may overlap or be conflated in any particular research. We will suggest that the assumptions in each represent a point of tension with postcolonial theory and that, furthermore, both are Eurocentric in nature.

The utilitarian, market-driven approach is particularly evident in much of the research and evaluation work carried out by the World Bank and some aid agencies. Here, the dominant principle or 'ethic' is 'value for money' driven by a utilitarian concern with the effectiveness and efficiency of education. The underlying assumptions are positivist and focus on the 'neutrality' and 'objectivity' of the research process. Favoured methodologies reflect these concerns and include, for example, forms of econometric and cost-benefit analysis and randomised control trials. However, whilst presenting the illusion of neutrality, much of the research undertaken within this approach can be interpreted as regulatory in nature and linked to neo-liberal governmentality (Tikly, 2003b, 2004). For Santos, the concern with value for money has the effect of privileging some kinds of research questions and problems whilst silencing others, for example around Indigenous concerns or social justice issues. When used in the context of country or programme evaluations, the utilitarian approach can also drive research governance by insisting on value-for-money principles. Typically, less attention is given to other aspects of research ethics, including, for example, the nature of the relationship between funders and researchers, within research partnerships or between researchers and researched. Research participants in this approach are viewed principally as informants, rather than as active participants in the research process and, in this sense, researchers can be viewed as 'predatory' by co-opting informants to the researchers' purposes (Cannella & Lincoln, 2007).

The rights-based approach, on the other hand, is more characteristic of the approach towards education and educational research sponsored by UN agencies, international and local NGOs. The underlying rationale for research and research questions within this approach is provided by appeals to human rights, including children's rights, or to associated entitlements or targets (for example, the Millennium Development Goals). A range of methodologies may be used within this approach, ranging from quantitative to more interpretative and participatory approaches. The research process itself is more likely to be governed with reference to an explicit code (or codes) of ethics, such as those emanating from UNESCO or from research associations or institutional review boards. The common principles underlying these guidelines, including non-maleficence, beneficence, respect for persons, fidelity and justice, arose in the context of the development of Western social science disciplines and share a common origin with human rights discourses in Western moral philosophy (Kitchener & Kitchener, 2009).[6] Whilst, as Santos notes, rights-based approaches (and for that matter, Western ethical codes) are often used as a basis for protecting the interests of the most vulnerable and for emancipatory purposes, there is a contradiction between this and their Eurocentric bias. As several commentators have noted (Barnes, McCreanor, Edwards, & Borell, 2009; Chilisa, 2009; Cram, 2009; Grande, 2004; Tuhiwai Smith, 1999) Western ethical codes can have the effect of silencing Indigenous approaches to ethics. They can also exclude consideration of ethical issues at key stages of the research process, particularly: who is involved in conceptualising the research and defining research questions; who 'owns' the data; and, who benefits from publishing and disseminating research findings (Silka, 2009). Cannella and Lincoln (2011) give several examples where implementing Western research ethics can appear irrelevant, problematic, or have unintended and contradictory consequences in non-Western settings. Many of these scholars have also illustrated the significance of non-Western codes of ethics for educational research.

The postcolonial condition as a context for considering ethics in educational research

Consideration of the postcolonial condition in education provides a context for identifying issues and questions for research and understanding ongoing inequalities in the research process. As with the postcolonial condition more broadly, there have been shifts in the ethical basis of colonial education including the ways in which colonial education has been legitimated with continuity and discontinuity between the colonial and independence periods. A few illustrative examples drawn from a range of postcolonial contexts may suffice to illustrate this shift.[7]

Colonial education was hugely disruptive for native knowledge systems and forms of pre-colonial education, which had their own ethical basis and value system, rooted in pre-colonial economies and social relations. In Africa, for instance, as Nyerere (1967) explained in his pamphlet on *Education for Self-reliance*, classic European-style colonialism and missionary education were justified in relation to the supposed inferiority of the colonised and in relation to an evangelical civilising mission. This existed in a state of tension with a more utilitarian, instrumentalist view of colonial schooling for servicing the colonial economy through developing the necessary basic skills and dispositions of servitude (Altbach & Kelly, 1978; Kallaway, 2009; Nyerere, 1967; Tikly, 2003a). These dual purposes were evident to education systems introduced by other colonial powers including the French (White, 1996) and, indeed, the Japanese (Takeshi & Mangan, 1997), although there were differences.[8]

Furthermore, within countries that developed as settler colonies, such as the United States, Canada, Australia, countries in the Caribbean and South Africa, the underlying 'logic' of Western rule also led to complex and often contradictory policies that were simultaneously assimilationist, exclusionary and segregationist (Altbach & Kelly, 1978). Schooling within European countries, such as England, was often used to support the imperial project. Text-books often contained racialised stereotypes of the colonised, with curricula that sustained the assumption of European cultural and racial superiority (Mangan, 1988, 1993).

By privileging a Eurocentric curriculum in both colonising and colonised countries, colonial education had the profound and lasting effect of devaluing Indigenous cultures, languages, and identities for both colonisers and the colonised. It also produced gendered subjects that reflected dominant European patriarchal attitudes (Mohanty, 1988; Unterhalter, 1991). Colonial education was also highly elitist in nature. This produced a disjuncture between Europeanised elites and the great mass of the colonised population, a disjuncture that continued into the post-independence period.

The moral imperative of education in the formerly colonised world began to shift after independence and the introduction of the new paradigm for 'development' introduced after the Second World War. The colonial order, based on the innate inferiority of the native, was transformed by the discourse of 'development', which sought to incorporate populations into a new capitalist world order, albeit on the periphery (Tikly, 2004). Education was central to this process. The dominant discourse for educational purposes was human capital theory. Whilst this had a predominantly instrumentalist ethic, namely to produce human capital for the national and global economy, there have been important shifts in emphasis over the years.

In the 1950s, the focus for much education policy was on manpower planning. From the early 1980s and in the wake of the oil shock, the debt crisis and the introduction of structural adjustment lending by the multinational agencies, the emphasis shifted to a focus on the rates of return from investments in different levels and sectors of education. The upshot was the prioritisation of primary education at the expense of higher levels. This has led to a reduction in the capacity of universities in the low-income world to undertake educational research, a point that we return to below (Tikly, 2003b). The hegemonic role of neo-liberal thinking during the 1980s, particularly in the context of the so-called Washington consensus, also resulted in the introduction of user fees in education, which had a disastrous impact on educational enrolments (Samoff, 1994).

The shift towards the post-Washington consensus in the late 1980s meant education increasingly deployed not only to economic growth but also to poverty reduction by promoting the health and welfare of populations. Rights-based discourses legitimise dominant economic discourses but also serve as a source of contradiction and tension. The tension is played out between, on the one hand, the in-egalitarian effects of neo-liberal policies through structural adjustment lending, increasing marketisation and privatisation of schooling, in contrast, on the other, to the more egalitarian aims of the Millennium Development Goals in education (Tikly, 2011a, 2011b; Tikly & Barrett, 2011).

The dominance of Western economic thinking, particularly neo-liberalism, has had a profound effect, not only on sustaining inequality in the low-income world but also in shaping power relationships between institutions of the global North and South concerning research. It explains the power of the World Bank and other, principally Western-led, donors in determining research agendas. It also provides one explanation for the uneven capacity between Southern- and Northern-based institutions in conducting educational research, with the lack of investment in higher education across the low-income countries.

Meanwhile, the increasingly diverse nature of the school-going population in former colonising countries and the struggles of Indigenous and immigrant groups to have their cultures, languages and histories recognised have raised ethical questions about how to engage with alterity and difference (Todd, 2003). The response has varied depending on the context and has involved a mixture of assimilationist and integrationist policies. More recently, the response to diversity in most Western countries has been by reference to variations of multiculturalism, arguably the preferred approach for managing difference under late capitalism. As many commentators have pointed out, however, this has often failed to challenge the underlying Eurocentric assumptions of the curriculum. There also remain marked differences in outcomes for different ethnic groups, reflecting the persistence of institutionalised racism (Banks & Banks, 2010; Ladson-Billings & Gilborn, 2004). Non-European ethnic groups often continue to be under-represented in higher education and other research institutions in Western countries. When combined with the relative poverty of universities in the low-income world, this is problematic for a field such as CIE because it reflects and reinforces wider global inequalities as consequences of the colonial legacy. It also further limits the possibilities for processes of intercultural translation to occur within the research process, as we argue below.

Postcolonial research ethics as emancipatory

As Edward Said and others (Hall, 1996; Loomba, 2004) have pointed out, the emancipatory intention of much postcolonial scholarship has been to bring to the fore the voices and experiences of those who have been historically marginalised by the colonial encounter. These studies have sought to highlight the contribution of Indigenous voices to research and the value of their perspectives to an understanding of research ethics. This is significant because it provides a basis for potentially reconstructing research ethics to take account of the interests of historically marginalised groups.

In some instances, research ethics are articulated with a critical humanist perspective relating to wider social justice concerns. This is true about Tuhiwai Smith's (1999) work, which focuses on *Decolonising Methodologies*, and Sandy

Grande's (2004) work on *Red Pedagogy*. Both of these texts present a dynamic and fluid view of Indigenous cultures, explaining how they have developed in relation to, but also resistant to, Western hegemony. The texts also present a view of cultures as being overlaid by different forms of inequality and oppression, based on gender and class, that articulate in complex ways with ethnic identities. In both cases, developing an Indigenous approach to research, methodologies and research ethics sees the research process as an instance of critical pedagogy that is inextricably linked to a wider emancipatory project for Indigenous groups.

A postcolonial perspective on 'situated ethics'

A product of the cultural turn in the social sciences and the influence of postmodernist and poststructuralist perspectives has been a growing interest for 'situated ethics' and their application to education (Danaher & Danaher, 2008; Piper & Simons, 2005; Simons & Usher, 2000). This approach recognises that, "research is a social practice, or more accurately a variety of social practices, each with its own set of ethical issues" (Simons & Usher, 2000, p. 2). Accordingly, "the whole point about a situated ethics is precisely that it is situated, and this implies that it is immune to universalization. A situated ethics is local and specific to particular practices" (p. 2). The pragmatic realities of undertaking research within the limitations of time and funding also tend to focus attention on a situated ethic appropriate to academic partners and the people being researched.

These ideas resonate with some core themes in both postcolonial perspectives and the significance attached to culture and context in much of CIE research (Crossley, 2000). Further, much of the critical literature on research ethics, including that addressing Indigenous and other postcolonial settings, derives its appeal from its attention to the particular and local. Indeed, it often implicitly assumes the local or the nation state as the principal unit of analysis for understanding and interpreting the relevance of Indigenous research ethics. Unfortunately, this is also a limitation of this literature because it does not sufficiently explore the ethical implications of unequal power relationships as an aspect of the postcolonial condition and the increasing significance of transverse cultural linkages across local and national boundaries.

From a postcolonial perspective, no approach to research ethics can ever be complete and claims to universalisation always need to be treated with suspicion. Nonetheless, this does not preclude imagining research ethics as operating in several ways simultaneously. Such a view is particularly important given the increasingly cross-national and cross-cultural nature of research in CIE. It is possible to imagine, for example, ethical guidelines evolving at a global level in the context, for example, of the World Congress of Comparative Education Societies, and that these would influence and be influenced by guidelines and covenants at the regional, national, and local levels. This would involve, however, a different view of ethical guidelines from the hegemonic, regulatory view. Here ethical guidelines would be developed through processes of cross-cultural dialogue and would seek to affirm diversity in ethical thought rather than seek to universalise a homogenised ethic. It would also seek to locate discussion of ethics at the appropriate level within a contextualised understanding of power relationships and of inequality in education (Bond, 2012).

There is a further sense in which a postcolonial research ethics need to be situated. That is in relation to a contextualised understanding of the research process itself. Part of this understanding would revolve around the politics of partnership in a context where CIE research increasingly takes place in cross-national teams (Barrett, Crossley, & Dacha, 2011; Silka, 2009). It involves engaging with the complexities of power relationships between researchers and researched in postcolonial settings, if research ethics are to be transformative (Mertens, Harris, & Holmes, 2009). Finally, but very importantly, a situated approach from a postcolonial perspective requires a critical understanding of self in relation to the research process (Cannella & Lincoln, 2011). This is to acknowledge in Foucauldian terms the micro-capillarity of power and the complex and contradictory ways in which discourses around research ethics construct the subjectivities of researchers and the researched in relationships of inequality. It is also to affirm the potential for a liberatory agency, in keeping with the critical humanist thrust of postcolonial scholarship.

Postcolonial research ethics as dialogical

The primary methodology for developing a situated ethic ought to be dialogue between the interested parties. A dialogical view of research ethics goes to the heart of the view of postcolonial research ethics presented here. Cannella and Lincoln (2011) define a dialogical approach to research ethics in terms of a, "philosophical concern for the equitable treatment of others, moral examination of self, and particularised understandings and responses that are infused throughout our research practices (engaging in ethical dialogue and negotiation that becomes the core of research practices)" (pp. 216–217). Importantly for our purposes, dialogical ethics can also be seen as a way to conceptualise how a process of diatopical hermeneutics might occur in the context of the research process. As Hall (2011) explains:

> Dialogical dialogue begins with the assumption that the other is also an original source of human understanding and that, at some level, persons who enter the dialogue have a capacity to communicate their unique experiences and understandings to each other. ... It can proceed only on the basis of a certain trust in the 'other *qua* other' – and even a kind of 'cosmic confidence' in the unfolding of reality itself. But it should not – indeed

cannot – assume a single vantage point or higher view outside the traditions themselves. The ground for understanding needs to be created in the space between the traditions through the praxis of dialogue. (p. 1)

This view of dialogical ethics has further implications for the conduct of research. For example, it speaks to the importance of human relationships as the basis for the research process. In this regard, it is suggestive of a covenantal rather than a contractual (Brydon-Miller, 2009) basis for conceptualising relationships between researchers from different cultural backgrounds and between researchers and researched that is itself the product of an act of translation but would be built on an ethic of trust (Bond, 2007), care, human dignity, and social justice.

Such an approach would recognise and make explicit, through dialogue, the workings of power on the subject matter and the research process itself. It would seek to identify key ethical questions at each stage of the research process. Who defines the research questions and in whose interests? How are the roles and responsibilities defined within cross-cultural teams? What are the theoretical and methodological assumptions guiding the research? How can the research be conducted ethically and in the best interests of the researched? Who benefits from the research findings? To what extent can the research contribute to the development of an ecology of knowledges and to an epistemology of the South that can act in the interests of the historically marginalised? Such a dialogic approach is not confined to cross-cultural research. Through actively engaging with the existence of diversity and different human interests based on ethnicity, language, identity, sexuality, and so on, the research process also becomes an act of a critical pedagogy, echoing Freire (1970) and Grande (2004).

Conclusion

Given the dominance of Western thinking, the application of postcolonial theory to research ethics presents profound challenges to researchers and their practices associated with ethical review and research processes. We suggest that a postcolonial perspective can provide a critique of the Western bias in research ethics in comparative education by deepening the existing critical literature through drawing attention to the complexities and contradictions inherent in the postcolonial condition. In contrast to the deconstructivist emphasis within poststructuralist and postmodernist approaches, it can also provide a basis for reconstructing a postcolonial research ethics, although this involves moving beyond a poststructural reading of the postcolonial condition to embrace the possibilities of a new critical humanism. A postcolonial approach draws attention to the importance of locating a discussion of research ethics within an account of the postcolonial conditions in former colonised and colonising countries. Extending the existing critical scholarship, which has tended to focus on the nation state as its primary unit of analysis, a postcolonial perspective can assist in drawing attention to the importance of situating a discussion of research ethics at a number of scales and levels within and between nation states. We have argued that the critical humanist perspective, evident in postcolonial scholarship, can contribute to an emancipatory view of research ethics in comparative education. Furthermore, a dialogical approach to defining research ethics can contribute, in Santos' terms, towards broader processes of intercultural translation and the development of an epistemology of the South.

What has been presented is just one reading of postcolonial theory and of the postcolonial condition. Nonetheless, we hope that the chapter has contributed to the emerging critical literature on research ethics in cross-cultural, postcolonial settings in ways that will provoke re-consideration of actual practice within the field of comparative and international education.

Notes

1 Tuhiwai Smith deploys key themes in postcolonial theory whilst remaining ambivalent to postcolonial theory as developed in the Western academy.
2 Although, as Harvey (2011) has observed, this hegemony is increasingly challenged by the emergence of the Brazilian, Russian, Indian, and Chinese economies, accompanied by a new form of colonial relationship between China and Africa.
3 Thus, we use the term 'postcolonial' to describe a general condition rather than 'post-colonial', which might imply that colonialism is 'over'.
4 Sen discusses at length the use of the concept *rahi aql*, the 'rule of the intellect', considered by the Muslim Murghal Emperor Akbar to be the basis for assessing differing ethical arguments put forward by different religious groups.
5 Foucault (1982) claimed that central to his work was the objective to "create a history of the different modes by which, in our culture, human beings are made subjects" (p. 777).
6 Particularly influential here are natural rights theory and versions of deontology (Kitchener & Kitchener, 2009).
7 Most of the examples here relate to contexts that the authors are more familiar with and the account is necessarily partial.
8 As these authors explain for example, education under British colonial rule tended to be culturally segregationist whilst under French rule it was assimilationist in orientation. Japanese colonial education has been characterised as having both segregationist and assimilationist aspects.

References

Altbach, P., & Kelly, G. (1978). *Education and colonialism*. New York, NY: Longman.
Ashcroft, B., Griffiths, G., & Tiffin, H. (Eds.). (1989). *The empire writes back: Theory and practice in post-colonial literatures*. London, England: Routledge.
Banks, J. & Banks, C. (Eds.). (2010). *Multicultural education: Issues and perspectives*. New York, NY: John Wiley and Sons.

Barnes, H. M., McCreanor, T., Edwards, S., & Borell, B. (2009). Epistemological domination: Social science research ethics in Aotearoa. In D. Mertens & P. Ginsberg (Eds.), *The handbook of social research ethics* (pp. 442–457). Thousand Oaks, CA: Sage.

Barrett, A. M., Crossley, M., & Dacha, H. A. (2011). International collaboration and research capacity building: Learning from the EdQual experience. *Comparative Education, 47*(1), 25–43.

Bhabha, H. K. (1984). Of mimicry and man: The ambivalence of colonial discourse. *October, 28*, 125–133.

Bhabha, H. K. (1996). The other question: Difference, discrimination, and the discourse of colonialism. In H. Baker, M. Diawara, & R. Lindeborg (Eds.), *Black British cultural studies: A reader* (pp. 87–91). Chicago, IL: University of Chicago Press.

Bond, T. (2007). Ethics and psychotherapy: An issue of trust. In R. Ashcroft, A. Dawson, H. Draper, & J. McMillan (Eds.), *Principles of health care ethics* (pp. 435–442). Chichester, England: John Wiley & Sons.

Bond, T. (2012). Ethical imperialism or ethical mindfulness? Rethinking ethical review for social sciences. *Research Ethics, 8*(2), 97–112.

Brydon-Miller, M. (2009). Covenantal ethics and action research: Exploring a common foundation for social research. In D. Mertens & P. Ginsberg (Eds.), *The handbook of social research ethics* (pp. 243–258). Thousand Oaks, CA: Sage.

Cannella, G., & Lincoln, Y. (2007). Predatory vs. dialogic ethics: Constructing an illusion or ethical practice as the core of research methods. *Qualitative Inquiry, 13*(3), 315–335.

Cannella, G., & Lincoln, Y. (2011). Ethics, research regulations, and critical social science. In N. Denzin & Y. Lincoln (Eds.), *The Sage handbook of qualitative research* (pp. 81–89). London, England: Sage.

Chilisa, B. (2009). Indigenous African-centred ethics. In D. Mertens & P. Ginsberg (Eds.), *The handbook of social research ethics* (pp. 407–425). Thousand Oaks, CA: Sage.

Christians, C. (2007). Cultural continuity as an ethical imperative. *Qualitative Inquiry, 13*(3), 437–444.

Coloma, R. (Ed.). (2009). *Postcolonial challenges in education*. New York, NY: Peter Lang.

Cowan, R., & Kazamias, A. (Eds.). (2009). *International handbook of comparative education*. New York, NY: Springer.

Cram, F. (2009). Maintaining indigenous voices. In D. Mertens & P. Ginsberg (Eds.), *The handbook of social research ethics* (pp. 308–322). Thousand Oaks, CA: Sage.

Crossley, M. (2000). Bridging cultures and traditions in the reconceptualisation of comparative and international education. *Comparative Education, 36*(3), 319–332.

Crossley, M., & Tikly, L. (Eds.). (2004). *Special issue (28): Postcolonialism and comparative education*. London, England: Taylor & Francis.

Crossley, M., Watson, K., & Bray, M. (2003). *Comparative and international research in education: Globalisation, context and difference*. London, England: Routledge.

Danaher, M., & Danaher, P. A. (2008). Situated ethics in investigating non-government organisations and showgrounds: Issues in researching Japanese environmental politics and Australian traveller education. *International Journal of Pedagogies and Learning, 4*(1), 58–70.

Escobar, A. (1995). *Encountering development: The making and unmaking of the third world*. Princeton, NJ: Princeton University Press.

Foucault, M. (1982). The subject and power. *Critical Inquiry, 8*(4), 777–795.

Freire, P. (1970). *Pedagogy of the oppressed*. London, England: Penguin.

Gandhi, M. (1910). *Hind swarak or Indian home rule*. Retrieved from https://www.mkgandhi.org/ebks/hind_swaraj.pdf

Gilroy, P. (1993). *The Black Atlantic: Modernity and double-consciousness*. London, England: Verso.

Gilroy, P. (2006). A new cosmopolitanism. *Interventions: International Journal of Postcolonial Studies, 7*(3), 287–292.

Goldberg, D. T. (1993). Modernity, race and morality. *Cultural Critique, 24*, 193–227.

Grande, S. (2004). *Red pedagogy: Native American social and political thought*. Oxford, England: Rowman and Littlefield.

Hall, S. (1996). When was the 'postcolonial'? In J. Chamber, & L. Curti (Eds.), *The postcolonial question* (pp. 242–260). New York, NY: Routledge.

Hall, G. (2011). *Raimon Panikkar's intercultural and interreligious hermeneutics*. Retrieved from https://gerardhallsm.files.wordpress.com/2018/08/panikkars-intercultural-interreligious-hermeneutics_ghall.pdf

Harvey, D. (2003). *The new imperialism*. Milton Keynes, England: Open University Press.

Harvey, D. (2011). *The enigma of capital and the crises of capitalism*. London, England: Profile Books.

Hickling-Hudson, A., Matthews, J., & Woods, A. (Eds.). (2004). *Disrupting preconceptions: Postcolonialism and education*. Flaxton, Australia: Post Pressed.

Kallaway, P. (2009). Education, health and social welfare in the late colonial context: The international missionary council and educational transition in the interwar years with specific reference to colonial Africa. *History of Education, 38*(2), 219–246.

Kitchener, K., & Kitchener, R. (2009). Social science research ethics: Historical and philosophical issues. In D. Mertens & P. Ginsberg (Eds.), *The handbook of social research ethics* (pp. 5–22). Thousand Oaks, CA: Sage.

Ladson-Billings, G., & Gilborn, D. (Eds.). (2004). *The RoutledgeFalmer reader in multicultural education: Critical perspectives on race, racism and education*. Oxford, England: Routledge.

Loomba, A. (2004). *Colonialism/postcolonialism: The new critical idiom*. London, England: Routledge.

Mangan, J. (1988). *Benefits bestowed? Education and British imperialism*. Manchester, England: Manchester University Press.

Mangan, J. (Ed.). (1993). *The imperial curriculum: Racial images and education in the British colonial experience*. London, England: Routledge.

Manzo, K. (1997). Critical humanism: Postcolonialism and postmodern ethics. *Alternatives: Global, Local Political, 22*(3), 381–408.

Mbembe, A., & Posel, D. (2005). A critical humanism. *Interventions: International Journal of Postcolonial Studies, 7*(3), 283–286.

Mertens, D., Harris, R., & Holmes, H. (2009). Transformative research and ethics. In D. Mertens & P. Ginsberg (Eds.), *The handbook of social research ethics* (pp. 85–102). Thousand Oaks, CA: Sage.

Mohanty, C. (1988). Under Western eyes: Feminist scholarship and colonial discourses. *Feminist Review, 30*, 61–68.

Morley, D., & Chen, K.-H. (Eds.). (1996). *Stuart Hall: Critical dialogues in cultural studies*. London, England: Routledge.

Nyerere, J. (1967). Education for self-reliance. *The Ecumenical Review, 19*(4), 382–403.

Panikkar, R. (n.d.). Diatopical Hermeneutics. *Raimon Panikkar*. Retrieved from https://www.raimon-panikkar.org/english/gloss-diatopic.html

Parry, B. (1995). Problems in current theories of colonial discourse. In B. Ashcroft, G. Griffiths, & H. Tiffin (Eds.), *The post-colonial studies reader* (pp. 36–44). London, England: Routledge.

Phillips, D. D., & Schweisfurth, M. (2007). *Comparative and international education: An introduction to theory, method and practice*. London, England: Continuum.

Piper, H., & Simons, H. (2005). Ethical responsibility in social research. In B. Somekh & C. Lewin (Eds.), *Research methods in the social sciences* (pp. 56–63). London, England: Sage.

Said, E. (2004). *Humanism and democratic criticism*. New York, England: Columbia University Press.

Samoff, J. (Ed.). (1994). *Coping with crisis: Austerity, adjustment and human resources*. London, England: Cassell.

Santos, B. (2002). Towards a multicultural conception of human rights. In B. Hernández-Truyol (Ed.), *Moral imperialism* (pp. 39–60). New York, NY: New York University Press.

Santos, B. (2007). Beyond abyssal thinking: From global lines to ecologies of knowledge. *Review, 30*(1), 45–89.

Santos, B. (2012). The public sphere and epistemologies of the South. *African Development, 37*(1), 43–68.

Sen, A. (1999). *Development as freedom*. Oxford, England: Oxford University Press.

Sen, A. (2006). *Identity and violence: The illusion of destiny*. London, England: Penguin.

Sen, A. (2009). *The idea of justice*. London, England: Penguin.

Silka, L. (2009). Partnership ethics. In D. Mertens & P. Ginsberg (Eds.), *The handbook of social research ethics* (pp. 337–352). Thousand Oaks, CA: Sage.

Simons, H., & Usher, R. (Eds.). (2000). *Situated ethics in educational research*. London, England: Routledge.

Spivak, G. C. (1988). Can the subaltern speak. In C. Nelson & L. Grossberg (Eds.), *Marxism and the interpretation of culture* (pp. 24–28). London, England: Macmillan.

Takeshi, K., & Mangan, J. (1997). Japanese colonial education in Taiwan 1895–1922: Precepts and practices of control. *History of Education, 26*(3), 307–322.

Tikly, L. (1999). Postcolonialism and comparative education. *International Review of Education, 45*(5), 603–621.

Tikly, L. (2001). Globalisation and education in the postcolonial world: Towards a conceptual framework. *Comparative Education, 37*(2), 151–171.

Tikly, L. (2003a). The African Renaissance, NEPAD and skills formation: An identification of key policy tensions. *International Journal of Educational Development, 23*(5), 543–564.

Tikly, L. (2003b). Governmentality and the study of education policy in South Africa. *Journal of Education Policy, 18*(2), 161–174.

Tikly, L. (2004). Education and the new imperialism. *Comparative Education, 40*(2), 173–198.

Tikly, L. (2011a). A roadblock to social justice? An analysis and critique of the South African education roadmap. *International Journal of Educational Development, 31*(1), 86–94.

Tikly, L. (2011b). Towards a framework for researching the quality of education in low-income countries. *Comparative Education, 47*(1), 1–23.

Tikly, L., & Barrett, A. M. (2011). Social justice, capabilities and the quality of education in low income countries. *International Journal of Educational Development, 31*(1), 3–14.

Todd, S. (2003). *Learning from the other: Levinas, psychoanalysis, and ethical possibilities in education*. Albany, NY: State University of New York Press.

Tuhiwai Smith, L. (Ed.) (1999). *Decolonizing methodologies: Research and indigenous peoples*. New York, NY: Zed Books.

Unterhalter, E. (1991). Can education overcome women's subordinate position in the occupation structure? In H. Unterhalter, T. Wolpe, & Botha (Eds.), *Education in a future South Africa: Policy issues for transformation* (pp. 56–70). Oxford, England: Heinemann.

White, B. (1996). Talk about school: Education and the colonial project in French and British Africa (1860–1960). *Comparative Education, 32*(1), 9–26.

Young, R. (2001). *Postcolonialism: An historical introduction*. Oxford, England: Blackwell.

3
RESEARCHING DISABILITY AND EDUCATION

Rigour, respect and responsibility

Nidhi Singal

Over the past two decades, there has been an increased focus on disability issues. This growing recognition of disability is evident in international and national policy discourses with disability being explicitly mentioned in the Sustainable Development Goals (SDGs) (UN, 2015). Such a focus is even more pertinent, given the complete absence of disability and related issues in the Millennium Development Goals (UN, 2000). These developments are particularly significant, given that global figures indicate an estimated 10 per cent of the world's population lives with a disability (WHO, 2011).

More recent evidence suggests that persons with disabilities are twice as likely to live in poverty and often are among the poorest of the poor (WHO, 2011). In more recent years, disrupting this strong cyclical relationship between poverty and disability has become an integral part of the development discourse (DfID, 2001; UN, 2015; WHO, 2011). Education is recognised as one of the most significant pathways in breaking this continued cycle of deprivation. The Global Monitoring Report (GMR) (GMR, 2014, p. 6) poignantly notes that "education transforms lives". The GMR estimates that if all students in low-income countries left school with basic reading skills, 171 million people could be lifted out of poverty, which would be equivalent to a 12 per cent cut in world poverty. Globally, 1 year of school increases earnings by 10 per cent on average. Additionally, education impacts on positive health prospects (GMR, 2014), fostering individual agency, and asserting citizenship (Arnot, Casely-Hayford, & Chege, 2012).

In his paper, Braunholtz (2007), upon analysing data on exit routes out of poverty, particularly for those who have been in long-term poverty, identifies two important routes, namely high dependency on their own labour (in the absence of financial and material assets) and formal education. Education, he

DOI: 10.4324/9781003355397-4

argues, is crucial as it helps individuals improve the quality of their labour and enables higher returns. Not surprisingly, there is a growing appreciation of the pivotal role of education in the field of disability and development (Grech, 2014; Singal, 2017).

The SDG 4 categorically states the need to 'ensure inclusive and quality education for all and promote lifelong learning'. While there is growing acknowledgement of the need to provide education for all, there is also a realisation that there is little understanding of how best to achieve this. The World Report on Disability (WHO, 2011) notes that the existing "lack of data and evidence ... often impedes understanding and action" (p. 263) in the field across various sectors including education. As its final recommendation, the report notes the "need to strengthen and support research on disability" (p. 267). Fundamentally, high-quality research on disability is needed to uphold and achieve the rights of people with disabilities as enshrined in the United Nations Convention on the Rights of Persons with Disabilities (UNCRPD) (UN, 2006). Article 31 of the Convention notes research is central to addressing discrimination, changing perceptions, and combating stereotypes and prejudices. It encourages member states to gather research data that can inform policy and monitor progress towards realisation of the rights of people with disabilities. The article goes a step further in emphasising the need for people with disabilities to monitor and evaluate the impact of UNCRPD on their lives and hence advocates for all research being available and accessible.

This chapter begins by reflecting on the current status of education for children with disabilities. It then moves on to reviewing the current state of research on disability issues in the field of education, highlighting key trends and gaps in knowledge. Drawing on insights from this analysis, I develop three key themes which I propose ought to support future research on disability and education.

Educational status of children with disabilities: data woes

UNICEF (2013) estimates that there are approximately 93 million children with disabilities; that is, 1 in 20 children aged under 14 years has a disability. In a report published by WHO (2011), it is suggested that the number of children with disabilities globally may be as high as 130 million (WHO, 2011). This discrepancy in numbers is not uncommon in the field of disability. One reason for the lack of reliability in data is the use of inconsistent definitions of disability and the subsequent impact this has on methodologies and analysis (UNICEF, 2013). There are significant concerns over the reliability of data relating to children with disabilities, specifically around under reporting. The World Report on Disability (WHO, 2011) highlights this issue when it notes that the prevalence of childhood disability ranges from under 1 per cent in Kenya and Bangladesh to about 20 per cent in New Zealand. Over a decade earlier, Robson and Evans (2003, p. 35) based on a comprehensive review of international data sets on children with disabilities concluded: "Good data sets do not currently exist. Existing data sets are fragmentary and inconsistent in their definitions of disability. They provide little basis for meaningful international comparisons and, with some exceptions, are of unknown reliability and validity". This observation still holds true. Ironically, the issue of inconsistency across data sets and lack of definitional clarity remains the case even for within country efforts (Jeffery & Singal, 2008). Therefore, not surprisingly, there is very little reliable data even on the number of children with disabilities enrolled in primary and secondary schools in Southern contexts.

The current estimate most widely used is the one from UNICEF (2014), which states that 90 per cent of children with disabilities in developing economies do not attend school. However, what is noteworthy here is the fact that this report does not provide any reference to how this figure was calculated. While the significant exclusion of children with disabilities from the education system cannot be underestimated, the lack of transparency when such figures are used does not instil confidence. Based on findings of the World Health Survey from 51 countries, WHO (2011) reports that 51 per cent of male children with disabilities who attend primary school are estimated to complete their studies in relation to 61 per cent of male children without disabilities. In comparison, 42 per cent of girls with disabilities are likely to complete primary school in relation to 53 per cent of girls without disabilities (WHO, 2011). This pattern, wherein young people with disabilities are less likely to be in school than their peers without disabilities, is more pronounced in poorer countries. Findings of the Plan survey, which analysed data across 1.4 million children living in 30 different countries, noted that children with disabilities are ten times more likely not to attend school than children without disabilities (Plan International, 2013).

Additionally, transition from primary to higher levels of education is extremely challenging. In India, a report published by Singal, De, and Khanna-Bhutani (2017) noted that approximately 90 per cent of enrolment for children with disabilities is in elementary level (I–VIII grades) and only 8 per cent at secondary level compared with the total number of enrolments of children with disabilities in formal education. In 2013–2014 school year, children with disabilities accounted for only 0.61 per cent of the total secondary school enrolment. While there are a number of challenges with this data (such as those in relation to identification), the lack of transition from primary to higher levels of education is a key concern across all countries. Across the board, children with disabilities remain the single largest group excluded from schooling (UNESCO, 2015) and those living in lower-income countries are significantly less likely to attend school than those in high-income countries (WHO, 2011).

Discussions around educational enrolment figures, even though lacking in reliability, are currently more widely available, compared to an understanding of what happens to these children when they do make it to school. There is little data on how many children actually attend school, their level of participation in these settings, and more crucially, the impact on their learning. Thus, there is very little understanding of the quality and levels of learning achieved by children with disabilities (Howgego, Miles, & Myers, 2014). I now turn my attention to a closer analysis of the current status of research on disability and education in Southern contexts.

Current status of research on disability in the field of education

In the following section, I begin by discussing some of the dominant trends in educational research on disability issues in Southern settings and how these have been influenced by changing understandings of disability. At the outset, it is important to acknowledge that majority of research studies on disability issues, including in education, have been conducted by either international organisations or academics/research teams largely based in Northern settings.

'Disability' research, specifically in Northern contexts, Barnes (2001) notes, has been undertaken by various social scientists since the 1950s. However, the focus of these has been primarily on dealing with 'doctor-patient' relations, stigma, institutional living, and large-scale surveys chronicling the number of persons with disabilities. While these studies have enriched our understanding of disability and related issues, they were nonetheless anchored in a medicalised view of disability – the notion that disability is an individual deficit and that impairments, whether physical, sensory, or intellectual, are the main cause of disability and disadvantage. In educational terms, this meant that there was a focus on developing tests which could identify different disabilities that children have and how their behaviour could be modified or managed in specialised classrooms. As Tomlinson (2015) argues, this was a time where professional and practitioner beliefs were based on well-worn 'theories' of disadvantage and deficit within individuals, families, and social and racial groups, devoid of any social, political, and economic perspectives.

This focus underwent a significant shift in the late 1960s and early 1970s with the rise of a strong disabled people's movement in the UK, among other Northern countries. There was a real push, based on personal experiences and narratives of people with disabilities, that disability is the result not of individual factors but societal conditions. The 'problem' was not the person but the social milieu in which he or she was located. Hence, the focus was on understanding barriers that prevented people with disabilities from participating in mainstream endeavours. Thus, in educational research, there was a move towards highlighting the social construction of special educational needs (Tomlinson, 1982). A considerable body of research literature focused on bringing about important systemic changes in school systems to make them inclusive of all children, including those with disabilities.

While these broad trends hold for the type of research undertaken in Northern settings, issues of disability in educational research in Southern settings have not had similar progression. Singal (2010) reflecting on the status of disability research in these contexts stated: "Research addressing issues of disability in Southern countries is rather limited and tends to be dominated with concerns such as establishing the prevalence of various disabilities and effectiveness of rehabilitation programmes" (p. 415).

Specifically, in relation to research on disability issues in education, Howgego et al. (2014) concluded that issues of teacher attitudes and self-efficacy in relation to inclusive education are over-represented. They noted that of the 60 articles they identified in the area of inclusive education, 23 focused on attitudes. In some ways, this is not surprising, given that initial struggles of the inclusive education movement in Southern contexts have focused on addressing attitudinal barriers and delivering key messages to popularise the concept. However, this has also meant the lack of research in many other important areas.

A systematic review funded by AusAID, which included literature on the accessibility of education for people with disabilities in both developed and developing economies, found that "there have been virtually no studies in the academic literature that have looked at the impact of an intervention to improve accessibility of children with disabilities to formal school settings in low- and middle-income countries in the past decade" (Bakhshi, Kett, & Oliver, 2013, p. 28). This review noted a dominance of "commentaries, discussion papers, opinion pieces or reviews" (p. 28), particularly in the literature on education of children with disabilities in Southern contexts. Thus, there is a significant absence in the literature around issues relating to inclusive learning processes, strategies and outcomes at both teacher education and classroom level.

In addition to the lack of insights concerning classroom-based processes, also evident in the literature is little regard to the voices of children/young people with disabilities. Singal (2010) noted a more or less complete absence of thick descriptions of the lives of people with disabilities in the literature. The irony of their exclusion is highlighted in a brief published by the Chronic Poverty Research Centre (2006, unnumbered), which observed:

> Whilst few research or development organisations would consider working with all male respondents or beneficiaries, it is still common practice to work with only non-disabled people. This is despite recognising that disabled people are disproportionately among those living in chronic poverty.

While engaging with people with disabilities is crucial, providing them opportunities to express themselves when they have been continually excluded is rather challenging. In contexts where people with disabilities are not only marginalised but have also been systematically made invisible in policy and academic discourses, the value of research which attempts to hear their voices is difficult to exaggerate.

Finally, there is a need to acknowledge that researchers working on disability issues and those working on broader educational issues have continued to work in parallel with little regard to obvious synergies. Even when researchers have looked at issues of educational development, they have focused on gender, caste, poverty but rarely disability. Analysing the number of articles published on disability in comparative education journals, Brown (2014) noted that of the four journals examined over a 13-year period (from 2000 to 2013), the number of articles published which had a focus on disability ranged between 0.81 per cent and 1.26 per cent with most increase from 2007 onwards. Some of the reasons for this absence of evidence are not only to do with the lack of funding but also due to lack of training among researchers, which makes them reluctant to focus on disability.

Additionally, Nuwagaba and Rule (2015) note the presence of, what they term as, the 'fear of doing disability research' among researchers. Based on a critical analysis of the research ethical review processes in different African countries, the authors argue that the "current practice suggests that postgraduate students intending to do research involving participants with disabilities may fear facing this ethical maze" (p. 5). They note that the uncertainty of the process, the lack of clear guidelines, etc., potentially reduce the number of postgraduate students pursuing studies involving persons with disabilities and eventually result in low numbers and quality of researchers in this area of study. Consequently, there is a reduction in knowledge generation regarding disability issues and further marginalisation of people with disabilities as "there is no new evidence on which to base decisions that affect them" (p. 7).

The absence of an active and critical academia has been identified as one of the biggest challenges in promoting rigorous research in Southern contexts (Swartz, 2014), impacting significantly on knowledge production (Chomba, Mukuria, Kariuki, Tumuti, & Bunyasi, 2014).

Acknowledging many of these challenges, it is not surprising that the World Report on Disability (WHO, 2011) identifies the need for promoting research through more focused investments in both human and technical capacity, particularly in Southern countries.

Moving the field forward

At a time when there is a growing emphasis on the need for more quality evidence, it is worth highlighting three important themes that are useful in shaping the future of research on disability issues in education. Each of these three themes – (i) need for research which builds on local realities and priorities, (ii) undertaking more sophisticated research explorations, and (iii) forming alliances and networks for research impact – is discussed next.

Need for research which builds on local realities and priorities

More recently, powerful accounts written by researchers have begun to highlight the significant disjuncture between research agendas and the priorities that need addressing. Providing a very passionate and reflexive account of her experiences of working with the disability community in post-conflict Sierra Leone, Berghs (2010) highlights the many ways in which researchers and the international development community can collude with structures and institutions that exploit people with disabilities. She argued that the research questions she was asked to pose by her international funders did not reflect the immediate needs of people.

Research must encompass a nuanced understanding and reflection of sociocultural specificities. This is best exemplified in the following observation by Swartz (2014, p. 149): "It is absolutely outrageous that most of what we know about disability issues across the board comes from wealthier countries, when by far the majority of disabled people in the world live in low- and middle-income countries". More recently, researchers such as Chataika and Mckenzie (2013) have undertaken the task of interrogating epistemological assumptions that researchers bring to the research endeavour, particularly when working in Southern settings. Others have questioned how disability is the legacy of inequality generated by imperialism and sustained through unequal power relations that have left majority of people with disabilities and their families in stark conditions of inequity and deprivation in almost every sphere of life, including health and education (Barnes & Sheldon, 2010; Meekosha & Soldatic, 2011). While such criticality of discourse is seen in the field of disability studies, many of these issues and concerns have remained in the background in research studies focusing on education and disability.

Reflecting on the focus and assumptions specifically underpinning educational research and disability in Southern contexts, Singal and Muthukrishna (2014) argue that current discourse in this field tends to be largely monolithic. In such a scenario, not only are the lives of persons with disabilities commonly constructed as backward or as victims of society but their parents are also seen as neglectful and disinterested in their child's education. Within such homogeneous representations, there is little desire to construct a deeper understanding of the lived realities of children/people with disabilities.

To illustrate this point further, it is useful to examine the contrasting ways in which disability is broadly construed in debates in countries of the North and South. In the former, as Goble (2014) notes, disability is primarily constructed in individualistic terms. Consequently, the disability movement has focused on the individual and his or her relationship with the state. This is further legitimised through prevailing neo-liberal ideologies. In Southern countries, where more traditional, agrarian and collective values still hold, disability is not merely understood in individualistic terms. Rather, in these contexts, the relational world is much more significant. Thus, it is only by locating the individual in the collective that one is able to develop a holistic appreciation of persons with disabilities in such contexts. In doing so, the endeavour is not to undermine the individual but to acknowledge the role of the family and other collective units. Finally, given the paucity of state-driven interventions in most of these countries, the family and community take on a more pivotal role.

Rather pertinently, in contexts where individual/personhood is strongly linked with family identity, Das and Addlakha (2001, p. 527) propose the notion of "connected body-selves". Here the presence of a family member with disability has an impact on the life opportunities available to others in the household. Thus, when understanding disability, it is not sufficient to focus on the individual; rather, one needs to also trace the impact on the family unit. So, for example, while access to school for children with disabilities is an important concern in research studies, less emphasis is placed on how having a sibling or a parent with disabilities might compromise another child's schooling and push him or her into 'adult carer' roles.

The few studies which have accounted for such contextual nuances provide powerful insights. For instance, Hoogeveen (2004) noted a significant education deficit in Ugandan households headed by a disabled person, as children in these households received less education. While this deficit could be attributed to children being pushed into adult carer roles, it could also be due to the reduced ability of the household to afford school fees because of the direct costs of disability. Thus, to the extent that education drives the ability to earn an income in the future, there is a greater likelihood that the "currently disabled are more likely to pass their poverty on to their children" (Lwanga-Ntale, 2003, p. 7). Not only is there an increased likelihood of intergenerational transfer of economic deprivation, but it is also likely to be the case that in managing their day-to-day survival, poor families with a disabled member do not have as much time to build social networks (or have different, possibly truncated ones) and hence have fewer mechanisms of support and limited social capital (Singal, Jeffery, Jain & Sood, 2011).

Reinforcing this need for addressing contextual sensitivities, Owusu-Ansah and Mji (2013) call upon researchers to include Indigenous knowledge in the design and implementation of research on disability issues. They note that for research to be empowering and meaningful, it must, of necessity, include "African thought and ideas" (p. 2). There is an urgency to redress this knowledge gap through sensitive research which takes account of local realities.

Similar perspectives echo strongly in the field of disability and education, where the research agenda continues to be driven with little regard to the real needs and concerns of local stakeholders. Here some insightful reflections can be garnered from the research discourse surrounding 'inclusive education'. While the case for inclusive education has been strongly advocated at various international and national policy forums, there is growing discontentment in relation to its efficacy among researchers working in Southern contexts. For example, Le Fanu (2014) makes a strong argument for questioning the assumed homogeneity around what inclusion should look like across different countries. He goes on to emphasise the importance of contextualising the concept of inclusive learning, to critique 'global inclusionism', as promoted by UNESCO, and argue instead for 'grounded inclusionism' rooted in, and sensitive to, local realities. Researchers such as Armstrong, Armstrong, and Spandagou (2011, p. 33) refer to the push towards inclusive education as "exhortations of first world agencies, and international donors", primarily as these proclamations disregard the realities of teachers and schools in many of these contexts. Analysing data gathered from teachers and classroom-based observations in six primary schools in Botswana, Mukhopadhyay (2015) observed how teachers "were confused about the conceptualisation of inclusive education, its terminologies and practices" (p. 28). A constant theme among the teacher interviews was the dominance of certain perspectives in the inclusive education debate, where the government was trying to mimic Western policies. He exemplifies this through a quote from a teacher, who stated: "most of the consultants undermine our knowledge and practice, and force us to believe that 'West is best'"(p. 30). In his conclusions, Mukhopadhyay highlights the perennial concern facing the field, wherein policies, such as inclusive education, are implemented through a top-down approach, while being completely neglectful of teachers' Indigenous knowledge.

Moreover, Singal and Muthukrishna (2014) argue that the focus in majority of the research studies is on what is not happening and what should be done, rather than identifying enablers which can help support the development of effective systems which support diversity. Thus, research which identifies and builds on strategies that are proven to be effective in different Southern contexts is needed. Here an interesting example is seen in the work of Lynch and colleagues (Lynch et al., 2011; Lynch, Lund, & Massah, 2014) who identify various low-cost efforts which can support the inclusion of children with albinism in Malawi. They discuss in depth the work being undertaken by iterant teachers in supporting children with visual impairment in mainstream schools. In both the projects, the researchers show how working with local stakeholders, encouraging them to share their 'knowledges', offers a deeper appreciation of the contextual opportunities and barriers facing different settings. Thus, forefronting local voices with a view towards building on the positives or enablers in the system should be a desirable and valued goal.

Undertaking more sophisticated research explorations

Over the past few years, understandings of disability have become far more nuanced. There is growing acceptance that there is no single definition of disability. It is acknowledged that disability is not a static condition, and it differs across both temporal and cultural dimensions. Thus, research approaches need to acknowledge that disability is only one part of the identity or experience (Shakespeare, 2006) and that people with disabilities do not exist in a vacuum. Research needs to engage with this fluidity and understand how disability experience unfolds across an individual's life course.

There is a growing call for collecting disaggregated data across many dimensions, such as geography, wealth, sex, age, and disability, as this can provide a reliable picture, which is essential for planning and adequate resourcing. Given the multidimensional and complex nature of disability, capturing such data is highly problematic. However, recent years have seen significant progress being made by the Washington Group (WG) on Disability Statistics. The WG is a United Nations sponsored City Group which was commissioned in 2001 specifically to improve the quality and international comparability of disability measure. Drawing on the bio-psycho-social approach proposed by the International Classification of Functioning, Disability and Health (WHO, 2001), it considers disability and functioning as outcomes of interactions between health conditions (diseases, disorders, and injuries) and contextual factors. It adopts a neutral language and does not distinguish between the type and cause of disability – for instance, between 'physical' and 'mental' health. Most importantly, it is universal because it covers all human functioning and treats disability as a continuum rather than categorising people with disabilities as a separate group. Disaggregated data can help examine, for example, how variables such as gender, poverty, and other social characteristics shape access to schooling. Having such insights can allow for the development of effective, targeted interventions to address educational exclusion.

In addition to this, we also need more nuanced understanding of teaching and learning processes in mainstream classrooms. In a review undertaken by Srivastava, de Boer, and Pijl (2015), they noted the limited evidence available on the effectiveness of inclusive learning for children with disabilities. Focused on identifying projects from 2000 to 2010, aimed at making education more inclusive in Southern contexts, they noted insufficient empirical evidence on the effectiveness of these efforts. However, they note how irrespective of this lack of evidence various NGOs and national bodies continue to promote similar approaches.

While there is evidence to suggest that teachers are positive about the social aspects of including children with disabilities, they are much more sceptical about the academic benefits (Donohue & Bornman, 2015). A commonly noted concern in the literature is the lack of pedagogical knowledge among teachers in relation to implementing effective teaching strategies for diverse groups of learners.

At a time of 'global learning crisis' (GMR, 2014), research has an important role to play in holding systems accountable to delivering quality education. Singal and Sabates (2016), based on an analysis of children's achievement on basic learning in reading, arithmetic and English tests administered as part of the Annual Status of Education Report (ASER) survey in Pakistan, concluded that children with disabilities are least likely to be learning. Findings from the survey showed that across the different types of disabilities, children reported as having moderate to severe disabilities were reported to be at the lowest level of the learning scale. These children were unable to read simple letters or recognise single-digit numbers. The percentage of children with disabilities assessed at this level in the reading task was nearly five times more than those reporting mild or no disabilities. These insights are significant in placing children with disabilities more firmly in the debates on quality of education.

Most importantly, we also need to understand the experiences of children and young people with disabilities in a range of educational institutions, if we are to make effective policy decisions. This demands undertaking in-depth qualitative work, focusing on narratives and rich exploration of perspectives and experiences. Choudhuri, Khandake, Hasan, and Rashida (2005) in an assessment of education for children with disabilities across Bangladesh, Nepal, Vietnam, and South Africa consulted a range of stakeholders, including children and young people with disabilities, and concluded: "There is definite scope, through further research, for more comprehensive and intensive investigations into how best existing educational systems for disabled children could be improved" (p. 41). This more sophisticated exploration of issues concerning and shaping the education of children with disabilities continues to be lacking in the field.

There is also a pressing need for the systematic inclusion of people with disabilities in the research process as investigators and, more importantly, as the ones posing the research questions and setting the agenda for research. Koistinen (2008), in her research focused on capturing the experiences of young people with disabilities on vocational training and employment in Zambia, used a life history approach. In gathering data for the project, she worked with two research assistants both having 'learning disabilities'. Reflecting on the experience, she noted that working with life stories offered an opportunity to share real-life experiences and raised important issues around empowerment, participation, and inclusion. Nevertheless, the voices of people with disabilities are largely excluded from research. As observed by Kembhavi and Wirz (2009, p. 289), "the move from rhetoric to reality is particularly slow in occurring for adolescents with disabilities, whose inputs and voices are largely left out of research and decision-making concerning their lives".

Chappell, Rule, Dlamini, and Nkala (2014) discuss how it is possible (and essential) to conduct participatory research with children and youth with disabilities in the South. Taking a reflexive stance, their article raises critical issues that underpin research with youth, in particular examining misconceptions surrounding disabled sexualities in the South African context and the competence of youth with disabilities in undertaking research. The authors conclude that such research, based on strong ethical principles, is very important and significant in terms of the impact it can have. Reflecting on their research they noted that "youth with disabilities as co-researchers learnt a considerable amount not only about doing research but also on a range of practical life skills and about themselves and their abilities" (p. 396). Additionally, the process was mutually informing and reflexive for the researchers themselves. Similar observations were noted in Singal (2010), where the process of research was found to be extremely positive for young people with disabilities who had been offered a unique opportunity to express their feelings and share their perspectives. In parallel, the research team, which had never previously worked with people with disabilities, developed a deeper and more nuanced appreciation of their lives.

Forming alliances and networks for research impact

The World Report on Disability (WHO, 2011) highlights the central need to collect data and information to inform national policies on disability in a wide range of places. It notes that collection of data should be the purview of statistical agencies, government agencies, international organisations, non-governmental organisations (NGOs) and Disabled People's Organisations (DPOs). These should be shared through various networks – both within countries and internationally – including via publications in academic journals. This drawing together of different data and information can only be done through alliances and strong networks.

It is only practical that in an emerging field the potential for impact is more likely to be maximised if the different stakeholders are connected. Therefore, the issue is not simply about doing more research on disability issues in education but also understanding how research insights can be harnessed for impact on policy and practice.

However, given that low priority has traditionally been accorded to disability in educational research funding, it is not surprising to see the scarcity of existing evidence. But as we move forward, developing a more coherent agenda for action must be based on rigorous research findings. While this is not something that researchers can simply do on their own, they can form strategic alliances with other key stakeholders. Swartz (2014, p. 5) rightly notes that "good research ... will not on its own change the world. It needs to be accompanied by sophisticated and strategic activism". It is fair to acknowledge that not everyone has the same set of skills; that is, activists are not necessarily good researchers, and neither are researchers good activists. However, alliances based on mutual respect and an appreciation of the value of research in advocacy can be powerful. Shakespeare (2006) observes that while focus in disability research has primary been on oppression, more attention needs to be paid to partnerships and alliances.

Researchers and DPOs/NGOs who are willing to work together, showing a commitment to establishing and developing a strategic working relationship, are important in taking the field forward. Interesting examples already exist in the field where international disability organisations such as CBM and Sightsavers successfully fund research centres in established universities in the UK and regularly draw on their findings to shape country programmes. However, much more is needed in bridging this divide. Aniekwe et al. (2012) on examining 'Academic-NGO Collaboration in International Development Research' note that while spaces seem to be opening for more engagement between academics and practitioners primarily driven by demands for evidence-based logic and demonstrable impact of research, key challenges exist arising from different perspectives around research, institutional time frames and philosophies, and also different outcome expectations and requirements.

Another common issue which is raised in the literature is the concern that a substantial amount of research on disability issues that occurs in the field in Southern contexts is not brought to publication in a form that is necessarily identified by academics as research. Here the main criticism in the field of disability and development is channelled towards NGOs. It is commonly argued that even though very interesting work is undertaken by many of these organisations, there is little documentation and publication of the process. What is important to acknowledge here is the difference in goals and approaches that underpins much of this work. For example, while academic researchers are influenced by the priorities of the academy and its career/promotion incentives, which are highly positively disposed towards publishing in high-status 'scientific' journals, NGOs, on the other hand, are working towards achieving behavioural or policy change in a specific community and do not necessarily prioritise knowledge building in the same way as the academic community (Olivier, Hunt, & Ridde, 2016).

This raises some interesting challenges, wherein NGOs, given their close direct connection with the field, do have rich grey literature and data, but it is very difficult to access many of these publications. Stubbs (1999) noted the difficulties she faced in accessing reports and articles written within local programmes or by local researchers. She elaborates on the challenges involved in physically going and finding such reports and important documentation on the shelves of organisations, rather than these being available in digital forms.

In reflecting on what might be done in the future to foster greater collaboration among academics and NGOs, Aniekwe et al. (2012) highlight the need for NGOs to better assert their role as shapers of research agendas, not just as consumers. NGOs and researchers together must engage in demands for access to data and research, more so when they have a stake in its generation and its use. As Albert and Harrison (2005, p. 9) note, "the most productive way forward research is to adopt an emancipatory approach that puts disabled people in the forefront but also embraces genuine partnership working with academics or other professionals".

In addition, there is a significant need for developing greater research literacy on part of NGOs and donors. It is important that they develop critical reading of research processes (data collection and analysis) in order to use research findings effectively. It will also help strengthen what they can demand of research (and researchers), to be realistic of time pressures, etc.

Finally, there is a need for researchers to become more skilled in communicating their research findings to a growing body of stakeholders such as NGOs and policymakers at both the national and international level if they are to have any impact on framing evidence-based policy. Albert and Harrison (2005) in writing up their 'messages from research' make a very useful distinction around how researchers "should be 'on tap' not 'on top'" (p. 8). This is imperative for researchers working in disability-related areas. It is important that researchers are trained to use their expertise in ways that have positive outcomes, challenge the exclusion of people with disabilities and are responsive to their real needs. Stubbs (1999), reflecting on the challenges of undertaking research in a cultural and national context very different from that of the researcher, powerfully argues that,

> development is a continuum from the personal to the global; research can bring the two ends of this continuum together. Spend your time on finding better, more authentic, more integral, more rigorous approaches to research which result in greater social justice and emancipation for all. (p. 20)

This observation holds true even though there have been advances in technology. In addition to this 'on tap/on top' distinction, I would like to add the 'on shelf' distinction – research which is left on the shelf and accessible only to a few is not worth pursuing. Meaningful research that can support the inclusion of people with disabilities is needed. Researchers have an ethical obligation to ensure that the research they undertake reaches a wide breath of stakeholders, and this would mean being aware of the pathways through which to get findings heard. Researchers need to be proficient in not only research literacies but also a range of academic literacies so that their messages can be disseminated. Indeed, the ethical dimension of research dissemination needs to be forefronted in current debates and developed upon (Robinson-Pant & Singal, 2013). The role of research in fostering change can no longer be undermined or overlooked; however, there continues to be a need to make sure that research (and researchers) is respectful of people and their contexts, while being rigorous in gathering evidence.

As disability-related issues are finally making it to the global centre stage, there is an urgent need for educational research to provide direction. However, this will require an in-depth appreciation of the realities and concerns of

Southern contexts. At a time when global discourse on disability is gaining more prominence, there is urgent need for increased rigour and respect for the local and heightened sense of responsibility among researchers committed to the educational inclusion of children/young people with disabilities.

References

Albert, B., & Harrison, M. (2005). *Messages from research: Disability knowledge and research (KaR) programme.* London, England: DFID.

Aniekwe, C. C., Hayman, R., Mdee, A., Akuni, J., Lall, P., & Stevens, D. (2012). *Academic-NGO collaboration in international development research: A reflection on the issues.* Retrieved from https://www.intrac.org/wpcms/wp-content/uploads/2016/09/Academic-NGO-Collaboration-in-International-Development_September-2012.pdf

Armstrong, D., Armstrong, A. C., & Spandagou, I. (2011). Inclusion: By choice or by chance? *International Journal of Inclusive Education, 15*(1), 29–39.

Arnot, M., Casely-Hayford, L., & Chege, F. (2012). Schooling, rights and urban poverty. In C. Colclough (Ed.), *Education outcomes and poverty: A reassessment* (pp. 36–54). London, England: Routledge.

Bakhshi, P., Kett, M., & Oliver, K. (2013). *What are the impacts of approaches to increase the accessibility to education for people with a disability across developed and developing countries and what is known about the cost-effectiveness of different approaches?* London, England: EPPI-Centre.

Barnes, C. (2001, October 24). *'Emancipatory' disability research: Project or process?* Public lecture at City Chambers, Glasgow. Retrieved from https://disability-studies.leeds.ac.uk/wp-content/uploads/sites/40/library/Barnes-glasgow-lecture.pdf

Barnes, C., & Sheldon, A. (2010). Disability, politics and poverty in a majority world context. *Disability and Society, 25*(7), 771–782.

Berghs, M. (2010). Coming to terms with inequality and exploitation in an African state: Researching disability in Sierra Leone. *Disability & Society, 25*(7), 861–865.

Braunholtz, T. (2007). *Chronic poverty: An introduction* (Policy Brief, No. 1). Retrieved from https://cdn.odi.org/media/documents/1768.pdf

Brown, A. M. B. (2014). Situating disability within comparative education: A review of the literature. *Global Education Review, 1*(1), 56–75.

Chappell, P., Rule, P., Dlamini, M., & Nkala, N. (2014). Troubling power dynamics: Youth with disabilities as co-researchers in sexuality research in South Africa. *Childhood, 21*, 3385–3399.

Chataika, T., & Mckenzie, J. (2013). Considerations of an African childhood disability studies. In T. Curran & K. Runswick-Cole (Eds.), *Disabled children's childhood studies: Critical approaches in a global context* (pp. 152–163). London, England: Palgrave Macmillan.

Chomba, M. J., Mukuria, S. G., Kariuki, P. W., Tumuti, S., & Bunyasi, B. A. (2014). Education for students with intellectual disabilities in Kenya: Challenges and prospects. *Disability Studies Quarterly, 34*(4). DOI: 10.18061/dsq.v34i4.3846.

Choudhuri, M. A., Khandake, A. J., Hasan, R., & Rashida, S. A. (2005). *Situational analysis and assessment of education for children with disabilities in Bangladesh, South Asia, East Asia and South Africa.* Retrieved from https://hpod.law.harvard.edu/pdf/Kar-thematic_edu.pdf

Chronic Poverty Research Centre. (2006). CPRC methods toolbox. Retrieved from https://www.chronicpoverty.org/uploads/publication_files/toolbox-4.pdf

Das, V., & Addlakha, R. (2001). Disability and domestic citizenship: Voice, gender and the making of the subject. *Public Culture, 13*(3), 511–531.

DFID. (2001). *Disability, poverty and development.* Retrieved from http://hpod.org/pdf/Disability-poverty-and-development.pdf

Donohue, D. K., & Bornman, J. (2015). South African teachers' attitudes toward the inclusion of learners with different abilities in mainstream classrooms. *International Journal of Disability, Development and Education, 62*(1), 42–59.

Global Monitoring Report. (2014). *Teaching and learning: Achieving quality for all.* Paris: UNESCO.

Goble, C. (2014). Dependence, independence and normality. In J. Swain, S. French, C. Barnes, & C. Thomas (Eds.), *Disabled barriers-enabling environments* (pp. 31–36). London, England: Sage.

Grech, S. (2014). Disability, poverty and education: Perceived barriers and (dis) connections in rural Guatemala. *Disability and the Global South, 1*(1), 128–152.

Hoogeveen, J. G. (2004). Measuring welfare for small but vulnerable groups: Poverty and disability in Uganda. *Journal of African Economies, 14*(4), 603–631.

Howgego, C., Miles, S., & Myers, J. (2014). *Inclusive learning: Children with disabilities and difficulties in learning.* Retrieved from https://www.heart-resources.org/wp-content/uploads/2014/09/Inclusive-Learning-Topic-Guide.pdf

Jeffery, R., & Singal, N. (2008). Measuring disability in India. *Economic and Political Weekly, 43*(12–13), 22–24.

Kembhavi, G., & Wirz, S. (2009). Engaging adolescents with disabilities in research. *ALTER: European Journal of Disability Research, 3*(3), 286–296.

Koistinen, M. H. (2008). *Understanding experiences of vocational training and employment for persons with learning disabilities in Zambia: Lessons for the future.* Sussex, England: University of Sussex.

Le Fanu, G. (2014). International development, disability, and education towards a capacities focused discourse and praxis. *International Journal of Educational Development, 38,* 69–79.

Lwanga-Ntale, C. (2003). *Chronic poverty and disability in Uganda.* Retrieved from https://www.chronicpoverty.org/pdfs/2003conferencepapers/lwangaNtale.pdf

Lynch, P., Lund, P., & Massah, B. (2014). Identifying strategies to enhance the educational inclusion of visually impaired children with albinism in Malawi. *International Journal of Educational Development, 39,* 226–234.

Lynch, P., McCall, S., Douglas, G., McLinden, M., Mogesa, B., Mwaura, M., & Njoroge, M. (2011). Inclusive educational practices in Kenya: Evidencing practice of itinerant teachers who work with children with visual impairment in local mainstream schools. *International Journal of Educational Development, 31,* 478–488.

Meekosha, H., & Soldatic, K. (2011). Human rights and the Global South: The case of disability. *Third World Quarterly, 32*(8), 1383–1397.

Mukhopadhyay, S. (2015). West is best? A post-colonial perspective on the implementation of inclusive education in Botswana. *Korean Educational Development Institute, 12*(1), 19–39.

Nuwagaba, E. L., & Rule, P. (2015). Navigating the ethical maze in disability research: Ethical contestations in an African context. *Disability & Society, 30*(2), 255–269.

Olivier, C., Hunt, M. R., & Ridde, V. (2016). NGO–researcher partnerships in global health research: Benefits, challenges, and approaches that promote success. *Development in Practice, 26*(4), 444–455.

Owusu-Ansah, F. E., & Mji, G. (2013). African indigenous knowledge and research. *African Journal of Disability*, 2(1). DOI: 10.4102/ajod.v2i1.30.

Plan International. (2013). *Include us! A study of disability amongst Plan International's sponsored children.* Retrieved from https://plan-international.org/uploads/2022/01/2013_include_us_full_report_en-1.pdf

Robinson-Pant, A., & Singal, N. (2013). Research ethics in comparative and international education: Reflections from anthropology and health. *Compare*, 43(4), 443–463.

Robson, C., & Evans, P. (2003). *Educating children with disabilities in developing countries: The role of data sets.* Retrieved from https://eprints.hud.ac.uk/id/eprint/475/1/RobsonEducating.pdf

Shakespeare, T. (2006). *Disability rights and wrongs.* London, England: Routledge.

Singal, N. (2010). Doing disability research in a Southern context: Challenges and possibilities. *Disability & Society*, 25(4), 415–426.

Singal, N. (2017). Education in disability and poverty debates: Research insights from Southern contexts. In M. T. Hughes & E. Talbott (Eds.), *The Wiley handbook of diversity in special education* (pp. 167–182). West Sussex, England: Wiley Blackwell.

Singal, N., De, A., & Khanna-Bhutani, S. (2017, July). *Secondary education for young people with disabilities in India. Critical analysis of provision under IEDSS.* Paper presented at the National Conference on Policy and Planning for Inclusion Education with focus on Children with Special Needs, NUEPA, New Delhi, India.

Singal, N., Jeffery, R., Jain, A., & Sood, N. (2011). The enabling role of education in the lives of young people with disabilities in India: Achieved and desired outcomes. *International Journal of Inclusive Education*, 15(10), 1205–1218.

Singal, N., & Muthukrishna, N. (2014). Education, childhood and disability in countries of the South: Re-positioning the debates. *Childhood*, 21(3), 293–307.

Singal, N., & Sabates, R. (2016, January 27). Access and learning are equally important for children with disabilities. *Global Partnership for Education.* Retrieved from https://www.globalpartnership.org/blog/access-and-learning-are-equally-important-children-disabilities

Srivastava, M., de Boer, A., & Pijl, S. J. (2015). Inclusive education in developing countries: A closer look at its implementation in the last 10 years. *Educational Review*, 67(2), 179–195.

Stubbs, S. (1999). Engaging with difference: Soul-searching for a methodology in disability and development research. In E. Stone (Ed.), *Disability and development: Learning from action and research on disability in the majority world* (pp. 257–279). Leeds, England: The Disability Press.

Swartz, L. (2014). Five challenges for disability related research in sub-Saharan Africa. *African Journal of Disability*, 3(2). DOI: 10.4102/ajod.v3i2.149.

Tomlinson, S. (1982). *A sociology of special education.* London, England: Routledge.

Tomlinson, S. (2015). Is a sociology of special and inclusive education possible? *Educational Review*, 67(3), 273–281.

UN. (2000). *The millennium development goals (MDGs) and disability.* Retrieved from https://www.un.org/development/desa/disabilities/issues/the-millennium-development-goals-mdgs-and-disability.html#about

UN. (2006, December 13). *Convention on the rights of persons with disabilities.* Retrieved from https://www.ohchr.org/en/instruments-mechanisms/instruments/convention-rights-persons-disabilities

UN. (2015, October 6). *The sustainable development goals (SDGs) and disability*. Retrieved from https://www.un.org/development/desa/disabilities/news/news/the-sustainable-development-goals-sdgs-and-disability.html

UNICEF. (2013). *The state of the world's children 2013: Children with disabilities*. Retrieved from https://www.unicef.org/media/84886/file/SOWC-2013.pdf

UNICEF. (2014). *Child development and education*. Retrieved from https://www.unicef.ca/en/discover/education

UNESCO. (2015). *The right to education for persons with disabilities*. Retrieved from https://unesdoc.unesco.org/ark:/48223/pf0000232592

WHO. (2001). *International classification of functioning, disability and health (ICF)*. Retrieved from https://www.who.int/classifications/international-classification-of-functioning-disability-and-health

WHO. (2011, December 14). *World report on disability*. Retrieved from https://www.who.int/publications/i/item/9789241564182

4
DECENTRING HEGEMONIC GENDER THEORY

The implications for educational research

Shailaja Fennell and Madeleine Arnot

The beginning of the twenty-first century witnessed a profusion of new thinking in the field of gender across the social sciences within North American and Western European universities. New philosophical and political conceptualisations of gender equality have been substantially reworked to consider new social agendas around multi-culturalism and diversity while new notions of citizenship and nationhood have required a reconsideration of how to position women in contemporary society (Benhabib, 2002; Yuval-Davis & Werbner, 2005). This re-engagement with the theoretical foundations of gender research occurs at a time when gender concerns have been placed on international agendas. Gender education today is now far more strongly linked to the drive to alleviate poverty through economic growth, universal human rights, and the development of democratic governance which, in turn, is assumed to provide the conditions for empowerment (Nussbaum, 2000; Sen, 2001). The emergence of global equality agendas associated with new frameworks and metrics for national growth also provides a unique opportunity to bring together the diverse understandings of gender that are emerging from the different trajectories taken by academic traditions in Western Europe/North America and other regional/national traditions of research (Tsing, 1993).

However, while the knowledge gathered and reviewed in the field of gender studies has been disseminated globally over the twentieth century, it has paid relatively little regard to the contexts and meanings that have simultaneously emerged in other regions of the world. Connell's (2007) work on *Southern Theory: The Global Dynamics of Knowledge in Social Science* shows how the hegemonic knowledge created in the powerful academic apparatus of global metropoles systematically denies the creativity and contribution of academic knowledge coming out of other regional and national academies.

Similarly, so often Indigenous knowledge has been denied. According to Bhola (2002), "howsoever development is defined, the regeneration of indigenous knowledge systems is part of the developmental challenge ... The dialectic between indigenous and modern knowledge will have to be self-consciously and systematically guided to be mutually enriching" (Bhola, 2002, pp. 3, 10).

Yet, gender scholarship in education has only relatively recently started addressing this challenge. Up till recently, it has been part of a one-way traffic that leaves Western Europe and North America without having been influenced by insights from Indigenous cultural traditions. Also, the channels through which this metropolitan knowledge is transmitted to the global periphery confirm the belief that policy is generated, if not internationally, then through state agencies and private enterprises (Fennell, 2007). Consequently, gender education research and policy-making appears to be located more within development studies departments, government ministries, and NGOs than in the university faculties of education or institutes for training new teachers. As a result, the impact of global gender education research on national educational systems tends to be diffuse and ill-defined. Thus, even though gender researchers located outside Western metropoles work in innovative ways within their own countries and cross-national boundaries in order to undertake comparative international research, their local research on gender and education (schooling, adult education, and informal education) has difficulty achieving international scholarly impact. Indeed, localised knowledge about education and the functioning of the school system appears to be less significant than research funded for an audience of global policy-makers.

National gender agendas in education, therefore, are in danger of being both the symbol of progress and the vehicle of contemporary neo-colonialism. Where international agendas uncritically import liberal individualising models for education into developing countries, they could undermine women's position and future and perhaps could even aggravate existing gender divisions. As Unterhalter (2007) and Mundy and Murphy (2001) point out, transnational declarations of gender and education, even those which highlight gender equality rather than gender access, can be Trojan horses – in other words vehicles for other ideologies, only some of which might be liberatory for women. The tendencies of such hegemonic gender education research are to recreate its own knowledge in distant geographies in its own image. It is noticeable that the new thinking in gender research relating to the Millennium Development Goals (MDGs), on the whole, does not tend to challenge the hegemony of Anglo-American gender education theory nor question its assumptions and conceptual suppositions. The concept of Education for All (EFA) with its implications for national growth is in effect an incentive to export current hegemonic gender theorising in education globally, encouraging other regions of the world to focus their attention on formal mass schooling (rather than informal education), open up individual 'choice biographies' and cultivate policies that release girls from the traditional cultures. In this context, the lack of critical engagement with and validation of 'Southern' gender theory arguably disadvantages precisely those countries which are the target of the MDGs.

According to Bhola (2002), writing in *Africa Today*, there are two intersecting dialectics – that between education and development and between modern knowledge and what he calls Indigenous knowledge. In resolving these conflicts especially in a context in which there is considerable international pressure to deliver certain targets, national institutions of education within a developing nation are in danger of losing the creative knowledge and imagination of their Indigenous cultures. Such nations are also likely to find it hard to feel ownership of what is seen as alien cultural/political agendas. A more productive response to new global education agendas is to confront and understand the particular historical and intellectual forces in different cultures/nations which generate specific conceptual and analytical frameworks. Connell (2007) suggests that the key is to return to the manner in which knowledge is gleaned, accumulated, and distributed across nations and the world. In the gender context, such accounts will constitute what Ramamurthy (2007, p. 1) called the "geographies of feminist knowledge formation". Using this approach, the millennium targets for gender and education could provide new arenas in which to conduct such studies, even if international agencies which promoted such targets did not include such South–North learning. In the case of gender and education, the MDGs offer a rather unique opportunity to start such dialogical work.

This chapter represents our own first attempt to engage with those global dialogues and to reposition gender theory in relation to education and development. The way we have structured the chapter is to think first about the national and international contexts within which gender education research has been situated. We compare the settings as they have been perceived and analysed in Western Europe and North America on one hand, and those analysing the dynamics of gender in education from locations within Africa and South Asia, on the other.[1] We then highlight four main themes which have been developed by gender theorists from this latter group, many of whom have been trained mainly in the United States, but are critical of the hegemonic tendencies of what they see as 'Western' or so-called 'Northern' gender theory. This much neglected group of gender theorists, we argue, have identified new ways of thinking about gender that are of great significance for the gender educational field internationally. We begin our discussion by contextualising Southern feminist challenges.

Southern feminist challenges to universalising agendas

EFA provides a particular and unique contemporary vantage point from which to view the international impact of gender research on education. The push for EFA was a response by international agencies and national governments to address the inability of economic development to ensure education for all citizens (Education International, 2003). The new agenda therefore breaks away from a long tradition of development thinking where economic development is centre stage, industrialisation dominated the agenda and education was regarded as the handmaiden to achieve this objective. The effect of this shift in thinking is that gender relations are now evidenced in the education policies and documents put out by governments.

However long before this policy shift, feminist researchers had questioned whether women's contribution to economic growth had been adequately recognised in the then prevalent approach to development.[2] Mainstream economic categories cast women into one of two roles – those of *productive workers* and *reproductive mothers* – in a manner powerfully reminiscent of the Western European and North American feminist debates of the mid-twentieth century. Critical feminist research brought to the fore both Marxist analysis (Barrett & McIntosh, 1982; Mies, 1986) and post-Marxist critiques (Tinker, 1990) of national planning for economic growth. The critiques of human capital set out by Western European and North American gender theorists offered a new global vantage point with which to understand the impact of development processes on gender relations. These critiques evolved into a more radical Gender and Development (GAD) approach to gender analysis within the UN system. Development feminists also revealed the lack of recognition of gender disparities within national planning with the education of women and children relegated to smaller government departments such as social welfare rather than powerful ministries such as those of finance or human resources.

The recent emphasis on gender education within the field of international development is both a cause and a consequence of the MDGs for 2005 and 2015 which focus on gender equality in access and participation. Surprisingly, however, despite a history of feminist pressure on international agencies, especially post Beijing, development feminists and Southern gender theory appears to have had little influence on the UNESCO Global Monitoring Reports (UNESCO, 2002, 2003, 2005). A sustained dialogue between metropolitan and Southern intellectual gender education traditions could have opened up an opportunity, if not a rationale, to engage development feminism with North American and Western European theorising on education and to encourage more interfaces between these two traditions and the writings of Southern gender theory. Growing numbers of international students migrating to universities in Europe and North America to study, research and teach have led to more critical interrogations of metropolitan gender theory. Such writing provides new voices within feminist education research that engaged critically with the colonial and postcolonial European and American epistemologies. Globalised feminists now use their lived experiences in specific Asian and African locations to identify postcolonial and Indigenous feminist standpoints. Such contributions challenge contemporary American and Western European feminism which does not have much room for the local specificities of African and Asian feminist history, epistemology, and analysis. The postcolonial predicament in which American/European feminism is caught is now increasingly evident. Arguably the time is ripe for researchers engaging in EFA to recognise the hegemonic influences of such gender education research traditions.

Bringing non-metropolitan voices to the centre and acknowledging the importance of the hegemonising aspects of metropolitan knowledge in social science is a huge task (Connell, 2007). At a less ambitious level, we have started on the process of 'hearing' African and Indian feminists' critical readings of metropolitan gender theory as a way forward in constructing a more globally informed field of gender education research. We have elicited four themes which are particularly relevant to educational researchers (even if not originally discussed as such) while recognising that there are many more complex arguments to be found in theorisations of gender in many other global locations. The first such theme is one that encourages us to deconstruct universalisations within gender theory.

De-universalising categories: the problematic 'Third World Woman' and by implication the 'girl child'

In 1988, Chandra Talpade Mohanty[3] who described herself as "a Third World feminist trained in the United States, interested in questions of culture, knowledge production and activism in an international context" (Mohanty, 2003a, p. 45) wrote a now celebrated piece 'Under Western Eyes: Feminist Scholarship and Colonial Discourses' (Mohanty, 2003b). Here she pointed out that what she regarded as 'Western feminist research' was 'colonising' in the manner in which it depicted women from other societies as an essential category of 'Third World Woman'. Women in the developing world were categorised by their female gender (read: sexually constrained) and Third World character (read: poor, uneducated, tradition bound, domesticated). The ideological construction of 'Third World Woman' was based on a presumed social homogeneity, or shared characteristic, despite the existence of major differences in race and social class and experiences in the real lives of these women. The effect was to create a single story of male violence and oppression on subjugated and powerless women who were seen as dependent on men, oppressed by religion and family systems and where the way forward was to create a single sisterhood that was united in its struggle for 'freedom'.

In 'Cartographies of Struggle', Mohanty (2003a) extended her analysis of Western hegemonic knowledge showing the ways in which the term 'Native', constructed in anthropology in the early twentieth century, drew on racial and sexual stereotypes to provide the epistemological basis for the term 'Third

World Woman'. This analysis offered a valuable examination of the paralysing power of binary forms of 'othering', creating in this case a distinction between the 'West' and the rest of the world.

The implication of Mohanty's analysis is that knowledge production in the literary and social-scientific disciplines as a "discursive site for struggle" is just as important as material struggle (Mohanty, 2003a, p. 76). Her call for a more nuanced and political understanding of the categories used by social scientists (particularly those involved in development studies) is equally relevant for gender educational research in today's global context. The concept of the universal 'girl child', for example, which is applied to Southern contexts and often used in relation to female educational access in EFA targets, may well be another example of such essentialising. Despite sophisticated awareness of the intersectionality of social class, ethnic, and gender identities in metropolitan social science, the concept of the 'girl child' in Southern countries is used to explore educational access, participation, and treatment. It too could be regarded as part of hegemonic knowledge production that infantilises girls, seeing them not only as 'childlike' hence without agency, but also as a homogenous (undifferentiated) group located within economic, familial, and legal structures and the product of oppressive age and gender power relations within Southern societies. As a result, the diversity of experiences of young women within such societies, the range of possible femininities, and indeed their contribution to the survival of their families and their own negotiations and resistances are likely to go unrecognised.

Mohanty (1988) also argued that, as a consequence of these discursive constructions of 'third world' women, only those aspects of their lives which relate to what she regarded as 'Western' epistemologies were opened up for investigation. When international development brings education into the centre of its aid agenda and political concerns, there could well be a similar danger – that new universals regarding gender (this time of young people) will again be based on, for example, the historical features of the Western European industrial experience and the way these models have been cast in theories of economic development. The plight of the 'girl child' (or boy for that matter) in relation to educational goals may be considered only within the framework therefore of individualised transitions from family to school and from schooling to work rather than through the deeper formations of subjectivity, identity, and belonging within complex colonial and traditional cultural heritages (Bhola, 2002).

Contemporary research about gender and education in Southern contexts today has to consider whether it recognises the influence of such historical and negative stereotyping of the 'third world' girl, her teacher and her community. As Mohanty pointed out, women (and we would argue, female children) cannot be studied as gendered beings without recourse to the histories that have created the nation states within which they are located and how these histories have been refashioned by the colonial encounter. Hegemonic gender discourses that are woven in these contexts permeate into the micro-politics and family practices that surround them. The plurality of gender relations in multicultural societies such as those in Africa and South Asia also requires that gender difference should be replaced by *differentiation* with regard to oppression, conflict, and struggle (Mohanty, 2003a). Mohanty argues that what is needed is a transnational multicultural feminism which is radical, antiracist, and non-heterosexual and which can challenge a hegemonic capitalist regime: thus, the "task that feminist educators, artists, scholars and activists face is that of historicising and denaturalising the ideas, beliefs and values of global capital such that underlying exploitative social relations and structures are made visible" (Mohanty, 2003c, p. 124).

The 'othering' of motherhood and the importance of relational worlds

The second theme we want to consider relates to the types of 'othering' of the relational worlds inhabited and experienced by women outside the metropoles of North America and Western Europe. Obioma Nnaemeka, a Nigerian Professor of French and Women's Studies at Indiana University, takes this critique of universal categories further in *The Politics of (M)othering: Womanhood, Identity, and Resistance in African Literature* (1997a). In the introduction to this collection Nnaemeka identifies the opposition between Western and African feminism as the failure of the former to examine the relational roles which women take on, as a basis for identity. Nnaemeka (1997b), like Mohanty, points to the apparent hostility of Western feminism to motherhood – which she calls the 'othering of motherhood' (p. 5). This process of 'othering' leads to an under-privileging of African women's roles and identities (p. 1).[4] In the Nigerian context, a woman gains the status of a mother through acts of bearing and nurturing her children. The denial of women's roles as mothers (or even sisters and daughters) in associational African contexts has impoverished the social scientific understandings of female power in these communities. This has meant that the role of mothering as a relational identity and a form of resistance in opposition to local power relations has been hidden from the gaze of Western feminist researchers (Nnaemeka, 1997a). Nnaemeka's emphasis upon the importance of relational gender roles recasts the domestic sphere as an active site for small acts of resistance. Indeed, recent educational research on female para-teachers working in domestic-based pre-schools and schools in India and Bangladesh points to the ability of young women to use the discourse of the familial and the communal and women's status in the domestic sphere to achieve small levels of empowerment. In some cases, they are able to employ gender roles in what Saigal (2007) calls 'acts of citizenship'. Teaching, for example, gives girls access to new educational and livelihood paths (Raynor, 2007). Bringing in notions of domesticity and mothering allows us to view the education and lives of women not as circumscribed between the private and the public (as in Western European thinking) but as developing a public role in the community that concurs with, rather than opposes, their life within the family.

Nnaemeka (2003) also argues that, in Nigeria, there is interplay between gender, temporality and spirituality and that bodies, time and space operate in a non-linear manner. Relational worlds that are mediated by members of a community cannot therefore be fully comprehended by models that follow single lines of causality, i.e., a woman's life does not fall into time-mediated compartments of girl, sister, mother, and grandmother, but these may overlap and coexist through her life (and across lives). In this context, it is also important to explore notions of female friendship that are present among women in the Yoruba tribe. These are not always mediated by kinship. Women's friendship groups are a long-standing part of communal life and provide African women with important pathways to survive, gain status, and assume positions of power in a community. Nnaemeka steers clear of imposing the Western concept of 'feminism' to describe such groups – the term, she argues, is not relevant to the African context. Oyeronke Oyewumi,[5] in her book *The Invention of Women* (1997), argues along similar lines, although she places more emphasis on the importance of kinship. Without a recognition of the role of kinship, faulty conclusions have been drawn by researchers that women living in societies outside Western Europe and North America are subjugated by their men and worse off than those who were located in Northern geographical regions (Oyewumi, 2003a, 2003b). The incomplete, and often faulty, learnings that feminist research has gained from the analysis of gender in African societies have usurped the local positions of power that women have access to as a consequence of their associational experiences (Nzegwu, 2003). It is the denial by Western feminists of African women's power within such Indigenous relational worlds, forms of negotiation, friendship and systems of knowledge construction that relegates them to the status of subject/victim, rather than their cultures.

The implication here is that policy recommendations to empower African women have created an epistemic basis for understanding gender relations that fails to recognise African women's right to community and forces them into the liberal market economics of a globalising world. Of great significance to researchers in the global educational field is the need to see female *friendship* and *kinship* as the framework and context for analysing gender relations in education.

Individualism and the sex/gendering of the body

The third theme we have drawn from African and Indian gender writing relates specifically to the critique of individualism and its focus on individual embodied selves. These concepts form the basis of so much Anglo-centric gender education research. In the African context (for example, the Nigerian), this bodily focus can distort the analysis of gender relations. Regarding bodies as gender and sexual sites is highly problematic, according to Nnaemeka (2003). There are epistemic consequences from representing the gendering of the body as necessarily linked to sexual acts. Here again Nnaemeka argues that, in African societies such as her own, it is the relational world that provides the context for individual acts and it is within these relational acts that bodies gain gender values. These values do not accrue from the sexual aspects of the body but from its age and experience as these are regarded as key in the relational world. For example, the older member's age and experience adds value to younger members who are their apprentices, in rituals and in social exchange.

Similarly, Oyewumi highlights the dangers of basing research on the needs of the individual and a view of bodies as merely biological entities (Oyewumi, 2005). This, she argues, is a false basis for research outside the American experience of modernity. American and European philosophical traditions, she reminds us, should be considered exceptional rather than the norm. In *The Invention of Women* (Oyewumi, 1997) she highlights the ways in which Western European and North American history and social science understands the body through its *visual sense*. Consequently, it is the body of the individual that is regarded as the central actor rather than the actions of the individuals which contribute to a particular act or ritual. In a fascinating analysis, she highlights how the practices of African body clothing, piercing etc. are regarded as degrading by European and American feminists because they involve placing the body in seemingly demeaning positions. Yet these very practices are regarded as important rituals by African theorists (Oyewumi, 2003a). Secondly, she argues that the visual world is downplayed in African societies where there is a greater emphasis on an oral tradition of learning. Learning by listening gives considerable significance to the *auditory senses*. Where a young man or woman is associated with a headman/headwoman in an oral discourse, they acquire the power of headship through these acts – they are not regarded as young and unlearned, since in such conversation they take on the attributes of the old and experienced (Oyewumi, 1997).

Agency, dislocation and positionalities in the global gender education field

The concepts which have emerged in a variety of Indian and African feminisms do not find an easy equivalence with the gender theorising in the West. Positioning oneself in relation to the tensions between colonial American and European discourses, postcolonial feminism, and Indigenous knowledge forms is a far more difficult task than most education researchers admit to.

Decentring hegemonic gender theory

The fourth theme which emerges from this literature relates to issues of *agency, dislocation, and positionality*.

The concept of *agency* that is being advocated in the world of African gender studies is that agency should not be seen "in terms of dependence or independence but interdependence and intersubjectivity" (Nyamnjoh, 2002, p. 118). By engaging with and reworking notions of agency found within American and European social science, a number of Indian and African theorists have subjected the internal contradictions that have emerged in Indigenous feminisms to an expanded Foucauldian framework (John, 2004).

This debate about agency and the value of the contribution of Foucault to that discussion lies at the heart of much feminist reaction to North American and Western European theorising. A number of writers outside these metropoles employ poststructuralist deconstruction methods to voice their discontent with the hegemonic intellectual apparatus. They have reworked the underlying concepts of structure and agency within American and European social science to privilege both contextual and Indigenous meanings. Many draw on Spivak's (1985) influential writing[6] where she points out that it is only by 'decentring' the individual at the heart of a Foucauldian analysis and removing the geographical imperialisms that lurk behind his analysis that agency can be fully understood. Spivak asked whether 'the subaltern can speak?' in poststructuralist research as long as her voice is directed by intellectuals who are unable to de-centre themselves or their established forms of epistemology. If 'subalterns' such as 'Third World Women' are to be heard then we need to change the way in which we as academics use and work with ideas or we will not be able to interpret the articulation of the subaltern woman. Subaltern Studies, which seeks to understand the position of an individual as a consequence of being situated within a particular set of relations, must ensure that postcolonial analysis does not continue to give central place to dominant knowledge systems – it must be willing to move away from such existing systems of knowledge to permit exchanges between speaker and listener (c.f. Connell, 2007).

From Nnaemeka's point of view Foucauldian theory also offers little help in redressing the *political* problems associated with Western European and North American epistemologies since "post structuralism's focus on discourse and aesthetics instead of social action encourages the egocentricity and individualism that undermines collective action" (Nnaemeka, 2003, p. 364). Escaping such egocentricity and individualism would involve the construction of a different sort of gender theory, other than that of poststructuralism. A recognition of the complexity of African countries requires in Nnaemeka's view what she calls '*Nego-feminism*' – a feminism of negotiation or the non-ego form of feminism. Essentially Nego-feminism challenges the Cartesian duality of public/private spheres and male and female forces on which North American and Western European research is premised. It also implies a full exploration of these relational worlds of young men and women without slipping back into the forms of individualism and individualisation associated with Western liberal democracy. The African sense of identity is located within the communal rather than individual space.

Despite its limitations, the attraction of poststructuralism for gender theorists outside North American and Western European metropoles is that it requires feminist researchers to unpack not just the epistemologies that they have encountered but to also be prepared to be equally scrupulous in the manner in which they unpack their own learnings. The opportunities provided by the principles of *reflexivity* and *positionality* to undertake such a journey are numerous, but the researcher must be prepared for the personal and professional consequences of turning one's gaze within. Reflexive writing by American and European gender researchers working on education in the development context is surprisingly low. In contrast, a number of the African and South Asian authors we have cited have considered their own journey across the divide and dislocations between metropolitan and Southern theory. For example, in her article 'Genealogies of Community, Home, and Nation', Mohanty (2003c) describes in great detail what it meant for her to arrive from India and to engage with feminism in the United States in the 1980s and 1990s. Her own genealogy is "partial and deliberate. It is a genealogy that I find emotionally and politically enabling – it is part of the genealogy that underlies my self-identification as an educator involved in a pedagogy of liberation" (Mohanty, 2003c, p. 136).

Mary E. John also writes eloquently about the difficulties and dangers of such *positionality*. Having completed her PhD in the History of Consciousness Program in 1991 at the University of California, John now heads the Centre for Women's Development Studies, in New Delhi. In her article 'Postcolonial Feminists in a Western Intellectual Field', John (1996a) described herself as a 'Third World feminist'. She put forward a notion of 'discrepant dislocations' to understand how:

> the dislocation from a sheltered Indian middle-class environment, where a consciousness of privilege predominates, to a milieu as highly sexualized, and with such intensified and refined technologies of gender as this one, does lead to the espousal of a more explicitly feminist politics.
>
> *John (1996a, p. 16)*

John critiques American and European feminist research for its inability to understand such complex positionality and she points to the need to construct a new politics consequent on such personal dislocations. She argues that it is the insistence of working with a notion of a primary process of knowledge construction that prioritises a single alien epistemology and a hegemonic system of knowledge production. One result of this hegemony was that

American feminist research drew on anthropological antecedents to place the non-American researcher in the position of the 'native informant', treating them as the object of research.

John also questioned poststructuralism's inordinate concern with epistemology and abstraction and decried the relative disregard for the specific. Interestingly John drew upon Spivak's critique of Foucault's notion of 'specific intellect' which relies upon an *unrecognised* specificity'. In not being specific enough himself, Foucault is understood to have glossed over imperialism and other historical inequities such that his theory was in danger of encouraging denigration and was unable to deal with the consequences of its own vagueness and lack of historical regard. John was thinking here not just of her own positionality but also the place of gender within specific locales. On the personal front, John (1996a) pointed out that feminism is a politics before it is an epistemology – where questions of representation must deal with who speaks for whom as much as with what is being said. John argued that the extreme marginalisation that Mohanty spoke of in the early 1980s was being replaced by a growing recognition of the contributions of postcolonial intellectuals, and "the emergence of Third World feminists ... eager to delve into archives or engage in fieldwork in order to lay claim to a lost and repudiated history" (John, 1996b, unnumbered).

These postcolonial critiques have constructed an intellectual apparatus which gives greater attention to history, and particularly to those power relations between colonial power and colonised subjects that continue to permeate social science research. The call for a decentring of hegemonic power is welcome but the promise can only become a reality if serious consideration is given to how to ensure that local and national specificities are brought into the centre of gender education research. The importance of positionality in directing feminist gender education to the need to understand the 'subject' of study is valuable but will not itself prevent the tendency to create binaries within the postcolonial exposition (Suleri, 1992). Decentring requires a repositioning which involves an overturning of the master narratives, a disordering of existing hegemonic knowledge construction.

While these discussions about postcolonial feminism have taken place *within* women's studies and gender studies and have, in turn, encouraged the development of precisely the forms of poststructuralist/postmodernist debates which the above authors address, it is fair to say that there has been little spill over into the world of gender education research. The volume *Disrupting Preconceptions: Postcolonial and Education* (Hickling-Hudson, Matthews, & Woods, 2004) raises important questions as to whether the tradition of postcolonial debate that is evident in India, and now in the region of South Asia, can be achieved in the metropole. The beginning of a two-way migration of epistemic knowledge proffers the promise of a new international agenda around national growth and poverty alleviation. Gender education researchers in Western European, North American, and developing nations will need to consider their own positionality in relation to such 'postcolonial' agendas in education and development.

Learning from gender education research in other regions

The writers we have quoted have raised important questions for global educational research on gender. The concepts of the body, the 'ego' and the self which lie at the heart of North American and Western European research currently frame our understanding of what it means to be an individual and 'a subject' within an economically developing nation. They lie at the heart of the concept of 'national growth'. As we have found in our own research, these assumptions are extraordinarily hard to challenge. On the other hand, European and later North American inspired Foucauldian discursive analyses can uncover the ways in which dualities of public and private, the 'othering' of motherhood, and how particular constructions of other regions into metropolitan paradigms are embedded within development agendas. Using this methodology, it is possible to understand the MDG goals and their targets as constructing a discourse about gender power around notions of individual 'educational disadvantage' rather than economic/material and cultural inequalities – an educational discourse that precisely embeds individualised notions of self within educational systems.

As we have shown, African and South Asian feminists aim to move gender research towards an 'Indigenous' approach to knowledge systems and their creation (John, 1996a) – a construction of knowledge that would derive from the specifics of location and history. Yet defining a research methodology that is based on 'building on the indigenous' (Nnaemeka, 2003) is not easy. In her later work, John (2004) uses the notion of Indigenous knowledge to explore the growth of the women's movement and feminism over the past two centuries in India – which is best captured by the tensions and conflicts between culture and politics. John argues North American and Western European researchers regard 'construct' rather than 'construction' as central so they look for categories rather than the forces that generate particular etymologies. They are equally caught up with the identification of results (i.e., the 'product') and do not devote their energies to understanding the dynamics/pathways (i.e., 'processes') of a relational world. Consequently, North American and Western European feminist researchers have found themselves in difficulties trying to understand the internal formation of Indian feminisms that have occurred through contestations in the local sphere.[7] In its place, they have sought to find a single Indian feminism located at the national level. National feminists within India similarly have privileged conflicts with the national state to interpret the meaning of Indian feminism (John, 2004).

Nnaemeka argues that hegemonic forms of knowledge production currently only recognise findings from North American and Western European feminist research projects rather than Indigenous systems of knowledge construction. This leads to the disempowerment of the Indigenous community especially with its blatant disregard for the latter's processes of learning, sharing, and communicating. The systems of 'Othering' continually and cumulatively dispossess Southern national and local communities as the keepers of knowledge (Nnaemeka, 2005). The displacement, even effacement, of local knowledge systems in Africa is a form of devaluation of the process-based learning that results from an individual's journey through different relationships and rites during the passage of life. The replacement of this form of community learning by an externally imposed system of knowledge has also eroded epistemic abilities within African academia, placing them in the position of subject rather than creator/makers of knowledge (Nnaemeka, 2003). If we take her argument further, we might consider the ways in which gender research, particularly within liberal and neo-liberal traditions, celebrates formal educational knowledge, individual achievement and identity, and transitions into a form of adulthood that separates the individual from the community. If applied to the African context, educational investigations using this epistemology could well negate community/collective educational knowledges and community/relation integration through learning and marginalise, without intention, the development of Indigenous gendered forms of education.

If the community is to be considered the repository of knowledge, then we need to have more discussion about social scientific research methodologies that are being constructed and applied outside North American and Western European academic spaces. The tracing of relational life in the community needs to recognise that the role of elders is central not just to the maintenance of the corpus of knowledge, but that their collective presence directs the transmission of knowledge and draws together the supernatural, the temporal, and the spatial aspects of life (Oyewumi, 2002). Indigenous methodologies which have emerged in the Southern hemisphere and in New Zealand are designed to work with the notion of community and its attendant collective knowledges. Researchers here tend to approach the maintenance of cultural protocols, values, and behaviours as an integral part of a research methodology (Tuhiwai Smith, 1999, p. 15). Indigenous researchers working among the Māori, for example, do not consider these elements as mere formalities to permit access to the research site, but give intrinsic value to the relational aspects of life; they work with locally emergent notions of space, time, and spirituality. Tuhiwai Smith points to the productive results that have emerged through bi-cultural research in New Zealand where researchers drew on the mapping of the community as set out by the elders, respecting it as a form of epistemic knowledge rather than beginning with their own academic notions of mapping. These emergent methodologies are also at the heart of the work undertaken by Alexander and

Mohanty (1997) where their joint research began with an intensive learning period, where they each read about the other's cultural context so that they became 'fluent in each other's culture'. This starting point allowed these authors to embark on their fieldwork from a position where they both had worked towards a more equal exchange regarding their positionality and understanding of the micro-macro politics of practice and praxis. The construction of a new feminist research agenda around education that works to reduce binaries, increase bi-cultural workings, and readdress the role of positionality would help take us forward in the field of gender education research.[8]

The contradictions between local, national, and international meanings of gender equality in schooling which we have identified have only now begun to come to the surface (Unterhalter, 2007). Any investigation into how education is regarded whether by a disgruntled local administration, an irate teachers' lobby or by agitated and often relatively powerless communities, all stakeholders in the education of the 'girl child', is likely to be severely hindered by the lack of a nuanced Indigenous feminist research tradition. Only a new approach to gender and education can take us away from the consequences of an essentialising definition of gender that is limited to the search for universal categories of analysis. By working more closely with the relational world of everyday lives, where education occurs within and through the community, the insights of global feminist education research could be situated within existing community pathways of knowledge dissemination.

The international project of EFA, the MDGs and the fast increasing interest of governments to prove that they are on track in terms of closing gender gaps in access, participation and outcomes of schooling, as well as the need to alleviate poverty, means that, in effect, there is now a common gender and education project. That project at a minimal level is about ensuring that all boys and girls have equal rights to schooling across the globe. More than that, we now need to develop a field of global gender education studies which engages with dynamic and textured rather than essentialised notions of culture, and ensures that the growing interaction between feminist, Indigenous and international knowledge about gender is garnered to identify the most important theoretical, political, and empirical questions to ask in order to achieve education for all.

Acknowledgements

This chapter was developed as a background paper for the project *Youth Gender and Citizenship: An inter-generational study of educational outcomes and poverty*, which is part of the RECOUP programme of research (2005–2010) funded by the Department for International Development in the United Kingdom. We would like to thank Anna Robinson-Pant and the reviewers for their helpful comments on early drafts of the chapter.

Notes

1 The focus on South Asian and African authors does not signify that critical reflection on gender education is not underway in other geographical locations. We have chosen particular authors because they provide a new core of feminist theorising on categories and processes of gendering within and between nations. We are aware that there is a related literature on gender education and the state that is being generated in the Latin American context that is situated within the changing NGO politics for women's empowerment (Alvarez, 1999; Stromquist, 2007).
2 It gave rise to the now famous progression from Women in Development (WID) to Women and Development (WAD) frameworks within the UN set of institutions.
3 Chandra Talpade Mohanty is Professor of Women's Studies at Syracuse University. She came from India to the United States significantly to study for her doctorate within the field of education.
4 Mothering was recognised within the category of reproductive women in the mid-twentieth-century Western gender analysis, and it re-emerged as a category of analysis in radical feminist work on feminist revolutionary action within the women's peace movement (Roseneil, 1995).
5 Having studied both in Nigeria and at the University of California, Berkeley, Oyeronke Oyewumi is now a Professor of Sociology at SUNY.
6 Subaltern Studies emerged in the 1980s as an alternative approach to history and social analysis more broadly. It focuses on the agency of non-elites, i.e., subalterns to bring about political and social change.
7 There has been considerable dissent among Indian feminists about whether all women's movements can be accurately regarded as feminist in their orientation and objectives.
8 In conceptualising our DFID funded project on Youth Gender and Citizenship: An inter-generational study of educational outcomes and poverty under the theme of social and human outcomes, Northern and Southern teams encountered difficulties of ensuring a two-way participatory research process due to the different understandings of gender across disciplines and partner countries.

References

Alexander, M., & Mohanty, C. T. (Eds.). (1997). *Feminist genealogies, colonial legacies, democratic futures*. New York, NY: Routledge.
Alvarez, S. E. (1999). Advocating feminism: The Latin American feminist NGO 'boom'. *International Feminist Journal of Politics*, 1(2), 181–209.
Barrett, M., & McIntosh, M. (1982). *The anti-social family*. London, England: Verso.
Benhabib, S. (2002). *The claims of culture: Equality and diversity in the global era*. Princeton, NJ: Princeton University Press.
Bhola, H. S. (2002). Reclaiming old heritage for proclaiming future history: The knowledge-for-development debate in African contexts. *Africa Today*, 49(3), 3–21.
Connell, R. (2007). *Southern theory: The global dynamics of knowledge in social science*. Cambridge, England: Polity Press.
Education International. (2003). *Education for all: Is commitment enough?* Brussels, Belgium: Educational International.
Fennell, S. (2007). Contested gender frameworks: Economic models and provider perspectives in education. In S. Fennell & M. Arnot (Eds.), *Gender education and equality in a global context* (pp. 35–50). London, England: Routledge.
Hickling-Hudson, A., Matthews, J., & Woods, A. (2004). *Disrupting preconceptions: Postcolonial and education*. Brisbane, Australia: Post Pressed.

John, M. E. (1996a). *Discrepant dislocations: Feminism, theory, and postcolonial histories*. Berkeley, CA: University of California Press.
John, M. E. (1996b). Postcolonial feminists in a Western intellectual field: Anthropologists and native informants. *Centre for Cultural Studies*. Retrieved from https://culturalstudies.ucsc.edu/inscriptions/volume-5/mary-e-john/#1
John, M. E. (2004). Feminism in India and the West: Recasting a relationship. In M. Chaudhuri (Ed.), *Feminism in India* (pp. 52–68). New Delhi, India: Kali for Women.
Mies, M. (1986). *Patriarchy and accumulation on a world scale: Women in the international division of labour*. London, England: Zed Books.
Mohanty, C. T. (1988). Under Western eyes: Feminist scholarship and colonial discourses. *Feminist Review, 30*, 61–88.
Mohanty, C. T. (2003a). Cartographies of struggle: Third world women and the politics of feminism. In C. T. Mohanty (Ed.), *Feminism without borders: Decolonizing theory, practicing solidarity* (pp. 43–84). Durham, NC: Duke University Press.
Mohanty, C. T. (2003b). Western eyes revisited: Feminist solidarity through anticapitalist struggles. *Signs: Journal of Women in Culture and Society, 28*(2), 499–535.
Mohanty, C. T. (2003c). Genealogies of home, country and nation. In C. T. Mohanty (Ed.), *Feminism without borders: Decolonising theory, practicing solidarity* (pp. 124–138). Durham, NC: Duke University Press.
Mundy, K., & Murphy, L. (2001). Transnational advocacy, global civil society? Emerging evidence from the field of education. *Comparative Education Review, 45*(1), 85–126.
Nnaemeka, O. (Ed.). (1997a). *The politics of (m)othering: Womanhood, identity and resistance in African literature*. London, England: Routledge.
Nnaemeka, O. (1997b). Introduction: Imag(in)ing knowledge, power and subversion in the margins. In O. Nnaemeka (Ed.), *The politics of m(o)thering: Womanhood, identity and resistance in African literature* (pp. 1–25). London, England: Routledge.
Nnaemeka, O. (2003). Nego-feminism: Theorising, practicing and pruning Africa's way. *Signs: Journal of Women in Culture and Society, 29*(2), 357–385.
Nnaemeka, O. (2005). Bringing African women into the classroom: Rethinking pedagogy and epistemology. In O. Oyewumi (Ed.), *African gender studies: A reader* (pp. 51–66). New York, NY: Palgrave MacMillan.
Nussbaum, M. (2000). *Women and human development: The capabilities approach*. Cambridge, England: Cambridge University Press.
Nyamnjoh, F. B. (2002). A child is one person's only in the womb': Domestication, agency and subjectivity in the Cameroonian grassfields. In R. Werbner (Ed.), *Postcolonial subjectivities in Africa* (pp. 111–138). London, England: Zed Books.
Nzegwu, N. (2003). Africa: Gender imperialism in academia. In O. Oyewumi (Ed.), *African women and feminism: Reflecting on the politics of sisterhood* (pp. 99–154). Trenton, NJ: Africa World Press.
Oyewumi, O. (1997). *The invention of women: Making an African sense of Western gender discourses*. Minneapolis, MN: University of Minnesota Press.
Oyewumi, O. (2002). Conceptualizing gender: The Eurocentric foundations of feminist concepts and the challenge of African epistemologies. *JENdA: A Journal of Culture and African Women Studies, 2*(1), 1–9.
Oyewumi, O. (Ed.). (2003a). *African women and feminism: Reflecting on the politics of sisterhood*. Trenton, NJ: Africa World Press.

Oyewumi, O. (2003b). The white woman's burden: African women in Western feminist discourse. In O. Oyewumi (Ed.), *African women and feminism: Reflecting on the politics of sisterhood* (pp. 25–43). Trenton, NJ: Africa World Press.

Oyewumi, O. (Ed.). (2005). *African gender studies: A reader.* New York, NY: Palgrave Macmillan.

Ramamurthy, P. (2007, May). *Feminist conundrums in post-socialist India.* Paper presented at the conference on Gender, Empire, and the Politics of Central and East Europe: A Gender Symposium at the Central European University, Budapest, Hungary.

Raynor, J. (2007). Schooling girls: An inter-generational study of women's burdens in rural Bangladesh. In S. Fennell & M. Arnot (Eds.), *Gender education and equality in a global context* (pp. 117–130). London, England: Routledge.

Roseneil, S. (1995). *Disarming patriarchy: Feminism and political action at Greenham.* Buckingham, England: Open University Press.

Saigal, A. (2007). Acts of citizenship: Women's civic engagements as community-based educators in Mumbai. In S. Fennell & M. Arnot (Eds.), *Gender education and equality in a global context* (pp. 131–145). London, England: Routledge.

Sen, A. (2001). *Development as freedom.* London, England: Oxford University Press.

Spivak, G. (1985). Can the subaltern speak. In C. Nelson & L. Grossberg (Eds.), *Marxism and the interpretation of culture* (pp. 271–317). Champaign, IL: Illinois University Press.

Stromquist, N. (2007). *Feminist organisations and social transformations in Latin America.* Boulder, CO: Paradigm Publishers.

Suleri, S. (1992). Women skin deep: Feminism and the postcolonial condition. *Critical Inquiry, 18*(4), 756–769.

Tinker, I. (1990). *Persistent inequalities: Women and world development.* New York, NY: Oxford University Press.

Tsing, A. (1993). *In the realm of the diamond queen: Marginality in an out-of-the-way place.* Princeton, NJ: Princeton University Press.

Tuhuwai Smith, L. (1999). *Decolonising methodologies: Research and indigenous peoples.* London, England: Zed Books.

UNESCO. (2002). *Education for all: Is the world on track.* Retrieved from https://www.unesco.org/gem-report/en/efa-world-track

UNESCO. (2003). *Gender education for all: The leap to equality.* Retrieved from https://en.unesco.org/gem-report/report/2003/gender-and-education-all-leap-equality

UNESCO. (2005). *Education for all: The quality imperative.* Retrieved from https://en.unesco.org/gem-report/report/2005/education-all-quality-imperative

Unterhalter, E. (2007). *Gender, schooling and global social justice.* London, England: Routledge.

Yuval-Davis, N., & Werbner, P. (2005). *Women, citizenship and difference.* New Delhi, India: Zubaan Books.

5
INDIGENOUS ANTI-COLONIAL KNOWLEDGE AS 'HERITAGE KNOWLEDGE' FOR PROMOTING BLACK/AFRICAN EDUCATION IN DIASPORIC CONTEXTS

George Sefa Dei

Situating the intellectual and political challenge

Of late, I have been thinking seriously about some questions: As African scholars how do we pioneer new analytical systems for understanding our Indigenous communities and what are the challenges we are likely to be faced with? What are the intellectual and political merits of developing and promoting our own "home-grown Indigenous perspectives steeped in culture-specific paradigms" (Yankah, 2004, p. 26) in the Western academy? Admittedly, I see this opportunity as an important challenge in the struggle to save ourselves from becoming "intellectual imposters" (Nyamnjoh, 2012) in the academy. For a start, we can work on replacing our 'cultural estrangement' with 'cultural engagement' in the pursuit and promotion of African/Black education in Diasporic contexts.

In thinking through this topic, I find it imperative to reiterate that in the current epoch of globalisation and advance capitalism, schooling, and education have become discursively configured to meet the needs of modernisation from the context of Euromodernity. For African learners, we need to develop theoretical prisms or perspectives that are able to account for our lived experiences and our relationality with other learners. Such prisms will be rooted in our cultures, histories, and heritage and be presented as frames of reference for the intellectual and political projects of designing positive (i.e., solution-oriented) educational goals for learners.

From curricula to pedagogies, dominant knowledge systems have been organised and inscribed through governing Eurocentric paradigms historically augured within colonial specificities. Education systems and processes, as well as ideas about what counts as education, have been entrenched in the reproduction of colonial ways of knowing which concomitantly limit possibilities for many learners. By way of my own personal educational experience, I have written how my colonial education in Ghana taught me less about my own communities than other distant places, which made it difficult to relate education to my lived experiences. Cultural community knowledges were not affirmed in my education and it has taken many years of struggle to shed the Eurocentric gaze and interpretations that have been ingrained in my thinking. Many of us, whether as Indigenous, colonised or racially minoritised scholars/learners, continue to struggle to convey liberatory ways of understanding for/in different socio-cultural, economical, and political spaces. For education to facilitate rather than limit learning possibilities and educational transformation, it is crucial that we develop and apply liberatory conceptual frameworks that are accessible to learners.

With this in mind, I intervene in the discussion through transgressive pedagogies, by way of Indigenous epistemologies, to seek different and effective concepts, theories, and processes for educational transformation for all learners. In producing knowledge as theory, I recognise that the worth of any social theory must be measured both by its philosophical grounding, as well as its ability to offer a social and political corrective. This point speaks to the notion of consciousness and responsibility to/of producing, sharing, claiming, and gaining knowledge. Being knowledge producers makes us deeply implicated in colonial power relations and means that we have a responsibility to consider the foundations and consequences of our work. An important theoretical supposition that frames my own academic scholarship is that the transformation of social realities must start with re-conceptualising education, for example, asking new questions about the whats, hows, and whys of education. Specifically, it is important for us to ask: What sorts of education should be taking place in our schools today? How do learners of today come to know using multiple lenses of critical inquiry? Given that no one tells the full story, how do we tell and understand multiple stories that, all considered, help us to understand the whole story? How do learners read and understand our worlds in different ways and share such multiple knowings as 'communities of learners'?

Such questions are important if education is to be understood as living and working with ideas of freedom, growth, or social change. These questions also help to challenge the dominance of one particular story or particular stories over others. Our institutions of learning, as sites for education of young learners and adults, must liberate all knowledges. Our educational institutions cannot be places for mere survival(ism) for learners and educators. We must see our schools as sites of contestations – over knowledge, power, and social transformation (Ladson-Billings, 2011). In this chapter, therefore, I affirm the centrality of local cultural ways of knowing and local voices in the dialogue on education, as broadly defined.

The cultural knowledge challenge

How have I come to understand 'African Heritage Knowledge'? No doubt culture as a social system is at the roots of coming to know. I see African heritage knowledge as a cultural fund of the individual and collective knowledge of African peoples, which has endured through time and draws on a critical linkage of culture, race, and politics in coming to know. In this context race is engaged critically as part of our identities (class, gender, sexuality, disability, sexuality, etc.) and importantly linked with knowledge production. This knowledge speaks to a politicised affirming of culture and race (as opposed to the problematic denial of the significance of race, and the purposeful racial labelling intended for negative/oppressive ends) as well as the affirmation of cultural identity (Ivy, 1959; King, 2005).

As poignantly asked at the beginning of this chapter: How do we African scholars stop ourselves from becoming "intellectual imposters" in the Western academy? In other words, how do we work and hold ourselves accountable, to be ourselves and to exercise our intellectual agencies? The Eurocentric mimicry usually comes as an emotional, psychological, mental, and material costs to us individually and collectively. Writing in African contexts and specifically about African scholarship, Nyamnjoh (2012) writes about colonial education as "cultural violence, self-hate and mimicry" (p. 4). African scholarship, research, and knowledge production must help us to recover and reclaim ourselves, our knowledges and our voices. The difficult question is how to do this. This is about more than challenging and subverting "epistemological imperialism". It is about rooting knowledges and practices into their appropriate soils, cultural contexts, histories, and heritages. That is, in addition to resisting colonial education and knowledges, it is important to work, learn, and engage in knowledge production, sharing, and critical inquiry in contexts that affirm or are suitable given the histories, heritages, and cultures that shape our ways of understanding the world. There is a need for a rebirth of Indigenous epistemologies informed by local languages, perspectives, social values, cosmologies, and worldviews (Nyamnjoh, 2012, p. 10).

Rather than being dismissive of culture we must replace our 'cultural estrangement' with a critical 'cultural engagement'. Within the literature there are psychological, sociological, and/or anthropological points of view reinforcing the relevance of the culture, pedagogy, and education linkage. For example, as I have noted elsewhere (Dei, 2012), the works of Clifford (1986), Geertz (1993), Cole (1992, 2006), Rogoff (1981, 2003), Wertsch (1985, 2002), and Tappan (2006). Within anthropology Clifford (1986) and Geertz (1993) demonstrate how knowledge is embedded within particular cultural contexts and resists appeals to master narratives, transcendent experiences, or a universal 'human nature'. Not only do appeals to universal ways of knowing ignore the diversity of human experiences and cultures, but they work within inequitable power frameworks to privilege Western ways of knowing. These authors argue that culture is at the essence of all human experience and is central to knowledge production. We should expect 'multi-epistemes' (Cajete, 2000) to emerge given the diversity of cultures involved in educational contexts.

Within psychology, Rogoff (1981, 2003) details the marked differences in human development across cultures and examines how individuals develop as participants in their cultural communities. This engagement of individuals and cultural communities is necessarily dynamic and refutes the view of culture as static and having the same effect on each individual. Individuals relate differently to their cultures but they are guided by shared understandings of the cultural systems and expectations and social roles of each constituent member of their cultures. Thus, we can understand culture as a system of shared knowledge. Wertsch (1985, 2002) further examines the complex relationships between individuals and culture. In his work, he extrapolates on how cultural tools are taken up to mediate the formulation of a collective memory. This mediation works through the complex interactions between individuals and their social, cultural, and historical communities as well as surrounding natural and physical environments. Similarly, Tappan (2006) extends Wertsch's ideas around cultural mediation by examining moral development as the accumulation of cultural tools and moral mediation means, which allow the individual to operate and make choices as part of the community.

Molefi Asante's long-standing work (among many others) firmly grounds African culture in understand the African human condition (Asante, 1991, 2003). Affirming the centrality of African culture offers intellectual and discursive agency to the learner and recognition of their responsibilities to a larger community. Culture is a powerful lens for reading the African world – it is the starting point for discussion of knowledge production, identity, and development. Culture is not necessarily as much about sameness as it is about a shared body of knowledge. Culture is about identity, history, and constitutes a form of pedagogy. Culture is also hotly contested and is saturated with power. It is the complex engagements of the individual within and with the dynamic entity of culture that shapes who they are and how they come to know the world. What these authors are pointing to is the fact that culture influences human and social action in very complex ways.

This cursory look at selected literature suggests that the engagement of local culture/cultural knowings demonstrates the power of culturally contextualised discourses to transcend geographical/physical borders and boundaries in the delivery of effective education to learners. Educators need to put new pedagogical approaches and classroom instructional practices in place to address schooling challenges and to ensure safe, secure, and healthy learning environments for learners. Cultural paradigms shape the construction of particular knowledges, as well as experiences of schooling. The work of

African educators (research, writing, and teachings) must affirm Indigenous/ African cultures, while pointing to the creativity, resourcefulness, agency, and value systems of our cultural knowledges. We must challenge current intellectual posture, which sees how we come to know and understand our relations through the prism of the dominant. For example, as Nyamnjoh (2012, p. 2) notes in writing about the colonial and Diasporic encounter, those of us who move and/or are forced to move cannot position ourselves simply in relation to those we meet along the way or on the journey; we must stake out our own positions as well. We must be true to our authentic selves as African subjects of knowing. We also need to appreciate and work with the fact that there is knowledge beyond the capacity of the human senses to comprehend and/or render what is observable or not (Nyamnjoh, 2012, p. 4). This is the idea of uncertainty of knowledge, where there is no inclination to dominate other knowledges through certainty. Rather, there is an inclination and need to create spaces for our knowledges to be considered and critically examined on our own terms, free from dominating perspectives. We must understand the Indigenous reality or condition on its own terms through an anti-colonial intellectuality and praxis (Abraham, 2011). To understand the Indigenous reality, we must go to the Indigenous source for knowledge and not rely on theories and theorists elsewhere whose work speaks to different realities.

In the pursuit of anti-colonial intellectuality and praxis we must use local cultural sources of knowledge to resist the everyday devaluation, denial, and negation of the creativity, agency, resourcefulness, and knowledge systems of African peoples. It is so important that, as we seek to decolonise ourselves and the academy, we develop an anti-colonial intellectuality that helps us to challenge and subvert the colonial mappings and colonial cartographies of our institutions of who owns and is entitled to certain spaces. It is also fundamentally about the particular and intellectual praxis that coming into a given space/land requires us to uphold. We must understand the relations of political power and geographical and social spaces, as well as the strategic importance of land as a place of affirmation of histories, identities, and cultures of resistance. Anticolonial intellectuality and praxis is about bringing ideas into fruition as social practice, as grounding and testing theories in the contexts of the liberatory struggles of our peoples as well as the people with whom we work in political solidarity (these must include the Indigenous peoples on whose land we currently reside). Recognising the links among culture, knowledge production, and colonisation of land and space, as African diasporic subjects our development of anti-colonial knowledge production and intellectualities should remain rooted in histories, cultures, and revolutionary political traditions of African people's radical resistance to colonialism. Our work benefits from rich legacies of committed and visionary political action and our theories must be sophisticated enough to broach and sustain good political practice. We must challenge the ways discourses and bodies of knowledges are controlled, policed, regimented, selected, organised, and distributed in our academies and public spaces without any grounding in meaningful or concrete political practice. Anti-colonial intellectuality does not remain abstract – it does not rely on separation of body, mind, and spirit – and in its integrity it necessarily involves a world sense and lifestyle that actively threatens oppressive power structures. Anti-colonial education should strengthen and be strengthened by the development of effective personal and collective decolonising practices as well as our involvement in collective political struggles against all forms of oppression.

Education for 'global good' is education for responsible global citizenry. However, dominant conceptions of global (citizenship) education is often easily touted for its virtues of the global interdependence of our worlds, commitment to fundamental freedoms and rights of all peoples, for acknowledgement of cultural diversity, tolerance of intercultural differences, and the belief in the efficacy and power of individual action (Mundy & Manion, 2008; Wright, 2011). But where is the recognition of the necessity to deal concretely with power, privilege, and our relative complicities in ensuring colonial and oppressive education and global structural inequities? When counter-narratives, knowledges and oppositional voices are raised, they are often ridiculed or responded to with threats, violence, erasure, or plain dismissiveness – as is often the case of the subjectification of Indigenous knowledges as a "racial subset of knowledge" (Battiste & Youngblood Henderson, 2000). Education for the 'global good' and responsible global citizenry in the context of an oppressive status quo must involve anti-oppression.

Producing counter/oppositional knowledge for transformation of Black/African education is about building critical social theory. Theory cannot remain a privileged discussion among so-called academics and intellectuals that fails to evoke or be directly informed by anti-oppressive actions and practice. There is the necessity to create discursive frameworks that affirm the inseparability of theory and practices, to create what can be called a definitional power of anti-textuality and idealism can be strengthened and combined with deep historical inquiry, critical reflection, and an understanding and interpretation of our material existence. All knowledges have profound material consequences and our material conditions ground our knowledges.

As Fanon (1963, 1967) noted, no jargon can substitute for reality, and even the colonialist knows this fact. Oppressed, colonised, and racial minority scholars must challenge our investments in colonial conceptualisations of intellectuality and admit that we cannot achieve academic and social excellence in our communities by mimicking colonial standards of what counts as 'intellectual'. To this end, I agree with Abraham (2011) that we must "conceptualise our intellectuality on our own terms" (p. 15) and Lebakeng's (2010) exhortation that our intellectuality cannot in all sincerity be decoupled from a 'sociality and polity'. Community is shared space, thought, and body. It is a collective more powerful than a sea of individuals. The power of community (however defined) prevails over the fragmentation of individuals, each locked in her/his own subjectivity and discursive agency. Fanon is right in noting that the struggle and contestation over knowledge can only take place in the field of (intellectual) 'combat'. As Abraham (2011) notes, Fanon "uses the notion of combat to indicate the colonised intellectual's mental decolonisation as a result of direct involvement in collective liberation struggle" (pp. 17–18). This is not a fight for individuals or individualism. It is within this field of 'combat' that we sow the seeds of our own collective decolonisation.

Dubois, Fanon and the question of Black education

In this section, I want to borrow the ideas of pioneering Black/African scholars like W.E.B. Du Bois and Frantz Fanon as I articulate an 'Indigenous anti-colonial framework' (or what one of my graduate students recently labelled an 'Indigenist anti-colonial' framework – Sium, 2011) for understanding issues of Black/African education for 'global good'.

I use my long-standing work in the Canadian school system[1] to ground some issues because educational research and policy relating to Black/African Canadian education leaves much to be desired. First, there is the disturbing history of simply adding 'African' stories to a weak foundation. As educators and policy-makers, how can we hope to address a nagging (and unacceptable) problem of schools failing some learners when our solutions have been to simply add to what already exists? We have to recognise that we cannot simply add new floors/structures to the currently crumbling building that is education until we address the cracks in the foundation. To ensure Black/African educational success, we must seriously consider and begin working on creating new educational systems and alternatives that hold the promise of excellence for all. Second, we cannot expect success while reproducing an unsatisfactory status quo or while continuing to do the same things that are failing us. Third, we need to redouble efforts at creating a level playing field. This means addressing the 'poverty of school culture'. This explicit investment in a level playing field recognises the unlevel and inequitable circumstances in which education is embedded – the *a priori* inequality exists among students, within school culture, within educational discourse at many levels, and with Euro-American curricula. Fourth, there are multiple complicities in the making of the 'educational crisis'. It appears that even many of those people who are quick to point to a 'crisis' do not always easily acknowledge the systemic undercurrents and causes of the crisis. Talk of institutional responsibility for failed systems of schooling and the ways current education is delivered to create educational failure is often muted or denied. Fifth, is the total neglect of the works of African scholars and educators in shaping public policy about Black/African education. We do have tremendous amount of research literature by Black and minority scholars on the school system and yet one has to ask: whose voices are being privileged in scholarly work and school policymaking? Research by Black and minority scholars – research that is crucial for understanding the school system's failure to appropriately serve Black/African and minority students – is usually not taken seriously or ignored altogether. This reflects the coloniality and racism of the school system.

Sixth, is the unquestioned faith in integration. Integration (as we know it) has not led to success for our youth, so we must be critical and ask: Integration for whom, how, and at what/whose expense? Increasingly, at the policy level, I am perplexed by the blind faith in integration, even while it leads our youth along the path of cultural destruction and to what Maulana Karenga identified as the 'cultural crisis' (Karenga, cited in Asante, 2009). We need to be asking some critical questions. For many of our youth, 'education sucks'. Interrogating policy and practice to decolonise education for our youth starts by asking four simple questions: (a) Who is making educational policies? (b) What are the particular experiences that policy-makers bring to their work? (c) What theoretical perspectives shape the ideas of these policy-makers? and (d) Whose interests have conventional educational policies served? Finally, I see a 'return to the source' as imperative. It is important to know where we are coming from in order to know where we are going. I invoke the West African symbol of the 'Sankofa' bird who is looking around behind to see where he is going. The search for new answers can only succeed if we carefully dissect and understand what has failed us in the years before. We must come to understand what practices and ways of knowing are liberatory for our learners, what conditions make those practices and ways of knowing possible, and how to use these to build effective education systems. This, I argue, has everything to do with reclaiming Indigenous African ways of knowing for promoting African education.

W.E.B. Du Bois (1965) in his *The World and Africa* articulated four crucial points for the cause and direction of Black/African anti-colonial intellectualism and education (see also Diawara, 1996). Du Bois argued that (a) the history and cultures of peoples of Africa and African descent need to be written as a necessary intellectual exercise for our decolonisation; (b) the search for knowledge about the African cause is valuable if it allows Africans in the Diaspora to identify with the continent and to place Africa on an equal footing with Europe, Asia, and North America; (c) it is important for us to posit Africa's humanism and rich heritage as a compelling argument against racism and colonialism (Diawara, 1996); and (d) that Black-African peoples everywhere would not be completely free until Africa was liberated and emancipated in (an anti-colonial) modernity. These ideas are central to articulating an Indigenous anti-colonial prism for understanding Black education. African educators need to write and speak our histories of struggle in our children's education as an exercise in the development of decolonised African education. There are important lessons about traditional/pre-colonial and Indigenous African education that are very relevant to the promotion of education of youth in Diasporic contexts. These lessons make it possible for us to strike the continuities and similarities of African and Diasporic experiences (e.g., the central role of the family and community in youth education; education as about culture, language, heritage, etc.). Indigenous African humanistic thought about community, peace, belonging, solidarity, mutual interdependence, and shared destinies is a counterpoint to the denial and negation of our knowledges and experiences, as well as the practice of racial oppression, injustices, and inequities that African learners experience and contend with in the mainstream Euro-American school system. We pursue anti-colonial education not simply in affirmation and self-defence of our knowledges and experiences, but also to liberate ourselves, bodies, and minds from Eurocentric mimicry.

Frantz Fanon wrote about the importance, imperative, and urgency of extricating ourselves from Euro-colonial modernity when he asserted poignantly "each generation must come out of relative obscurity, discover its mission, fulfil it, or betray it" (Fanon, 1967, p. 206). He speaks to our responsibility as Black/Indigenous scholars, educators, researchers, and community workers to discover and fulfil our mission. Fanon's critique of the Negritude Movement in terms of seeking currency for the Black/African body through a negotiation of White colonial spaces and an uncritical evocation of the African past/culture/tradition is equally informative. There is a concern about engaging in an unending colonial mimicry and Fanon offers an opportunity to rethink transformative pedagogy and education. While the importance of Fanon for schooling, education, and pedagogy have largely been underexplored, we need to read Fanon's work as more than a mere theoretical exercise. Instead, we must read this African anti-colonial scholar politically, practically, and pedagogically. For example, his views on politics of identity, culture, national liberation, and resistance, the 'dialectic of experience', offer lessons for the contemporary African learner in extending our explorations of the 'colonial encounter' and the 'colonising experience' into a cohesive theoretical and practical contribution to social and educational thought and political action. Fanon reminds us of the power of the revolutionary consciousness and that the plight of the African intellectual in his colonial mimicry is itself an obstacle to our thinking outside the dominant box of knowledge. We need a revolutionary consciousness to understand and deal with the role of schools in both producing and resisting the creation of a 'pathological personality'. There is a Black/African ontology, a science and an essence of being, a personality (if you will) that exists and must exist outside the construction of the 'African' within Euro-American hegemony, ideology, imagination, and thought. A cultural decolonisation is critical to address cultural colonisation – i.e., through developing critical consciousness, a radical and mobilising new awareness to knowledge and knowledge production.

Resistance to dominant and colonising knowledges in order to transform our educational institutions should be an end goal of intellectual and political exercises. This will mean declaring the falsity of the independence of scholarship and activism divide. As African scholars and educators we should challenge ourselves by asking: "How are we complicit in Western hegemony?" "How does the search for knowledge create an ethical responsibility to share relevant knowledge with our communities?" "As producers of knowledge, how does our work contribute to the oppression or liberation of our people?" Change does not lie outside our purview. The power of individual and collective agency lies in the ontological primacy of interpretations – how we define and make sense of our worlds. The 'ontology of the (black) body' rests on recognition of race and racial identity as embodied knowing. We must use knowledge and practice to resist the violence of the 'inferiority complex' syndrome, which wounds us to our very core. The violence that Fanon diagnosed was violence intended to "heal the spiritually wounded" and was a cleansing measure.

Fanon's ideas are helpful in pointing to the intellectualising of transformative political projects, as well as the revolutionising of intellectuality. We must resist colonising knowledge if 'fulfilling education' is ever going to be a reality. Our education must make a difference and create space for our learners to work with(in) communities. The affirmation of the anti-colonial intellectuality is to address the major problems that oppressed and marginalised learners have to deal with: (a) negation of historical experiences and collective and cultural memories; (b) negation of our subjectivities; (c) the denial of the embodiment of knowledge; (d) the persistent and continuing struggles against our dehumanisation; (e) the 'spirit injury' of perpetual resistance; (f) the often times easy and seductive slippage into the form, logic and implicit assumptions of the very things we are contesting, as well as (g) the lack of mental/bodily/spiritual nourishment and accommodation (including food, shelter, clothing, and so on) that often accompany the systemic oppressions many of our people experience.

Broader implications for producing African Indigenous knowledge as 'heritage knowledge'

I now advance an Indigenous and anti-colonial framework for the study of Black/African education in the Diasporic context. Claiming 'Indigenous' is about a perspective anchored in Indigenous knowledge and local cultural knowing. The Indigenist perspective makes a distinction between 'Indigenous' and 'local/traditional' knowledge. 'Indigenous knowledge' is knowledge of the Indigenous peoples of a particular land used for everyday living, self and collective actualisation, survival and social existence. Local knowledge, on the other hand, can be possessed by any group (not necessarily Indigenous to the land) who have lived in a particular place/location or space for a period of time and come to know by experiencing that social environment through time (Fals Borda, 1980, 1991; Purcell, 1998; Roberts et al., 2004).

Both Indigenous and traditional/local knowledge work with the nexus of society-culture-interface, as well as the interrelations of the body, mind, and soul. They avoid a Cartesian split of body and mind and acknowledge the power of ancestralism and ancestral knowings. Indigenous knowledge affirms spirituality as a site of knowing and further argues that knowledge and resistance go hand in hand. For African peoples such knowing is a form of 'heritage knowledge' (King, 2005). This heritage knowledge is characterised by a philosophy of 'world sense', i.e., systems of thought and ontologies speaking to the realities and workings of the cosmos, and the nexus of nature, society, and culture. The uncertainty of knowing is appreciated along with the power of 'not knowing'. In effect within Indigenous knowledge 'the fear of not knowing' is acceptable and inconsequential (Dei, 2011, 2016). The idea of Indigeneity speaks to the ways of knowing as a body of epistemology connecting place, spirit, and body (Meyer, 2008). The spiritual is embodied and learners' spiritual identities are engaged in education. Spiritual identity is connected to the Land/Mother Earth and to one's inner self/soul and their physical and social surroundings. Spirituality is a way of knowing (Dillard, 2000; Dillard, Abdur-Rashid, & Tyson, 2000) including emotions. Indigenous cultural knowledge is about searching for wholeness and completeness.

The anti-colonial discursive framework (borrowing from the pioneering works of Cesaire, 1972; Fanon, 1963, 1967; Memmi, 1965; wa Thiong'o, 1986) involves a theorisation of colonial and re-colonial relations and the aftermath and the implications of power and imperial structures on: (a) the processes of knowledge production, interrogation, validation and dissemination; (b) claims of Indigeneity and Indigenous knowings; and (c) the recourse to agency, subjective politics and resistance. "Colonial" is defined as more than simply anything 'foreign' or 'alien'. Rather 'colonial' must implicate anything that is "imposed" and "dominating" (Dei, 2000a; Dei & Asgharzadeh, 2001; Dei & Kempf, 2006). The concern of the anti-colonial is also with re-organised 'colonial' relations rather than a supposedly 'new colonial' and, particularly, the ways re-organised colonial relations and mindsets structure and dominate social relations of knowledge production, ruling and social practice. Such analysis allows for the interrogation of power relations structured along lines of race, ethnicity, gender, class, religion, language, disability, and sexuality.

Anti-colonial theorising should seek transformation, not merely understanding of complexities, messiness, disjuncture, contentions, and contradictions of social realities. The anti-colonial perspective argues that mutual 'co-existence' cannot simply be assumed to exist; it must be fought for and realised. Thus, an anti-colonial pursuit is to subvert and decentre power and not necessarily to share or contest power. In this subversion, there is a central place for local cultural knowings, as well as local (subject) voices in the dialogue on Black/African education. Teasing out points of contention, resistance, and opposition in these voices offer possibilities for transforming current social systems. An anti-colonial approach to understanding the challenges of Black and African education allows us to learn from the intellectual agency of African peoples in providing education for their children. It affirms our agencies and voices in designing educational futures for our children. The anti-colonial is also about asking new and different questions. Current formal schooling is a colonial and oppressive system and transforming the educational system calls for an anti-colonial questioning stance. How do we subvert the ways the education of peoples of African descent has denied heterogeneity in local populations through the project of 'sameness'? How do educators provide anti-colonial education in ways that allow learners to develop a strong sense of identity, self and collective respect, agency, and empowerment to participate in community building? How do learners and educators work to create schools as healthy, working communities? What is the role of local knowledge in subverting the internalised colonial hierarchies of conventional schooling by promoting Indigenous teachings that focus specifically on social values, community, and character education? How do we revise schooling and education to espouse, at its centre, such values (and the subsequent struggle for them) as social justice, equity, fairness, resistance, and collective responsibilities?

When fusing together an Indigenous anti-colonial framework, we can examine how local African voices shift beyond mere critiques of the current educational order to transformative options that genuinely educate all learners. There is also the importance of upholding the idea of experiential, embodied knowings. Claiming Indigeneity necessarily entails an anti-racist, anti-colonial, and anti-imperialist stance. Indigeneity and anti-coloniality are about resistance, subjective agency, and collective politics. They each centre the agency and the authenticity of voice and political and intellectual interests of Indigenous, local, and oppressed subjects in accounting and resisting oppression and domination. What the politics of Indigeneity and anti-coloniality teach is that to learn is to act. Knowledge must compel action. Thus, there must be recognition of the interdependence of 'scholarship', 'politics', and 'activism'. It is not about prescribing a particular political ideology. Rather, it is about creating a space to legitimise politics in the intellectual/academic realm.

The Indigenous anti-colonial framework is about using an Indigenous lens to trouble Western science hegemony, specifically in the Western intellectual tradition. The Indigenous anti-colonial framework is anchored in the theoretical supposition that there are multiple knowledge forms with respective ways of knowing. European and Western scientific tradition is just one aspect of science knowledge. In other words, as Okeke (2005) long ago noted, "the West is one of the many producers of science" (quoted in Lebakeng, 2010, p. 27).

The Indigenous anti-colonial framework is about resistance and contestation of ideas. I see a particular responsibility for Indigenous scholars and our institutions of higher learning in the promotion of Indigenous knowledge.

Throughout the Western academy the dominance of the Western intellectual tradition is clear. I do not hear many accusations of inappropriate or essentialist intellectual engagement when Western science is paraded as the only valid knowledge. Contrast this with the charge of 'essentialism' when those of us who engage in counter-hegemonic intellectual work through claims of Indigenous knowledges, Indigeneity and authenticity of self, voice, culture history, and identity as part of the multiple ways of knowing! When we hear calls for the validation of our Indigenous truth claims, it is important to ask: Through what lens and perspectives are we being asked to engage in these validation processes? Who has power to determine validity? And, as discussed above, how do we develop the power to determine for ourselves the validity of our truth claims, without hegemonic impositions? In fact, we must see some of the reactions to Indigenous knowledges in the Western academy as more a question of how such knowledge reacts with certain bodies (in terms of threatened identities and politics), more so than where such knowledge sits (in terms of whether it is robust, sophisticated, or shows theoretical clarity).

The African-centred paradigm is an important theoretical and pragmatic space for African peoples to interpret and critically reflect upon their own experiences on their own terms and through the lenses of their worldviews and understandings, rather than being forced to understand the world through a Eurocentric lens. African-centred perspectives become an African worldview. As Molefi Asante and many others have argued, the African-centred perspective is about developing an African worldview. This worldview, as a system of thought, is shaped by the lens of Africology and stresses the centrality of culture, agency, history, identity, and experience. Consequently, African-centred education stresses notions of culture, centring learners' histories, identities, and experiences, and focusing on the learner's agency to bring about change in their personal and community lives. We need to work with the notion of the 'centredness' of the learner in her or his learning in order to engage knowledge. A culturally grounded perspective that centres African/Indigenous peoples' worldviews helps resist the dominance of Eurocentric perspectives. There is the need to centre the agency of marginalised and colonised peoples such that African learners, and all learners, become subjects of their own histories and stories and experiences (Asante, 1991, 2003; Mazama, 2001; Ziegler, 1996).

Conclusion

A re-visioning of Black/African education must have a place for local cultural knowledge. Local cultural resource knowledges of African peoples are sometimes least analysed for their contributions to schooling, education, and development. The teachings of local cultural knowledges about community, social responsibility, mutual interdependence, and solidarity usually conflict with the neo-liberal economic values of competitive individualism, consumerism, efficiency, productivity, etc. Building on what African learners know, school teachings can be affirming in helping to develop the agency, voice, and power of learners to own their education. Working with cultural knowledge as a form of African cultural inheritance, a fund of knowledge through a process of anti-colonial knowledge construction (e.g., using the instrumentality of African Indigenous languages) education can ensure the complete development of the learner to be aware of their social responsibilities and to combine academic success with social success.

An Indigenous education is characterised by knowledge production, interrogation, validation, and dissemination (including teaching and learning) which utilises what was available, what people know and sought to know, how African learners come to understand and interpret their worlds (social, physical, and metaphysical) and acted within such worlds for effective social existence. Such education is a teaching and learning about the past, present and future continuum that emphasises the place of local culture, traditions, and history. It makes the individual subject a whole being, belonging to a community and with societal responsibilities. Education is defined as more than going to school. It is learning about family, community, nature, and society interconnections through everyday practice and social activity. The educational site is not just the 'school' but within and throughout communities, homes, and families. An educated person is one who understands herself/himself as a whole person – mentally, spiritually, culturally, emotionally, physically, and materially – and as continually guided by the mutual obligations to, and interdependence with, the wider community. We need an Indigenous anti-colonial education to challenge the compartmentalisation of education into separate social, cultural, spiritual, political, biological dimensions. We need to challenge the split between the social and natural sciences and narrow conceptualisations of what counts as science, intellectuality, and critical inquiry. We need to do whatever it takes to build liberatory ways of educating our young people and ourselves. This means that, as we resist – from the inside or the outside – the current education system that oppresses us, we must be building better alternatives for the mental/physical/spiritual health, safety, and well-being of all learners.

Acknowledgements

A version of this chapter was given as an "Invited Paper" on the Presidential Session: "*In Consciousness and With Responsibility: Marshalling African/Black Heritage Knowledges, Identities and Practices for the Global Good*" organised by Cynthia Dillard for the Annual Meeting of the American Educational

Research Association (AERA), Vancouver, BC, 16 April 2012. I want to thank Andrew Abraham and Mairi McDermott all of the Department of Sociology and Equity Studies of the Ontario Institute for Studies in Education of the University of Toronto, as well as the editors of *Decolonization*, for their critical comments and input into this chapter.

Note

1 Over the years a central research concern and preoccupation has been how to promote minority youth education in Canada through exemplary practices of inclusive schooling. I see the current project as part of the search for viable educational alternatives for youth. Working with OISE/UT graduate students, my past and on-going research has identified some of the problems of minority youth disengagement from school, as well as educational innovations that can successfully promote effective learning for youth and enhance their educational outcomes (Dei, Holmes, Mazzuca, McIsaac, Campbell, 1995; Dei, Mazzuca, McIsaac, & Zine, 1997; Dei, James-Wilson, Karumanchery, & Zine, 2000b; Dei, James-Wilson, & Zine, 2002). Through these studies, it has been possible to learn about the challenges and possibilities of inclusive schooling. Inclusive schooling involves recognition of the important role of Indigenous/local cultural resource-based knowledge base for the contemporary learner. All learners come to school with particular and shared histories, cultures, identities, experiences, and knowledge bases. Their communities constitute rich sources of knowledge and schools must find ways to work with these cultural knowings. In 2009, I completed a three-year Social Sciences and Humanities Research Council (SSHRC) funded study examining the life histories and personal accounts of 'high academic achievers' in high schools, colleges, and universities. The study offers poignant insights into the power and efficacy of students' school and off-school/community knowledges, cultural histories, and experiences and how learners link their myriad identities to knowledge production. Informed by past and on-going research, my teaching and scholarly writings have always viewed local knowledges as part of the multiple knowings that exist within communities and as containing possibilities for enhanced learning for diverse learners (Dei et al., 2010). In my current, on-going research on African Indigenous philosophies, I am exploring Indigenous knowledge systems in Ghana, Nigeria, and Kenya. This SSHRC-funded study has four (4) objectives: (i) to document and explore the particular teachings are emphasised in local cultural resource knowledge base through local proverbs, songs, fables, folktales, myths, and mythologies; (ii) to critically examine the specific instructional, pedagogic, and communicative values and challenges contained in these teachings; (iii) to understand the ways these bodies of knowledge can be engaged to enhance learning for a diverse group of students using Indigenous/local cultural resource knowledge as sites of multiple knowings; and (iv) to tease out the extent to which such local cultural knowledges deal with social difference and the implications for promoting inclusive learning in pluralistic contexts.

References

Abraham, A. (2011). African and Western knowledge synthesis. *SES 1924H: Modernization, development and education in African context*. Toronto, Canada: Ontario Institute for Studies in Education of the University of Toronto.

Asante, M. K. (1991). The Afrocentric idea in education. *Journal of Negro Education*, 60(2), 170–180.

Asante, M. K. (2003). *Afrocentricity: The theory of social change*. Chicago, IL: African American Images.
Asante, M. K. (2009). *Maulana Karenga: An intellectual portrait*. Cambridge, England: Polity Press.
Battiste, M., & Youngblood Henderson, J. (2000). What is Indigenous knowledge? In J. Youngblood Henderson (Ed.), *Protecting Indigenous knowledge and heritage* (pp. 35–56). Saskatoon, Canada: Purich.
Cajete, G. (2000). *Native science: Natural laws of interdependence*. Santa Fe, NM: Clear Light Publishers.
Cesaire, A. (1972). *Discourse on colonialism*. New York, NY: Monthly Review Press.
Clifford, J. (1986). On ethnographic allegory. In J. Clifford & G. E. Marcus (Eds.), *The poetic and politics of ethnography: Experiments in contemporary anthropology* (pp. 98–121). Berkley, CA: University of California Press.
Cole, M. (1992). Context, modularity, and the cultural constitution of development. In L. T. Winegar & J. Valsiner (Eds.), *Children's development within social context, Vol. 2: Research and methodology* (pp. 5–31). Mahwah, NJ: Lawrence Erlbaum Associates Publishers.
Cole, M. (2006). *The fifth dimension: An after-school program built on diversity*. New York, NY: Russell Sage.
Dei, G. J. S., Holmes, L., Mazzuca, J., McIsaac, E., & Campbell, R. (1995). *Drop out or push out?: Understanding the dynamics of Black students disengagement form school*. Retrieved from https://ia600100.us.archive.org/30/items/dropoutorpushout00deig/dropoutorpushout00deig.pdf
Dei, G. J. S., Mazzuca, J., McIsaac, E., & Zine, J. (1997). *Reconstructing 'dropout'*. Toronto, Canada: University of Toronto Press.
Dei, G. J. S. (2000a). Rethinking the role of Indigenous knowledges in the academy. *International Journal of Inclusive Education, 4*(2), 111–132.
Dei, G. J. S., James, I. M., James-Wilson, S., Karumanchery, L. L., & Zine, J. (2000b). *Removing the margins: The challenges and possibilities of inclusive schooling*. Toronto, Canada: Canadian Scholars' Press.
Dei, G. J. S., & Asgharzadeh, A. (2001). The power of social theory: Towards an anticolonial discursive framework. *Journal of Educational Thought, 35*(3), 297–323.
Dei, G. J. S., James-Wilson, S., & Zine, J. (2002). *Inclusive schooling: A teacher's companion to removing the margins*. Toronto, Canada: Canadian Scholars' Press.
Dei, G. J. S., & Kempf, A. (Eds.). (2006). *Anti-colonialism and education: The politics of resistance*. Rotterdam, the Netherlands: Sense Publishers.
Dei, G. J. S., Butler, A., Charamia, G., Kola-Olusanya, B., Opini, B., Thomas, R., & Wagner, A. (2010). *Learning to succeed: The challenges and possibilities of educational development for all*. New York, NY: Teneo Press.
Dei, G. J. S. (Ed.). (2011). *Indigenous philosophies and critical education*. New York, NY: Peter Lang.
Dei, G. J. S. (2012, April). Learning from Indigenous cultural stories: The case of Ananse stories. Paper presented at the Annual Meeting of the American Educational Research Association (AERA), Vancouver, Canada.
Dei, G. J. S. (2016). Reclaiming schooling and higher education in Africa. In B. Akomolafe, M. K. Asante, & A. Nwoye (Eds.), *We will tell our own stories* (pp. 107–133). New York, NY: Universal Write Publications.
Diawara, M. (1996). Pan-Africanism and pedagogy. *Black Renaissance, 1*(1), 178–187.

Dillard, C. B. (2000). The substance of things hoped for, the evidence of things not seen: Examining an endarkened feminist epistemology in educational research and leadership. *International Journal of Qualitative Studies in Education, 13*(6), 661–681.

Dillard, C. B., Abdur-Rashid, D., & Tyson, C. A. (2000). My soul is a witness: Affirming pedagogies of the spirit. *International Journal of Qualitative Studies in Education, 13*(5), 447–462.

Du Bois, W. E. B. (1965). *The world and Africa: An inquiry into the part which Africa has played in world history.* New York, England: International Publishers.

Fals Borda, O. (1980). *Science and the common people.* Ljubljana, Yugoslavia: International Forum on Participatory Research.

Fals Borda, O. (1991). Some basic ingredients. In O. Fals Borda & M. A. Rahman (Eds.), *Action and knowledge: Breaking the monopoly with participatory action-research* (pp. 3–12). New York, NY: The Apex Press.

Fanon, F. (1963). *The wretched of the earth.* New York, NY: Grove Press.

Fanon, F. (1967). *Black skin, white masks.* New York, NY: Grove Press.

Geertz, C. (1993). *Local knowledge: Further essay in interpretive anthropology.* London, England: Fontana Press.

Ivy, J. W. (1959). The semantics of being Negro in the Americas. *Presence Africaine, xxiv–xxv* (1–2), 133–141.

King, J. (2005). A transformative vision of Black education for human freedom. In J. King (Ed.), *Black education: A transformative research and action agenda for the new century* (pp. 3–17). Mahwah, NJ: Lawrence Erlbaum Associates Publishers.

Ladson-Billings, G. (2011). Yes, but how do we do it?" Practicing culturally relevant pedagogy. In J. Landsman & C. W. Lewis (Eds.), *White teachers/diverse classrooms: Creating inclusive schools, building on students' diversity and providing true equity* (2nd ed., pp. 33–46). Sterling, VA: Stylus Publishing.

Lebakeng, T. G. (2010). Discourse on Indigenous knowledge systems, sustainable socio-economic development and the challenge of the academy in Africa. *CODESRIA Bulletin, 1–2,* 24–29.

Mazama, A. (2001). The Afrocentric paradigm: Contours and definitions. *Journal of Black Studies, 31*(4), 387–405.

Memmi, A. (1965). *The colonizer and the colonized.* Boston, MA: Beacon Press.

Meyer, M. (2008). Indigenous and authentic: Hawaiian epistemology and the triangulation of meaning. In N. Denzin, Y. Lincoln, & L. T. Smith (Eds.), *Handbook of critical and Indigenous methodologies* (pp. 217–232). Thousand Oaks, CA: Sage.

Mundy, K., & Manion, C. (2008). Global education in Canadian elementary schools: An exploratory study. *Canadian Journal of Education, 31*(4), 941–974.

Nyamnjoh, F. B. (2012). Potted plants in greenhouses: A critical reflection on the resilience of colonial education in Africa. *Journal of Asian and African Studies, 47*(2), 129–154.

Purcell, T. W. (1998). Indigenous knowledge and applied anthropology: Question of definition and direction. *Human Organization, 57,* 258–272.

Roberts, M. B., Haami, R., Benton, T., Satterfield, M. L., Finucane, M. H., & Manuka, H. (2004). Whakapapa as a Maori mental construct: Some implications for the debate over genetic modification of organisms. *The Contemporary Pacific, 16,* 1–28.

Rogoff, B. (1981). Schooling and the development of cognitive skills. In H. C. Triandis & A. Heron (Eds.), *Handbook of cross-cultural psychology: Developmental psychology* (Vol. 4, pp. 233–294). Rockleigh, NJ: Allyn and Bacon.

Rogoff, B. (2003). *The cultural nature of human development*. New York, NY: Oxford University Press.

Sium, A. (2011). Dreaming beyond the state: A critical look at the role of Indigenous governance in Africa's development from within. *SES 1924H: Modernization, development and education in African context*. Toronto, Canada: Ontario Institute for Studies in Education of the University of Toronto.

Tappan, M. B. (2006). Moral functioning as mediated action. *Journal of Moral Education, 35*(1), 1–18.

wa Thiong'o, N. (1986). *Decolonizing the mind: The politics of language in African literature*. Nairobi, Kenya: Heinemann.

Wertsch, J. V. (1985). *Vygotsky and the social transformation of mind*. Cambridge, MA: Harvard University Press.

Wertsch, J. (2002). *Voices of collective remembering*. Cambridge, England: Cambridge University Press.

Wright, L. (2011). Transforming Canada's hegemonic global education paradigm through an anti-colonial framework. *SES 1924H: Modernization, development and education in African context*. Toronto, Canada: Ontario Institute for Studies in Education of the University of Toronto.

Yankah, K. (2004). *Globalization and the African scholar* [Monograph]. Accra, Ghana: University of Ghana.

Ziegler, D. (Ed). (1996). *Molefi Kete Asante and Afrocentricity: In praise and in criticism*. Nashville, TN: James C. Winston Publishing.

6
POSTCOLONIAL MODELS, CULTURAL TRANSFERS AND TRANSNATIONAL PERSPECTIVES IN LATIN AMERICA

A research agenda

Gabriela Ossenbach Sauter and María del Mar del Pozo

This chapter introduces a debate on postcolonialism and its role in Latin American education. Postcolonial historiographic perspectives are yet to be applied in one of history's great empires, namely, the Spanish Empire. This is surprising because debate about postcolonialism has been common in Latin America for many years, and the postcolonial approach can be found in the historiographic debate surrounding the Portuguese Empire and education in Portugal and Brazil. We apply a genealogical and conceptual analysis of the defining terms in this field, namely, 'postcolonial', 'transnational', and 'cultural transfers', analyse postcolonial studies in the history of Latin American and Iberian education, and point out lines of investigation that concur with postcolonial theory.

Postcolonialism secured its place in academic and intellectual discourse in the mid-1980s, along with poststructuralism and postmodernism. The genealogy of postcolonialism can be found in an increased sensitivity towards intellectuals from what were, until quite recently, known as the Third World countries. Postcolonialism came to refer to the collective thoughts and views of these intellectuals; whose views included the reformulation of old geopolitical concepts such as 'centre' and 'periphery', a new definition of national and regional borders, and the introduction of new categories of collective identities. It also questioned the classic narrative regarding progress and modernity, subjugated as it had been until then by Eurocentric concepts and an enduring colonial mentality. Originally, the term postcolonial had three different meanings: "as a literal description of conditions in formerly colonial societies"; "as a description of a global condition after the period of colonialism", in which case it substituted the term and the paradigm 'Third World' (Dirlik, 1994, p. 332);

DOI: 10.4324/9781003355397-7

and "as a description of a discourse on the above-named conditions that is informed by the epistemological and psychic orientations that are products of those conditions" (Shohat, 1992, p. 100).

Many have pointed out the multiplicity of meanings that the term postcolonial acquired after its first use when the decolonisation of the European empires took place. Some authors stuck to its original meaning in the understanding that it encompassed two levels of comprehension: "a particular period in history – after the colonial era – and the state of mind from which, as it were, the colonial has been expunged" (Coté, 2005, p. 15). Two new meanings grew from this. The first was aligned with political and ideological postures which understood postcolonial critical thought to mean the production of discourses of resistance to colonialism and imperialism. The second, which would become a new intellectual and cultural tradition strongly influenced by globalising tendencies, is associated with concepts such as diasporas, internationalism, transnational migrations, and cultural exchange. The contributions of non-European artists and intellectuals to European culture have led to the concept of a "transnational imaginary" which proposes to redefine the idea of culture as "a space for a renegotiation of identities and the projection of hybrid identities" (Miampika & García de Vinuesa, 2009, p. 100).

It is in this place – where identities are renegotiated – that the concepts of postcolonialism and transnationalism find their connection. However, in order to describe common traditions, it is important to analyse the intellectual genealogy of the terms. For certain authors, transnational is synonymous with globalisation, while for others it is identified with cosmopolitanism and international critique. Since the mid-1990s, transnational has been a substitute conceptual framework for postcolonial in the analysis of contemporary culture, to such an extent that a "transnational turn" has even been proposed (Heise, 2008, p. 381). Whereas the term international was defined as a genuine relation between nations, transnational seemed to refer to spaces without national jurisdiction; to processes and entities that transcended national borders and were not subject to the control of any government (Union of International Associations, 1982, p. 10). Galtung proposed, in opposition to the idea of international organisations, the idea of the 'individual human', as an entity that would transcend all borders and become the true, basic unit of political action (Galtung, 1980, p. 23).

The transnational turn was attributed to the influence of postcolonial academics and intellectuals. Comparisons have even been proposed of the biographical trajectories of the term's transnational and postcolonial, where the ever-broader interpretations of the latter seem to evidence a kind of competition between the two words in the field of academia (Bayly et al., 2006). However, while the meaning of postcolonial has broadened considerably, the transnational has remained true to the terms by which it was first coined and is still easily identifiable. Transnational history took on a different meaning from international history, which deals with the relations between nations. Transnational history examines units that spill over and seep through national borders. It conceptualises categories and identities, discovers networks united by bonds stronger than social class or ideology, and links narratives and experiences that transcend time and location, while it "… consider[s] cross-national comparison as subject rather than method" (Seigel, 2005, p. 66). The principal concern of a transnational approach is the interpretation of history in terms of movement, ebb, and circulation, not only as themes of study but as points of view, and as an analytical framework in which to generate new historical discourse.

In some circles, transnational history has begun to be considered as a new paradigm of historiography. The origins of the cultural transfer concept can be found in attacks on the kind of comparative history which presented an artificial juxtaposition of isolated national cases that avoided any dynamic interpretation of the contact between cultures. The analyses of the cultural transfer method, based on the categories of introduction, transmission, reception, and appropriation, acknowledge the importance of comparing both cultures, the importer, and the exporter, in order to understand how the system of relations reaches across geographical locations. Werner and Zimmerman stated that the study of cultural transfers belongs to a "family of 'relational' approaches" (2006, p. 31) and introduced the term '*histoire croisée*' (2003, p. 7), meaning 'entangled history', to describe narratives that share strong bonds, and "connected histories", "shared history", and the historian's job of piecing such histories together (Ther, 2009, p. 209). The *histoire croisée* concept may shed light on some of the blind spots of transfer studies. Among these are the problems of reciprocity and reversibility, which, although only vaguely defined, seem to indicate the multidirectional interrelationships, successive transfers, and triangular configurations, all of which could make research on cultural transfer extraordinarily complex (Werner & Zimmermann, 2006, p. 37). It also allows for other related concepts, such as 'cultural spaces', which may contribute to the creation of new mental maps of the continents where the subjects of analysis are no longer nations or territories but rather the places and networks of cultural exchange. Within this family of 'relational' approaches there are also concepts such as connected histories and shared histories, both of which have grown out of postcolonial studies.

Looking beyond the terminology, historians need to develop critical perspectives regarding how these cultural exchanges take place. This is where education could become a central element in this field of study, given the privileged position it occupies in the observation and interpretation of phenomena such as acculturation and enculturation, the transmission and adaptation of culture, and the relationship between dominant and receptive cultures. Pedagogic culture also has the advantage of being built upon a foundation of ideas, terms, institutions, and practices that 'travel', crossing borders, connecting spaces, and serving as models of transnational history. The rediscovery of this model and this subject opens up new possibilities for evaluating the relationship between the different players in the educational field, as well as for building new categories of intercultural transfers that will include new ways of forging individual and collective identities.

Postcolonial approaches in cultural studies: the Latin American case

The relationship between 'centre' and 'periphery', upon which postcolonial theory has been developed, has had an important influence on thought, culture and politics in Latin America, as well as on the way that history has been written. Naturally it has also left its mark on education. This complex, tense relationship, in which the centre is represented not only by the Iberian metropolis but also by Europe and the United States, has shown itself to be invariably characterised by dichotomies such as colony/metropolis; dependence/independence; civilisation/barbarism; development/underdevelopment.

Weinberg attempted to establish a chronological framework for the complex relationship between internal development and external influence, and between originality and imitation in Latin American culture. He defined three stages: "imposed culture", "accepted culture", and "criticised or disputed culture" (Weinberg, 1972). "Imposed culture", which was of a functional nature for the metropolis, corresponds to the colonial era, while "accepted culture" is associated with the organisation of the national societies as they strove to *progress* after political emancipation from the Iberian metropolis. This phase includes the assimilation of foreign cultural and philosophical tendencies by Latin American countries, which adopted them due to their usefulness for solving the theoretical and practical problems involved in organising the new nations. This receptive attitude towards tendencies coming from more advanced countries was due to a growing awareness of the way in which Latin America was 'out of sync' with progress in Europe and the United States. Independence brought its political structures that imitated those of the most advanced countries, and those in power sought ideas and inspirations that would help these countries 'catch up', "homogenizing the diversity of times" (Weinberg, 1993, p. 38). Liberal intellectuals from erstwhile Spanish colonies did not find this receptiveness to foreign ideas contradictory with regard to the new spirit of emancipation; they actually considered it a way of overcoming a colonial legacy. They even developed a discourse on spiritual emancipation from Spain, with clear echoes of English and French literature that had created a sort of 'black legend' surrounding the history of Spain. The peculiar access to independence by Brazil, which declared itself an Empire under the reign of the descendants of the Portuguese royal family, resulted in Brazilian intellectuals viewing the Portuguese legacy quite differently from other Hispanic

Americans. Brazilian intellectuals adopted an eclectic position which facilitated reconciliation of their present with their colonial past.

The phase of "accepted culture" came to an end around 1930, coinciding with the Great Depression. This marks the beginning of the "criticised or disputed culture", in which "docility is gone forever, while it is ever more difficult to admit influences or even passively recognise them" (Weinberg, 1972, p. 21). One notorious precedent for this critical discourse is the reaction of Latin American thought to the surge of Anglo-Saxon utilitarian values, promoted primarily by territorial expansion and economic penetration of the United States, which culminated in the domination of Cuba and Puerto Rico. This gave rise to a new generalised consciousness of a need to gain a 'second independence', this time from the United States. A generation of influential thinkers emerged from this context; the Uruguayan José Enrique Rodó appealed to American youth to adopt spiritual values other than those of *nordomanía* or North American materialism (Rodó, 1900), while the Mexican José Vasconcelos made a case for the creative power of a *mestizo* (mixed European/Indigenous) culture for forging a new Latin American consciousness (Vasconcelos, 1925). This marked an abrupt departure from the strong positivist tendencies present in policies for organising Latin American nations in the last quarter of the 19th century. These ideas became associated with student movements and reached their culmination in the Reform of the University of Córdoba (Argentina), in 1918. This movement represented a clamour for breaking "the remaining chains that, here in the 20th century, were still tying us to a monarchic, monastic domination" (Barros et al., 1918, p. 194), an allusion to the colonial past. Out of this sentiment would grow an extensive continental movement calling for Latin American unity to oppose imperialism.

In this context of anti-imperialistic, socially oriented discourse, another movement, *indigenism,* began to take root in the 1920s and 1930s. This movement was encouraged by the Mexican Revolution, by an emerging Marxist thought represented principally by the Peruvian José Carlos Mariátegui, and by the initiatives of certain intellectuals who were actively involved in addressing social problems in the Andean countries, in Mexico, and in Guatemala. The emancipation of Indigenous people, the abolition of pre-capitalist labour practices that bound them to the *haciendas*, the right to own the land they worked, and the right to receive an education were all important elements in the new discourses and policies, which favoured emancipation of native Latin Americans.

From the late 1950s, the dialectic between dependence and independence focused more and more on the originality of Latin American thought. Intellectuals that stood out in this debate were Ardao (Uruguay), Bondy (Peru), and Zea (Mexico). These authors emphasised the importance of Ortega y Gasset's ideas in helping Latin Americans understand the validity of forming a philosophical framework out of their own circumstances (Zea, 1969).

Another turning point in the interpretation of Latin American history through the centre/periphery perspective came about in the 1970s with the so-called 'dependency theory', which was of a markedly economic nature and which would exercise an especially strong influence on the social sciences. However, many dependency theorists favoured an exclusive interpretation of American developments as reactions against unidirectional pressures coming from the exterior. In failing to consider the importance of external as well as American factors, and in considering 19th century dependence as a mere continuation of a colonial legacy (neo-colonialism), these authors failed to acknowledge the importance of the independence movements and the creation of new, sovereign states. Dependency theorists, such as Cardoso and Faletto, responded to some of these simplistic approaches by encouraging more complex analyses that would include the study of internal relationships among groups struggling for power at a *national* level, as well as their links to the exterior, thus revealing the contradictions inherent in national, sovereign states operating within an international economic framework that determined them (Carmagnani, 1984; Kaplan, 1981; Lechner, 1983; Oszlak, 1981).

The development programmes carried out in Latin America during the 1960s and 1970s led to profound changes in urban and rural locations (migration, industrialisation, more inclusive social policies). This new reality, which quickly generated a political and intellectual pan-continental consciousness, provided fertile ground for the emergence of modern postcolonial theories in Latin America. These theories have had an impact on anthropology, philosophy, cultural studies, literature, and history, giving rise to numerous categories for the analysis and critical evaluation of Latin American reality. These theories criticise the fact that the mutual dependence between modernity and colonialism has been ignored, with colonialism being portrayed merely as an undesired by-product of modernity, or as a historical phase of modernity whose time has passed. Postcolonial theory is unambiguous in denouncing the epistemic violence of Eurocentrism, which created devices that would guarantee its expansion: the coloniality of power, the coloniality of knowledge, and the coloniality of being (Calderón, 2008, pp. 10–16).

In the field of philosophy one of the discourses that have a major impact is the exiled Argentinean Enrique Dussel whose thesis contained the idea that while the philosophy of the 'centre' becomes an instrument of oppression and an expression of European intellectual colonialism, at the periphery it becomes an instrument of liberation (Dussel, 1985). Another important postcolonial theory emerged in the 1990s with the critique of Latin American 'cultural studies' in numerous US universities taught by intellectuals from Latin America. The Argentinean Walter Mignolo argued that the European Renaissance of the 16th and 17th centuries had another invisible, forgotten side: the colonisation of America (Mignolo, 1995). Other Latin American postcolonial theorists were associated with the 'World-system approach' developed by the North American sociologist Immanuel Wallerstein, which emphasised the mechanisms of economic distribution among central, semi-peripheral, and peripheral countries (Lander, 2000).

Another fertile area of study is 'interculturality', which criticises not only the imposed subjugation to the logic and reason of Eurocentricity, but also the creation of a *racial* imaginary, with its consequences for the definition of European superiority (Calderón, 2008). From a political perspective, interculturality encourages the struggle among Indigenous sectors – as well as those of African descent – but neglects their integration into the *modern* national project. Rather, these diverse sectors are encouraged to become a kind of 'nation' among many others, with their own ways of producing knowledge, of administering economy and justice, of relating to their environment, etc. In other words, interculturality does not recognise the Indigenous as another element in the multicultural diversity of the nation (a concept found within Eurocentric universalism) but rather aspires, as a political project articulated from the colonial difference to a pluri-nationality (Walsh, 2009). This debate has led to the definition of the 'postcolonial national state' and has produced an intense discussion about citizenship and exclusion, issues which invariably touch on ethnicity. This phenomenon has spilled over into the political space that used the Marxist category of social class to analyses in terms of identity (Figueroa, 2007).

Arturo Escobar argued that the Third World does not actually exist as an objective reality, but rather as an intervention created on the basis of the geopolitics of power, and upon which certain governmental technologies are applied. According to Escobar, the Third World was invented after the Second World War, in the contexts of the Cold War and North American interests in Latin America, and in the recently emancipated nations of Africa and Asia (Escobar, 1995).

Lastly, there is the association between these postcolonial theories and liberation theology, the movement in which certain Catholic groups supported underprivileged sectors of society in Latin America. In education, this movement led to a clamour for "education as a practice of freedom", a powerful slogan that came from Paulo Freire's book, published for the first time in English in 1976 (Freire, 1976). This book enjoyed unprecedented international success, symbolising the unfinished process of emancipation in Latin America.

Postcolonial studies in Iberian and Latin American history of education: state of art, critical reviews and the research agenda

The story of transnationality and postcolonialism in education began with a conference in 1993 having the title *Education Encounters People and Cultures: The Colonial Experience (16th–20th Centuries)*. The word 'encounters' in the title suggested an analysis of a theme that had only been previously analysed through the lens of the influence of the colonisers on colonised peoples and cultures. António Nóvoa introduced postcolonialism into the history of education at this conference (Nóvoa, 1995). The postcolonial point of view became increasingly evident in subsequent publications (Allender, 2010; Barthélémy, Picard, & Rogers, 2010; Goodman, McCulloch, & Richardson, 2009; Madeira, 2005; McCulloch & Lowe, 2003), while there is a noticeable interest in the transnational approach in subsequent historiographic analysis (Caruso, 2007; Fuchs, 2007; Trethewey & Whitehead, 2003). The concept of educational transfer (Steiner-Khamsi, 2000), meanwhile, has been developed to explore the possibilities offered by adopting a world history or global history of education (Caruso, 2008; Myers, Grosvenor, & Watts, 2008).

Goodman et al. (2009) looked beyond the traditional colonial interpretative model, which always moves in a unidirectional manner from the centre to the periphery, and incorporated a more flexible analysis in which reciprocity allows us to discover reciprocal and multidirectional influences between the metropolis and the colonies. This in-depth and thoroughly documented essay on the categories of analysis used in postcolonial studies is based almost exclusively on the case of the British Empire, which is the symbolic space which has generated the most literature on the subject.

Educational historiography in the Iberian Peninsula, home to the Spanish and Portuguese metropolis, can be approached from three perspectives. The first perspective is an analysis of the themes of investigation undertaken in the past 30 years and their possible consideration as postcolonial studies. Analysis of two Spanish publications coming out of the V Centenary of the Discovery of the Americas – the minutes of the National Colloquium of the History of Education (V Coloquio Nacional de Historia de la Educación, 1988) and the monographic issue of the journal *Historia de la Educación* (Lozano Seijas, 1992a) – provide a clue: they are the volumes with the fewest number of pages in their respective collections. The 50 papers presented at the Colloquium were divided equally between the colonial era and the era of independence: numerous papers focused on Spanish pedagogues and their influence in Latin America; others dealt exclusively with Spain, and only two included the concept of 'mutual relations', even though this was the theme of the conference. On the other hand, the monographic issue on the History of Ibero-American Education called for the history of Latin American education to be studied "parallel to" Spanish and European education and to try to "imagine a view of Spanish education as seen from the other shore", which sounded like a novel approach, a "history under construction" (Lozano Seijas, 1992b, p. 19). Yet only one of the articles in that issue presented a parallel history of Spanish and American educative histories as being somehow connected (Ossenbach, 1992).

In the following two decades, three lines of research developed in Spain. Interest in educational exile began in the early 1990s, in particular the massive exile of Republican pedagogues and teachers who were forced to leave Spain after the Civil War (1936–1939) and who emigrated to Latin American countries. Generally, studies have focused on specific teachers, their Spanish trajectory (pre-Civil War), their Latin American trajectory (post-Civil War), and especially on the institutions and projects that they started in their countries of reception (Almendros, 2005; Canellas & Torán, 2003; Cruz Orozco, 2004, 2005; Lozano Seijas, 1999; Marqués Sureda, 2003, 2005; Marqués Sureda & Martín Frechilla, 2002). The second line of research concerns the *indianos* schools (Cuenca, Fernández, & Hevia, 2003; Malheiro Gutiérrez, 2005; Peña Saavedra, 1991; Zapater Cornejo, 2007) which were created in Spain by Spaniards who emigrated to Latin America and later provided funds to build schools in their home towns. A third line of research is focused on the idea of America, as it is presented in school textbooks, and is closely associated with the commemoration of the bicentenary of the emancipation of the American nations (Cruz, 2007; Valls, 2007).

The second perspective for the analysis of the educational historiography in the Iberian Peninsula is that of examining the investigative approaches used to discern how they conform to the discourses of postcolonial theory. There is an evolution of concepts which go beyond the idea of the 'influence' of the metropolis on the colonies. Yet many of the studies of the exiles continue to adopt a metropolitan perspective; they provide a context and background for the exile's trajectory previous to the war but they are not familiar with the circumstances of the countries that have taken them in; they analyse the way in which the exiles transferred and applied their pedagogical knowledge in their new professional surroundings, but they do not take into account how that knowledge interacted with and was transformed by contact with the existing educational traditions. Investigations about the *indianos* schools have been influenced by studies of the social history of emigration, which tend to delve into the routes of transmission, the formation of migratory networks and, above all, the consequences of the emigrants' return; the returned exiles not only brought back material wealth, but they transmitted ideas on political and social progress which they then tried to apply in their places of origin (Núñez Seijas, 1998). They tried to implement the public Argentinian education model which was an original model that had been elaborated and contributed to by a number of Spanish intellectuals (Malheiro Gutiérrez, 2007).

The centenary of the creation of the *Junta para Ampliación de Estudios e Investigaciones Científicas*, an institution which between 1907 and 1936 granted thousands of scholarships for Spanish scientists, educators, and artists to travel and study abroad, brought renewed attention to reciprocal cultural relations between centre and periphery. The experience encouraged a historiographic production that places an emphasis on cultural exchange, as is evidenced in publications referring to the networks created among Spanish and Latin American intellectuals (Fernández Terán & González Redondo, 2010; Naranjo Orovio, 2007).

The third study perspective is the analysis of the trajectory of Spanish historiography of education by comparing it to that of Portugal. Notwithstanding the many common issues, there is a difference between them in terms of the creation of spaces for postcolonial research. Portuguese historians have constructed a common tradition with their Brazilian colleagues, one that is based on reciprocity and mutual production, circulation, and connection. The driving force behind this was António Nóvoa, who encouraged the creation of 'spaces of relation' between Portugal, Brazil, and Mozambique, and who found inspiration in postcolonial theories for the establishment of theoretical frameworks for future investigative agendas. Among other ideas, he recommended substituting the traditional histories of colonisation – with their unidirectional and simplistic vision of the coloniser–colonised relationship – with the postcolonial concept of 'hybridity', allowing for intersecting areas of contact and encounter with the 'other' (Nóvoa, 2001, p. 141; Paulo, 2001). The unequivocal adoption of this agenda facilitated the construction of an investigative tradition (Pintassilgo, Freitas, Mogarro, & Carvalho, 2006) based on the discovery of communication networks among the three national communities. Since 1996, the tradition has been reaffirmed in the Portuguese-Brazilian Congresses of the History of Education, and its influence has begun to have an effect on comparative approaches regarding the history of education in Brazil and other Latin American countries (Mignot & Gondra, 2009; Vidal & Ascolani, 2009). And yet we see no desire to establish comparable 'spaces of relation' between Spain and the Latin American countries with which they shared their colonial adventure.

Situating ourselves on 'the other shore', we observe that while the investigative approaches based on postcolonial theory in Latin America have been many and varied, their impact on the history of education is negligible. Historians have given little attention to education during the colonial era and no significant critical discourse has emerged (Pimenta, 2010). This brings to mind the observation made by some historians of the colonial era that the postcolonial paradigm should not be used to study colonial situations in America (Klor de Alva, 1992).

Latin American historians of education have focused on the national histories of the independent countries; especially in the period when national educational systems were being established (Ossenbach, 2000). These histories have paid little attention to transnational tendencies or to the complex modes of exchange of educational models between centre and periphery or between peripheral regions. There are exceptions, such as the investigation of the transatlantic book trade in the first decades of the 19th century by Roldán Vera (2003) and the network analysis that this author undertook on the introduction of the monitorial system of education in early independent Spanish America (Roldán Vera & Schupp, 2005).

Certain overly simplistic views of the history of education – possibly a consequence of dependency theory itself – have conveyed the idea of unidirectional movement in which models are always circulating from the central regions to Latin America. Acknowledgement of the capacity for the colonised or peripheral countries to appropriate these models, make them their own, and produce significant changes in them can be found in the important work by Sáenz, Saldarriaga, and Ospina (1997), and in the investigations that Vera undertook with Caruso concerning the 'acclimatisation' of the monitorial system of education in Latin America (Caruso & Roldán Vera, 2005; Roldán Vera & Caruso, 2007). A different approach, based on the history of concepts, was used by Caruso, who applied the term semantic emancipation to refer to the transformation and weakening in post-independent America of the category, so imbued with Spanish connotations, of *primeras letras* (a form of designating the realm of elementary education) (Caruso, 2010).

An emerging area of study in which postcolonial theories could be applied is the education of Indigenous and African descendants. Attention to Indigenous education has increased significantly in recent years as a part of the history of rural education and because of the proliferation of regional, local, and provincial studies in Mexico, Brazil, Argentina, and Colombia. There is a tendency for studies of rural education to ignore the specific conditions of the Indigenous, merely including them as a part of the rural peasantry. Nonetheless, that studies of rural education are being carried out is a gesture in keeping with the subaltern approach proposed by postcolonial theories, because the focus moves away from urban contexts in which the Eurocentric legacy is more likely to have left its imprint. In other cases, Indigenous education has been studied as a part of the history of Indigenous groups, separate from the specific field of the history of education. Such studies identify some of the educative strategies designed by the Indigenous themselves (Cajías de la Vega & Cajías de la Vega, 2010; Escalante, 2005). Other studies, perhaps affording a greater critical potential, have attempted to approach the perception of the Indigenous through the application of theories of 'otherness'.

The idea that Latin America has proved itself capable of producing changes in its metropolis represents another approach to the postcolonial perspective on the history of education. As Pineau has stated, "making progress in giving America the 'right to history' requires thinking that America was capable of producing deep changes in Europe and seeing both continents in passive and active modes" (2008, p. 747). Proposing an inverted circulation for Latin America in which models flowed from the periphery to the centre stirs up the accepted consciousness of this continent as a region that did nothing but receive outside influences. In 1936, Lovejoy proposed another line of investigation for the history of ideas that would surely help to identify and reveal much of the phenomena of inverted circulation of influences and models. Lovejoy proposed a history of 'unit-ideas', ideas which upon circulating would become nuanced and, in some cases, acquire more strength than the original idea. From this perspective, Latin America can be seen to have produced countless nuances on ideas that arrived from the metropolis; then, in a process of refraction, these ideas circulated with even greater strength back towards the centre (Lovejoy, 1936).

We also propose introducing the concept of 'hybridity' into the academic debate on the history of education in Latin America. This not only facilitates the creation of cultural exchange and the definition of meeting places among cultures, it also helps to better comprehend all those individuals, such as exiles and emigrants, who lived between two worlds and were forced to negotiate and construct a new personal identity, in which the colonial aspect was an important part. Zulueta stated that "truth is essentially a *mestizo* creation" (Zulueta, 1952, p. 101). This paraphrasing of Rostand was Zulueta's way of affirming, there at the crossroads of colonisers and colonised, his new identity, which no longer belonged to either of these categories.

Postcolonialism is, above all, an attitude, a way of looking at the world that encourages reflection on the way relations with the past can mark the present and the future of national communities. The notion of 'time-lag' introduced by Bhabha suggests that "the colonial past is present and informs the postcolonial now, that is, in the colonialist stereotype that surfaces in the present and troubles the linearity of modernity by repeating the past" (Bhabha, 1994, p. 253). Postcolonialism makes us question our most deeply felt identities and reveals dark corners of our consciousness in which remnants of imperial constructs persist. But it also allows us to invent new spaces for reflection, spaces that encourage transnational communication.

References

Allender, T. (2010). Understanding education and India: New turns in postcolonial scholarship. *History of Education, 39*(2), 281–288.
Almendros, H. (2005). *Diario de un maestro exiliado.* Valencia, Spain: Pre-Textos.
Barthélémy, P., Picard, E., & Rogers, R. (Eds.). L'enseignement dans l'Empire colonial français (XIXe–XXe siècles). *Histoire de l'éducation,* 128, 5–190.
Barros, E. F., Valdés, H., Bordabehere, I. C., Sayazo, G., Castellanos, A., Méndez, L. M., & Garzón, E.. (1981). La juventud argentina de Córdoba a los hombres libres de Sud América: Manifiesto del 21 de Junio de 1918. *CLACSO,* 194–199.
Bayly, C. A., Beckert, S., Connelly, M., Hofmeyr, I., Kozol, W., & Seed, P. (2006). AHR conversation: On transnational history. *American Historical Review,* 5, 1440–1464.
Bhabha, H. K. (1994). *The location of culture.* London, England: Routledge.
Cajías de la Vega, M., & Cajías de la Vega, B. (2010). Apuntes para repensar la educación indígena a la luz de su historia y de los procesos de liberación del indio en Bolivia. *Historia de la Educación: Revista Interuniversitaria,* 29, 103–116.
Calderón, L. T. (2008). *La violencia epistémica y sus dispositivos eurocéntricos: Una mirada desde la teoría de la decolonización.* La Paz, Bolivia: Centro de Estudios para la América Andina y Amazónica.

Canellas, C., & Torán, R. (2003). *Dolors Piera, mestra, política i exiliada*. Barcelona, Spain: Ajuntament de Barcelona y Publicacions de l'Abadía de Montserrat.

Carmagnani, M. (1984). *Estado y sociedad en América Latina, 1850–1930*. Barcelona, Spain: Crítica.

Caruso, M., & Roldán Vera, E. (2005). Pluralizing meanings: The monitorial system of education in Latin America in the early nineteenth century. *Paedagogica Historica*, 41(6), 645–654.

Caruso, M. (2007). Disruptive dynamics: The spatial dimensions of the Spanish networks in the spread of monitorial schooling (1815–1825). *Paedagogica Historica*, 43(2), 271–282.

Caruso, M. (2008). World systems, world society, world polity: Theoretical insights for a global history of education. *History of Education*, 37(6), 825–840.

Caruso, M. (2010). La emancipación semántica: 'Primeras letras' en Hispanoamérica (ca. 1770–1840). *Bordón*, 62(2), 39–51.

Coté, J. (2005). Memory and history, community and nation: Telling the story of the Indisch Dutch in Australia. In J. Coté & L. Westerbeek (Eds.), *Recalling the Indies – Colonial culture & postcolonial identities* (pp. 9–27). Amsterdam, Netherlands: Aksant.

Cruz Orozco, J. I. (2004). *Maestros y colegios en el exilio de 1939*. Valencia, Spain: Institució Alfons el Magnànim.

Cruz Orozco, J. I. (Ed.). (2005). *Los colegios del exilio en México*. Madrid, Spain: Residencia de Estudiantes.

Cruz, M. D. (2007). '*Portugal gigante*': Nationalism, motherland and colonial encounters in Portuguese school textbooks. *Goiânia*, 5(2), 395–422.

Cuenca, C., Fernández, F. F., & Hevia, J. (2003). *Escuelas de indianos y emigrantes en Asturias: Rehabilitación de las escuelas de Vidiago*. Gijón, Spain: Trea.

Dirlik, A. (1994). The postcolonial aura: Third world criticism in the age of global capitalism. *Critical Inquiry*, 2, 328–356.

Dussel, E. (1985). *Philosophy of liberation*. New York, NY: Orbis Books.

Escalante, C. (2005). Indígenas e Historia de la Educación en América Latina (siglos XIX y XX. Un primer acercamiento biblio-hemerográfico. *Revista de la Escuela de Ciencias de la Educación*, 59–86.

Escobar, A. (1995). *Encountering development: The making and unmaking of the third world*. Princeton, NJ: Princeton University Press.

Fernández Terán, R. E., & González Redondo, F. A. (2010). Las cátedras de la Institución Cultural Española y de Buenos Aires: Ciencia y educación entre Eespaña y Argentina, 1910–1940. *Historia de la Educación: Revista Interuniversitaria*, 29, 195–219.

Figueroa, J. A. (2007). Etnización de la política: Una lectura desde la teoría crítica. In C. Büschges, G. Bustos, & O. Kaltmeier (Eds.), *Etnicidad y poder en los países andinos* (pp. 43–59). Quito, Eucador: Corporación Editora Nacional.

Freire, P. (1976). *Education: The practice of freedom*. London, England: Writers and Readers Publishing Cooperative.

Fuchs, E. (2007). Networks and the history of education. *Paedagogica Historica*, 43(2), 185–197.

Galtung, J. (1980). *The true worlds: A transnational perspective*. New York, NY: The Free Press.

Goodman, J., McCulloch, G., & Richardson, W. (2009). Empires overseas' and 'empires at home': Postcolonial and transnational perspectives on social change in the history of education. *Paedagogica Historica*, 45(6), 695–821.

Heise, U. K. (2008). Ecocriticism and the transnational turn in American studies. *American Literary History, 20*(1–2), 381–404.
Kaplan, M. (1981). *Aspectos del Estado en América Latina*. México City, México: UNAM.
Klor de Alva, J. (1992). Colonialism and postcolonialism as (Latin) American mirage. *Colonial Latin American Review, 1*(2), 3–23.
Lander, E. (Ed.). (2000). *La colonialidad del saber. Eurocentrismo y ciencias sociales. Perspectivas latinoamericanas*. Buenos Aires, Argentina: CLACSO.
Lechner, N. (Ed.). (1983). *Estado y política en América Latina*. Coyoacán, México: Siglo XXI.
Lovejoy, A. O. (1936). *The great chain of being: A study of the history of an idea*. Cambridge, MA: Harvard University Press.
Lozano Seijas, C. (1992a). Historia de la educación iberoamericana. *Historia de la Educación: Revista Interuniversitaria, 11*, 11–20.
Lozano Seijas, C. (1992b). La educación iberoamericana: Presentación. *Gredos Principal*, 11–20.
Lozano Seijas, C. (1999). *1939, el exilio pedagógico: Estudios sobre el exilio republicano español de 1939*. Barcelona, Spain: Cooperativa Universitària Sant Jordi.
Madeira, A. I. (2005). Portuguese, French and British discourses on colonial education: Church-state relations, school expansion and missionary competition in Africa, 1890– 1930. *Paedagogica Historica, 41*(1–2), 31–60.
Malheiro Gutiérrez, X. M. (2005). *Herdanza da emigración ultramarina: Catálogo fotográfico da arquitectura escolar indiana na provincia de Pontevedra*. Pontevedra, Spain: Diputación Provincial.
Malheiro Gutiérrez, X. M. (2007). Una nueva luz: La influencia de la escuela argentina en la intervención de los emigrantes gallegos en sus lugares de origen. *Historia de la Educación: Revista Interuniversitaria, 26*, 341–366.
Marqués Sureda, S., & Martín Frechilla, J. (2002). *La labor educativa de los exiliados españoles en Venezuela*. Caracas, Venezuela: Universidad Central de Venezuela.
Marqués Sureda, S. (2003). *Maestros catalanes del exilio*. Zapopan, México: El Colegio de Jalisco.
Marqués Sureda, S. (2005). *Els Mestres i l'exili del 39*. Barcelona, Spain: Universitat de Barcelona.
McCulloch, G., & Lowe, R. (2003). Introduction: Centre and periphery – Networks, space and geography in the history of education. *History of Education, 32*(5), 457–594.
Miampika, L.-W., & García de Vinuesa, M. (2009). Migration, racism and postcolonial studies in Spain. In G. Huggan & I. Law (Eds.), *Racism, postcolonialism, Europe* (pp. 92–101). Liverpool, England: Liverpool University Press.
Mignolo, W. (1995). *The darker side of the renaissance: Literacy, territoriality, and colonization*. Ann Arbor, MI: University of Michigan Press.
Mignot, A. C. V., & Gondra, J. G. (Eds.). (2007). *Viagens pedagógicos*. São Paulo, Brazil: Cortez.
Myers, K., Grosvenor, I., & Watts, R. (2008). Education and globalisation. *History of Education, 37*(6), 737–741.
Naranjo Orovio, C. (2007). La Junta para la Ampliación de Estudios y América Latina: Memoria, políticas y acción cultural (1907–1939). *Revista de Indias, 67*(239), 283–306.
Nóvoa, A. (1995). On history, history of education and history of colonial education. In A. Nóvoa, M. Depaepe, & E. V. Johanningmeier (Eds.), *The colonial experience in education: Historical issues and perspectives* (Vol. 1, pp. 23–61). Ghent, Belgium: CHSP.

Nóvoa, A. (2001). Tempos da Escola no Espaço Portugal-Brasil-Moçambique dez digressões sobre um programa de investigação. *Currículo sem Fronteiras*, 1(2), 131–150.

Núñez Seijas, X. M. (1998). *Emigrantes, caciques e indianos: O influxo sociopolítico da emigración transoceánica en Galicia (1900–1930)*. Vigo, Spain: Ediciones Xerais.

Ossenbach, G. (1992). Pedro Alcántara García y las relaciones pedagógicas entre España e Hispanoamérica a finales del siglo XIX. *Historia de la Educación: Revista Interuniversitaria*, 11, 125–142.

Ossenbach, G. (2000). Research into the history of education in Latin America: Balance of the current situation. *Paedagogica Historica*, 36(3), 841–866.

Oszlak, O. (1981). The historical formation of the state in Latin America: Some theoretical and methodological guidelines for its study. *Latin American Research Review*, 16(2), 3–32.

Paulo, J. C. (2001). What does indigenous education mean? Portuguese colonial thought and the construction of ethnicity and education. *Paedagogica Historica*, 37(1), 231–250.

Peña Saavedra, V. (1991). *Éxodo, organización comunitaria e intervención escolar: La impronta educativa de la emigración transoceánica en Galicia* (Vol. 2). La Coruña, Spain: Xunta de Galicía.

Pimenta, J. P. G. (2010). Education and the historiography of Ibero-American independence: Elusive presences, many absences. *Paedagogica Historica*, 46(4), 419–434.

Pineau, P. (2008). Education and globalisation: A Latin American perspective. *History of Education*, 37(6), 743–755.

Pintassilgo, J., Freitas, M. C., Mogarro, M. J., & Carvalho, M. M. C. (Eds.). (2006). *História da escola em Portugal e no Brasil: Circulação e apropriação de modelos culturais* Lisboa. Portugal: Edições Colibrí/Centro de Investigação em Educação da Faculdade de Ciências da Universidade de Lisboa.

Rodó, J. E. (1900). *Ariel*. Montevideo, Uruguay: Imp. de Dornaleche y Reyes.

Roldán Vera, E., & Caruso, M. (Eds.). (2007). *Imported modernity in post-colonial state formation: The appropriation of political, educational, and cultural models in nineteenth-century Latin America*. Frankfurt, Germany: Peter Lang.

Roldán Vera, E., & Schupp, T. (2005). Bridges over the Atlantic: A network analysis of the introduction of the monitorial system of education in early-independent Spanish America. *Comparativ*, 15(1), 58–93.

Roldán Vera, E. (2003). *The British book trade and Spanish American independence: Education and knowledge transmission in transcontinental perspective*. Aldershot, England: Ashgate.

Sáenz, J., Saldarriaga, O., & Ospina, A. (1997). *Mirar la infancia: Pedagogía, moral y modernidad en Colombia, 1903–1946* (Vol. 2). Medellín, Colombia: Colciencias.

Seigel, M. (2005). Beyond compare: Comparative method after the transnational turn. *Radical History Review*, 91, 62–90.

Shohat, E. (1992). Notes on the "post-colonial". *Social Text*, 31–32, 99–113.

Steiner-Khamsi, G. (2000). Transferring education, displacing reforms. In J. Schriewer (Ed.), *Discourse formation in comparative education* (pp. 155–187). Frankfurt, Germany: Peter Lang.

Ther, P. (2009). Comparisons, cultural transfers, and the study of networks: Toward a transnational history of Europe. In H.-G. Haupt & J. Kocka (Eds.), *Comparative and transnational history: Central European approaches and new perspectives* (pp. 204–225). New York, NY: Berghahn Books.

Trethewey, L., & Whitehead, K. (2003). Beyond centre and periphery: Transnationalism in two teacher/suffragettes' work. *History of Education, 32*(5), 547–559.

Union of International Associations (1982). *World forum mondial 1980. proceedings: From international to transnational, Document no. 23 for the study of international non-governmental relations.* Brussels, Belgium: Union of International Associations.

V Coloquio Nacional de Historia de la Educación (1988). *Historia de las relaciones educativas entre España y América.* Sevilla, Spain: Departamento de Teoría e Historia de la Educación.

Valls, R. (Ed.). (2007). *Los procesos independentistas iberoamericanos en los manuales de Historia, Vol. I: Países andinos y España; Vol. II: Argentina, Chile, Paraguay, Uruguay; Vol. III: Brasil e Portugal; Vol. IV: Costa Rica, México, Nicaragua y Panamá.* Madrid, Spain: OEI/Fundación Mapfre.

Vasconcelos, J. (1925). *La raza cósmica, misión de la raza Iberoamericana: Notas de viajes a la América del Sur.* Madrid, Spain: Agencia Mundial de Librería.

Vidal, D. G., & Ascolani, A. (Eds.). (2009). *Reformas educativas no Brasil e na Argentina: Ensaios de historia comparada da educação (1820– 2000).* São Paulo, Brazil: Cortez.

Walsh, C. (2009). *Interculturalidad, estado, sociedad: Luchas (de)coloniales de nuestra época.* Quito, Eucador: Universidad Andina Simón Bolívar.

Weinberg, G. (1972). Sobre el quehacer filosófico latinoamericano: Algunas consideraciones históricas y reflexiones actuales. *Revista de la Universidad de México, XXVI*(6–7), 19–24.

Weinberg, G. (1993). *Tiempo, destiempo y contratiempo.* Buenos Aires, Argentina: Leviatán.

Werner, M., & Zimmermann, B. (2003). Penser l'histoire croisée: Entre empirie et réflexivité. *Annales, 58*(1), 7–36.

Werner, M., & Zimmermann, B. (2006). Beyond comparison: *Histoire croisée* and the challenge of reflexivity. *History and Theory, 45*(1), 30–50.

Zapater Cornejo, M. (2007). *Escuelas de Indianos en La Rioja.* Logroño, Spain: Instituto de Estudios Riojanos.

Zea, L. (1969). *La filosofía americana como filosofía sin más.* Coyoacán, México: Siglo XXI.

Zulueta, L. (1952). *El rapto de América (Ensayo sobre la colonización española).* Buenos Aires, Argentina: Editorial Sudamericana.

PART II
Reframing the codes, rules and rituals of educational research practice

7
REFLEXIVITY AND THE POLITICS OF KNOWLEDGE

Researchers as 'brokers' and 'translators' of educational development

Arathi Sriprakash and Rahul Mukhopadhyay

In this chapter, we interrogate the ways in which 'reflexivity' has proliferated as a normative methodological discourse in qualitative social research. In the field of international and comparative education, and the social sciences more broadly, reflexive research has become synonymous with 'good' research practice: it signals the researcher's intent to be sensitive to local contexts and to the representation of research participants. Often this is done through an acknowledgement of how the researcher's own knowledge frames (social positions and theoretical perspectives) relate to the knowledge frames of the 'other' under study. Sometimes, particularly in research that purports to be participatory, emancipatory, or critical, the epistemological standpoints of the researched are privileged over the researchers. While these intentions are certainly important in orienting us towards ethical research endeavours, we explore the limitations of this kind of 'reflexivity'. We argue that in foregrounding, and even monumentalising, the standpoints of 'knowers' in research (whether the researcher or the researched), such approaches to reflexivity do not attend to the situated, contingent, and relational dynamics of 'knowing' itself. Moreover, these approaches too easily bypass the *performative* effects of research; how disciplinary ways of knowing (through associated methods and discourses) enact particular realities of the world. In the domain of education development, where policy and research are often clearly entwined, and where the stakes for the marginalised are so high, the ways in which realities are assembled through research must be a central consideration for the reflexive researcher.

We suggest that a second-order engagement with the notion of reflexivity is necessary in social research – and in educational development research more specifically. A second-order engagement with reflexivity encourages us to trace the ways in which knowledge about educational development is *assembled*: how particular 'truths' about educational development are produced through empirical studies, how these 'truths' circulate, and how they gain an apparent stability and durability. As Law (2004, p. 149) writes, we need to attend to the ways in which different versions of social science research operate "to make certain (political) arrangements more probable, stronger, more real, whilst eroding others and making them less real". Reflexivity, then, is not only concerned with individual researchers' engagement with their subjects under study, but it is also about tracing the *politics of knowledge* with respect to their field of study and beyond.

Drawing on theoretical devices from actor–network theory (ANT), we put forward the perspective that social researchers, through the methods and disciplinary discourses they deploy, are 'brokers' and 'translators' of knowledge. Broadly speaking, ANT is interested in the interconnections of 'actors' to understand how things come together and how they appear to hold together. If research is understood as a network of relationships, then a researcher would be one actor in that network, as would research participants, and also non-human entities such as policies and research tools that all come to bear on the network. ANT takes an anti-foundationalist approach, whereby "nothing exists prior to its performance or enactment" (Fenwick & Edwards, 2012, p. x). That is, the associations (or networks) of diverse sets of actors are seen as mechanisms through which meanings of phenomenon are constituted. This means ANT is attentive to both contingency and change: it endorses a processual research approach that traces the contingent transformations of actors, their interests, and their associations.

Central to this approach is the notion of 'translation' which foregrounds the processes through which interconnections between actors are contingently negotiated, resisted, defended, moved, and transformed. It is through a process of translation that knowledge is assembled. Useful to our explorations of reflexivity, then, the ANT perspective signifies the ways in which social research itself brings together multiple actors, educational discourses, scripts, and performances which, through a process of translation, produce particular understandings of the world. Building on this view, we propose that social researchers can be understood as 'brokers' and 'translators' of knowledge. They are 'brokers' of knowledge, in the sense that they are mediators in the research process. But they are also 'translators' in the sense that the salience of their mediations is contingent on the role and agency of other actors connected to the research network and on the negotiations of these interconnections.

We consider how these ideas play out by looking at research on teachers and teachers' work in the Indian educational development context, an area of ongoing research enquiry for us. Our reading of this field using the metaphors of brokers and translators foregrounds the politics of knowledge in social research. What we want to emphasise is not the 'reflexivity' that assumes its significance *ex post* a process of research, but 'reflexivity' as a means of apprehending the interplay of a multiplicity of actors. It is through this interplay that particular educational realities are constituted and circulated in research communities and are reinforced in policy discourses. By looking at the case of teacher research in India, we attempt to explicate the limitations of a first-order reflexivity and allude to the potential of understanding reflexivity as a second-order engagement that arises from the performative elements of a research endeavour. The shift from standpoints of knowers to processes of knowing in this view encourages reflexive research to account for the contingencies and complexities of its claims. We begin our discussions by critically examining the dominant discourses of reflexivity in social research.

Reflexivity: a tool of methodological power?

In a broad-brush sense, reflexivity in social research refers to an ongoing process of reflection through which the relations between the researcher, research subjects, and knowledge production are made explicit, and in turn shape the research process. Following the constructivist turn in the social sciences, reflexivity has become a normative methodological discourse in educational research, and the visibility it brings to these relations plays a number of roles in how good, rigorous, or valid research is now understood. For example, Pillow (2003, p. 185) discusses the ways in which reflexivity is commonly used in research: as "recognition of self; recognition of other; reflexivity as truth; and reflexivity as transcendence". Recognition of the self often involves the disclosure of one's own subjectivities and their connections to the research subjects. Such forms of self-reflection are often used to validate 'insider' research, and tend to be predicated on an assumption that the researcher and researched are fully knowable subjects. Recognition of the other is based on similar assumptions and can be seen in research which privileges the voices of the research subject as a claim to greater validity for the production of knowledge about the other. What is often not adequately addressed in such validity claims are the conditions under which the other (the research subject) is asked to define oneself or one's social practices.

Pillow goes on to describe how "reflexivity as truth" is a common strategy used in social research to "authorise our texts" (2003, p. 186); it is a methodological tool through which the 'contexts' of knowledge production are revealed in order to make claims to a 'truthful' representation of the research subject. Moore and Muller (1999, p. 203) call this a "displaced" reflexivity whereby 'reflexivity' is presented as a theoretically sustainable approach in and of itself. Reflexivity has also been identified as part of radical or critical research endeavours, a way of flattening power dynamics in the research process (cf. Lynch, 2000). While this form of reflexivity intends to make research processes more mutual or participatory, it can also work to "situate the researcher's own need and desire for 'truth' as primary" (Pillow, 2003, p. 186).

Indeed, Pillow suggests that 'reflexivity' is often used in social research as a tool for 'transcendence': it allows researchers to release themselves from "the problematic of representation" (p. 186) through confession and absolution. The processes of "confession, catharsis, and cure" engendered by such reflexive strategies act as a "tool of methodological power" (p. 192) with which researchers validate their work. On an almost benign level, reflexivity appears in research as indulgent narcissism, but in a much more problematic way it is used as a means of obscuring the inequities of power in the production of 'knowledge' about the other.

Thus, we cannot see 'reflexivity' as a neutral process, despite it being often "reduced to a question of technique or method" (Trinh, 1991, cited in Pillow, 2003, p. 180). Such critiques about reflexivity have led to a number of scholars seeking ways to reconfigure its role in social research. For example, Visweswaran (1994) argues that the shifting and multiple subjectivities brought into relation during the research process require ways of illuminating the plays of power involved in research interpretation – by both the researcher and the reader. This is not to lapse into a cycle of 'confession' through which the dilemmas of research can be resolved. Rather, the messiness and "uncomfortable realities" (Pillow, 2003, p. 193) of doing research are to be acknowledged, and as Visweswaran suggests, the ethics of research is not about seeking claims to 'truth', but about "whether we can be accountable to people's struggles for self-representation and self-determination" (1994, p. 32).

The stance of 'reflexivity', therefore, can be seen to privilege a certain knowledge (that of the researcher) over other knowledge(s). This form of posturing can be said to characterise any meta-theoretic position which gestures towards a distance taken by the researcher, either with respect to the objects of analyses (cf. Mannheim, 1936; Schütz, 1976), or with respect to a disciplinary domain that already operates at a distance from its objects of analyses (cf. Bourdieu & Wacquant, 1992). As Chia (1996) observes about such positions:

> The common thread which runs through these meta-theoretical preoccupations is the search for a higher vantage point from which commentaries about the field of study can be legitimately defended without being caught up in a reflexive tangle. This widespread practice of *ontological gerrymandering* enables these meta-theorists temporally to defer the question of reflexivity by positioning themselves *out of the research/theorising equation*. (pp. 41–42; emphases in original)

A path forward, suggested by Maton (2003), is a greater focus on the epistemic relation between the object of study and knowledge itself.[1] Maton argues that reflexivity in research has bypassed 'knowledge' by focusing on the *social* relations between the researcher and knowledge, and the researcher and research subject: "the emphasis is thus on the socialised gaze of people rather than explicit procedures, knowers rather than knowledge" (p. 60). Thus, building on Bourdieu's theory of epistemic reflexivity, Maton calls for greater attention to the 'structuring significance' of knowledge itself in shaping the validity of knowledge claims. "Reflexivity should not be reduced to viewing intellectual practices as being solely oriented (consciously or otherwise) by social interests" (p. 61). This is to acknowledge the cognitive interests in knowledge production in addition to social interests. Reflexivity in research is thus not only about the social resources and social power brought to the research relationship, but also about 'epistemic capital'; "the ways in which actors within the intellectual field engage in strategies aimed at maximising ... epistemic profits, that is, better knowledge of the world" (p. 62).

Over the past decade, there have been promising developments in the field of comparative and international education (CIE) regarding the complex politics of ethics and 'reflexivity' in research. These engagements go far beyond a simplistic notion of reflexivity as a navel-gazing pursuit in research. For example, reflecting on the field at the turn of the twenty-first century, Crossley (2000) notes the need not only for culturally and contextually sensitive research, but also for research that is critically attentive to its own (re)production of neo-colonialism and western world views. Here, postcolonial analyses have made a valuable contribution, as recently demonstrated by Tikly and Bond (2013). The authors use postcolonial critiques of global power relations to suggest a more situated understanding of research 'ethics' in an unequal world. For example, and as we also elaborate in this chapter, Tikly and Bond point to the ways the privileging of certain kinds of research methodologies and research questions over others is itself a question of ethics that requires reflexive consideration. Similarly, Canagarajah's (2002) book *A Geopolitics of Academic Writing* raises important ethical issues about the publishing practices of academic research that are pertinent for the CIE field. He argues that the western conventions, both implicit and explicit, which govern academic writing and publishing have profoundly shaped the ways knowledge is constructed and legitimised, and have marginalised knowledge practices from the periphery.

Indeed, CIE researchers have critically examined the ways in which institutional practices such as university research ethics protocols in the west often risk narrowing understandings of 'ethics' (cf. Holliday, 2013; Robinson-Pant & Singal, 2013; Sikes, 2013). Robinson-Pant and Singal (2013) question the assumptions underlying the norms and processes of ethics clearance procedures in northern universities, their relevance and sensitivity to Southern contexts, and the ways the process itself values one set of knowledge production over another. They call for a more situated understanding of research ethics: "researching ethically is not just a matter of understanding and adapting research tools to specific cultural and social contexts, but also about researchers interrogating and responding to unequal power relations at both micro and macro levels" (Robinson-Pant & Singal, 2013, p. 444). As we also develop in this chapter, the authors discuss the ways the field of anthropology has provided a rich resource for CIE researchers to think about the hierarchies of culture and power which influence knowledge production.

In the next section, we draw on devices from ANT to suggest that knowledge production in research is a process of mediation and organisation of the social, cognitive, and the material. Therefore, there is the need for 'reflexive' research to attend to the relational aspects that produce specific orderings of 'knowledge', as these recent engagements in CIE have suggested, rather than a thin preoccupation with the social relations between the researcher and the researched. As Chia (1996, p. 52) puts it: "the greatest value of any theorizing process, therefore, is not so much what it purports to have 'discovered' as the extent to which the process sensitizes us to the materially related organized complexities of the human condition".

A way forward? The researcher as a 'broker' and 'translator'

Writing from the sociology of science, scholars such as Latour (1987, 1988) and Law (1994) have sought to orientate research inquiries to explanatory frameworks which foreground the ways in which knowledge is assembled through research processes. The focus of these scholars has been on "the complex and heterogeneous micro-organizational processes involved in the ongoing enactment of social reality including any forms of organized complexity" (Chia, 1996, p. 50). In doing so, they take an explicitly processual orientation to research practice which makes two important simultaneous moves for us to consider. First, it provides a means of problematising the allusions implicit even among 'reflexive' researchers to privileged knowledge positions. Second, the processual orientation of these scholars' gestures towards the incompleteness of any research endeavour where 'things' receive primacy over 'relationships'. Their engagement with 'how things come to be what they are' displaces both the primacy of 'things' and also a preoccupation with *which* representation of an external reality is more accurate. Implicit in these two moves is a notion of 'agency' which challenges structure/agency dualisms that configure agency as an "individuated source of empowerment rooted in conscious intentions that mobilize action" (Fenwick & Edwards, 2010, p. 21). Rather, 'agency' in the ANT ontology comes into being through heterogeneous relationships of a network of humans, materials, and discourses.

Foregrounding the complex and multiple processes that are involved in any stable representation of what we deem to be an external reality necessarily demands a supreme attention to detail – "a commitment to recovering the concreteness of our brute experiences as they emerge – a form of ultra-empiricism'"(Chia, 1996, p. 47). This in turn helps to devalue the relativist position that is often assumed by researchers to portray the ideological complexities built into their own research endeavours. It challenges researchers to reflect not only on their positionality, but also on "the fields of power within which their knowledge production becomes (or fails to become) authoritative" (Lewis & Mosse, 2006, p. 8).

But is there a useful conception of the role of the researcher that can illustrate what would possibly underline this processual orientation that has been variously labelled as 'infra-reflexivity' (Latour, 1988) and as 'relational materialism' (Law, 1994)? There is a body of anthropological work in the area of development studies which has sought to understand development actors as 'brokers' and 'translators' (Lewis & Mosse, 2006). In a similar vein, we propose that understanding of the role of the researcher as a 'broker' and 'translator' provides meaningful insights not only into what underlies a processual orientation in contemporary educational research endeavours, but also into a more politically nuanced reassessment of the constitutive effects of such research on the project(s) of development.

The idea of development actors as 'brokers' taken up by Lewis and Mosse stems from the work by French anthropologists (Bierschenk, Chauveau, & de Sardan, 2002) who drew attention to the increasingly diverse actors involved in development processes, and how their practices and concepts, strategies, and contextual constraints related to broader national and international sociopolitical dynamics. With the decentralisation and denationalisation of development aid and activity, these development 'brokers' are not only connected to the state apparatus, but are also increasingly associated with civil society and non-state organisations, stretching beyond national boundaries. The broker perspective is one that underlines the diversity of actors involved in development processes – "actors of different statuses, with varying resources and dissimilar goals" – actors who come to shape the development 'project' itself (Lewis & Mosse, 2006, p. 1).

We suggest that it is useful and necessary to explicitly acknowledge that development researchers, including social and educational researchers working in sites and spaces of development, are themselves one of the 'brokers' of development knowledge and practices. In a sense, it is easy to see how the concept of 'brokers' as "intermediary actors ... operating at the 'interfaces' of different worldviews and knowledge systems ... negotiating roles, relationships, and representations" (Lewis & Mosse, 2006, p. 10) could be used interchangeably for the social/educational researcher, especially one working in cross-cultural, development contexts. Drawing primarily upon the work of Bruno Latour, the authors challenge the normative and stable understanding of 'brokers' as intermediaries in institutional interstices who negotiate development ideas and actions. Advocating a more sophisticated conceptualisation of the role of 'brokers' in development, the authors aptly underscore that such a conceptualisation

> should be far less confident about the a priori existence of social and institutional realms. All actors (and not just sociologists) produce interpretations,

and powerful actors offer scripts into which others can be recruited for a period. In this sense their interpretations are performative: they prove themselves by transforming the world in conformity with their perspective on the world.

Lewis & Mosse (2006, p. 13)

Taking this view, then, the educational researcher is positioned not as the interpreter (reflexive or otherwise) of an a priori world. But rather, the process of research itself engages actors (of which the researcher is one), scripts, and performances which produce particular understandings of, and effects on, the world. This figuration of the researcher is developed further through the concept of 'translation' which, in the sociology of science, has been used to understand and trace the mutual enrolment and interlocking of interests that produce knowledge, practices, and 'realities'. As Lewis and Mosse describe, translation is not about how actors operate and strategies within existing institutional or social arrangements of 'development', but how "development projects – always unforeseeable – become real through the work of generating and translating interests, creating context by tying in supporters and so sustaining interpretations" (Lewis & Mosse, 2006, p. 13).

As a 'broker', the education development researcher is oriented towards composing a particular order and creating a coherent representation of the world. However, as a 'translator', this effort is necessarily incomplete as both the researcher and the other actors involved in constituting the research enterprise undergo and effect transformations while associating themselves in a network. Thus, the nature and extent of the 'coherence' of the 'research knowledge' generated are achieved through a network of alliances involving other actors (such as other researchers, policymakers, educational discourses, research journals, and research publications) and by a process where individual interests of actors are 'translated' in the act of constituting these alliances. Even the most 'reflexive' of researchers is engaged with and alongside other actors and brokers of development in the task of creating order out of difference, fragmentation, and dissent, "through political acts of *composition*" (Lewis & Mosse, 2006, p. 14; emphasis in original).

This has a number of implications for how we understand the research process and role of the development researcher. First, it underscores that research perspectives are not "brought to bear on anything stable" (Latour, 1996, p. 79); 'development' is not a fixed 'entity' to be known but a shifting, contingent, and unforeseeable process. The act of composition by the researcher is thus always 'political' in the sense that it involves the foregrounding of particular orders, perspectives, and practices over others. However, this 'political' work can be understood as methodological and not just ideological. Methodologically, the notion of 'translation' draws attention to the interlocking, tying in, and enrolment of actors and their interests. Returning to Chia's notion of 'ultra-empiricism', the attention to methodological detail, especially with respect to 'how things come to be' within the research process, is part of the researcher-as-translator's work.

The concept of the researcher as broker and translator makes a particularly useful contribution to the reflexivity debates outlined earlier in this chapter. It is able to cut through self-referential relativism by engaging with the micro-workings of power. It continues to place importance on interpretation and representation in research, but this is not just about acknowledging different points of view. Rather, it is also to trace the ways in which the object of research inquiry itself can "appear or disappear depending upon the interpretations given to them by people of different standing" (Lewis & Mosse, 2006, p. 8). Significantly, the attention to the processes and contingencies of translation enables researchers to eschew methodological 'blackboxing' (Latour, 1999) in which the internal complexities of the research are made invisible in the depiction of coherent representations of development. A 'reflexive' approach in this sense is about addressing the "epistemological possibilities and limits" of the research endeavour (Sobe & Kowalczyk, 2012, p. 64), and entering into an engagement with the politics of knowledge production.

The politics of knowledge production: researching teachers' work in India

We turn now to consider the contemporary research terrain on the role and work of the teacher in India in order to develop our critique of existing notions of reflexivity. The body of teacher research in India usefully illustrates the ways in which research has played a significant part in foregrounding particular scripts about teachers in terms of the limitations, hopes, and efficacy of education development reform. Indeed, we look at two broad approaches of research on teachers which engage in different ways, politically and methodologically, with the issue of teacher accountability and the shortcomings of India's education system that have emerged in recent public discourse. We map this body of research on teachers' work to demonstrate how different 'realities' about teachers and Indian education reform are assembled in and through research. In doing so, we consider the ways in which the brokers and translators' perspective might add a more politically nuanced reading of the constitutive effects of this research in India and on education development research more broadly.

Though key Education Commissions such as the Kothari Commission (1964–1966) and the Chattopadhyaya Commission (1983–1985) have recognised the centrality of the role of teachers in the Indian education system and argued for reforms in teacher education, educationists have now for long observed how the role and work of teachers in India seem marginalised from both policy discourses and substantive processes of educational reforms

(Batra, 2009; Dyer, 2000; Government of India, 1966, 1985; Sriprakash, 2012). As Batra (2009) perceptively observes: "contemporary educational practice in India tends to view the teacher as an 'implementing agency' of larger interests: national interest as defined by the State; a channel of reproduction of the officially approved curriculum often via rote learning" (p. 132).

The classic formulation of the role and work of the teacher in India has been through the image of the 'meek dictator'– an actor whose dominance in the classroom is counterpoised against his or her disempowered role within the hierarchy of the education administration system (Kumar, 2005). A colonial legacy like many other features of the post-independence education system, the image of the teacher as a 'meek dictator' resonates with the work of other educationists who have emphasised and continue to stress how the teachers are neglected in the overall education policy reforms processes in recent years. For example, Dyer's (2000) work on Operation Blackboard, one of the large-scale programmes consequent to the National Policy of Education 1986, reveals that:

> Teachers articulated their sense of the vast gap between themselves and the educational administration; and between themselves and educational policy. That teachers were still not central to educational policy, despite the words of the NPE 1986, was evident in the way the scheme, and indeed the policy itself, was formulated without any input from practicing teachers. (p. 146)

In contrast to this apparent lack of agency that defines the meekness of teachers in relation to the educational administration and higher authorities, other researchers have dwelled on the overpowering presence of teachers within classroom settings (Clarke, 2001; Sarangapani, 2003). These studies, ethnographic in their methodological orientation, focus on school and classroom microprocesses to understand the role and work of teachers in terms of the interactions between the beliefs and cultural models of the teachers. It was found that these cultural models were not necessarily embedded in the cultures and philosophies underlying the modern institution of schooling. For example, Sarangapani (2003) has noted how authority relations between the teacher and student draw upon relationships such as that of the adult–child, parent–child, *guru–sishya*, and patron–protégé. As she analyses from her observations:

> It is clear that there is much in the acceptance of the teacher's authority which is prior to and independent of the considerations of the context of school or school knowledge. These representations emphasise the moral, cultural and epistemic superiority of the teacher and attribute a benevolent intention to his or her actions. (p. 117)

Besides culturally mediated relationships of authority that define teacher–student interactions in classrooms, these ethnographies underline how the social distance between teachers and their underprivileged students strengthens deficit theories of the child's educability. They also critically examine the ways in which textbooks play a dominant role in classroom pedagogic practices of the teachers.

Steeped in a broadly similar methodological tradition, newer studies have provided further insights into the ways the relationships between teachers, colleagues and superiors, school administrative authorities, and students are mediated in the Indian context (Majumdar, 2011; Majumdar & Mooij, 2011; Mukhopadhyay & Sriprakash, 2011; Sriprakash, 2012; Vijaysimha, 2013). These studies have challenged the image of the non-agentic teachers in terms of their interactions with their superiors and school administrative authorities, and in terms of their role as 'implementers' of education policy. They seek to foreground the socio-material realities within which the work of teachers is located and which, in turn, defines their professional engagement. For example, using the notion of 'translation' from the work of the actor–network theorists, our own work has shown how a large-scale standardised assessment programme is reinterpreted and reworked through the agency of teachers, despite teachers being bypassed as state functionaries by the programme (Mukhopadhyay & Sriprakash, 2011). In a sense, the new research seeks to explicate in clearer terms the socio-material realities of the work settings of teachers and their mediation of classroom processes, thus placing in context the exclusionary practices for which teachers are often indicted.

There is a parallel body of research that has approached the role and work of the teachers in a distinctively different manner. Indeed, a number of education researchers have used the lens of accountability and the qualitatively poor performance of government schools to advance a stringent critique of the role that teachers play in the government school system in India. For example, Kingdon and Muzammil (2003) have analysed in detail the political affiliations of teachers through teacher unions and argued how teachers use such political connections to improve their own service conditions to the detriment of any efforts to improve the larger school system. A natural outcome in such a scenario is that of low levels of teacher accountability and increased teacher absenteeism, issues that have received attention in the works of a number of other researchers (Banerjee & Duflo, 2006; Kremer, Chaudhury, Rogers, Muralidharan, & Hammer, 2005). In fact, these studies on teachers' absenteeism in India often juxtapose the abysmal levels of loss to the public exchequer through large-scale teacher absenteeism with the service conditions of teachers in private schools and contract/para-teachers who, in spite of their significantly lower salaries, show comparable or better attendance rates. For example, based on the findings from an experimental design in the state of Andhra Pradesh, Muralidharan and Sundararaman (2013, p. 23) conclude,

> expanding the use of contract teachers could be a highly cost-effective way of improving primary education outcomes in developing countries.

In particular, expensive policy initiatives to get highly qualified teachers to remote areas may be much less cost effective than hiring several local contract teachers to provide much more attention to students at a similar cost.

Other studies, conducted in a similar vein, have advocated for managerial approaches to ensure accountability among teachers – through more monitored school environments and incentive-based compensation, interventions which have been found to lead to better students' achievements (Duflo, Hanna, & Ryan, 2012; Kingdon & Teal, 2007). These studies, using education production functions or randomised experiment designs, pose their findings as prescriptions emerging from the realm of the private school system that could go a long way to address the lack of professional engagement among government schoolteachers. For example, based on an experimental study in a non-governmental organisation and a similar experiment of the delivery of health services in India, Duflo et al. (2012) make the case for the deployment of monitoring cameras which can be used by students to record attendance of teachers to support an attendance-linked salary incentive scheme:

> A recent experiment demonstrates the external validity of these results outside the NGO context (Banerjee, Duflo, & Glennerster, 2007). Following the results of the cameras program, the government of Rajasthan created a similar system for government nurses, whose absence rate was about 44 percent. The nurses were monitored using time and date stamps. The announced incentive system was severe: it called for a 50 percent reduction in the pay of nurses who were absent 50 percent of the time, and termination of persistently absent nurses. In the first few months, when these punishments were carried out, the program lead to about a 50 percent reduction in absenteeism. However, after a few months, the government started granting a large number of 'exemptions' (although the monitoring did continue). The absence rate in the treatment group quickly converged to that of the control group. This further confirms that monitoring is effective, but only when coupled with real incentives, as is suggested by the results of our structural model. (p. 35)

It is apparent from these sets of studies on education in India that they produce, broadly, two distinct scripts of teachers and their work. Let us dwell a bit more on these different orderings of 'knowledge' on teachers. The former set of studies draws primarily upon the disciplinary areas of history, sociology, and anthropology, and is attentive to the diachronic and socio-material contexts that shape the work of the teachers. For example, both the historical and the material become important in the imagining of the teacher as a 'meek dictator':

> The material basis and status of the vocation of teaching went through a drastic change with the establishment of the colonial system. Whereas earlier the teacher was supported by the local community, he now became a functionary of the state, working for a salary. Teaching became part of government service, and a teaching job now carried with it considerable clerical work, such as maintaining records of admission, attendance, examination and expenditure.
>
> *(Kumar, 2005, p. 75)*

Besides, this imagination also encompasses the relational network of teachers with other actors, the imbrications of their vocational identities with teachers' social identities, and the articulation of teachers' agency through the social and material conditions of their lived experience. Majumdar and Mooij (2011) capture such an imagination in terms of the 'multiple ambivalences and contradictions' in the work life of teachers:

> Among others, these have to do with grand policy goals on the one hand versus inadequate resources on the other; their lofty ideas regarding the role of teachers versus their own lack of motivation; the declining social status of teachers versus their upward social mobility; and the simultaneous stranglehold and neglect that characterises their relationship with the educational administration. (p. 67)

Through such an understanding, these studies converge on a trope that highlights the absence of both 'voice and agency' in the professional life and work of teachers (Batra, 2005).

On the other hand, the latter set of studies emerges from the discipline of economics and underlines a more synchronic understanding of teachers and their work that is limited to the extent of its contribution to the efficiency of a public service delivery system such as education. For the education production function approach adopted by a number of these studies, combined in recent times with randomised experiments, a teacher is more an input among other inputs that go into the education system, while the work of teachers as rational actors is often guided by rent-seeking behaviour. This imagination of the work and behaviour of teachers is evident in studies that have variedly focused on teacher absenteeism, teacher accountability, and school efficiency. For example, it is such an imagination of rationally motivated agents that underlie Muralidharan and Sundararaman's

(2011) observations in their randomised experimental study of the effect of performance-based incentives on teachers' work:

> We measure changes in teacher behaviour in response to the program with both teacher interviews and direct physical observation of teacher activity. Our results suggest that the main mechanism for the impact of the incentive program was not increased teacher attendance but greater (and more effective) teaching effort conditional on being present. (p. 41)

In addition, these studies position teachers as an input in the education process, drawing an equivalence and comparative efficiency between teachers and other material inputs to the education process. From the same set of studies as the previous one, Muralidharan and Sundararaman (2009) conclude how they "find that performance-based bonus payments to teachers were a significantly more cost-effective way of increasing student test scores compared to spending a similar amount of money unconditionally on additional schooling inputs" (p. 3).

Indeed, the two sets of studies become the site for invoking two distinct policy tropes and discursive frameworks about education development, especially in terms of their relation to the role and work of teachers. Majumdar (2011), though somewhat caricaturing these two positions, aptly demarcates the outlines of these two discursive frameworks:

> Imagined in the role of either political power or professional powerlessness, discussions on the involvement of teachers in primary schooling range from a 'scornful' view, on the one hand, to a 'smug' view, on the other. The former smacks of extreme pessimism and often degenerates into full-fledged teacher bashing ... The smug view, on the other hand, underplays, or even ignores, the hard evidence of dereliction of duties on the part of at least some teachers ... and its damaging effects on students' learning abilities. (p. 39)

The 'scornful' view endorses an understanding of teachers and their work through an input–output model of schooling with efficiency and accountability as key conceptual parameters of this model. Policy directions emerging from this discourse draw upon organisational and operational principles of the corporate/private sector to emphasise the application of scientific management techniques – performance-based incentives, para/contract teachers, and teacher-proofing of pedagogic processes. On the other hand, the 'smug' view offers a socio-historical lens to understand teachers as disempowered professionals. Policy imperatives that are, therefore, central to this view are teacher education, teacher professional development, continuous personal support, and teacher autonomy in pedagogic processes. As Batra (2012) succinctly observes on the position of teachers and their work in the contemporary education scenario in India,

> two parallel strands of thought can be discerned within the current policy discourse in India: the neoliberal frame of standardisation, teacher accountability and learning outcomes; and the academic-led perspective on school curriculum (NCERT, 2005) and teacher education curriculum (NCTE, 2009) that regard education as critical for social transformation. (p. 226)

Conclusions and reflections: reflexivity and the politics of knowledge

In examining two broad sets of studies on teachers' work in India, we set out to look at the ways research has created different and distinct understandings of teachers and their worlds. The first set emphasised the social-material contexts of teaching in India, foregrounding the teacher as an individual with distinct life histories. The a priori understanding of the teacher here is that he or she is a person who lacks or is denied agency with respect to the social, cultural, and political contexts of his or her work. The research emphasises that the actions of teachers must be explained with respect to the social-material contexts of their work, over which they have little or limited control. The second set of research took a starkly different view of teachers: it was primarily interested in teachers as a collective (rather than as individuals with distinct life histories), and emphasised that teachers are rational agents within their social, cultural, and political worlds. Proceeding on this assumption, this body of work emphasised the ways in which teachers as agents must be accountable in terms of their role in the public delivery system of education.

For our argument, a first-order reflexivity in educational research goes only as far as problematising these two distinct understandings of teachers and their work as emerging from the different paradigms (disciplinary, theoretical, methodological, and political) of the researchers and their allied communities. In this, reflexivity is addressed to the extent which the agency of the researchers is able to problematise their distinct paradigms. However, there is a second-order reflexivity that can be alluded to through the two distinct research tropes on teachers and their work. Evidently there are numerous and different actors – or mediating entities – which constitute the networks that go into the making of the two tropes. For example, actors include the particular actions or practices of teachers, which leave out other actions or practices, and thus do not become 'known'. Furthermore, these networks are constituted through particular disciplinary foci and methodological approaches which orient the researcher and reader towards particular 'realities' of teachers' worlds. Actors also include the tools within research processes which make certain data visible and render other data invisible. Policy discourse itself shapes the understanding of teachers' worlds, as research differentially circulates and gains currency through policy 'knowledge'. Finally, as we saw, researchers who are aligned with specific disciplinary and discursive frameworks are themselves implicated as 'brokers', acting as powerful intermediaries between academic, research, and policy communities, in the circulation of distinct but equally persuasive understandings of teachers' worlds.

However, a conception of educational research as a network of multiple actors – the objects and subjects of research, the researchers, disciplinary and methodological paradigms, policy discourses, and allies from research and policy communities – signifies the inherent 'incompleteness' of the role researchers might play as brokers. The interruptions, and new political possibilities of research efforts, in such an understanding, could arise from any of the multiple actors and the relationships of the research network. Here, researchers are simultaneously 'translators' of knowledge, negotiating associations in the network. This is seen in the ways 'realities' of Indian teachers' work have been negotiated in education development research: on the one hand, "many public school protagonists are acutely aware of how poorly some government schools and teachers are functioning; still, they contend that government schools need to be defended on equity grounds and improved to bridge quality gaps" (Majumdar, 2011, p. 37), and on the other hand, those in favour of more market-oriented options such as para-teachers concede and contend that "while concerns for equity, professional status and security remain valid, the concerns about condemning children to poorer quality para-teachers are not borne out by the available evidence" (Kingdon & Sipahimalani-Rao, 2010, p. 67).

Where does this leave us, in terms of encouraging 'reflexive' practice in the field of educational development research? The trope of researchers as 'brokers' and 'translators' usefully draws attention to the ways in which researchers are themselves actors who put together particular assemblages of their research subjects. However, we also caution against forms of 'reflexivity' that overstate the individual agency of the researcher, or present a form of determinism whereby the researcher alone determines what constitutes valid 'knowledge'. As we have attempted to illustrate in regard to the body of teacher research in India, researchers are enacting particular discursive traditions and disciplinary norms of their fields.

The view of researchers as brokers and translators, that is, not only as powerful intermediaries but also as actors among a multitude of other actors within a network, acknowledges that researchers are themselves situated by a set of discursive practices and their work is thus politically mediated. This helps us go beyond self-referential forms of reflexivity to consider the ways in which the researcher, pre-existing discourses, disciplinary practices, as well as the research subjects themselves are all 'actors' involved in the assemblage of knowledge. In the case we explored in this chapter, all these 'actors' have come together to perform different understandings of teachers' work in India.

We call for a 'reflexivity', then, that is alive to the processes of knowledge assemblage in which researchers are themselves enmeshed, as well as to the politics of knowledge that is made possible by the inherent incompleteness and performativity of research endeavours.

Note

1 Here, we are cautious about the ontological positions of 'objects of study' and 'knowledge' being unchallenged in Maton's thesis. As we discuss in this chapter, the ANT ontology challenges agency/structure dualisms by focusing on the multiple, contingent circulating forces that act upon one another.

References

Banerjee, A., & Duflo, E. (2006). Addressing absence. *The Journal of Economic Perspectives, 20*(1), 117–132.
Batra, P. (2005). Voice and agency of teachers: Missing link in National Curriculum Framework. *Economic and Political Weekly, 40*(40), 4347–4356.
Batra, P. (2009). Teacher empowerment: The education entitlement-social transformation traverse. *Contemporary Education Dialogue, 6*(2), 121–156.
Batra, P. (2012). Positioning teachers in the emerging education landscape of contemporary India. In IDFC Foundation (Ed.), *India Infrastructure report 2012: Private sector in education* (pp. 219–231). New Delhi, India: Routledge.
Bierschenk, T., Chauveau, J.-P., & de Sardan, J.-P. O. (2002). *Local development brokers in Africa: The rise of a new social category* (Working Paper No. 13). Mainz, Germany: Johannes Gutenberg University.
Bourdieu, P., & Wacquant, L. J. D. (1992). *An invitation to reflexive sociology*. Chicago, IL: University of Chicago Press.
Canagarajah, A. S. (2002). *A geopolitics of academic writing*. Pittsburgh, PA: University of Pittsburgh Press.
Chia, R. (1996). The problem of reflexivity in organizational research: Towards a postmodern science of organization. *Organization, 3*(1), 31–59.
Clarke, P. (2001). *Teaching and learning: The culture of pedagogy*. New Delhi, India: Sage.
Crossley, M. (2000). Bridging cultures and traditions in the reconceptualisation of comparative and international education. *Comparative Education, 36*(3), 319–332.
Duflo, E., Hanna, R., & Ryan, S. P. (2012). Incentives work: Getting teachers to come to school. *American Economic Review, 102*(4), 1241–1278.
Dyer, C. (2000). *Operation Blackboard: Policy implementation in Indian elementary education*. Oxford, England: Symposium Books.
Fenwick, T., & Edwards, R. (2010). *Actor-network theory in education*. New York, NY: Routledge.
Fenwick, T., & Edwards (Eds.). (2012). *Researching education through actor-network theory*. London, England: Wiley Blackwell.
Government of India (1966). *Report of the Education Commission (1964–66): Education and national development*. New Delhi, India: Ministry of Education.
Government of India (1985). *Chattopadhyaya Committee Report (1983–85): The teacher and society*. New Delhi, India: Ministry of Human Resource Development.

Holliday, A. (2013). The politics of ethics in diverse cultural settings: Colonising the centre stage. *Compare, 43*(4), 537–554.

Kingdon, G. G., & Muzammil, M. (2003). *The political economy of education in India: Teacher politics in Uttar Pradesh*. New Delhi, India: Oxford University Press.

Kingdon, G. G., & Sipahimalani-Rao, V. (2010). Parateachers in India: Status and impact. *Economic and Political Weekly, 45*(12), 59–67.

Kingdon, G. G., & Teal, F. (2007). Does performance related pay for teachers improve student performance? Some evidence from India. *Economics of Education Review, 26*(4), 473–486.

Kremer, M., Chaudhury, N., Rogers, F. H., Muralidharan, K., & Hammer, J. (2005). Teacher absence in India: A snapshot. *Journal of the European Economic Association, 3*(2-3), 658–667.

Kumar, K. (2005). *Political agenda of education: A study of colonialist and nationalist ideas*. New Delhi, India: Sage.

Latour, B. (1987). *Science in action*. Milton Keynes, England: Open University Press.

Latour, B. (1988). The politics of explanation: An alternative. In S. Woolgar & M. Ashmore (Eds.), *Knowledge and reflexivity: New frontiers in the sociology of knowledge* (pp. 155–176). London, England: Sage.

Latour, B. (1996). *Aramis, or the love of technology*. Cambridge, MA: Harvard University Press.

Latour, B. (1999). *Pandora's hope: Essays on the reality of science studies*. Cambridge, MA: Harvard University Press.

Law, J. (1994). *Organizing modernity*. Oxford, England: Blackwell.

Law, J. (2004). *After method: Mess in social science research*. London, England: Routledge.

Lewis, D., & Mosse, D. (Eds.). (2006). *Development brokers and translators: The ethnography of aid and agencies*. Bloomfield, CT: Kumarian Press.

Lynch, M. (2000). Against reflexivity as an academic virtue and source of privileged knowledge. *Theory, Culture & Society, 17*(3), 26–54.

Majumdar, M. (2011). Politicians, civil servants or professionals? Teachers' voices on their work and worth. *Contemporary Education Dialogue, 8*(1), 33–65.

Majumdar, M., & Mooij, J. (2011). *Education and inequality in India: A classroom view*. London, England: Routledge.

Mannheim, K. (1936). *Ideology and utopia*. New York, NY: Harvest Books.

Maton, K. (2003). Reflexivity, relationism, & research Pierre Bourdieu and the epistemic conditions of social scientific knowledge. *Space and Culture, 6*(1), 52–65.

Moore, R., & Muller, J. (1999). The discourse of 'voice' and the problem of knowledge and identity in the sociology of education. *British Journal of Sociology of Education, 20*(2), 189–206.

Mukhopadhyay, R., & Sriprakash, A. (2011). Global frameworks, local contingencies: Policy translations and education development in India. *Compare, 41*(3), 311–326.

Muralidharan, K., & Sundararaman, V. (2009). *Teacher performance pay: Experimental evidence from India* (Working Paper 15323). Retrieved from National Bureau of Economic Research website: https://www.nber.org/system/files/working_papers/w15323/w15323.pdf

Muralidharan, K., & Sundararaman, V. (2013). *Contract teachers: Experimental evidence from India* (No. w19440). National Bureau of Economic Research. https://www.nber.org/papers/w19440

Muralidharan, K., & Sundararaman, V. (2011). Teacher performance pay: Experimental evidence from India. *The Journal of Political Economy, 119*(1), 39–77.
NCERT. (2005). *National Curriculum Framework 2005*. New Delhi, India: National Council of Educational Research and Training.
NCTE. (2009). *National Curriculum Framework for Teacher Education: Towards preparing professional and humane teacher*. New Delhi, India: National Council for Teacher Education.
Pillow, W. (2003). Confession, catharsis, or cure? Rethinking the uses of reflexivity as methodological power in qualitative research. *International Journal of Qualitative Studies in Education, 16*(2), 175–196.
Robinson-Pant, A., & Singal, N. (2013). Research ethics in comparative and international education: Reflections from anthropology and health. *Compare, 43*(4), 443–463.
Sarangapani, P. (2003). *Constructing school knowledge: An ethnography of learning in an Indian village*. New Delhi, India: Sage.
Schütz, A. (1976). The stranger: An essay in social psychology. In A. Brodersen (Ed.), *Collected papers II: Studies in social theory* (pp. 91–105). The Hague, the Netherlands: Martinus Nijhoff.
Sikes, P. (2013). Working together for critical research ethics. *Compare, 43*(4), 516–536.
Sobe, N. W., & Kowalczyk, J. (2012). The problem of context in comparative education research. *Journal of Educational, Cultural and Psychological Studies, 3*(6), 55–74.
Sriprakash, A. (2012). *Pedagogies for development: The politics and practice of child-centred education in India*. Dordrecht, Netherlands: Springer.
Tikly, L., & Bond, T. (2013). Towards a postcolonial research ethics in comparative and international education. *Compare, 43*(4), 422–442.
Vijaysimha, I. (2013). "We are textbook badnekais!': A Bernsteinian analysis of textbook culture in science classrooms. *Contemporary Education Dialogue, 10*(1), 67–97.
Visweswaran, K. (1994). *Fictions of feminist ethnography*. Minneapolis, MN: University of Minnesota Press.

8
NON-CHINESE RESEARCHERS CONDUCTING RESEARCH IN CHINESE CULTURES

Critical reflections

Kokila Roy Katyal and Mark Edward King

This chapter examines methodological and ethical issues faced by two non-Chinese researchers whilst conducting educational research projects in the context of Hong Kong's predominantly Chinese society in 2005. The two research domains appear to be vastly dissimilar – Study One, the seemingly innocuous world of schools, schooling, and teacher leadership, and Study Two, the stigmatised world of transgender – but an in-depth look reveals striking similarities and contradictions in the realm of research methodology and complexities of conducting research where the dominant culture is not one's own. More specifically, we explore the intricacies of applying models of research methodology, grounded as they tend to be in Western modes of thinking, to Confucian cultures.

The central argument here is that research methodology is not neutral in relation to the enterprise of comparison. Rather, the adoption of a comparative perspective, with its emphasis on the importance of context, also applies to the tools of inquiry that researchers use. Thus, we claim that just as substantive theoretical perspectives, practices, and policy prescriptions may fail to cross Confucian Heritage Cultures (CHCs) because of unique and individual contextual qualities, so too may matters of inquiry and inference fail to cross these contextual boundaries. Issues raised in this chapter will need re-theorising to provide a more realistic and comprehensive view of the need to re-examine the paradigms that guide research methodology in Confucian societies.

The Hong Kong context: the Confucian way of life

The notion of culture brings with it complexity and confusion – there is no one definition of culture. Nonetheless, culture is typically defined in terms of shared orientations that hold a unit together and give it a distinctive identity.

Scholars such as King (1995) and Ho (1994) define culture as a group's individual and collective ways of thinking, believing, and knowing, which includes the group's shared experiences, consciousness, skills, values, forms of expression, social institutions, and behaviours. We used this definition in order to build up our conceptual understanding of the culture of Hong Kong and its people.

At the time of the research, approximately 95% of the population of Hong Kong was ethnically Chinese, mainly of Han origin. Han Chinese residents generally refer to themselves as *Hèung Góng Yàhn* ('Hong Kong People') and were referred to as Hong Kong Chinese people. Although Hong Kong has been a cosmopolitan and Westernised city, social attitudes still tend to be conservative and strongly influenced by Confucianism (Hsu, 1985; Wilson, Greenblatt, & Wilson, 1977).

Confucian tenets are practical and social in nature and without religious content – being a set of practical rules for daily life. Consequently, Chinese society places a high value on the adjusted equilibrium, harmony, conformity, loyalty, and the strict controlling of one's emotions. According to Ma (1999), any individual's deviation from the societal norms would be regarded as bringing shame to his or her parents and ancestors. The social order of traditional Chinese society was built upon the *Wu Lun*, the Five Cardinal Relationships (Bellah, 1970), namely, ruler/subject; father/son; older brother/younger brother; husband/wife; and older friend/younger friend. These relationships are based on an inherent sense of deference and a firm hierarchy of being and comprise the central value system through which fundamental relationships are governed (Hofstede & Bond, 1988). Societal stability according to Confucius is based on these unequal relationships between people – in the educational realm, this is the teacher–student dyad or the principal–teacher dyad. The social order of the unit can be maintained through conformity with the demands of collective uniformity in terms of ideas and behaviours (Ho, 1994; Yang, 1959). The principle of *xiao* (filial piety) is at the very centre of personal, family, and social existence and constitutes the basic ideal against which any other form of self-image has to be judged. Confucian societies are known to be collectivist in nature; that is, people are integrated into strong cohesive in-groups and the virtue of harmony reigns supreme, and confrontations are to be avoided at all costs (Hofstede & Hofstede, 2005).

Maintaining 'face' (*mianzi*) is deemed important in such societies, and losing face inflicts significant personal damage, leading to disharmony (Hofstede & Hofstede, 2005). Face refers to an individual's self-image as perceived by others. It is also how individuals respond to other's tacit and explicit expectations, and face can be saved or lost by two individuals engaging in harmonious interactions or confrontations. Junior members in a hierarchical structure tend to play the role of enhancing the face of the seniors. On the other hand, seniors may give more face to their juniors in an effort to increase the prestige of the juniors in front of others, so both the juniors and seniors have face and maintain harmonious relationships. In losing face, individuals fail to play the social roles expected of them and thus people try to save face in all social interactions. In the context of research methodology, allowing a person to save face is important. Individuals in these societies tend to use indirect styles, such as avoidance (not discussing topics of conflict) and assuming an obliging style to avoid loss of face and its consequent disharmony. Pratt, Kelly, and Wong (1999) noted that such Confucian tenets dominated the beliefs and understandings of the local teachers and students; specifically, they noted that "Faculty and students were understood to be part of a hierarchy that is so pervasive in Hong Kong (and traditional Chinese) social structures as to be invisible" (p. 247).

Pang (2005) notes that there is a growing drive for countries worldwide to become more 'Asia literate', and even a cursory reading of the research literature in international and comparative education supports this claim. Many of these contexts are both research-ripe and complex. In this chapter, we limit ourselves to exploring CHCs. CHCs are unique in their socio-cultural composition (Walker & Dimmock, 2000) and the inherent intricacies of these cultures make them difficult to comprehend, even for Asian researchers. Conducting research in CHCs requires researchers to be aware of the multi-dimensional complexities of the social mores of these countries.

Sensitivities associated with research

Traditionally, sensitive research covers areas viewed as being taboo (such as death or sex). Lee (1993) questions this view of sensitivity, as it does not account for contextual significances. Sieber and Stanley (1988) define socially sensitive research "as studies in which there are potential consequences or implications, whether directly for the participants in the research or for the class of individuals represented by the research" (p. 49). As Lee and Renzetti (1993) assert, defining sensitive research in this way broadens the scope and includes topics that might not ordinarily be thought of as sensitive. The wider implication of this is that researchers recognise the responsibilities attached to their research and to the wider society, and this adds an ethical dimension to such research. Although this definition of sensitive research ties in with the paradigms that define our studies, it does not consider the specific "technical and methodological" (Lee, 1993, p. 3) issues that researchers may face.

Initially, the research on teacher leadership was not considered overtly sensitive since it did not investigate taboo subjects or deal with sensitive participants and therefore the ethical considerations merely emphasised protection of the research participants. The research on transgender people was ripe with sensitivity and was subjected to rigorous ethical examinations. However, the research on Hong Kong teachers raised unforeseen sensitivities because what constitutes sensitive research in the mainly Western literature that had informed the theoretical background of the study and the researcher's own beliefs, differed from what emerged from a Confucian dominated socio-cultural society. Paradoxically, the other study was less sensitive, and found surprisingly open attitudes towards non-normative gender identity.

Outsider versus insider research

Researcher A is a South Asian female teacher, albeit never having taught in Hong Kong. The focus of her research was the impact that teacher leadership has on student engagement in schools (Study One). Researcher B is a North American male whose research assessed the attitudes held by Hong Kong Chinese people towards male-to-female transgender people and the implications that this had on public policy and education (Study Two). Both were residents of Hong Kong at the time of the study (Researcher A three years, Researcher B more than two decades). This added a further dimension of complexity since both researchers were reasonably familiar with the research context, thus 'insiders', but at the same time 'outsiders', being racially non-Chinese.

A concern that dominated both studies was the relationship between our own cultural cognition and that of the culturally different community we were studying. We were aware of our own cultural conditioning and were keen not to overlook the different cognitive frameworks of the participants and thus address questions about their beliefs and attitudes through appropriate lenses.

Eisenhart (2001) points out that "culture may mean one thing to bilingual educators, another thing to educational anthropologists and something else to ethnic scholars or cognitive psychologists" (p. 16). This becomes important in a wider research context where there are scholars who argue that only those who have shared in a particular experience can have a true understanding of what it is like. Arising from this school of thought is the eye-catching slogan 'Nothing about us without us' that came from the disability camp (Charlton, 1998). Though similar views may be noted in research linked to potentially sensitive areas, there are also scholars who believe that although individuals from one community have access to a particular form of cultural cognition, or "privileged access" (Merton, 1972, p. 11), this does not automatically attach authority to this cognition (Kreiger, 1982). Furthermore, the very 'outsiderness' of the researchers may reveal information that may otherwise be overlooked. The world view of the insiders, as insiders, may exhibit confirmation bias. Subjects were willing to talk of sexual matters with a *gweilo* (a colloquial Cantonese term denoting a Caucasian) – the racial difference making the subjects less inhibited than they would have been talking to somebody from their own community. Similarly, the very outsiderness of Researcher A enabled the students to speak freely with her and indeed her racial difference was a point of interest to the groups.

A critical question for all cross-cultural studies is that it is not always obvious who is inside and who is outside the group. It is only when descriptors are added to define the identity of any given community (for example, Black, female, teacher) that demarcations may be formed, placing someone on the inside or on the outside.

The two studies

Considering the differences between the two studies, where can areas of similarity be located? We brought to the study our own cultural cognitions, coupled with our Western-trained researcher selves, which were then brought into play with cultural understanding, beliefs, and behaviours of our Chinese participants (Katyal & King, 2011). This meant that we had data that sometimes lay beyond the cognitive framework of our cultural understandings and thus we had to critically evaluate these differences and be aware of our ability to be reliable and truthful in terms of our analysis whilst avoiding the pitfalls of "misguided rationalism" and thus attempt to "make sense of concrete circumstances" (McNamee, 2001, p. 313).

Study One (Researcher A)

This study explored the impact of teacher leadership on student engagement in three Hong Kong schools using on-site participant observation, semi-structured interviews, and written standardised question interviews with the teachers, students, and parents. Teacher leadership was perceived to be centrally and exclusively concerned with the idea that all organisational members can lead and that leadership is a form of agency that can be distributed or shared. It is fundamentally connected to Gronn's (2000) view of leadership as "a flow of influence ... which detangles it from any presumed connection with headship" (p. 334) and falls with the theoretical traditions associated with distributed and transformational theories of leadership.

Purposive sampling was used to select participants in order to identify information-rich cases. Consequently, the schools selected were ones where teacher leadership was recognised informally as a significant feature of school life. Five teachers, five parents, and groups of 10–14 students, formed the participant pool in each school. The data from the students were collected from group discussions and through written standardised question interviews. The questions asked of the teachers, parents, and students were complementary and informed by systems theory, and dealt with the participants' beliefs about the impact of the external environment on schools, knowledge of the school teaching and learning systems, teacher influences, and the issues related to home–school communication.

Hue (2007) noted that "an essential component of Hong Kong schools is the cultural context" (p. 22) and Li, Leung, and Kember (2001) point out that understanding how Chinese teachers' function is problematic if studies are based on frameworks of Western cultural research. This study exemplifies the validity of this point of view.

Hong Kong schools are relatively unfamiliar with being research sites. Therefore, the first hurdle was access. In one instance, whilst the principal supported the study at the school, the 'in-house collaborator' (teacher) was less enthusiastic. After wasting considerable time and resources I realised that the obstacles being put in my way were her way of informing me that I should withdraw because she was hesitant to openly oppose her principal. Deference to those in higher echelons is a part of the local culture, and openly questioning the feasibility of running the study in the school would have meant engaging in a behaviour that was inconsistent with the expected social norms (Katyal, 2011).

Second, gaining access eventually highlighted the importance of having the 'right' connections (*guanxi*) to obtain the necessary permissions – another aspect of the collectivist CHC. Bell (2000) demonstrated that *guanxi* has roots in traditional Confucian values of 'perfect virtue' (*ren*), in situations of hardship where "reliance on one's family is often not sufficient and an extension of familial forms of support has been sought through membership in a village, work group or kin group" (p. 132). Hence, a more correct translation of the term, according to Bell would be 'relation'; a deeper and more valuable relationship than a simple 'connection'. In the current research, *guanxi* in most contexts, and especially in business language, has been translated into the term 'interpersonal connections' or the establishment of 'networks of assistance'. Indeed, Nordtveit (2011) notes that researchers undertaking research in CHCs may need to cultivate and use *guanxi* and concurrently understand the methodological challenges that this entails.

The notion that 'every one counts' is a "perspective that might reasonably be taken in many societies but might not be true in a highly stratified society as China" (Stening & Zhang, 2007, p. 128) and may apply to the Hong Kong Chinese people as well. Communication is very hierarchical in Chinese organisations and as "one's relative place in the hierarchy is closely correlated with one's power, who is included in the sample takes on greater significance than in more egalitarian societies" (Stening & Zhang, 2007, p. 129). An interesting manifestation of this was where newer or younger teachers saw themselves as 'just staff' and were reluctant to voice their opinions, as opposed to the more senior teachers who were more eager to talk about education-related matters, both during the interview process and elsewhere. However, these were just the initial teething problems associated with gaining access to sites and participants.

First, though the participation of teachers was to be voluntary, it transpired that in some cases, despite getting informed consent from the teachers, there was a 'directive' consent at play – the principal had directed the teachers to participate. This led to concerns that these participants would give socially desirable responses, and care had to be taken to elicit valid responses, rather than 'right' ones. Furthermore, obtaining informed consent was difficult in the case of students. For various reasons, "The procedure for informing consent and for making it clear that participation is voluntary is often suspended in the case of children" (Homan, 2001, p. 31). Whilst the original research design sought to redress this problem, in two of the three cases studied the principals' 'gatekeeping' responsibilities extended to them granting a blanket approval for interviewing students – without involving the students' themselves or asking the parents. At one level, I realised that this was a way by which the principals, presumably more cognisant of the Hong Kong people's reluctance of being interviewed, was facilitating the study by granting permission *in loco parentis*, but as a researcher I faced an ethical problem, based on Western frameworks of understanding informed consent and as an institutional requirement in terms of gaining ethical approval for the study and of whether to go ahead and interview students or not (Katyal, 2011).

Second, the literature on teacher leadership is awash with instances of principals intruding on the professional spaces of teachers (Katzenmeyer & Moller, 2001), and principals occasionally tend to make teachers "subordinate in a world full of super-ordinates" (Barth, 2001). Initially, when the principal of School 2 wanted to see a teacher's responses and check these (via a native English speaker), I took this to be one such instance; more so, because of the tight hierarchical structure of the school – hierarchy being long perceived as a bulwark against teacher leadership (Boles, 1992; Wasley, 1991). Later, after further interaction with the principal and the native English teacher, I realised that this was not done to change the content or tone of the responses but to 'correct' any possible linguistic errors the teachers might have made. Taking the contextual beliefs into consideration, I realised that as a senior member of a partnership, the principal owed junior members (in this case, teachers) protection and consideration. Thus, by presenting linguistically correct answers to me, the principal would be sparing the teachers any possible embarrassment or loss of face.

Third, a subtler form of hierarchy was evident within the school community. It soon became apparent that many teachers realised that there was a communication gulf between the school and the parents because the teachers were in a higher social position, being university graduates.

More obvious were the barely contained prejudices that the Hong Kong teachers and students had about the Mainland students who were viewed as troublesome and academically weak, and were believed to be in a lower position in the hierarchical scale. Although, at first glance, the student body appeared to be fairly homogeneous, with all the students being ethnically Chinese, this subtle social hierarchy would be difficult for an outsider to detect.

Fourth, what became increasingly apparent was that there is "a cult of secrecy" (Simon, teacher, School 2) in Hong Kong schools. There was a marked lack of transparency in administrative procedures and, as one teacher who is a Westerner pointed out, "Basically, you have to respect and adapt to the hierarchy ... The principal ... dictates a lot".

Paradoxically, teachers were content to be a part of this hierarchy and found the system "easy and comfortable" to work in and that the hierarchy is "very clear and from top ... down it is very coherent". Stening and Zhang (2007) argue that, in general, Western conceptualisations of Chinese culture are intrinsically flawed as they present a Chinese world view that is a 'rational structural perspective' rather than one that is full of paradoxes and contradictions. In essence, the views held by the teachers are a case in point.

Given this rather tight control in schools, where there is, at least superficially, an orderliness that comes close to maintaining equilibrium, it gradually transpired that the issues being discussed – such as teachers critiquing school administrators or students – created, at least notionally, disharmony. For example, the principal of one of the schools believed in teachers being involved in key decision-making processes, with this being a critical factor in promoting teacher leadership. Nonetheless, the teachers at this school complained that "there are so many people involved, so many panels, so many committees that ... it is hard for us to get the consent or come to a consensus".

When the respondents were asked to comment on the bureaucracy and the administrative structure of their schools, teachers in leadership positions or higher up in the school hierarchy tended to be less critical of the organisation. This varied from skirting controversial questions altogether or merely mouthing the official school platitudes. The teachers who were lower in the hierarchy were willing to talk, but often resorted to gestures or whispers when talking about the school administration and the principal or used other subtle channels to make their feelings known. The participants would hint that the 'power' and 'authority' that principals had over them were absolute, almost as if the principals held a quasi-pater/materfamilias role in the school. Often, the questions had to be re-phrased in order to evaluate their answers, as the participants seemed to fear social censure. Seen in this light, the data were far more contentious than was previously believed. Consequently, whilst perhaps not formally falling into the category of 'sensitive' study, nonetheless it required a great degree of sensitivity to deal with both the participants and the data.

Study Two (Researcher B)

Study Two investigated Hong Kong Chinese people's attitudes towards transgenderism with a view to changing public educational policy. The study was conducted in two stages using a mixed-methods research design. Initially, the study used qualitative methodology to obtain data that reflected an insider perspective, based on the assumption that the unique ideas, concepts, beliefs, values, and norms that are specific to Hong Kong Chinese people's culture are key factors to understanding attitudes towards transgender people. Based on the research design, and it being a sensitive study, purposive sampling was used according to specific inclusion criteria – academic and medical professionals (specialising in Psychiatry, Social Work, and Education) with direct knowledge and experience of transgenderism and transsexuality.

The second phase involved a telephonic structured interview, administered by professional interviewers (all Chinese). Throughout the interviewer training, Chinese cultural issues regarding sexuality and identity were instilled in the interviewers. This meant that the interviewers had to understand all terms in the questionnaire and nuances in their approach to the participants as well as be comfortable using sexually sensitive terms themselves. The participants of this study were 856 (362 men and 494 women) Hong Kong Chinese residents ranging in age from 15 to 64 years. A random sampling technique was used to select the households and a random method was employed in sampling each individual within the household. In total 856 respondents agreed to participate in the phone interview and 149 dropped out or only partially completed the interview.

It had been anticipated that with sexual mores being viewed as a taboo subject in Hong Kong, it might prove difficult to get participants. However, at the time of data collection the film *Brokeback Mountain* was being screened in theatres and had received extensive media coverage and, as a result, the participants were willing to discuss issues that heretofore would have remained unspoken. Also, the subject matter of this study was quite different from any other public opinion surveys conducted in Hong Kong, and for this reason, the interviewers were able to maintain the participants' interest. Moreover, when it was made known that the person analysing these data was a non-Chinese, participants were less inhibited than they would have been otherwise (King, Winter, & Webster, 2009).

A comparison between the results of the quantitative and qualitative parts of the study revealed discrepancies. The quantitative study showed surprisingly open attitudes towards transgenderism insofar as the institutional dimensions of legislation and public policy were concerned. The findings of the qualitative study were more complex as they concurrently indicated both substantial and pervasive negative attitudes and anti-transgender bias, as well as support for the very same people. This led to a closer examination of the contextual factors as these dichotomies suggested that understanding the social mindset of Hong Kong people by someone with a different socio-cultural heritage may be more difficult than is generally believed.

Hong Kong people have a strong family oriented culture as Confucian ideals value kinship ties and harmony. Consequently, it is important to maintain the homogeneity of the social fabric in order to avoid disharmony. In practical terms, there is a tendency to stigmatise people seen to be different and non-normative, be it because of an illness (Fong & Hung, 2002), or physical disability (Tam, Chan, Lam, & Lam, 2003), as these individuals were seen to threaten the perceived harmony of the society or a family. As a long-term resident of Hong Kong, I anticipated that it would be highly likely that the participants would be biased against transgender people. Transgender participants were also aware of the reasons for their being stigmatised:

> It is important to understand the ways Hong Kong people deal with things they don't understand ... anything that is not considered 'normal' or 'conforming' is treated as 'ugly ... revolting ... or disgusting' ... especially when it comes to sexual things ... and transgender combines all of these things ... so Hong Kong peoples' understanding of transgender is confused and very negative.
>
> *Participant TG1, Transgender*

However, the challenge was not the expected biases, but that a majority of the heterosexual people whom I interviewed *denied* the very existence of transgender people in Hong Kong, saying that they existed in foreign countries only. This meant that the interview had to be modified to include a 'pre-interview session' that explained in detail that mental illnesses, physical disabilities, differences in sexual orientation, and other differences existed in every human population and that it was logical to assume that transgender people existed in Hong Kong, even though in other societies, such as in Thailand, they were more visible. Since I spoke from what the participants believed to be an 'expert' point of view, they conceded the point (deference to authority being a characteristic of many Asian societies, Confucian, in particular). The suicide of a young transgender Chinese woman that was widely reported in the press at this time also increased awareness of the issue.

As a non-Chinese researcher, it was difficult to understand why, given the bias against non-normative people, many participants supported legislation protecting these people. It was only after much probing that support for transgender rights emerged from the value that the Chinese place on privacy. As a Westerner, I come from a socio-cultural tradition where civil rights are in the forefront of public discourse. Consequently, during the early stages of data collection and subsequent analysis, I veered towards accepting the support for transgender people at face value, as it echoed my personal beliefs and that of many Western civil rights scholars about equality. Confirmation also appeared to come from the quantitative part of my own study. It is only when

I investigated further to determine why there was a seeming anomaly between the biases that people held towards transgender people and the belief that they should have legislative rights, that I arrived at a picture that, though complicated, could be explained through the lens of Confucian beliefs. That is, this support for the privacy of transgender people was not because of an inherent belief about the rights of all humans but because people believed in hiding non-normative individuals:

> Chinese people tend not to interfere in another person's private life ... and we expect to be treated the same ... I can see how these issues are even more important for the *yen yiu* [colloquial term for transgender people], because they have something more important to hide
> *Participant LG2, 36-year-old heterosexual male*

During the course of the study, I realised that what could be framed as a source of bias proved not to be so. In the initial stages of the study, whilst examining the sources of biases, it seemed that the influence of the linguistic conceptualisations of transgender, as colloquially expressed by Hong Kong Chinese people, reflected their bias as the term was derogatory in meaning:

> the typical language people use is '*yen yiu*' ... in a way, if you try to analyse it, '*yiu*' means evil ... something evil ... and '*yen*' of course means 'man' ... an 'evil man' or even as a 'human monster' ... that is the direct interpretation of the Cantonese
> *Participant SWI, academic social worker*

But it was soon apparent that apart from the scholars working in the field, the only people who used the politically correct terms for transgender people were the transgender people themselves. However, after repeated interactions with the participants, I realised that whilst the general attitudes of the Hong Kong people regarding transgender people reflect relatively negative attitudes, the words *yen yiu* did not carry negative connotations *per se*. It was rather like the usage of the word *gweilo*, which means 'white ghost', a seemingly negative word, but one that is now a part of everyday usage to describe Caucasians and does not have any particularly positive or negative connotations.

Challenges of data interpretation

As suggested by Dinges and Baldwin (1996), even deep immersion in a particular culture will not guarantee flawless interpretation of data. This is because although competence in the given culture may be achieved at a cognitive level, residual affective effects from one's own culture make objective assessments difficult. The challenge, therefore, is not to eliminate these cultural and personal values but to consider (and even document) the effects of personal bias that may influence one's perspective and positionality in research.

Bevan-Brown (2001) voices concern about the differences in language and concepts expressed by linguistic means. Generally, even fluent bilingual individuals differed in the amount of information that they offer in one language (usually the first) to another. In our studies, almost all the participants were Cantonese speakers, and although in Study One most were fluent in English, it required great patience and a conscious attempt on our part to make the participants feel at ease. Huer and Saenz (2002, p. 270) note that the "very act of interviewing may be foreign to the members of some cultures", and we found it so in Hong Kong.

Indeed, at the initial stages of Study One, the participants believed that the interviewer was connected to the Education Bureau and some parents only engaged in the preliminary discussion because they believed this was the case. Later, after knowing the real background of the study, they invested 'authority' to the interviewer and thus spoke of their concerns. Therefore, to build trust, different strategies had to be built into our design. In some cases, there were follow-up written interviews and often the participants (especially the student participants) expressed themselves more freely in writing than during the oral interview. This is in keeping with the work of other scholars who have found that direct questions about perceived sensitive topics are more difficult as the participants may be culturally accustomed to communicating indirectly (Huer & Saenz, 2002), and thus there is a basic concern that their community would judge them harshly as a result of their opinions. Many of the participants did not vocalise their thoughts whilst raising criticisms and resorted to body language and gestures instead. There are, as other researchers have noted (see for example, Bevan-Brown, 2001), pitfalls in trying to interpret non-verbal cues because they too may be misunderstood because of cultural differences. Consequently, in interpreting data, we had to come to terms with a socio-linguistic frame of reference that was quite different from our own.

In Study Two, there was an additional dimension to this factor. As non-Cantonese-speaking researchers, one of the critical issues was the linguistic conceptualisation of transgenderism, namely that transgender people were commonly referred to as *yen yiu* or 'human monsters'. This seemingly highly negative representation, it was thought, must have a significant effect on attitudes. Coming to terms with the data on the impact of aetiological and biological essentialist beliefs on attitudes required an extensive review of the literature and referral back to the data from the qualitative interviews. Experts in Hong Kong culture were consulted to confirm that the interpretations were accurate and plausible within the Chinese cultural context. A final area of consideration was understanding the effect of demographic variables on attitudes towards transgenderism and transgender civil rights and interpreting the data in a way that understood the pathways in which Hong Kong Chinese people codify, abstract, and diffuse information relevant to their attitudes, ways that are fundamentally and markedly dissimilar to the researcher's way of being.

Stening and Zhang (2007) point out another key factor – they note that concepts such as trust, loyalty, and justice have different meanings in Chinese societies from their commonly held meanings in other societies. They note "the very way that these issues [pertaining to conducting research in China] have been framed reflects, to some extent at least, a positivist Western bias" (p. 194). Unique characteristics have resulted in response biases being noted in studies conducted in China (Fu & Tsui, 2003), which the researchers explain is related to a deep-rooted Confucian idea that emphasises the 'doctrine of the mean' that emphasises the maintenance of harmony. The emphasis on maintaining harmony has implications, as discussed earlier in the chapter, for the conduct of research. Additionally, in our own research, we found that notions of 'informed consent' and the ethics of 'gate-keeping', key elements of Western-based notions of research ethics, failed to hold up in a culture that is more paternalistic in nature.

In sum, it was important that we acknowledged our locations within the social world in which we worked and explored how our locations influenced our particular world views in terms of settling upon a 'researchable question', sampling issues, the development of research instruments, and issues regarding data collection and interpretation. These are all significant issues for any researcher, but also for non-Chinese researchers conducting social science investigations in Chinese societies. In Chinese societies, people's meaning is often deeply embedded in what they are saying and people with the same orientation would be able to gauge the sub-context of such meanings. This may be much more difficult for researchers who come from entirely different cultures. According to Dennett (1995, p. 340), "what we are is very much a matter of what culture has made us", and we found this to apply to us and the participants equally.

Implications for research and practice

A great deal of cross-cultural research has been conducted across a wide range of societies, but very few studies have focused on the particular methodological issues canvassed in this discussion. A synthesis of the methodological challenges that we faced may also provide implications that these issues have for other researchers who like us are non-Chinese, but pursue research agendas in Confucian dominated Chinese societies. These implications can in fact be viewed as a set of recommendations to guide further research.

Although some of the challenges that we faced may be found in other contexts, there is little argument that CHCs display unique characteristics that impacted our respective studies. Furthermore, we would argue that cultural contexts influence research methodology, particularly the kinds of inferences that methodology can sanction. In studies such as ours, knowledge of culture is more than just another feature that needs to be investigated. This knowledge plays a decisive role in the kinds of inferences that can be made. For example, in a culture that is hierarchical in nature and where relationships are seen to be governed as quasi-familial structures, fear of losing face or of not giving face, or disrupting harmony by articulating the truth, may result in the data falling prey to confirmation bias or affirmation bias. Researchers may thus need several levels of analysis or triangulation in order to arrive at veracious conclusions. This is easier said than done because it is difficult to determine when a participant has confirmed or affirmed responses based on contextual factors.

As both our studies have highlighted, being an insider does not necessarily add strength and authority to a researcher's cultural cognition. Indeed, we found that outsiders can shed light on taken-for-granted assumptions. Moreover, as Merton (1972) has pointed out, individuals may have status sets. In any case, in an increasingly globalised world, the insider–outsider dilemma has acquired far more complex undertones. Nonetheless, a significant factor is first understanding one's own cultural conditioning and then its relationship with a culturally different context in terms of evaluating and drawing inferences about the different frameworks of understanding held by the participants. And there is enough literature in existence that highlights the uniqueness of Confucian influenced contexts.

Evers and Mason (2011) argue from an epistemological perspective that cultural knowledge is critical in terms of understanding the social realities in the contexts that are being investigated in the context of drawing critical inferences, and this brings us to another important implication, that there is a fundamental need for researchers to conduct studies that provide contextually sensitive evidence for the design or evaluation of issues. A simple solution to the problem is for researchers to adopt what has been called 'context-embedded' modes of investigation, mainly by using co-researchers from the contexts that are to be studied. This model, we argue, has some immediate shortcomings. On a practical level, it may not always be feasible, or even desirable, to co-opt co-researchers. Moreover, there are research-related advantages of being outsiders, especially in Hong Kong where due to socio-cultural factors, participants are more open to discussing certain issues with non-Chinese researchers. We do not believe that CHC or Western conceptual frameworks are incommensurable or mutually exclusive. It would be difficult to construct CHC-inspired research methodology without applying the rigour demanded of Western research processes (Park, 2011) though researchers may react to the nuances of such contexts when they occur. For example, research design must be flexible and it may be justifiable to assume that formal ethical considerations for most research projects are based on Western frameworks of understanding. We found this to be problematic. For instance, emphasis on individual autonomy guiding our studies was at odds with the norms of a collectivist, hierarchical, CHC. Viewed through Western frameworks of understanding, this has negative connotations as it compromises the fundamental concept of the individual's right to choose, but when seen through a Confucian lens, this was not a deliberate or an intentional infringing of rights but a manifestation of familial and paternalistic relationships that guide interpersonal interactions in these societies. Similarly, research does not need to concern sensitive topics in order for its participants to fall in the sensitive category. Consequently, researchers need to be finely attuned to the needs and vulnerabilities of the participants they are investigating – even though at the beginning of the study, the participants may display no such qualities. Our view is that instead of institutional requirements focusing on the sensitive nature of the research project, it may be better to focus on the sensitivities associated with the participants.

Though the studies reported here are in the context of Hong Kong, even a cursory look at the literature affirms that the issues raised here have transnational applicability. Many of the CHC contexts are complex in that they are unique in their socio-cultural composition, and as we have found in our own research, the inherent intricacies of these cultures make them difficult to comprehend. We hope that the issues raised in this chapter provide useful guidelines for researchers and open pathways for future research endeavours in these contexts.

References

Barth, R. S. (2001). Teacher leader. *Phi Delta Kappan, 82*(6), 443–449.
Bell, D. (2000). Guanxi: A nesting of groups. *Current Anthropology, 41*(1), 132–138.
Bellah, R. N. (1970). *Tokugawa religion.* Boston, MA: Beacon Press.
Bevan-Brown, J. (2001). Evaluating special education services for learners from ethnically diverse groups: Getting it right. *Journal of the Association for Persons with Severe Handicaps, 26*(3), 138–147.
Boles, K. (1992). *School restructuring by teachers: A study of the teaching project at the Edward devotion school.* Paper presented at the American Educational Research Association, San Francisco, CA.
Charlton, J. I. (1998). *Nothing about us without us: Disability oppression and empowerment.* Berkeley, CA: University of California Press.
Dennett, D. C. (1995). *Darwin's dangerous idea: Evolution and the meanings of life.* New York, NY: Simon & Schuster.
Dinges, N., & Baldwin, K. (1996). Intercultural competence: A research perspective. In D. Landis & R. Bhagat (Eds.), *Handbook of intercultural training* (pp. 106–146). Thousand Oaks, CA: Sage.
Eisenhart, M. (2001). Educational ethnography past, present, and future: Ideas to think with. *Educational Researcher, 30*(8), 16–27.
Evers, C. W., & Mason, M. (2011). Context based inferences in research methodology: the role of culture in justifying knowledge claims. *Comparative Education, 47*(3), 301–314.

Fong, C.-y. G., & Hung, A. (2002). Public awareness, attitude, and understanding of epilepsy in Hong Kong special administrative region, China. *Epilepsia, 43*(3), 311–316.

Fu, P. R., & Tsui, A. S. (2003). Utilizing printed media to understand desired leadership attributes in the People's Republic of China. *Asia Pacific Journal of Management, 20*(4), 423–446.

Gronn, P. (2000). Distributed properties: A new architecture for leadership. *Educational Management and Administration, 28*(3), 317–338.

Ho, D. Y. F. (1994). Filial piety, authoritarian moralism, and cognitive conservatism. *Genetic, Social, and General Psychology Monographs, 120*(3), 347–365.

Hofstede, G., & Bond, M. H. (1988). The Confucius connection: From cultural roots to economic growth. *Organizational Dynamic, 16*(1), 4–21.

Hofstede, G. H., & Hofstede, G. J. (2005). *Cultures and organizations: Software of the mind* (2nd ed.). New York, NY: McGraw Hill.

Homan, R. (2001). The principal of assumed consent: The ethics of gatekeeping. In M. McNamee & D. Bridges (Eds.), *The ethics of educational research* (pp. 23–41). Oxford, England: Blackwell.

Hsu, J. (1985). The Chinese family: Relations, problems, and therapy. In W. S. Tseng & D. Wu (Eds.), *Chinese culture and mental health* (pp. 95–112). New York, NY: Academic Press.

Hue, M.-T. (2007). Emergence of Confucianism from teachers' definitions of guidance and discipline in Hong Kong secondary schools. *Research in Education, 78*(1), 21–33.

Huer, M. B., & Saenz, T. I. (2002). Thinking about conducting culturally sensitive research in augmentative and alternative communication. *Augmentative and Alternative Communication, 18*(4), 267–273.

Katyal, K. R. (2011). Gate-keeping and paternalism: Ambiguities in the nature of 'informed consent' in Confucius societies. *International Journal of Research & Method in Education, 34*(2), 147–159.

Katyal, K. R., & King, M. E. (2011). 'Outsiderness' versus 'Insiderness' in a Confucian society: Complexity of contexts. *Comparative Education, 47*(3), 327–341.

Katzenmeyer, M., & Moller, G. (2001). *Awakening the sleeping giant: Helping teachers develop as leaders* (2nd ed.). Thousand Oaks, CA: Corwin Publishing.

King, J. E. (1995). Culture-centered knowledge: Black studies, curriculum transformation, and social action. In J. A. Banks & C. M. Banks (Eds.), *Handbook of research on multicultural education* (pp. 265–290). New York, NY: Macmillan.

King, M. E., Winter, S., & Webster, B. (2009). Contact reduces transprejudice: A study on attitudes towards transgenderism and transgender civil rights in Hong Kong. *International Journal of Sexual Health, 21*(1), 17–34.

Kreiger, S. (1982). Lesbian identity and community: Recent social science literature. *Sign, 8*(11), 91–108.

Lee, R. M. (1993). *Doing research on sensitive topics*. London, England: Sage.

Lee, R. M., & Renzetti, C. M. (1993). *Researching sensitive topics*. Newbury Park, CA: Sage.

Li, N., Leung, D. Y. P., & Kember, D. (2001). Medium of instruction in Hong Kong universities: The mismatch between espoused theory and theory use. *Higher Education Policy, 14*(4), 293–312.

Ma, J. L. C. (1999). Social work practice with transsexuals in Hong Kong who apply for sex reassignment surgery. *Social Work in Health Care, 29*(2), 85–103.

McNamee, M. (2001). Introduction: Whose ethics, which research? *Journal of Philosophy of Education*, 35(3), 309–327.

Merton, R. (1972). Insiders and outsiders: A chapter in the sociology of knowledge. *American Journal of Sociology*, 78(1), 9–47.

Nordtveit, B. H. (2011). Politics, guanxi and the search for objectivity: The intricacies of conducting educational research in Chinese contexts. *Comparative Education*, 47(3), 355–367.

Pang, D. (2005). Educating for location? The policy context of a 'becoming Asialiteratea TM' in five Western countries/regions in the 1990s. *Comparative Education*, 41(2), 171–198.

Park, J. (2011). Metamorphosis of Confucian Heritage Culture and the possibility of an Asian education research methodology. *Comparative Education*, 47(3), 367–381.

Pratt, D., Kelly, M., & Wong, W. S. S. (1999). Chinese conceptions of 'effective teaching' in Hong Kong: Towards culturally sensitive evaluation of teaching. *International Journal of Lifelong Education*, 18(4), 241–258.

Sieber, J. E., & Stanley, B. (1988). Ethical and professional dimensions of socially sensitive research. *American Psychologist*, 43(1), 49–55.

Stening, B. W., & Zhang, M. Y. (2007). Methodological challenges confronted when conducting management research in China. *International Journal of Cross Cultural Management*, 7(1), 121–142.

Tam, S. F., Chan, M. H., Lam, H. W., & Lam, L. H. (2003). Comparing the self-concepts of Hong Kong Chinese adults with visible and not visible physical disability. *Journal of Psychology*, 137(4), 363–372.

Walker, A., & Dimmock, C. (2000). Leadership dilemmas of Hong Kong principals: Sources, perceptions and outcomes. *Australian Journal of Education*, 44(1), 5–25.

Wasley, P. (1991). *Teachers who lead*. New York, NY: Teachers College Press.

Wilson, A. A., Greenblatt, S. L., & Wilson, R. W. (1977). *Deviance and social control in Chinese society*. New York, NY: Praeger.

Yang, C. K. (1959). *Chinese Communist Society: The family and the tillage*. Cambridge, MA: MIT Press.

9
(RE)CENTRING THE SPIRIT

A spiritual Black feminist take on cultivating right relationships in qualitative research

Christina S. Morton

Anxiously watching the clock, I waited for my first student to arrive for his academic coaching appointment. Hearing a soft knock at the door, I stiffened awkwardly in my chair and attempted to look as confident as I possibly could, calling out: "Come in, the door is open". Then I saw my supervisor's smiling face as she eased the door open and ushered in the young man behind her. She proceeded to sit across from me, invited the student to do the same, and began a round of introductions. Noticing my nervousness, she inquired if I would be comfortable with her beginning the conversation to help us all get better acquainted. I gratefully obliged, and as I observed her gentle but purposeful probing, coupled with her attentive and affirming demeanour, I knew that I wanted to emulate her approach in my own practice. As the meeting continued, I felt calm, supported, and reassured that I could do what was asked of me. I imagine the student felt the same way. What I realise now is that my supervisor's humanising, spiritually edifying approach to working with students continued to guide me long after my tenure as an academic success coach was over. Whether I was supervising undergraduates in residence life, teaching, or conducting higher education research, I wanted the people I interacted with to feel as seen, heard, and cared for as I did when working alongside her.

Reflecting on the lessons my supervisor taught me early in my career, I wanted to bring them to bear in my philosophical and methodological approach to conducting qualitative research. Interested in conceptual frameworks that complemented the strategies that I observed my supervisor – a Black woman – employ in her professional practice, I was drawn to Black feminist thought (Collins, 2000, 2009) and endarkened feminist epistemology (Dillard, 2000, 2006). I have used these frameworks to inform and examine my methodological approach to conducting qualitative research. I also make linkages between these frameworks and my professional practice in higher education. Using examples from my own research concerning the role of spirituality in the lives of Black women pursuing engineering doctorates, I elaborate upon how I engage in what Dillard (2006) referred to as a *methodology of surrender* in endarkened feminist epistemology. I embrace a meditative and faith-filled research space that promotes love, compassion, reciprocity, and ritual. In such a space, researchers can (a) see and listen carefully to their participants to recognise their truths; (b) bridge the divide between researchers and participants by recognising the participants' dignity and equality; and (c) intentionally challenge factors that may create distance between researchers, participants, and participants' experiences. Additionally, from a Black feminist epistemological standpoint, I describe how I (a) privileged lived experience – my participants' and my own, including my spirituality – as a criterion of meaning and as an index of credibility and believability, (b) used dialogue (i.e., humanising conversations between people) to assess knowledge claims, and (c) engaged in ethics of care and personal accountability as inherent parts of the knowledge validation process (Collins, 2000).

Furthermore, I illuminate the applicability of these frameworks in guiding the cultivation of right relationships, in research and higher education practice, that are both humanising and healing. Parallel with discussions of right relationships that have been advanced in Indigenous scholarship, I assert that right relationships in research and practice, as informed by Black feminism, are spiritually grounded and responsibly fostered through ethics of accountability and care. In discussing the importance of relationships in her work, Indigenous scholar Sandy Grande (2000) wrote: "I understand if my work is to have any meaning at all that it must evolve from the central concerns of my life" (p. 357), a perspective that included the health and welfare of her communities, social transformation, and improving the educational experiences of Indigenous children. As a Black woman scholar and higher educational professional, my pursuit of right relationships in my own work and practice is aimed at cultivating socially just and liberating educational environments for all students, particularly Black, Indigenous, and People of Color.

Epistemology informs research and practice. Through a reflexive examination of my own scholarship and career through the conceptual frameworks of Black feminist thought and endarkened feminist epistemology I demonstrate how our epistemologies, as researchers and practitioners, can provide valuable principles by which we can engage our participants and students in ethical, intentional, and meaningful ways.

Positionality statement

My commitment to cultivating right relationships in higher education research and practice is largely driven by my personal experiences navigating various institutional contexts as a Black woman. As an undergraduate in engineering,

I sought out spaces where I could feel affirmed in my identities and would receive the support I needed to succeed. Such spaces were often the offices of academic and student affairs practitioners on campus. Later, as I pursued a career in higher education and eventually graduate studies in this field, I wanted to offer students and research participants spaces of uplift and respite like the ones that had been created for me by my mentors. Furthermore, throughout my academic and professional career, I have relied heavily on my Christian faith to inform the ways I approach my scholarship and practice. My epistemological standpoint as a researcher and practitioner is largely influenced by and aligned with scholars such as Dillard (2000), who names research as an inherently spiritual enterprise. I believe my purpose in higher education is to extend love, hope, and joy to those I encounter in my work and research, which I consider to be a spiritual endeavour. The views expressed in this chapter reflect the spiritual subjectivities of myself and my Christian participants; however, I fully acknowledge that there are other spiritual ways of being and knowing outside of Christianity. Further, I do not presume that a Christian spirituality is the only or best way to pursue right relationships in research and practice. I encourage scholars and practitioners to consider what spirituality means to them and how it may inform their work.

Conceptual frameworks

By referring to Black feminist thought (Collins, 2000, 2009) and endarkened feminist epistemology (Dillard, 2000, 2006) as conceptual frameworks, I am denoting my use of them as analytical tools to examine my research practice. My intention is not to test a series of propositions used to explain particular phenomena, as one might with theory, but rather to examine my methodological approach through the lens of these frameworks, to consider their applicability to higher education practice, and to reflect on my own work.

Black feminist thought

As Collins (2000, 2009) asserted, within Black feminist thought there is a set of principles that Black women use to assess and validate knowledge claims. These principles are derived from the collective wisdom of Black women, which she suggested is established through the sharing and preservation of Black women's experiences throughout history. From a Black feminist epistemological standpoint, lived experience is a criterion of meaning, dialogue is used to assess knowledge claims, and ethics of personal accountability and care are inherent in the knowledge validation process.

According to Collins (2000), lived experience confers credibility onto someone positioning herself as an expert on a particular topic. For instance, a student may be more responsive when a trusted mentor offers advice based on her own lived experience, which adds credibility to her guidance. Through dialogue, ideas are examined and proven in conversation with others rather than in isolation. The ethic of personal accountability refers to the expectation that a person is responsible for their knowledge claims, which makes that person's character, values, and ethics subject to evaluation. In other words, being accountable for her words and actions is a testament to her character.

The ethic of care comprises three components: personal expressiveness, emotion, and empathy. Personal expressiveness speaks to the value of individual uniqueness within Black communities. Collins (2009) shared: "Rooted in a tradition of African humanism, each individual is thought to be a unique expression of a common spirit, power, or energy inherent in all life" (p. 282). For instance, a teacher who honours students' personal expressiveness celebrates the individuality found within the collective class. Emotion serves as evidence of the speaker's belief in her argument. Using the example of Black women's blues tradition, Collins asserted that powerful lyrics combined with a singer's emotional delivery inspire conviction in the audience and denote the performer's belief in the song's message. Within higher education, remaining attentive to students' emotions can entail checking in with them after a troubling event on campus or in the national news. Empathy refers to a Black woman's ability to see herself in another's experience and thereby better understand that person. In educational research, allowing the experiences of participants to resonate with the researcher's own could be one way of demonstrating empathy.

Endarkened feminist epistemology

Rooted in Black feminist scholarship, endarkened feminist epistemology aims to disrupt what is considered known and taken for granted in educational research (Dillard, 2000, 2006). Endarkened feminist epistemology describes Black women's ways of knowing, with attention to their intersecting identities: "Thus, an endarkened feminist epistemology has as its research project the vigilant and consistent desire to 'dig up' the nexus of racial/ethnic, gender, and other identity realities: of how we understand and experience the world as Black women" (Dillard, 2000, p. 678). Central to endarkened feminist epistemology is a critique of the "violence perpetuated in the universal generalization from the particular White male knowledge of the nature of reality to describe everyone's realities, including those Black and female" (Dillard, 2006, p. 17). Further, *endarkened* is intentionally used to describe such an epistemology in an effort to encourage the use of new language to describe the knowledge and lived realities of People of Color from the perspective of Black feminist thought (Dillard, 2000):

> Therefore, in contrast with the common use of the term 'enlightened' as a way of expressing the having of new and important feminist insights (arising

historically from the well-established canon of White feminist thought), I use the term *endarkened* feminist epistemology to articulate how reality is known when based in the historical roots of Black feminist thought, embodying a distinguishable difference in cultural standpoint, located in the intersection/overlap of the culturally constructed socializations of race, gender, and other identities and the historical and contemporary contexts of oppressions and resistance for African American women. (p. 662)

Moreover, an endarkened feminist epistemology draws on a spiritual tradition that acknowledges Black women's historical and contemporary reliance on various forms of spirituality to resist oppression and find purpose in their pursuits (Dillard, 2000, 2006). An endarkened feminist epistemology also recognises that individuals, though unique, possess a common spirit that imbues them with inherent worth and validates their expressed truths (Dillard, 2006). Situated in an Afrocentric worldview, from an endarkened feminist epistemological perspective, "one's selfhood is understood and constituted as body, mind, and spirit and affirmed in relationship to both one's group and one's creator" (Dillard, 2006, p. 32).

In my research, I engage in what Dillard (2006) refers to as a methodology of surrender, which embraces a meditative and faith filled research space that promotes love, compassion, reciprocity, and ritual. Love involves reconceptualising the researcher-participant relationship. To love the people and communities being researched, the researcher must look and listen carefully to her participants in order recognise their truths (Dillard, 2006). Writing about love in the ethnographic research tradition, Carspecken (2018) suggested that love in research implies a recognition of the importance of emotion and a prioritisation of participants' wellbeing by the researcher:

> By doing social research we are making an implicit claim that other human beings concern us emotionally as well as intellectually and that their wellbeing *should* concern both authors and readers. We are tacitly positioning an ethical ideal, a value on which the other values build, although it is not one we ever fully live up to. I translate this ideal as love. (p. 2)

Aligned with Carspecken (2018) and informed by Dillard (2006), I consider love to be an ethic that encourages researchers and higher education professionals to strive for more humanising practices. These begin with careful observation of and listening to the communities we research and the students we serve, to recognise their full humanity and truths.

Compassion refers to the "intention and capacity to relieve and transform suffering through our research work" (Dillard, 2006, p. 84). Being compassionate towards the people or communities one is researching means caring deeply and desiring to bring them joy. Reciprocity entails bridging the divide between the researcher and the participant by recognising all human beings as equal and eradicating the artificial boundaries created to distance one from the other. "Imagining one's self as another – and all of us as spirit beings having human experience – is the only way to narrow the chasm between the 'differences' that are so often the topics of our academic discussions and work" (Dillard, 2006, p. 85). To engage in ritual involves remembering that research is not only an intellectual pursuit, but also a spiritual one, "unifying the human and the divine" (Dillard, 2006, p. 85). This study provided the context for me to examine my own research practice through the lens of Black feminist thought and endarkened feminist epistemology.

Study overview

The examples and excerpts provided for this chapter come from earlier research in which I examined the role of spirituality in the lives of Black women pursuing doctorates in engineering at historically Black and White institutions. There were seven specific research questions for the study.

- How do Black women in engineering doctoral programmes understand, describe, and express their spirituality?
- When, where, and with whom do Black women in engineering express their spirituality?
- To what extent, and in what ways, does spirituality inform resilience, resistance, and transcendence among Black women pursuing engineering doctorates?
- How do Black women in engineering doctoral programmes describe their experiences in their educational environments, and how does spirituality help them to navigate the challenges and affordances of those contexts?
- How are race and gender implicated in the challenges and successes that Black women in engineering experience, and how does spirituality help them navigate those particular challenges?
- How, if at all, is spirituality implicated in Black women's work as engineers (e.g., in their knowledge claims, in the ways that they understand what is valid, in the creative process, in problem solving, and in engaging others in collaborative processes)?
- To what extent do Black women in engineering experience conflict between spiritual and scientific epistemologies?

Participants

The sample consisted of 16 self-identified Black women of various ethnicities, including Brazilian, Cameroonian, Ghanaian, Kenyan, Nigerian, and Panamanian. All were pursuing doctorates in engineering; their majors included biomedical, chemical, civil, computer science, electrical, environmental, industrial, materials science, mechanical, and nuclear engineering. Of the 16 participants, 7 attended historically Black institutions, and 9 attended historically White institutions. Participants ranged from first-year precandidates to seventh-year candidates in their programmes at the time of the first interview. Participants ranged from 22 to 48 years of age, and all 16 participants identified with Christianity to some degree.

Method

Data collected for the study included three semi-structured interviews with each participant, totalling 48 interviews, over the course of six months between January and June 2019. Participants also engaged in journaling and photo elicitation – the use of photos to explore how individuals make meaning of particular topics (Denton, Kortegast, & Miller, 2018) – based on specific reflective prompts prior to the second interviews (Figure 9.1). Participants were each given six prompts to provide photos and write journal entries about particular academic and spiritual spaces they occupied while in their engineering doctoral programmes, which were used to seed the second interview for elaboration and reflection. Throughout the interview process, I also captured my own thoughts and reflections with written and audio recorded memos, which served to facilitate my analytic thinking about the data (Maxwell, 2013). Each audio recorded interview and memo was transcribed verbatim.

Analysis

For the purpose of this chapter, I engaged in a deep reading of the memos recorded during and shortly after the third round of interviews. Returning to these memos, I coded for evidence of methodological decisions and applications of Black feminist thought and endarkened feminist epistemology's methodology of surrender. Utilising Black feminist thought's ethics of personal accountability and care, I created codes to capture my discussion of instances when my participants and I validated one another's knowledge claims through dialogue. For instance, in my memos I looked for examples of participants' claims about the nature of their doctoral experiences and my responses to such claims as we engaged in conversation. I also coded for evidence of attention to personal expressiveness, emotion, and empathy during the interviews.

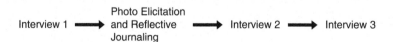

FIGURE 9.1 Data collection process

Regarding methodology of surrender, I specifically coded for instances of love, compassion, reciprocity, and ritual as discussed in the memos, utilising Dillard's (2006) descriptions of these concepts as guiding definitions for my codes. For example, in coding for love, I looked for instances when I demonstrated concern for the wellbeing of my participants – such as remaining attentive to their physical or verbal cues during difficult moments in the interviews to discern whether or not we needed to take a pause or perhaps change direction entirely. After coding the memos, I revisited the interview transcripts to pinpoint key moments, which further illuminated the methodological decisions and framework applications referenced in my memos. Excerpts from the personal memos and interviews illustrate how Black feminist thought and endarkened feminist epistemology informed my methodological approach to the study, particularly the interview process and the content of conversations with participants.

Insights from my research and practice

Endarkened feminist epistemology and Black feminist thought provide useful frameworks for considering how to (re)centre the spirit in qualitative research and professional practice. Both frameworks foreground Black women's ways of knowing, and they call for a humanising, caring approach to conducting research. Furthermore, these frameworks complement each other well. Adopting an ethic of care (i.e., attending to personal expressiveness, emotion, and empathy) involves love, compassion, and reciprocity. For a spiritual person, an ethic of personal accountability may encourage the use of ritual (e.g., prayer, meditation) prior to making knowledge claims and possibly using similar strategies to discern the believability of another person's claims after engaging in dialogue. These frameworks guided my own research practice and allowed me to reimagine the research enterprise and to cultivate meaningful, mutually healing relationships that extended beyond the study; these frameworks and my reflections on them were also applied in my professional practice in higher education.

Endarkened feminist epistemology (methodology of surrender)

Love

Guided by Dillard's (2006) methodology of surrender, I intentionally infused love, compassion, reciprocity, and ritual into my process of conducting research. As Dillard suggested, love entails careful listening to and observation of participants to recognise their truths. In my research, I showed participants love by remaining attentive to their body language, tone, and delivery as we engaged in conversation. If a normally open and vivacious participant appeared to be guarded and more reserved, I noted those shifts and acknowledged them during the dialogue. For instance, during my third and final interview with Parker (participants identified with pseudonyms), I noticed that her demeanour was downcast, and her responses to my questions appeared to be purposefully vague. In that moment, I could tell that she wanted to share what was going on, but not as a study participant, rather as a friend:

Parker: I honestly ... this you don't need to put it in your write up, okay?
Me: Okay. You just tell me how much of that is not going in the writings.
Parker: This is off the record. And I'll tell you when it's on the record. But right now, we're off the record.

Parker went on to fully disclose the situation, and afterwards we had an open conversation about what she did and did not want included in the writing of my research. Later, as I reflected on the experience, I was humbled by the faith she placed in me to respect the boundaries she outlined while entrusting me with her story. That evening, in my audio memo I spoke of how much I valued that moment between us, because we were able to move beyond research and into deeper relationship with one another:

And then there's this interesting moment when the interview was over and suddenly the real sharing begins. And spiritually, that's something I think I value even more than some of the quotes or moments in the conversation where I think, "Oh my gosh, I have to make sure that makes it into the dissertation," or "I have to make sure that gets into a journal article," or "I have to make sure that goes in the book." Really, I think the real purpose of this work is beyond just the work. I feel very strongly now more than ever that God has a greater purpose for me being in contact [with] and encountering these women ... beyond just how this research might go forward to help other people who are in similar situations, but for me specifically to be connected with them specifically as people.

In that instance, enacting love meant forgoing my agenda as a researcher for that interview and attending to my participant's needs as a person. The choice gave us the freedom to have a more meaningful conversation and ultimately a friendship that transcended the purpose of the study.

My interaction with Parker also reminded me of moments in my professional career when I extended love to and witnessed love from students. While working as an academic success coach, I remember having a conversation with a student about his academic and professional aspirations. He was explaining to me that his primary motivation for attending college was to make money, and he had no intentions of continuing his education after earning his bachelor's degree. He even considered leaving school altogether so he could devote more time to working. As I was mentally preparing my argument for why school should be his top priority, I paused and realised that I was ready to convince him to do what I felt was best without fully listening or understanding his reasoning. I took a breath, put my pen down, and asked him to tell me why making money was so important. He then shared that he was financially supporting his younger sister who was in high school, regularly sending money to his mother back home, and working multiple jobs as an undergraduate to make ends meet for himself and his family.

After he left, I wondered how many times for the sake of my own agenda I had missed an opportunity to extend love to my students. Love, in that particular moment, meant taking a pause and actually listening to what my student was trying to tell me. As Dillard (2006) suggested, extending love to my student required careful listening and attentive observation to recognise his truths. He needed to share the weight of his caregiving responsibilities with another person, even if I did not have a perfect solution to offer immediately in response. Attending to his actual needs, as opposed to what I believed to be his needs, shifted my coaching approach. We began to discuss scholarships, work-study options, and other ways he could provide for his family and remain in school; however, that conversation would not have been possible without love.

Compassion

Just as I allowed love to inform my approach to conducting research, I also considered how I could demonstrate compassion during the research process. According to Dillard (2006), compassion involves researchers' intending to have and having the capacity to relieve suffering. While love entails careful listening and observing to uncover another's truths, compassion compels researchers and practitioners to consider how their involvement in the lives of participants and students may alleviate suffering, or at least provide support in times of distress. Applying this principle in my work, I purposefully strived to encourage my participants as they described moments of uncertainty and doubt over the course of our interviews. A specific strategy I employed was sharing quotes with participants from their previous interviews when they spoke of overcoming obstacles or having faith that they would achieve their goals. This strategy was particularly helpful for Bree who, at the time of her third interview, was feeling anxious about her next steps professionally as she was attempting to finish her doctorate.

Bree: I'm in no rush to be at work at 8:00 in the morning five days a week anyway. But it's still like, the uncertainty is what drives me crazy. I don't know when I'll be done. I don't know where I'm going to be. And everyone that knows I've been in college this long keeps asking me,

"How much longer you got? You know where you're going to work? Where you want to work? You going to work on the other side of the country?" I'm just like, "I don't know yet."

Me: Yeah.
Bree: I wish I had some answers for you. I want the same answers.

Shortly after Bree expressed her thoughts, I looked through my notes and shared two passages that I highlighted from her first and second interview transcripts.

Me: You actually have a moment in your first interview when you talk about faith. And yeah, I think that this part might be helpful for you to hear again. You said: "I don't know if I would've come to grad school if I didn't have faith, because it was like that was still a tough time with the family. I wanted to go out and make money. And I probably would've chose that option. It's like I needed to do that now. I probably would've gotten the job. They called me back, said, 'You need to apply [for] full time.' But because I had the faith, I was like, I don't know anybody that went to grad school or got a PhD. So, it was scary for me, because I don't have anybody to talk to or to give me advice on this. But I just really had to step out on faith. And I figure, I'm just going to figure it out as it goes, and it's going to work out. So that's just what I did." So, you've used faith before. What'd you say?
Bree: Said I'm still figuring it out as it goes.
Me: You are. You are. But it's good. You're working it out.
Bree: It's been working, right?
Me: Mm-hmm [affirmative]. You also said that faith is kind of like the biggest question for any believer. Yeah, you said: "I guess my biggest challenge of faith is just accepting what is and trusting what will be." So, yeah. Yeah. It's interesting.
Bree: I need to write that one down.
Me: Mm-hmm [affirmative]. That was from your second interview.
Bree: Yeah.
Me: I could tell you again. So, you said: "I mean, the challenge of faith is just accepting what is and trusting what will be."
Bree: That's going to be in a poem one day.

After I recited Bree's own words back to her, I watched her countenance change as she recalled how she felt when she made those statements months before. For Bree and several other participants, it was powerful to be encouraged by her past self in a present moment of uncertainty. My decision to share those quotes was driven by compassion towards my participants as they navigated difficult moments of transition over the course of our time together.

I realised that as a researcher I had the privilege of being able to listen to the recordings and review the transcripts of our interviews, which allowed me to see their progress and be uplifted by their wisdom. My participants, however, did not have the benefit of easily revisiting these conversations as I did; therefore, bringing my participants' previous words back into the conversation was an intentional move to remind them of the strength of their faith.

Reciprocity

Dillard's (2006) methodology of surrender urges researchers to bridge the divide between themselves and their participants by recognising participants' dignity and equality. Reflecting on Dillard's principle of reciprocity, I recorded a memo about my interpretation of this idea and how it translated into my interactions with my participants:

> Being in academia, I think there's a fearfulness around connection and this intellectualising of contact between people. So, it's like … "I, as the researcher, am approaching this participant as a well which I will draw data and knowledge from, and then I will take that water from said well, and I will go and use it for whatever purpose. I'm going to write these papers, write these books, do what I want to do, and forget about the well until I need to go and tap into it again." For me, I can't do that. Not spiritually, not ethically, not as another human being. That idea of the well doesn't make sense to me, but if I think of myself as a pitcher full of water and my participants as another pitcher full of water, there are moments when we both are pouring into one another, and maybe I'm more full at one point and I can pour some of what I have into them, and perhaps they're more full at some points and they are pouring into me. There's this exchange that we have when we're sharing. Then there's moments when we both are full and we're overflowing, and then I believe that when we leave those interviews, we could share what happened in the overflow with other people, which is so powerful.

Reconceptualising the researcher-participant relationship as a mutually beneficial and spiritually edifying experience helped me to move away from exploitative, one-sided notions of the research enterprise and to imagine new possibilities. In doing so, I began to heed Dillard's (2000) call to move from the metaphor of research as recipe – implying a detachment from my participants as people – towards research as responsibility:

> This *necessitates* a different relationship between me, as the researcher, and the researched, between my knowing and the production of knowledge. This is also where Black feminist knowledge provides an angle of vision

from which to construct an alternative version of this relationship and a new metaphor in educational research, one that moves us away from detachment with participants and contexts and their use as "ingredients" in our research recipes and towards an epistemological position more appropriate for work within such communities. Thus, a more useful research metaphor arising from an endarkened feminist epistemology is *research as a responsibility*, answerable and obligated to the very persons and communities being engaged in the inquiry. (p. 663)

Contemplating how my participants and I could both leave the research experience full and perhaps overflowing gave me great hope for what could be achieved if engaging in reciprocity was an intentional aim in the research process.

Ritual

Aligned with Dillard's (2006) proposition that research is inherently a spiritual enterprise, I remained attuned to my own spirituality throughout the research process. Through prayer, reflection, and journaling I engaged in what Dillard describes as ritual, or the honouring of the divine forces that imbue researchers with the strength to take part in the research endeavour. The process helped me to have courage as I took methodological risks in my research. For example, despite Dillard's encouragement to dismantle artificial boundaries between researchers and participants, there were moments during the research process when I found myself questioning whether or not I was maintaining a suitable amount of distance from my participants. Then, I questioned where these concerns were coming from, and I realised that somehow, in spite of my qualitative methods training, notions of objectivity and boundary making still preoccupied my thoughts. However, through ritual (e.g., seeking divine guidance and reflection), I had a personal revelation, which I recorded in an audio memo:

> To kind of bring this whole personal reflection full circle ... for me, as a child of God, I have a very clear identity in a spiritual sense, and that spiritual sense allows me to do things naturally that perhaps I wouldn't have the courage or the boldness to do on my own, because my position might inform my behaviour in other ways, so take just being a researcher for example, right? As a researcher, someone might caution me about getting too close to participants, to being worried about influencing them in such a way, about commenting too much, about inserting myself too much, about feeling just in relationship too much ... If you are outside of the bounds of ... ethical responsibility, by all means, yes, but ... I think that some of those cautions are around this idea of objectivity and wanting not to bias

your sample or bias the data in some way, but that is just a completely unrealistic, inhumane way of understanding research and people. When you separate your humanity from the work that you're doing, you inherently are dehumanising the very people that you're attempting to understand, and that to me makes no sense whatsoever. That is unethical to me, and so my identity as a child of God tells me that if I'm in a position to encourage, to uplift, to help, to heal, to support, then that is my job … [which] gives me a freedom, and a boldness, and a courage.

Incorporating ritual into my research process emboldened me as a researcher by helping me understand that it is not by my own strength that I am able to do this work. Furthermore, remaining attuned to my spirit helped me to be attentive to the spirits of my participants, which transformed my research study into a faith filled, healing experience for all of us. During my final interviews with participants, several shared with me that our time together was cathartic and even therapeutic for them in some way, which was something that I had truly hoped for and had also felt. Professionally, I have had similar moments with students, when I chose to trust my instincts and not hide behind barriers that kept me distant and misaligned with my purpose.

Black feminist thought

Just as I had looked to Dillard's methodology of surrender to inform my research process, I looked to Black feminist thought (Collins, 2000) to examine the content of my conversations with participants. Grounded in an ethic of personal accountability and care, Black feminist thought describes how knowledge is produced and validated by Black women. Black feminist thought influenced the nature of my interviews with participants.

Personal accountability

Collins (2000) foregrounded the importance of dialogue in the production and assessment of knowledge claims among Black women. This knowledge production and validation process was consistent throughout my interviews with participants. An especially noteworthy example of this process was revealed during my third interview with Nadia. In the interviews, Nadia recounted several moments when she felt marginalised in her research lab. Through our conversations, Nadia came to a pivotal realisation about her peers' and advisor's perceptions of her as a Black woman:

> It's probably I'm not seen as equal. I don't know. Maybe that's what I'm saying. I know that I didn't see myself as equal, because I've been at that level for so long that I need to not even see myself as an equal, but just

see myself as the best that I can be, and love the people who perceive whatever it is, and that's what I'm building to be. That's where I'm trying to be now.

Notably, in the midst of this realisation, Nadia began to affirm herself by stating that striving to be seen as equal by her colleagues may not be a worthwhile endeavour, but she should aim to be her best anyway and trust that those who care for her will see her as she truly is and aspires to be. Later in the conversation, Nadia revisited her earlier statement about not being seen as an equal to her engineering colleagues:

Nadia: I'm still thinking about that thing I said like not [being] seen as equal, because I think that that pretty much summed it up.
Me: Right now, has that been one of the first times you've said that out loud?
Nadia: Yes. Right now. That was the first time I ever said that and thought about that. It's so clear. It's just good to get something clear and concise, because it's easy to process.
Me: I see it turning around in your mind, like, "Did I just say that?"
Nadia: I did.
Me: And then you're like, "Is that what it is? That's what it is." I see it's solidifying.

At the conclusion of the interview, I asked Nadia how participating in this research study influenced her, if at all. She responded:

It's helped me to process my thoughts. Even today I realised that I'd actually – this whole time – never thought that I was equal. That was what it boils down to, and I never would've thought about that if it wasn't for this study … Also, it just helps me to keep things more in perspective, and validate my own thoughts and know that I'm right. Just [diving into] the dialogue helps to know these things are actually real. Because at first, during the interview, the first interview, I was like, "I'm a Black student in engineering," but I think that I might've been imagining all of this stuff that's happened to me. I remember you've done a lot of head nods and said, "Actually, no, that's real. That's real stuff that's happening to you." And I said, "Okay, well maybe this is why I feel the way I have been feeling the last five or six years." And that was a decision to make too, to actually believe those things [were] actually happening, that I wasn't imagining them. That happened within the last year, probably six months. And what would it be like if I had never realised that? Just who – I don't even want to imagine, because I didn't have anybody to talk to about it. Yeah, this is a very helpful interview.

By engaging in dialogue with me about being a Black woman in engineering, Nadia was able to articulate and validate her experiences. Through conversation, she felt affirmed in her perception that her encounters with her peers and advisor were actually real and not imagined microaggressions. Further, in disclosing these experiences, she was able to reach a new truth about her feelings over the past six years: as a result of their mistreatment, she did not view herself as her colleagues' equal. However, in speaking that truth, Nadia felt encouraged to trust her instincts and validate her own thinking.

Personal expressiveness

In describing an ethic of care, Collins (2000) conveyed the importance of remaining attentive to the individual uniqueness among Black community members. With this principle in mind, I wanted each of my participants to have a unique interview experience where the questions asked were catered specifically to them. At the time of the second interview, I used excerpts from their journal reflections and incorporated the photos they took in their interview process. In the third interview, we revisited passages from their previous interviews and discussed how their thoughts had evolved over time. Further, there were moments of improvisation and impromptu questions that were raised in response to participants' remarks, which led to new directions and insights during the conversations. In the end, participants each had a personalised interview experience while they still attended to my original research questions. In an audio memo, I recorded a reflection about the personalisation of the interview process:

> If they were really excited and interested in music, like Harmony and like Bree were ... I mean we dug in. "Tell me. Tell me about the soundtrack to your life. Tell me what worship songs really move and get you going. Tell me how you feel when you play music." I mean we were talking about all sorts of things, and it was so cool, because I felt as though no matter what came up, even if it wasn't uniform between all of the participants, it made the experience so much richer, because it was unique to them. I was able to have a unique experience with each of them.

As I embraced the natural flow of conversation with my participants, while also intentionally bringing in content that was specific to each one, their personal expressiveness was able to shine through in the interviews.

Attending to participants' personal expressiveness in the study reminded me of how in my professional practice I seek to understand the unique talents and strengths of the students I work with. When I was a hall director in residence life, I learned that my staff members thrived when I tailored my supervision to who they were as individuals. For instance, when one of my staff members described his passion for engineering during a meeting, I suggested that he craft a programme engaging his residents in a hands-on, interactive activity that applied engineering design principles. The prospect of sharing his interests with others allowed his creativity to flourish and inspired me to invest more time in learning about and uplifting the unique gifts my staff members possessed.

Emotion

In Black feminist thought's ethic of care, another concept is emotion, which, according to Collins (2000), indicates a speaker's belief in the validity of their argument. As a researcher, I listen carefully for emotion in participants' expression, tone, and delivery as they share their stories. Such observation is essential in understanding participants' beliefs and how they make meaning of their experiences. During an interview with Nadia, I paid particular attention to the emotion she conveyed as she recounted several examples of being slighted, ignored, or disrespected in her research lab. After naming these incidents, she said:

> And then another thing I was thinking about today is – do you remember when there was some lion in Africa that got shot and it raised a lot of publicity? Like people were very, very upset that this lion was shot and killed, and around the same time I think it was a Black church that got burned to the ground. That moment was the moment I realised, to me – and I would love to be proven wrong – that in America an animal's body is seen or perceived as being more valuable than a Black body or a group of them. So just that event while I was in grad school made me realise the worth of being African American in America. Yeah that really upset me, because I still remember it, and I'm surprised at how much I thought about that quite a lot, you know.

When Nadia shared this, I was also grappling with emotions. After hearing example after example of the mistreatment she endured during her doctoral programme from peers and faculty, then sitting with her conclusion about the devaluation of Black people in America, I transitioned from disbelief to disappointment to anger, and it felt both appropriate and necessary to share those feelings with Nadia:

> I felt myself getting very angry, because you described what [your colleagues] did and I felt it's necessary to tell you that, that it's so wrong. And exactly what you said: that sometimes all of that passive aggression can make you feel like, "Am I imagining this?" Especially when they [say], "Oh, you're overreacting – I was giving you a compliment." Like no, that's not

what that was. So, I just want to affirm that, yes, those things are very much so real. And you are amazing because you are still making it through step by step, and these people aren't going to define or determine your future.

In remaining attentive to Nadia's emotions and expressing my own, we engaged in a shared process of knowledge validation. My response to Nadia's emotional account of her experiences affirmed their reality and further justified how she felt about those moments.

Empathy

Finally, from a Black feminist epistemological standpoint, empathy refers to a Black woman's ability to see herself in another's experience and thereby better understand that person. Over the course of six months, I had conducted a total of 48 interviews, and pored over the journals and photos thoughtfully provided by my 16 participants. After a final interview with one of the participants, she asked me how I felt after hearing so many women's stories. She specifically wanted to know whether I carried the weight of their experiences as a heavy burden. In the audio memo recorded after our conversation, I recounted my reply to her question:

> It's actually the opposite. I feel so light, because rarely do people – and I was thinking, specifically Black women – get a chance to put the bags down, the burdens, all the things that we carry all the time, the thoughts, fears, the worries, the stressors, the drama, the insecurities, everything. Here in this interview setting, I watched women put their bags down, and in turn I was able to put some stuff down. It's funny because even though I may not be directly in conversation, this is my experience, this is what happened to me, too. Hearing them articulate these moments of breakthrough and triumph and joy and revelation, I feel like they are describing some of the things that I am feeling, the things that I am going through as a person, as a student, as a Black woman. It is so powerful to have these shared moments. Whether they know it, shared or not, I know in my heart that that's what I was going through too, and that's what I needed to hear just then. I told her that she, without even realising it, was ministering to me.

As I listened to my participants' stories, I could see myself in them, which helped me understand them, and myself, better. Their wisdom was applicable to my life, and I could easily relate to their stories. By adopting an empathetic stance, I was able to take part in a mutual healing experience with the participants that led to understanding ourselves and one another more deeply.

Implications for research

As exemplified by my own research experience, the frameworks outlined by Dillard (2000, 2006) and Collins (2000) certainly have applicability for qualitative researchers. For instance, to love one's participants entails treating their truths with the care and dignity they deserve. One way to do that is by honouring participants' boundaries and welcoming authentic dialogue outside the confines of research. Showing compassion for participants could mean intentionally considering how to bring them joy through the research experience, by acknowledging their growth over the course of their interviews, for example, or offering a word of encouragement when participants share that they are going through challenging times. Reciprocity entails remembering that participants are not merely wells to be drawn from; rather, both the researcher and the participant are pitchers of water that have the capability of pouring out and being poured into. Adopting such a mindset can help researchers remember that the aim of research should not solely be to gain, but also to give. Engaging in ritual serves to remind researchers they have the potential to create sacred spaces where healing and transformation can occur with their participants. Being personally accountable for one's knowledge claims involves researchers acknowledging participants as producers and cocreators of knowledge, which can be assessed and validated through dialogue. Finally, adopting an ethic of care encourages researchers to better understand and care for participants by embracing their own emotions in addition to those of the participants while recognising participants' individuality and attempting to see themselves in participants' lives.

Implications for academic and student affairs practice

Black feminist thought and endarkened feminist epistemology have implications not only for research, but also for academic and student affairs practice. A useful question for student affairs practitioners to consider would be: What might a meditative, faith filled praxis look like? From an endarkened feminist epistemological perspective, it could mean listening carefully to students in the interest of ascertaining their truths and forgoing personal agendas to remain attuned to students' needs. It might entail actively working towards dismantling artificial boundaries that keep practitioners distant and indifferent to the humanity of students. Practitioners might also consider incorporating their spirituality into their practice, not in the interest of imposing particular belief systems, but rather to honour their own and students' spirits with the aim of engaging in more humanising and healing practice. Referring back to principles from Black feminist thought, student affairs practitioners should hold themselves accountable for their words and actions, remain attentive to the unique needs of students, take heed of students' emotions, express their own emotions as an act of affirming and understanding, and, finally, attempt to see themselves in their students' experiences to better reach and understand them.

Conclusion

The reimagining of researcher-participant relationships in qualitative research (re)centres the spirit from a Black feminist standpoint. Black feminist thought and endarkened feminist epistemology helped me reflect on my experiences as an academic and student affairs practitioner. These frameworks have provided me with the language to name the humanising, spiritually grounded approaches I have witnessed and employed in my professional practice. Although the examples were taken from my research with Black women, I would suggest that Black feminist thought and endarkened feminist epistemology offer principles that can be applied in work with participants and students of various backgrounds and identities. In essence, I find these frameworks useful in expanding notions of what good research and practice can look like. They raise considerations of how people might bring their full selves to interactions with participants and students and begin to take up the ethical, philosophical, and spiritual work of enacting principles of love, compassion, reciprocity, ritual, care, and accountability in practice. I encourage researchers and practitioners alike to reflect on how their own identities and experiences may influence their application of these principles. Cognisant that Black feminist thought and endarkened feminist epistemology are situated in the lived realities of Black women, researchers and practitioners should also thoughtfully consider how power, privilege, and oppression are implicated in their interpretations and use of these frameworks.

Utilising Black feminist thought and endarkened feminist epistemology to inform and examine my research practice illuminated possibilities in cultivating research relationships that are both humanising and healing:

> As researchers, whether we choose to be in more intimate and human relationship with the subjects of our work, and whether we choose to be subjects within the work ourselves will make the ultimate difference between the lessons we learn and the lessons we just "think about".
>
> *Dillard (2006, p. 81)*

In sharing the lessons that I have learned from applying Black feminist epistemologies to my research practice, it is my hope that researchers and higher education professionals will be encouraged to foster more intimate, humane, and right relationships with participants and students.

References

Carspecken, L. (2018). Introduction: Love in the time of ethnography. In L. Carspecken (Ed.), *Love in the time of ethnography: Essays on connections as a focus and basis for research* (pp. 1–14). Lanham, MD: Lexington Books.

Collins, P. H. (2000). *Black feminist thought: Knowledge, consciousness, and the politics of empowerment* (2nd ed.). New York, NY: Routledge.

Collins, P. H. (2009). *Black feminist thought: Knowledge, consciousness, and the politics of empowerment* (3rd ed.). New York, NY: Routledge.

Denton, J. M., Kortegast, C. A., & Miller, C. (2018). Overview of the use of visual methods in research. In B. Turner Kelly & C. A. Kortegast (Eds.), *Engaging images for research, pedagogy, and practice: Utilizing visual methods to understand and promote college student development* (pp. 13–28). Sterling, VA: Stylus.

Dillard, C. B. (2000). The substance of things hoped for, the evidence of things not seen: Examining an endarkened feminist epistemology in educational research and leadership. *International Journal of Qualitative Studies in Education, 13*(6), 661–681.

Dillard, C. B. (2006). *On spiritual strivings: Transforming an African American woman's academic life.* Albany, NY: State University of New York Press.

Grande, S. (2000). American Indian identity and intellectualism: The quest for a new red pedagogy. *International Journal of Qualitative Studies in Education, 13*(4), 343–359.

Maxwell, J. A. (2013). *Qualitative research design: An interactive approach* (3rd ed.). Thousand Oaks, CA: Sage.

10
FIELDWORK FOR LANGUAGE EDUCATION RESEARCH IN RURAL BANGLADESH

Ethical issues and dilemmas

M. Obaidul Hamid

It is common for scholars and researchers from developing countries to pursue higher degrees in research in Western academia. Often these researchers, particularly in the social sciences, humanities and education fields, base their research on fieldwork in their own societies. This 'insider' perspective, as is commonly suggested, may help to avoid cultural, ethical, and also epistemological concerns associated with research conducted by Western researchers (i.e., the 'outsider' perspective) in developing countries (Tuhiwai Smith, 1999). However, the insider perspective is also susceptible to ethical questions that are related on the one hand to researchers' identities and the ethical orientation of their research in Western academia, and local norms of social and cultural behaviours and the absence of institutionalised research ethics in their societies on the other. To date, these issues have received far from adequate attention in the literature.

I highlight here ethical dilemmas faced by insider researchers and invite discussion by presenting an experiential account of fieldwork in my own country, Bangladesh. With this end in mind, I discuss the relevance of the ethical codes emphasised by the ethics committee of an Australian university to the context of my fieldwork in rural Bangladesh. The discussion highlights personal ethical dilemmas, which resulted from an irreconcilable gap between the expectations of research ethics in Western academia and cultural realities and behavioural norms in the field. The contribution is divided into three sections. First, I introduce my research and its goals, and the specific social context in which it was located. Second, I position myself in relation to this research and its social context. This section emphasises the problematic nature of researcher identity and offers a critique of the insider–outsider dichotomy. In the final section, I relate a number of incidents from my fieldwork, which best reflect my ethical dilemmas and, consequently, my vulnerability as a fieldworker. I describe the implications of my experiences in the conclusion.

The PhD research and its setting

Fieldwork played an important part of my PhD study at the University of Queensland in Australia (Hamid, 2009). Using mixed methodologies, I investigated the relationship between Year 10 students' social biographies and their academic achievement in English in a rural sub-district in Bangladesh. The quantitative phase of the study involved two major instruments of data collection: (1) a questionnaire survey which elicited information on different aspects of the students' family economic, cultural, and social capital and their *habitus* (i.e., the students' attitudes, motivation and other dispositional characteristics) and (2) an English proficiency test. The qualitative phase included selective student ($n = 14$), parent ($n = 10$), and teacher (six English teachers and six head teachers) interviews. I limit my discussion to student and parent interviews. Student interviews focused on students' attitudes, motivations, English-learning experiences, future education plans and career goals, and their perceptions of the influence of their family situations on academic achievement. The parent interviews elicited information on parental perceptions of the importance of education and English learning for their children and parental involvement in children's schooling and academic achievement. For cultural, ethical as well as practical reasons all interviews were organised in the homes of students (Hamid, 2009).

Nadiranga

The study was situated in a rural, peripheral sub-district called Nadiranga (a pseudonym) in northern Bangladesh, a South Asian nation of 160 million Muslim-majority people. Nadiranga with a population of 115,000 is one of the poorest sub-districts in Bangladesh (Hamid, 2009). The literacy rate of people aged seven and over in Nadiranga is 33%, compared to the national literacy rate of 45%.

Nadiranga is situated 500 km from the Bangladeshi capital, Dhaka. The sub-district has a rural, agricultural base with a small central town, in which the local government headquarters, a marketplace, three colleges and two secondary schools are located. Ten other secondary schools exist in more remote areas of the region, in addition to 116 primary schools, which offer free education to children up to Year 5.

Poverty and underdevelopment characterise the socio-economic profile of Nadiranga. The famine which took place in Bangladesh in 1974 (after the nation's independence from Pakistan in 1971) was experienced most severely in Nadiranga. This human disaster gained international attention from donors and agencies that set up non-governmental organisations (NGOs), such as the Switzerland-based Terre des Hommes (locally known as *Chhinnamukul*) and Rangpur Dinajpur Rehabilitation Services (RDRS), to run rehabilitation programmes in the area for starving children. Dozens of NGOs, funded by government and international agencies, were operating microfinance, health and sanitation, non-formal education and livelihood programmes at the time of my fieldwork in the last quarter of 2006.

Challenges in researching English language education in Nadiranga

The focus of my research was the teaching and learning of English in Nadiranga. I developed an interest in understanding the social circumstances and academic experiences of low-income and disadvantaged students in Nadiranga as a result of my own experience as a child, having been rehabilitated in Chhinnamukul from 1977 until 1987 along with hundreds of other children. Towards the end of my stay at the rehabilitation centre, I saw firsthand that my fellow rehabilitees were not able to continue their schooling once they were sent back to their homes, as their impoverished and uneducated parents could ill afford the educational expenses. After I left Chhinnamukul permanently, I continued my education although I was forced to earn my own living and educational expenses. I gained valuable insider experience, and after two decades my PhD project provided an opportunity to investigate the English learning experiences of students in Nadiranga in relation to their social backgrounds.

English came to Bangladesh in the wake of British colonial rule. It is widely believed to be a language of power, prestige, and social mobility which is required for higher education and employment in the country. Bangladeshi state policies have made English compulsory for Year 1–12 students throughout the country (Hamid, 2011). I was interested in investigating whether and to what extent poorer students from a rural region such as Nadiranga could utilise the benefits of English learning to ensure their economic and social mobility in a competitive society. The appropriateness of the teaching and learning of English in socio-economically disadvantaged regions such as Nadiranga might invite ethical questions, particularly when one considers the issues of limited resources and spending resources on priority areas such as poverty alleviation or literacy development in the first language (Bruthiaux, 2002). However, discussing ethics in relation to English language education in marginalised societies is too broad and complex of an issue to be incorporated into the scope of the present contribution.

I had anticipated several problems for the fieldwork in a familiar social setting. First, Nadiranga had gained the reputation of being 'aid-dependent' and its consequences continued in the mindset of local people. I held concerns that my research could be misconstrued as being commissioned by an international aid agency and would result in a development programme for the socio-economic benefit of local residents. Indeed, when I was making copies of my survey instruments in a local copy shop during my fieldwork, the shop owner (who did not know me) remarked that I must be working for an NGO. His observation was understandable given the number of NGOs operating in the locality and the extent of fieldwork carried out by NGO workers and activists. Fieldwork for educational research was unknown in this locality and one of the challenges I anticipated was how to communicate to the local people that fieldwork could be carried out for independent educational research and, more importantly, that not all fieldwork is commissioned by aid agencies. I was unsure whether or how this issue was relevant to the Ethics Committee of the University of Queensland. Therefore, I did not elaborate on this issue in my application for ethical clearance. However, this was a crucial issue in my judgement. Fortunately, at the end of my fieldwork I was pleased that the local people did understand and appreciate the nature and purpose of my research which became widely known in the locality.

The second challenge was related to my identity and its implications for research and fieldwork. I was born and raised in Nadiranga. Although I left Nadiranga for higher studies and employment, I remained connected to the locality through regular visits to my parents, relatives, and friends. I was well-known in the region first as a 'high-achieving' student and later as an academic at the University of Dhaka. I was the only person to embody that professional identity in the region. My new identity as a researcher was added to these established identities, which invited ethical questions. As Sikes (2006, p. 110) observes:

> People considering embarking on insider research have to think very carefully about what taking on the role and identity of researcher can mean and involve in a setting where they are normally seen as someone else with particular responsibilities and powers.

I had anticipated that my professional identity and its valuation, particularly in a disadvantaged region, would create social distance between me and my interviewees. In hindsight, this identity had an impact on my interactions with different groups of participants in complex ways. For instance, I was addressed as 'Sir'[1] by the majority of student interviewees. It is interesting that these students gave preference to my professional identity and muted my local identity in our conversations. The remaining students did not use an address form. Is it plausible that these students preferred my researcher identity (distant and objective) and considered me an outsider? In comparison, the English teachers whom I interviewed accepted me 'as one of them', although this may have been tempered by a misunderstanding of my professional identity with possible connections to the central education authority in Dhaka, and could have made them cautious of expressing their views on English teaching in schools. I suggest that it is irrelevant whether researchers claim an insider or outsider perspective. What is important is to identify to which of our multiple identities our participants refer at a particular moment, and to recognise that not all participants may refer to the same identity.

Although claiming an insider perspective is common in the description of researchers' relationships with their research and/or their social contexts, this position-taking can actually be more complex. Apparently, I had good reasons to claim an insider perspective. I was a member of the local community by virtue of birth, upbringing, and permanent home address.[2] Unlike many researchers in developing societies who belong to the local elite (Rizvi, 1993), I was born into a lower-class family and as such could claim affinity with the students and parents with whom I worked. My class and self-consciousness enabled me to empathise with my student interviewees who expressed a strong desire for social mobility through education but felt constrained by economic necessity. Nevertheless, I questioned whether I could really claim to be an insider in Nadiranga. I had left the area 20 years earlier, the locality would have changed substantially over time, as had my own values and outlook. I studied English literature at university which brought me closer to the values of British society, and later moved to Australia to study, where my orientation changed again to reflect the research and ethical norms of Western academia. Could I still claim to be an insider in Nadiranga simply because of birth and upbringing?

Making sense of Western research ethics and ethical dilemmas

Before I could start my fieldwork in Nadiranga, I had to apply for ethical clearance from the Ethics Committee within the School of Languages and Comparative Cultural Studies at the University of Queensland. The Committee emphasised the principles of informed consent, privacy, confidentiality, anonymity, participants' right to withdraw from research and avoiding harm to 'vulnerable groups' (children, in the case of my research, who were aged 15–16 years). These are standard ethical codes which are more or less common to institutional review boards (IRBs) in Western academia (Israel & Hay, 2006).

Given that my application for ethical clearance was in a prescribed form which contained a fixed set of Western ethical issues previously noted, I found myself in a situation where I was forced to view the social, cultural, and ethical questions in Nadiranga through the prescribed ethical criteria. I was required to conform to these criteria for the sake of my research and the research degree towards which I was working. Said differently, I felt more concerned about research ethics *in theory* (i.e., in the application) than *in reality* (i.e., in the field). I had conversations with my fellow PhD scholars in social sciences and education who had already obtained ethical clearance for their research. I came to understand that they had similar experiences when they worked on their ethical clearance applications.

This engagement with the ethics in theory, which to some extent compromises ethical concerns, in reality is required for successful ethical clearance application.[3] Nevertheless, it was difficult to satisfy the Ethics Committee which required that I revise my application, although not substantially. The issues raised by the Committee were mostly related to language, style, and conventional expectations of ethical clearance application with which I was not sufficiently familiar on account of my inexperience and inadequate socialisation. More importantly, the Committee raised issues concerning the sociocultural appropriateness of some fieldwork documents in terms of language and discourse:

> A few of the committee members feel that the consent and information sheets are overly wordy and not necessarily socio-culturally appropriate. The committee requests that you consider more user-friendly and simple language for your information packet. It is important to create documents that can be genuinely read, understood, and signed. At present some members feel the wording is too dense.[4]

The emphasis on simple and user-friendly language conveyed through this feedback is generally appreciable. However, the judgement that the documents were 'overly wordy' and 'not necessarily socio-culturally appropriate' was based on Western modes of discourse and communication, although implicitly it was assumed to be universal. Conventional expectations of written communication in Bangladesh are different from those in the West. In government departments letters from the public are expected to be verbose. Anecdotal evidence shows that letters sent to government offices can be returned to their writers if conventional expectations of format, content and the degree of formality or verbosity are not considered. Since the two documents in question along with the application for gatekeeper permission (see the discussion that follows) had to be submitted to central education authorities in Dhaka, those social expectations of written communication were taken into consideration while drafting them. Interestingly, documents prepared by a local researcher for local use were judged 'socio-culturally inappropriate' by a non-local IRB who had little knowledge of the society or the culture in question.

In addition, the committee's feedback had implications for translation in ethics clearance application. I had noted in my application that the two documents would be translated into Bangla[5] which was the dominant language of communication in Bangladesh. Although the documents were found dense and verbose *in English*, they might not be necessarily so *in Bangla*. This was not taken into consideration in the Committee's feedback. What was the issue was the questions of language and social reality as well as Western modes of discourse and communication; IRBs can be guided by a monolingual (English) view of the world.

Revising my application in the light of the feedback, I eventually obtained provisional ethical clearance for my research and was advised by the Committee to obtain gatekeeper permission from educational authorities in Bangladesh for final clearance. I applied for this permission from the Directorate of Secondary and Higher Education (DSHE), which reports to the Ministry of Education of the Government of Bangladesh. In Bangladesh bureaucracy is slow, and intervention is often sought. I requested approval from the official responsible in person and obtained an official letter of approval in two weeks. Importantly, the authorities did not offer comment or raise concerns about the fieldwork on ethical grounds. Either the Bangladeshi authorities were satisfied with the ethical clearance from the Ethics Committee of the University of Queensland or they were not concerned about ethical issues in educational research. In the absence of any ethical prescriptions from the DSHE, I was bound now only to abide by the principles prescribed by the Australian IRB. However important in theory, many of these principles either did not make sense or were impossible to abide by once I started my fieldwork. I will demonstrate this with examples in the following pages.

Informed consent and right to withdrawal

The concept of informed consent requires that research participants be fully informed of the research, the nature and extent of their participation and their right to withdraw from the study at any stage of the research (Israel & Hay, 2006, p. 61). Accordingly, I briefed student participants in groups about the research in their schools and requested their participation. Although I explained clearly that participation was voluntary, the students were not free in reality to decide whether or not to participate because of: (1) my professional and local identity and (2) the obligation created by head teachers in asking for the students' full cooperation. As to (1), probably the students could not refuse a university academic who was a former student of one of their schools and who was researching *their* experience in English learning in Nadiranga. With regard to (2), showing respect and obeisance to (head) teachers is socially binding for Bangladeshi students. All students from whom I requested participation in the eight schools in Nadiranga instantly agreed to contribute to the study. Whether or not their participation was voluntary could not be ascertained.

Once the students verbally agreed to participate in the study, I handed them the participant information package along with consent forms for them and their parents to sign. The consent forms were returned with student and parent signatures by the deadline agreed. However, it remains unclear whether parents were fully informed of the research by the information package. This was the case particularly with parents of little or no formal education who may not have comprehended what was involved, and may have been persuaded to sign the consent forms by their children. In the case of parents without the ability to write their names, the children themselves might have signed the forms on their behalf.

From a different perspective, however, informed consent is not an issue in a social context like Nadiranga where being able to participate in the work of people with higher education is considered an honour bestowed upon those who participate. For many students and parents, the invitation to participate in the research was an opportunity to help a university academic (who also belonged to the local community) and therefore there was no question of non-participation. In fact, failure to participate could mean loss of opportunity. For instance, I selected only small samples of students from three schools for pilot testing of my survey instruments. In one of these schools a few students who were not selected asked me why I had deprived them of the opportunity to participate. My explanations of the purpose of the pilot test did not prove convincing, and their understanding was that they had been denied an experience that their friends alone would be able to relate to family and other locals.

The problem of exclusion arose again on a larger scale when I began working with students on the questionnaire survey and English proficiency test. For resource and time constraints I planned to work with selected secondary schools in Nadiranga. A few schools were excluded when the criteria of school location and gender of the student population were considered. One day I met the headteachers of two of the excluded schools in the marketplace who enquired why I decided not to work in their schools. They informed me that their students were aware of my research and had requested that I be invited to work with them as well. I explained my research constraints and was able to convince the headteachers why I could not work with students in all schools. Even then I had to offer assurances that I would visit their schools and talk to students, although they were not going to be my research participants.

The home setting and issues of hospitality, politeness and obligation

As previously noted, the students and their parents were interviewed in their homes for social, cultural, and practical reasons. Ethical issues arising from fieldwork in the home setting have been discussed by Yee and Andrews (2006). These researchers pointed out identity conflicts in the home setting – between a professional researcher and a guest – since they had to suppress their researcher identities and act as proper guests. My fieldwork with students and parents in their homes presented similar conflicts. However, in my case the ethical issues were more complex than those suggested by these researchers.

For the majority of the interviews, I visited the homes and requested appointments with the parents and students. With a few families, I was able to request an appointment by mobile phone.[6] When I spoke to the father of one female student, one of the few wealthy men in Nadiranga, and asked for an appointment, he agreed on one condition: that I interview him and his daughter and have lunch at his residence. His condition placed me in a difficult ethical situation. On the one hand I wanted to conduct the interview in order to understand the economic, social, and cultural capital that was invested by the family in the schooling and academic experiences of this high-performing student. On the other hand, as a researcher I was hesitant to accept the invitation as it would mean much time and effort on the part of the family. I attempted to avoid accepting their hospitality as politely as possible, but the father was insistent. Finally, I relented and accepted his luncheon invitation as well as his consent to the interviews. Although my researcher self was not entirely happy with the resolution, I justified myself on several grounds. First, it was important that I interview the daughter and the father of this wealthy family. Second, although the lunch was going to cost the family in terms of time, effort, and money, at least money was not a concern. I decided to take some local sweets, the most appropriate gift to take on such occasions. However, the crucial reason for not declining his invitation was related to my insider identity. He was a socially distinguished man and as such deserved my respect and obedience. Saying 'no' to him (or to any person of his standing in Nadiranga) would be interpreted as conceit based on my professional academic and researcher identity, which I could not allow. I admit I could not hold fast to my researcher identity, and not at the expense of my other identities associated with the place of my birth.

Interviewing students and parents from poor and disadvantaged families also presented ethical dilemmas. Bangladeshi people, particularly in rural areas, are very hospitable and offer food to their visitors, whatever the purpose of their visit. A show of hospitality to me was predictable particularly as I was a familiar person in the locality. Moreover, I was considered 'a role model' for their children seeking social mobility through education. Almost all the homes I visited for interviews offered me food; some provided light refreshments while others substantial meals. Although I tried to reciprocate by bringing local sweets, I felt uncomfortable, particularly in those homes where it became clear to me that spending even a little extra money on food was a sacrifice on their part given their socio-economic status. However, I could not refuse the food offered to me. I was aware that doing so would send an inappropriate message: that I considered the food not good enough for my (recently achieved) social standing.

Privacy and confidentiality

The concept of privacy as defined in Western academia was not applicable to the context of my fieldwork in the home setting. The homes of the poor students and their parents where the interviews took place cannot be called 'private spaces' in the sense used in the West. Their dwelling places were open to their next-door neighbours, friends, and relatives. Most of the houses (made of bamboo, thatch, and corrugated iron sheets) are so close to one another that a neighbour can hear everything that is said in the house next door. My conversations with interviewees would have been audible to neighbours. Consequently, privacy and confidentiality of the views expressed by the interviewees could not be maintained.

The confidentiality of the views of interviewees was affected in yet another way. The interview was a special event for the family and their next-door neighbours. Although it was arranged inside the house, once I started conversations, I found that we were being observed by other family members and neighbours. Yee and Andrews encountered the same problem in their fieldwork in the home setting and found it "impossible to identify beforehand who will be present at the interview" (2006, p. 408).

In the West this would be considered a breach of privacy and confidentiality. However, I felt helpless to do anything. Did I have the right to ask people to leave and let us continue conversations in private? No, I did not. I myself was an outsider in the house. I could not ask them to leave, although allowing them to stay and listen to my interview was a breach of privacy, both morally and ethically.

Although these incidents demonstrate the breach of privacy and confidentiality of the views of the interviewees from the Western perspective, this was not considered so in the context of the fieldwork. The people I interviewed had lived their entire lives in privacy-deficient environments. There was nothing wrong with entering a neighbour's house without permission. In fact, asking for permission would be considered unusual. Similarly, their conversations with an outsider (the researcher) would not be considered private or confidential in their judgement; it was a public event and therefore accessible to other family members and neighbours. It was probably unfathomable to them how one of them (the interviewee) could hold private conversations with someone (the researcher) who was not one of their family members or neighbours.

Occasionally, privacy had to be sacrificed for the sake of social and cultural appropriateness. Being a male adult, it is socially and religiously inappropriate to interview a female student by myself inside the house. Therefore, I was required to request a parent or sibling to be present while I conducted the interview. Doing so was to compromise the privacy of her views, but not to do so would have compromised social norms of appropriate behaviour. This example clearly demonstrates that despite the ethical requirement to adhere to the researcher's identity, an individual's other identities (gender in this case) and their implications for fieldwork cannot be ignored or superseded.

In sum, the hegemony of Western academia assumes that the concepts of privacy and confidentiality are universal. In reality, however, they are not, as

I have discussed in relation to my fieldwork. Western approaches to ethics are based on an individualistic view of society which does not characterise many societies in Asia or Africa. These societies, in general, view individuals as closely integrated into community and social networks. Therefore, the concepts of self and 'other' and related notions of privacy and confidentiality as applied to research ethics in Western academia appear significantly different, if not entirely irrelevant, in these societies.

Avoiding harm

The ethical requirement of avoiding harm to my Year 10 participants and their parents proved problematic. The research, inspired by critical approaches to applied linguistics (Pennycook, 2004), aimed at highlighting geographic and socio-economic differences in English learning opportunities and their consequences in the Bangladeshi society. Asking students about personal and experiential issues evoked unhappy experiences of meeting socio-economic challenges at this 'vulnerable' age. The inner struggles of the students surfaced during the course of interviews. Struggles existed between their desire for a better life through educational achievement and their frustration at the manifold constraints their social origins brought upon successful learning and academic achievement (Baldauf & Hamid, 2009). For example, Afrin, a self-conscious student from a remote school whose parents had lost their lands to the river and were about to lose their home, observed that she held no expectations of her forthcoming school-leaving examination or her future education or career. She implied that it was meaningless to 'dream' about future education or career aspirations as she knew well her parents could not support her in pursuing those dreams. Sathi, whose mother headed their family after her father's death, wished to have an MA qualification in the future. However, she said, "I wish, but it seems I won't be able to make it". Her explanation was, "Our family income is not adequate enough to maintain our family. How can my mother bear my educational expenses up to that level [MA]"? (Hamid, 2009, p. 168). Similarly, Rajib, a young man who was responsible for his mother and siblings in the absence of his father who had gone to Dhaka in search of manual work, indicated his feelings of helplessness, his desire for a university education, and the reality of his socio-economic situation:

Researcher: Do you have a wish to go to university?
Rajib: Yes, I do ... But I am not sure if my dream will come true because of our economic problems.

Hamid (2009, p. 168)

The interviews did cause distress, however temporary, by requiring students to talk about their experiences of socio-economic marginality and their hopelessness in pursuing educational aspirations. The psychological impact of the interviews is undeniable in the case of Monir who recollected how his family's socio-economic condition had affected his self-determination:

Researcher: Do you get all the things that you need for your studies – for example, books, pens, papers and then, money for taking private lessons – from home?
Monir: No, not as much as I need.
Researcher: What sort of problems is caused by this?
Monir: Sorry?
Researcher: I mean you said you don't get all the things that you need. How does it affect your studies?
Monir: Not getting the things affects my studies. It changes my mentality.
Researcher: Ok, what kind of change in your mentality?
Monir: For instance, I need a book but I can't buy it, and it affects my studies. I can't prepare my lessons before I go to the class.
Researcher: Yes.
Monir: That's why I feel bad and think about giving up my studies. In those moments I become upset and keep myself away from my studies. I suffer from tensions and agonies.

Hamid (2009, pp. 164–165)

On another occasion the impact of the interview was dramatic and left me embarrassed. I was interviewing Mitun's father, who was a manual worker. When asked to explain his family contribution to his daughter's education, he expressed worry and frustration: his income was not enough even for regular family meals. It was beyond his means to provide Mitun with study requirements such as books and private tutoring. He was well aware of the importance of education and of English for his 15-year-old daughter. Although he wanted Mitun to continue her studies to secure a better future, he knew how little he was able to help her academically and financially. The interview reminded him of his 'failure' to fulfil this parental duty. Suddenly, he burst into tears and kept sobbing. I was ill-prepared for such emotional moments and did not know how to respond. I remained silent and allowed the powerful emotions to subside.

It was difficult for me to wear the mask of a dispassionate researcher in the wake of the distress occasioned by the interviews. The helplessness of the students who belonged to my community called for the activation of a different identity – that of a counsellor and supporter. I deliberately took up the role of counsellor and friend to many of the young men and women whose hearts I was able to read having passed through similar experiences of distress in my struggle for social establishment. After each of the interviews I encouraged the students to carry on despite their struggles and encouraged hope in a better future. I offered myself as a source of inspiration, reminding the students that I was not unlike them at their age. In doing so, I abandoned my researcher identity and assumed the role of confidant and activist for educational reform to ensure a better future for the young men and women of Nadiranga.

Implications and conclusions

My experience in working with the students and parents in a peripheral, rural community in Bangladesh has implications for IRBs in Western academia as well as for ethical fieldwork in developing countries. The account suggests that insider researchers can draw on their tacit knowledge of local social, cultural norms, and values to understand their research participants and make sense of the latter's thoughts, words, and experiences. In addition, this knowledge enables these researchers to behave in socially and culturally appropriate ways with their participants in their fieldwork. However, as I have argued in this chapter, the insider perspective is more complex than is commonly assumed. Not all local researchers are truly insiders because they may have social status differences with their research participants. Moreover, their training in Western academia with regard to research ethics and methodology raises questions about their insider identity in their own societies.

The absence of local IRBs for social and educational research in developing countries leaves local researchers necessarily accountable to their own conscience and professional ethics. In addition, there is a requirement that researchers follow the ethical principles prescribed by ethics review boards in their affiliated institutions in the West. As discussed in this chapter, this creates a different set of ethical dilemmas for researchers as many Western ethical principles are not applicable to the social contexts of the developing world. Institutionalisation of local research ethics is apparently a solution to the problem. However, if there are discrepancies between local and Western review boards in terms of the definition of research ethics and ethical rules, the question will be, which ethics review board to follow – the local or Western?

In the absence of locally institutionalised research ethics, IRBs in the West could take a more flexible stance in granting ethical clearance to researchers seeking to research their own societies. If the fieldwork is to be carried out in a Bangladeshi local context, for example, it is questionable why the fieldwork should strictly follow the prescriptions of an Australian IRB. Signing memoranda of understanding between institutions in the developing and developed world may be a good step towards devising common platforms based on negotiations with regard to ethics for social and educational research.

The experiential account presented lends support to the contention that IRBs in Western academia may not fully prepare researchers for the unexpected in the field in developing societies (Gallagher, Creighton, & Gibbons, 1995). Therefore, the unexpected is to be expected and should be 'thought over' (Wilson, 1993) and handled locally and contextually with reference to appropriate social norms and professional conduct. The researcher should remember that adhering to an objective, dispassionate researcher identity, however desirable, is not always feasible.

Acknowledgements

I would like to acknowledge the contributions of Nanette Gottlieb, Roland Sussex and Richard Baldauf to my PhD research, and Jo Grimmond who provided valuable feedback on an earlier draft.

Notes

1. It is common practice in Bangladesh to address teachers as 'Sir' by students (and other people), even if the latter were never taught by the former.
2. Every Bangladeshi citizen has a permanent address which remains his/her address forever. My permanent address no longer exists because the home as well as my village was destroyed by the river. Even then my passport carries this address since it cannot be changed.
3. This is evidenced by the ethical dilemmas described and analysed in this chapter. Although I obtained ethical approval for my research and the fieldwork, I could not abide by the ethical prescriptions of the IRB when faced with real people and their economic, social, and cultural values and givens.
4. Copied from the feedback of the Ethics Committee on my ethical clearance application in July 2006.
5. I had not enclosed Bangla translations of the documents because the Committee or the School did not have access to this language.
6. Bangladesh has made significant progress in spreading the mobile phone network throughout the country. Mobile phone numbers are treated as private and confidential information in the West. However, this is not so in Bangladesh, particularly in rural areas. One can easily obtain someone's mobile phone number from another person and make a phone call. The issue of privacy or confidentiality is not relevant here.

References

Baldauf, R. B., & Hamid, M. O. (2009, August). *English, socio-economic disadvantage and ELT policy: Insights from rural Bangladesh*. Paper presented at the Asia TEFL International Conference, Bangkok, Thailand.

Bruthiaux, P. (2002). Hold your courses: Language education, language choice, and economic development. *TESOL Quarterly, 36*, 275–296.

Gallagher, B., Creighton, S., & Gibbons, J. (1995). Ethical dilemmas in social research: No easy solutions. *British Journal of Social Work, 25*, 295–311.

Hamid, M. O. (2009). *Sociology of language learning: Social biographies and school English achievement in rural Bangladesh* (Doctoral dissertation, University of Queensland, Brisbane, Australia). Retrieved from https://espace.library.uq.edu.au/view/UQ:178929

Hamid, M. O. (2011). Planning for failure: English and language policy and planning in Bangladesh. In J. Fishman & O. Garcia (Eds.), *Handbook of language and ethnic identity* (Vol. 2, pp. 192–203). Oxford, England: Oxford University Press.

Israel, M., & Hay, I. (2006). *Research ethics for social scientists: Between ethical conduct and regulatory compliance.* Thousand Oaks, CA: Sage.

Pennycook, A. (2004). Critical applied linguistics. In A. Davies & C. Elder (Eds.), *The handbook of applied linguistics* (pp. 784–807). Oxford, England: Blackwell.

Rizvi, S. (1993). Fieldwork in a familiar setting: The role of politics at the national, community and household levels. In S. Devereux & J. Hoddinott (Eds.), *Fieldworks in developing countries* (pp. 153–163). Boulder, CO: Lynne Rienner.

Sikes, P. (2006). On dodgy ground? Problematics and ethics of educational research. *International Journal of Research & Method in Education, 29*, 105–117.

Tuhiwai Smith, L. (1999). *Decolonizing methodologies: Research and indigenous peoples.* London, England: Zed Books.

Wilson, K. (1993). Thinking about the ethics of fieldwork. In S. Devereux & J. Hoddinott (Eds.), *Fieldworks in developing countries* (pp. 179–199). Boulder, CO: Lynne Reinner.

Yee, W. C., & Andrews, J. (2006). Professional researcher or a 'good guest'? Ethical dilemmas involved in researching children and families in the home setting. *Educational Review, 58*, 397–413.

11
INFORMED CONSENT IN EDUCATIONAL RESEARCH IN THE SOUTH

Tensions and accommodations

Fauzia Shamim and Rashida Qureshi

The codes of educational research ethics developed by the American Educational Research Association (AERA), and the British Educational Research Association (BERA), as well as those produced by Institutional Review Boards of different universities of the North, are available aplenty, and educational researchers are expected to abide by these international guidelines in order to be considered 'rigorous' for academic purposes and 'authentic' for publication of findings. At the same time, there is a growing body of literature on the inadequacy of these ethical codes/guidelines, particularly for conducting research in known and emerging contexts in the South (Nolen & Puten, 2007; Shamim & Qureshi, 2010; Small, 2002). While the principles – for example, protecting the rights of human subjects can be universal, their application requires contextual knowledge, particularly in terms of culturally appropriate norms of behaviour in a given research context. To the point that research is as specific as it is universal, researchers from varied research contexts have highlighted multiple complexities in following the international codes of research ethics (Ashraf, 2010; Rarieya, 2010; Shamim, 1993; Taylor, Plaice, & Perley, 2010).

The purpose of this chapter is to underscore the need for an ongoing dialogue among academic scholars in the North or Centre, dominated by Anglo-American culture and philosophies, and the scholars in the South in regard to ethical standards and their application in varied research locales, particularly in the peripheries. This will be done by highlighting some tensions and accommodations required in the translation of a 'universal' ethical principle in the field, that is, informed consent (IC). Our aim is to build a case for a hybridity[1] or a global perspective that is a position of "limited cultural pluralism" (Qureshi, 2010, p. 94). This position differentiates between principles and their application(s) somewhat similarly to Howe and Moses (1999), who state that it is necessary in contemporary research, defined by them as research after the "interpretive" turn, to differentiate between contemporary fundamental principles, such as that of IC, and operating principles, that is, the methodological "nitty-gritty of techniques and principles" (p. 39). This is an important distinction for the purposes of our argument in this chapter. We contend that the former should be broad and eco-transferable, while the latter needs to be eco-specific (cf. Sikes, 2006), that is, rooted in local cultures (and subcultures) and specific research environments (Hsiung, 2012; Qureshi, 2010; Simon & Usher, 2000).

A subsidiary purpose of our chapter is to 'increase the visibility of those (who are sitting) on the peripheries' of the academic community (Cisneros Puebla, Figaredo, Faux, Kolbel, & Packer, 2006; Mruck, Puebla, César, & Faux, 2005). For illustrating our position, we will use specific examples from previous research, our own observations and accounts of students and colleagues, mainly from Pakistan (and some from Saudi Arabia), to examine tensions and accommodations that relate to a widely accepted ethical principle, that is, gaining IC from participants, including negotiating entry into the field. While we draw on examples from research conducted mainly in Pakistan, an Islamic country in the South, the issues raised, the scenarios discussed and the interpretations presented are relevant to similar contexts elsewhere.

The rationale for choosing the principle of IC is that: (1) IC is at the heart of field research, (2) for many researchers, getting IC may appear a straightforward procedure following a standard research methods textbook with its 'dos' and 'don'ts', while, in a context like Pakistan, even negotiating entry in the field before IC can be gained requires wading through layers of social controls. More importantly, as discussed later, other variables, such as gender roles in these communities, give rise to questions such as 'Who has the right to give consent and on whose behalf?', which adds to the overall complexity of the process of acquiring IC.

The rationale for confining our discussion to the principle of IC only is the limitation of space.

Research environment in Pakistan

Professional research as an academic activity is slowly emerging in Pakistan. However, like many other peripheral countries, the research culture in Pakistan is not strong, despite the fact that almost all institutions of higher learning require research work as part of their degree programmes.[2] The inception of the Higher Education Commission (HEC) in 2002 has played a positive role in promoting the research culture in Pakistan by providing incentives to researchers and taking measures to build the capacity of academics and by linking selection/promotion of teaching faculty on the bases of their research publications (Lodhi, 2012). However, the HEC has not taken any explicit position with respect to the Code of Ethics, except for plagiarism, for 'Pakistani' researchers or research studies conducted in Pakistan with local 'subjects'.[3] Similarly, the majority of universities in Pakistan, both public and private, do not have their own research policy or a requirement for ethical clearance by their students or staff. This leaves Pakistani researchers without any 'official' or uniform ethical standards of practice to adhere to. However, relevant to the purpose of our chapter is the fact that Pakistani researchers, in order to publish their research studies in international journals in particular, have to show evidence of following some code of ethics. Consequently, the majority of the higher education faculty in Pakistan use AERA/BERA and the Institutional Review Boards' codes of ethical conduct as reference points in their research.

A number of non-governmental organisations, both national and international, and community-based organisations mostly working in the social development sector also produce monitoring and evaluation reports and monographs. However, as these are mainly meant for internal consumption, adherence to any ethical standards is neither emphasised nor shared with the wider research community.

Hsiung (2012) asserts that the 'Anglo-American core' principles are introduced in the periphery through 'returnees', that is, scholars who are educated in Western universities. The Pakistan Association for Research in Education (PARE) fits the description.[4] The large majority of the founding members of this fledgling organisation, created a few years ago, have received degrees from Anglo-American institutions of higher learning. The goal of the association is to promote educational research in Pakistan. However, the members have not even started debating the ethical dilemmas and issues related to international ethical standards and local research environment in Pakistan. In the history of research methodologies of the South, it was the use of 'common sense' that gave practitioners the genre of participatory research approaches, more Indigenous in character than any other so-called rigorous positivist approaches (Halai & Wiliam, 2012).

Informed consent (IC) in theory

The principle of IC, first enunciated in the Nuremberg code, has been refined and legally defined, especially in the field of biomedical and behavioural research. Important for our purposes, however, is the Belmont Report, published by the National Commission for the Protection of Human Participants of Biomedical and Behavioral Research [National Commission] (1978). Consistent with our position in this chapter, the Belmont Report outlines the basic ethical principles and their applications, thus distinguishing clearly between 'research and practice'. 'Respect for persons', which embodies the consent of the participants is one of the three basic principles outlined in the Belmont Report (the other two are 'Beneficence' and 'Justice').

Informed consent of the research participants, according to the Belmont report (National Commission, 1978), includes at least two ethical convictions:

> first, that individuals should be treated as autonomous agents, and second, that persons with diminished autonomy are entitled to protection. The principle of respect for persons thus divides into two separate moral requirements: the requirement to acknowledge autonomy and the requirement to protect those with diminished autonomy. (pp. 3–4)

The first ethical conviction – autonomy – requires that subjects, to the degree that they are capable, be given the opportunity to choose what shall or shall not happen to them (Howe & Moses, 1999, p. 24). When made operational through the notion of IC, 'autonomy' refers to voluntary consent of the participants in a research study after they have received adequate information about the study objectives and methodology and what their participation would entail in terms of 'burdens and benefits' to health or welfare of individuals or society at large. Normally, there should be documentation to show that IC was gained from the participants – it is recommended that participants' consent be gained by giving them an IC form to sign prior to the study or at the start of data collection. The participants also have the right to withdraw their consent at any point during the study without fear of any negative consequences. Similarly, refusal to participate on the part of research participants is binding even if their refusal results in a failure to maximise assumed benefits (AERA, 2011; BERA, 2011).

The second ethical conviction – protection – as part of IC seeks to protect research participants with 'diminished autonomy' or vulnerable populations, for example, children, prisoners, from deceit and coercion. Predominantly, in the discourse of research, however, the first ethical conviction prevails; research participants are considered autonomous and capable of deciding for themselves; their decision whether to participate in a study or not is based on information provided by the researcher. Thus, research participants, rather than the researcher or funding agencies, have the right to weigh the risks and possible harm of participating in a study (Howe & Moses, 1999, p. 23).

Respect for persons also includes privacy, which is protected by the IC principle as:

> part of the informed consent process is describing to participants just what the risks to their privacy might be and what measures will be taken to ensure anonymity and confidentiality; in this way, how important privacy might be, and why, largely devolves to individuals' exercise of autonomy.
>
> *Howe and Moses (1999, pp. 25–26)*

It is important to note that some qualitative researchers, such as Christians (2005), question the relevance of both autonomy and privacy, mainly derived from positivism, to contemporary qualitative research. However, we regard them as essential aspects of the IC construct, along with the three major components of IC outlined in the Belmont Report (National Commission, 1978) as follows:

1 *information*: the participants are given adequate information about a study;
2 *comprehension*: the information should be provided in a manner and language that is comprehensible to them; and
3 *voluntariness*: the consent should be 'voluntary', that is, there should be no 'brokers' or 'translators', except in the case of children and mentally challenged people.

The application of each of these three components of IC is problematic in many research environments characterised by oral cultures and/or high rates of illiteracy in the population. This will be illustrated in the next section.

As mentioned earlier, the IC principle is also part of the AERA (2011) 'code of ethics' as "a basic ethical tenet of scientific research on human populations" (p. 115). The AERA also extends the theoretical boundaries of the notion of 'vulnerable populations' by acknowledging the power differential between researchers, say a professor, and their students and employees in university and other hierarchical settings. Furthermore, guidelines are provided to safeguard research participants against deception as well as for using recording technologies by researchers.

Additionally, BERA's (2011) guidelines for educational researchers add the word 'voluntary' before 'informed consent', perhaps to highlight the importance of the concept of 'autonomy' as 'voluntary informed consent' is, "the condition in which participants understand and agree to their participation without any duress, prior to the research getting underway" (p. 5). Researchers are expected to ensure that, "all participants in the research understand the process in which they are to be engaged, including why their participation is necessary, how it will be used and how and to whom it will be reported" (p. 5). Articles 12–31 of the BERA guidelines cover other aspects regarding information, comprehension and voluntariness (similar to the Belmont Report) that may facilitate or unduly influence participants in giving their consent to participate in a research study (for details, see articles 10–31, 5–8).

All the guidelines discussed above are intended to help researchers (and bodies like Ethics Review Committees) to adhere to one of the basic principles espoused in the Belmont Report, that is, 'respect for persons' and operationalised through gaining the IC of the research participants prior to a research study.

In order to ensure compliance, it is mandatory for all research concerning human subjects to be approved by Ethics Committees or Institutional Review

Boards set up for this purpose. This approval is granted after assuring that the research will be conducted, "at an institution within the constraints set forth by the IRB and by other institutional and federal requirements" (Department of Health and Human Services, 2009, p. 4). The US Office of Human Research Protections (2009) has also issued a checklist of 'Basic and additional elements' to facilitate IRBs and individual researchers. The Requirements of Informed Consent form, approved by the Office of Management and Budget (56 FR 28,012, 28,022, June 18, 1991, as amended at 70 FR 36,328, June 23, 2005), emphasises the documentation of IC – either by subjects or by their legal representatives by signing the IC form. The amendment allows the researcher to gain informed consent by reading out the form to the research participants and documenting this process in a systematic way.

In the next section we will examine how this principle – gaining IC – leads to a number of tensions when applied 'locally' in diverse research environments. These situations require accommodations by researchers to ensure the quality of their data and the overall rigour of their research study.

IC in practice: tensions and accommodations

Here we share examples of tensions in the application of the IC principles as well as the accommodations made by researchers to maintain rigour in their research while following the social norms and culture of their research contexts. As stated earlier, while most of these examples are from our work and that of our colleagues and graduate students in Pakistan, we believe that the discussion will be useful for both novice and experienced researchers working in this context and similar contexts elsewhere.

The first, and perhaps the most recurring, ethical dilemmas in educational research in Pakistan arise from identifying power hierarchies and accommodating 'gatekeepers' (see also Welland and Pugsley [2002] for ethical dilemmas). Holloway and Wheeler (2002) define gatekeeping as the process of allowing or denying another person (researcher) access to someone (research participants) or something.

The entry negotiations in the vignette below are a classic example of "formal gatekeepers in positions of power in bureaucracies" who have "the authority to grant official permission" (Wanat, 2008, p. 192):

Research supervisor: Did you share with her [the school principal] the purpose of your research?
Student: I did and she got so excited; 'yes, now I will know exactly what my staff thinks about me' were her exact words. When I told her that I was ethically bound not to share my data with her she looked annoyed; 'then what is in it for me? I mean for my school? What utility

	then your research has for the system?' She was quiet for a long time and when I asked her if I could start my data collection she told me to check with her the following day; but her demeanour was telling me that I will not be allowed to access her teachers.
Research supervisor:	And? I mean did you get the permission to collect data?
Student:	No, the next day I was told that due to examination related activities whole staff would be too busy to create time for me but I could see this was an excuse to dissuade me.

The above exchange between a research supervisor (one of the authors) and her research student took place in an institution of higher learning in Pakistan. While the discussion may be seen as reflective of having a young scholar/inexperienced student carry out the research, the contextual pointers were indicating more of a tension due to the requirement of anonymity and confidentiality in internationally developed 'research standards' and local 'research environments' characterised by a lack of respect for privacy of the research participants (Qureshi, 2010).

It is noteworthy that "gatekeepers at the top may deny approval when the researcher already has gained acceptance at lower organisational levels" (Wanat, 2008, p. 193). This was true in the case of the student above, who was formally blocked by the principal though, according to her, she had already been informally welcomed by the schoolteachers.

Our experiences of research and those of our graduate students show that in the majority of schools in Pakistan the institutional heads consider it their privilege to identify research participants for a study. For example, in a study that aimed to build communities of practice in three schools in Karachi, Pakistan, one of the principals justified their selection of participants by saying that they wanted to nominate teachers who they felt would gain most from this experience (Shamim, 2005). Similarly, a coordinator in another school used the 'power' of the researchers to get her teachers to submit their exam papers and grades on time. She informed the teachers that the researchers required to see these things in their next meeting. This stressed the teachers and changed the nature of their participation in the project as well as developing mistrust of the researchers and the study objectives (Shamim & Farah, 2005). However, as Bogdan and Biklen (2003) have warned, official permission may not guarantee cooperation from participants. This was observed in the above study, where one teacher was vocal about her displeasure over her 'selection' and requested the researchers to 'release' her from this commitment.

Gatekeeping does not occur only at the institutional or organisational level, but family set-up and the prevailing decision-making practices also set rules for entry negotiation by controlling, excluding or blocking certain people and ideas (Roberts, 2005). For instance, women of any age may not have the right to give free consent, particularly in rural settings in Pakistan (Qureshi, 2010). Besides women, in Pakistan (and many other contexts), it may not be appropriate or possible for researchers to gain access to participants like members of a lower caste in a feudal village to get their voluntary consent (Asif, 2010). In situations like these, gatekeepers have to be identified and used as 'middle men' or agents to gain access to the participants. Due to the enabling role of the gatekeepers, Asif was able to access her research participants, an otherwise inaccessible group of people in her research environment. However, the role of gatekeepers is contradictory: a gatekeeper may enable and promote people and ideas by providing opportunities, as was the case in Asif's research, or may control, exclude or block people and ideas, as was the experience of our graduate student above.

Jafarey and Farooqui (2006), though not educationists, encountered a scenario as physicians/researchers that may have parallels in educational research (teachers/principals as locus parents). They interviewed physicians in a leading hospital in Karachi, Pakistan, about their perceptions and practices regarding IC in the prevailing socio-cultural set-up, where the family elders are often delegated the responsibility of making important decisions, including those about medical treatment. At times, either these elders, or the patients themselves, hand over this power to the physician(s) as being the best judge. This delegation of power to a physician is not only a recognition of the physician's professional competence, but is also a sign of trust as 'one of us'. This can cause a major ethical dilemma for the physicians: should they insist on involving the patient, as per standard ethical guidelines and practices, or respect the patient's right to exercise autonomy in delegating decision making either to their family members or to them? Hence, "this change of focus from the individual to the family or the physician raises the question of the role of individual autonomy in this culture and the whole concept of informed consent" (Jafarey & Farooqui, 2006, p. 133). This central role of the family in decision making in the Pakistani context was recognised by all the study participants and, as reflected in one of the participant's remarks, "there is no difference between the patient as an individual and his family; both are one and the same" (p. 135). In such an environment, the physicians felt uncomfortable with using a Western approach "thrusting upon them [patients] unwanted and unsolicited autonomy" (p. 135). This situation is even more pronounced in cases of female patients and research subjects, who often willingly delegate decision making to their spouses.

It is important to note that international ethical guidelines do not recognise voluntariness by proxy. The implicit assumption is that all adult members of society have the power and capacity to accept (or refuse) participation in a research study by signing the IC form. This may be true for certain cultures, particularly in the North, where 'vulnerable' populations mainly include children who may not be mature enough, and mentally challenged and institutionalised people, who are not in a condition to give voluntary consent. However, in developing countries and hierarchical societies in particular, poverty and lack of human rights accorded to certain sections of society, such as 'bonded labour', also enter as variables in the equation of gaining IC. Hence, poor people and those on the lowest rung of the social ladder can often be defined as 'vulnerable' in the Southern context due to their 'diminished autonomy', though not recognised as such by the international standards. Hence, accommodations need to be made in such research environments without compromising the rigour of research.

Once a researcher has entered the research site gate, the second dilemma is 'when and how' – the timing and method of obtaining IC. The first author had completed a study at a university in Saudi Arabia. When she gave the IC forms and explained their rights to the research participants before their in-depth interviews, their first reaction was that of fear, evident in the comment by one participating teacher: 'Oh, you are scaring me'. Hence, to put the research participants at ease, the researcher postponed the signing of the form until after the interview, pledging that the data would not be used until then. Later, all the participants returned the signed forms to her 'as a favour' as she had told them that signing the IC form was a formal requirement for her research study (Shamim, 2013). Our observations and experiences from other studies also suggest that participants may be happy to sign the IC form at different stages of the study and only after a degree of trust has been established between the researcher and the research participants.

International guidelines, implicitly as well as explicitly, recognise IC as a 'written' document, a form to be read and signed by the research participant(s). In some cultures, like Pakistan, oral or informal consent is more binding on the participants than formal written consent. In fact, often, signing a written consent form is regarded with suspicion, especially in non-literate communities, where signatures or thumb impressions (in cases of non-literate participants) are often required for legal documentation only (Asif, 2010; Pardhan, 2007; Qureshi, 2010). Similarly, in research environments characterised by oral cultures, the power of the written word can also be invoked for shifting the blame onto someone else. For instance, in a study of the curriculum and practices of English Language teaching in university classrooms, the Heads of higher education institutions in Pakistani universities, as primary gatekeepers, showed a great deal of reluctance in signing the IC forms, even after it was explained to them that the IC form was for the protection of the participants' rights. One of these gatekeepers shared informally with the researcher later that he was afraid that the signed IC form might be used against him by the higher authorities, particularly if the research findings were not very complimentary for their institution (Shamim, 2006).

A major concern regarding the 'how' of IC is related to the non-tangibility of oral consent and the difficulty of documenting it for the public gaze. Some researchers suggest the use of formal procedures such as audio recording, while others recommend the use of field notes for this purpose. In our experience, differentiation between informal and formal ways of gaining consent, and use of appropriate methods accordingly, helps in addressing many a dilemma faced in this regard, without compromising either the research participants' autonomy or the quality and quantity of data collected. Finally, it is the researchers' integrity that helps them decide on context-appropriate strategies and processes, as long as their aim is to uphold the principle of respect for persons and to protect the research participants from the risk of potential harm, both physical and psychological.

To sum up, the application of the seemingly simple principle of informed voluntary participation in a research study is fraught with complexities arising from an interplay of socio-politico-cultural factors that impinge upon participant selection through societal norms, practices, and institutions. The first set of ethical dilemmas, outlined above, is related to research participants' lack of autonomy to give IC for participation in a study. In such an environment, the next logical question would be: Can the consent of the participants gained indirectly be termed as voluntary consent? Or, more simply put: How voluntary is IC in different research environments? As established earlier, voluntarism is an essential component of the IC principle, hence, coercion of any kind – explicit or implicit – is considered unethical. The second set of dilemmas arise from when and how to document IC. Ethical standards recommend that IC be gained prior to beginning the study. However, in many contexts the signing of IC forms or oral consent does not necessarily mean that participants have been given full information and/or comprehend the given information about the research study they have been 'selected' to become part of. This brings us to the third and last issue related to obtaining IC, that is: How much information should researchers share about the research purpose and its expected outcomes? In other words: 'How "informed" should IC be in different research environments'?

Jafarey and Farooqui (2006), in their qualitative study of the perceptions of physicians mentioned earlier, found a great deal of diversity in the amount of information shared with patients, ranging from complete details to "excluding distressing facts and outright deception" (p. 136) in the interest of not causing undue anxiety to the patient, as noted by one participant: "The job of the doctor is to reassure and comfort the sick and not to frighten them" (p. 136). This proved to be true for Shamim (1993) when her efforts to come 'clean' became a cause of anxiety for the participants. Shamim shared her research aims and methodology with teachers in a school (a potential research site) in a meeting called for this purpose by the institutional head at the request of the researcher. The teachers misunderstood 'classroom observation for data collection' as evaluation of their teaching – something they were apparently familiar with in this setting. Since the meeting had been called by the institutional head, the teachers didn't think they had a choice regarding their participation in the study and they were terrified of the consequences for their future career. After the meeting, the teachers sent a message to the researcher 'not to be after their jobs'. Later, more locally acceptable strategies were used to access the participants, mainly as 'friend of a friend' and only a few general details were given at the outset about the purpose of research. More importantly, the researcher, during her visit to teachers' classrooms and in subsequent conversations with them, had to be very diplomatic in not giving any evaluative or judgmental comments in response to their questions about their classroom performance. The Head was initially unhappy about this but later agreed that anonymity and confidentiality were necessary to obtain 'authentic' data. This helped develop a relationship of trust with the teachers. In fact, in subsequent interviews, the teachers provided details they would have feared to disclose earlier. Similarly, Asif (2010) maintained a degree of ambivalence about her research purpose with her research participants from a rural village in Pakistan (also see Pardhan [2007] and Qureshi [2010] for the discussion of similar issues) to avoid causing them undue anxiety.

The implementation of 'when' and 'how' has another aspect, too – that of providing information about the research in a way comprehensible to participants. For example, sharing of information becomes problematic when the parties involved – the researcher and research participants – do not share the same language. The use of interpreters who may not be able to translate (or sometimes be unwilling to convey all the details of the IC form to the participants) compounds the problem, especially if the interpreters are untrained (Jafarey & Farooqui, 2006). Researchers are normally required to translate the form in one or more languages familiar to the participants. However, the tensions embedded in the process of translation are well documented by researchers working in varied cultural settings (Halai, 2007; Regmi, Naidoo, & Pilkington, 2010).

Another dimension of sharing information as part of IC comes into play at the writing stage of the research methodology and findings – the issue of anonymity and representation of research participants in a study. These issues can be extenuated in small close-knit communities in qualitative studies in general and case studies in particular. Ashraf (2010) reports a number of ethical dilemmas in writing up her study findings and how she addressed them so as not to compromise her research participants – six women teachers in a small rural community in Pakistan. Similarly, one of our graduate students went back to her research participants for a member check (also called member or respondent validation) and the participants disowned the material presented in written form as theirs. The explanation given to the researcher was that they perceived the interpretation of what they had said earlier did not match with what 'they really meant'. Like Ashraf (2010), the graduate student in question also had to make a number of accommodations.

Ferris and Sass-Kortsak (2011) suggest that, "Researchers need to include stakeholders, such as groups and communities, in these discussions [related to the disclosure of research findings] and in planning for the dissemination of research findings" (p. 172). The most important, however, is that "these discussions need to occur early in the research process" (p. 172). This also emphasises the timing and method of obtaining consent, especially in studies involving groups and communities.

While there is no disagreement between researchers from the South and North on 'respect for persons' as a universal principle, the local application of the IC principle has the largest potential for creating tensions (or disagreement perhaps) and hence requiring accommodation. As illustrated above, the ethical dilemmas faced by researchers in applying the principle of IC mainly revolve around three major concerns regarding the alleged autonomy of the individual that underlies this principle: (1) Can the consent be termed as voluntary when gained indirectly or through 'proxy'? (2) When and how should IC be gained? (3) How much information should researchers share about the research purpose and its expected outcomes?

Informed consent is often considered, especially by novice researchers, as a one-time activity, normally undertaken at the beginning of field work. In real research settings, the accounts of field experiences show that IC involves a continuous process of negotiation and reaffirmation of participants' commitment (Halai, 2006; Shamim, 1993, 2005).

Before we conclude this section, it is important to differentiate between moral misconduct, as in the Tuskegee case (Brandt, 1978), and practical accommodations of the kind mentioned above. Fine (1993 as cited by Welland, 2002, p. 136) points out the difficulty of having clear boundaries between informed and uninformed consent and that some amount of 'deceit' is unavoidable in 'grounded projects'. However, while the intention of the researchers in the Tuskgee case was to wilfully deceive the subjects by withholding important information from them, the researchers in the cases reported in this chapter disclosed only as much information as was required by different participants in the research setting so as not to lead to mistrust of the researcher or cause undue anxiety for the participants.

Conclusion and recommendations

We now look at some strategies to address the issues explored around IC in earlier parts of the chapter. On one hand, we realise the importance of having general ethical codes of conduct for reminding the researchers of their responsibilities towards their research participants. The example of our graduate student illustrates that the research student's bind to the general code of anonymity and confidentiality made her refuse to serve the agenda of the principal. Though this experience was very frustrating for her personally and professionally, adherence to general ethical standards prevented her from exploiting her research participants to achieve her research goals. On the other hand, we feel it equally important to have 'local' ethics review of research studies, and particularly the methodological approach to the application of general principles like IC. We quote an incident here to illustrate our point about local ethics review, in addition to the review by the university/organisation in the North (if applicable), to remind researchers about their responsibilities towards the subjects and prevent them from exploiting them, particularly in research environments in the South. A researcher (a graduate student enrolled in a university in the North) wanted to work with children in a school in Pakistan for her research study. She had received ethical clearance from her parent university. However, when questioned about the application of these principles in her specific research setting in Pakistan, by the local university's Ethic Review Committee with which she was affiliated, it emerged that she was planning to give the children an IC form in English to be signed by their parents. In that specific community, the English language was not used or even understood by the majority of the parents. She assumed that 'silence implies consent', that is, parents who failed to return the form, by default, will be deemed to have agreed for their children to participate in the study. She was not only dissuaded from an unethical practice, which could be construed as 'cheating' the children and their parents, but also advised about the use of other locally acceptable practices without compromising the principle of IC. If there had been no review procedure of the *application* of general ethical principles, the researcher might have used the 'pre-text' of adherence to local culture to do something in a country in the South that she would not have been allowed to do with her research participants in the North.

We do not know whether the above student made her experience a formal part of her written account of entry negotiations in her dissertation. However, in our formal and informal discussions with other researchers and research supervisors, we have come across many such examples of tensions and accommodations, which, if documented properly, will highlight transcultural applications of "how to preserve contextual nuance across disciplinary and/or geopolitical boundaries" (Hsiung, 2012, p. 14) while gaining IC in Pakistan and similar contexts.

A pertinent question that can be asked at this juncture is: What if facilities for ethics review of research or advice from the 'local' researchers are not available in a research setting? One way of avoiding and/or dealing with ethical dilemmas is to pre-empt issues and challenges in applying the basic principle of IC in specific research contexts and share strategies and techniques for addressing them with the ethics committees prior to starting data collection. Halai (2006) provides a good example of this process by considering the nature of the research process and roles and relationships between the researchers and study participants in the field prior to data collection. She was involved in a five-year, three-country participatory action research project to study the process and outcomes of the 'implementation of curriculum changes for reducing poverty and improving gender equity'. Relevant questions were asked by the research team when the project was in its initial stage and baseline information was being collected in the three countries (Pakistan, Rwanda, and South Africa). Ways to address possible issues and challenges in implementing ethical guidelines were sought by team members in consultation with each other and also from previous literature outlining ethical dilemmas and strategies used to address them in these and similar contexts elsewhere.

In cases where this kind of information gathering may not be possible, it should be mandatory for researchers to write a 'thick description' (Geertz, 1973) of the tensions and accommodations with regard to gaining IC.[5] These accounts will enhance our collective wisdom and add to the existing repertoire of similar stories from the field (Shamim & Qureshi, 2010; Simon & Usher, 2000; Welland & Pugsley, 2002).

Finally, we need to acknowledge that while cultural descriptors such as South Asian or the Pakistani culture may be useful for the purposes of making broad distinctions, they fail to capture the essential differences between various cultures and sub-cultures within a broader culture defined by ethnicity or geography. Holliday (2010) argues that cultural descriptions are, in fact, political acts. In the same vein, Holliday and Aboshiha (2009), while discussing British teachers' perceptions of non-native speaker teachers, posit a 'multi-active-political' picture of culture that is best viewed, "not as sets of discrete describable entities, but as shifting, sometimes indescribable, phenomena that are deeply interconnected as and politically and economically placed within worldwide processes such as globalisation and Centre–Periphery relations" (pp. 682–683). Hence, it is inevitable that universal or general ethical principles will give rise to ethical dilemmas or tensions when transported to different cultures and sub-cultures in varied research environments. This further highlights the need for accommodations and therefore hybridity in developing ethical practices for research.

To conclude, IC is a complex process as it "implies a dialogue, a relationship between two subjectivities" (Brenda, 2010, p. 19). As illustrated above, the "relationship between two subjectivities" is even more complex as the subjectivity of the researcher is constantly in battle with the 'objectivity' of his/her academic research culture and the demand of this latter culture may not be in harmony with the local culture the research participant is an embodiment of. This relationship of subjectivities with a pinch of 'objectivity' is a *raison d'être* for the hybridity of universal ethical standards and local ethical environments.

The pathway to hybridisation may not be built without the collective efforts of individuals and institutions across countries in general and within countries in particular. Our specific recommendation, therefore, is that ethics clearance should be mandatory for research in all institutions in the South. In fact, obtaining ethical clearance locally should be a pre-condition even for researchers enrolled in or coming from the North to do research in varied contexts in the South for funding and/or recognition and publication of their work at both national and international levels. While this may not be a unique demand, it needs to be reiterated as research ethics is still not practised in many institutions in the South. In case facilities for ethics clearance are not available locally, researchers should be obligated to report the application of 'general' principles in their specific research contexts, providing details of the tensions and the strategies and methods used to make accommodations to suit the requirements of the local socio-cultural context. Efforts should be made to actively pre-empt the ethical issues and challenges in a research environment without falling into the trap of stereotyping cultural practices and milieus. More important, the tensions caused by the conflict between the requirements of universal ethical principles and specific socio-cultural contexts should not be used as an argument for exploiting research participants in the guise of using 'local standards'. We therefore advocate the creation of an 'ethical space' (Kushner, 2000) between Northern standards and Southern research environments that allows researchers to be both 'responsive and fair' in making ethical judgments regarding IC. How this ethical space is created is a challenge for all researchers, especially working in the South, which, due to its colonial past, is a vulnerable context (Qureshi, 2011).

Another relevant question is: 'Who' can create the desired ethical space? Given that knowledge is often produced in the North and consumed in the South (Hsiung, 2012), "researchers from the core ... are ... obligated to change the uni-directional flow of knowledge ... from the core to the periphery into an intellectual dialogue" (p. 13). This should not absolve researchers from the periphery of their role. Our assumption is that in the wake of globalisation, a meeting of cultures is inevitable. In view of the fact that interdisciplinary research is encouraged within the research community as a means of obliterating subject boundaries and the meeting of minds and cultures for mutual learning and for overall benefit to society at large, hybridisation in education ethics could be achieved through international collaboration. It will allow researchers from both 'poles' to learn with and from each other in their joint quest of improving their ethical practices in educational research.

Notes

1 Hybridity, which originated in biological studies, was first defined as, "the creation of new transcultural forms within the contact zone produced by colonisation" (Ashcroft, Griffiths, & Tiffin, 2003, p. 118). In postcolonial studies, not only has the term a negative connotation but it also suggests the presence of an overarching core: the discourse of oppressor. However, our position regarding global regulations is comparable to that of Ashcroft et al. (2003), who consider hybridity positively: a two-way process leading to mutual learning rather than the 'oppressor' silencing the voice of the 'oppressed'.

2 This is verifiable by their published programmes of study.
3 The HEC has linked university faculty promotions to their research output. As some cases of plagiarism were reported, the HEC now requires all universities to set up 'plagiarism committees' for arresting this trend among students and faculty in higher education institutions in Pakistan.
4 The PARE aims 'To promote a vibrant educational research culture in Pakistan; To enhance the impact of educational research on policy and practice'. As such, it organises training sessions in research methodology, and conferences to facilitate exchange of expertise, knowledge, and ideas. However, it has not taken up, until now, the issue of research ethics in a significant way (for details see, description http://pare.org.pk/).
5 In Geertz's tradition, a thick description would include the contextual details of the when, where, and how of the action, besides the researcher's intentions in doing so. This would allow other researchers to see all the possible meanings of the action (Geertz, 1973).

References

American Educational Research Association. (2011). *Code of ethics*. Retrieved from https://www.aera.net/Portals/38/docs/About_AERA/CodeOfEthics(1).pdf

Ashcroft, B., Griffiths, G., & Tiffin, H. (2003). *Post-colonial studies: The key concepts*. London, England: Routledge.

Ashraf, D. (2010). Using a feminist standpoint for researching women's lives in the rural mountainous areas of Pakistan. In F. Shamim & R. Qureshi (Eds.), *Perils, pitfalls and reflexivity in qualitative research education* (pp. 101–126). Karachi, Pakistan: Oxford University Press.

Asif, S. (2010). Obligations, roles and rights: Research ethics revisited. In F. Shamim & R. Qureshi (Eds.), *Perils, pitfalls and reflexivity in qualitative research education* (pp. 59–77). Karachi, Pakistan: Oxford University Press.

Bogdan, R. C., & Biklen, S. K. (2003). *Qualitative research for education: An introduction to theories and methods* (4th ed.). Boston, MA: Allyn & Bacon.

Brandt, A. M. (1978). Racism and research: The case of the Tuskegee syphilis study. *The Hastings Center Report*, 8(6), 21–29.

Brenda, M. J. M. (2010). Behind the informed consent. *International Journal of Bio-Anthropological Practice*, 1(1), 19–22.

British Educational Research Association. (2011). *Ethical guidelines for educational research*. Retrieved from https://www.bera.ac.uk/wp-content/uploads/2018/06/BERA-Ethical-Guidelines-for-Educational-Research_4thEdn_2018.pdf

Christians, C. G. (2005). Ethics and politics in qualitative research. In N. K. Denzin & Y. S. Lincoln (Eds.), *The Sage handbook of qualitative research* (3rd ed., pp. 139–164). Thousand Oaks, CA: Sage.

Cisneros Puebla, C. A., Figaredo, D. D., Faux, R., Kolbel, C., & Packer, M. (2006). Editorial: About qualitative research epistemologies and peripheries. *Forum: Qualitative Social Research*, 7(4). DOI: 10.17169/fqs-7.4.158.

Department of Health and Human Services. (2009). *Protection of human subjects*. Retrieved from https://www.hhs.gov/ohrp/sites/default/files/ohrp/humansubjects/regbook2013.pdf.pdf

Ferris, L. E., & Sass-Kortsak, A. (2011). Sharing research findings with research participants and communities. *Ethics Corner*, 2(3), 172–181.

Fine, G. A. (1993). Ten lies of ethnography: Moral dilemmas of field research. *Journal of Contemporary Ethnography*, *22*(3), 267–294.

Geertz, C. (1973). Thick description: Toward an interpretative theory of culture. In C. Geertz (Ed.), *The interpretation of cultures* (pp. 3–30). New York, NY: Basic Books.

Halai, A. (2006). *Ethics in qualitative research: Issues and challenges* (EdQual Working Paper No. 4). Retrieved from https://www.edqual.org/publications/workingpaper/edqualwp4.pdf/

Halai, N. (2007). Making use of bilingual interview data: Some experiences from the field. *The Qualitative Report*, *12*(3), 344–355.

Halai, A., & Wiliam, D. (Eds.). (2012). *Research methodologies in the 'South'*. Toronto, Canada: Oxford University Press.

Holliday, A. R. (2010). Cultural descriptions as political cultural acts: An exploration. *Language and Intercultural Communication*, *10*(3), 259–272.

Holliday, A. R., & Aboshiha, P. (2009). The denial of ideology in perceptions of 'nonnative speaker' teachers. *TESOL Quarterly*, *43*(4), 669–689.

Holloway, I., & Wheeler, S. (2002). *Qualitative research in nursing* (2nd ed.). Oxford, England: Blackwell.

Howe, K., & Moses, M. (1999). Ethics in educational research. *Review of Research in Education*, *24*(1), 21–60.

Hsiung, P. (2012). The globalization of qualitative research: Challenging Anglo-American domination and local hegemonic discourse. *Forum: Qualitative Social Research*, *13*(1). DOI: 10.17169/fqs-13.1.1710.

Jafarey, A. M., & Farooqui, A. (2006). Informed consent in the Pakistani milieu: The physician's perspective. In G. Irfan (Ed.), *Ethics, values and society: Social transformation conference proceedings* (pp. 132–139). Karachi, Pakistan: Oxford University Press.

Kushner, S. (2000). 'Come into my parlour': Ethical space and the conduct of evaluation. In H. Simon & R. Usher (Eds.), *Situated ethics in educational research* (pp. 56–68). London, England: Routledge.

Lodhi, A. S. (2012). A pilot study of researching the research culture in Pakistani public universities: The academic's perspective. *Procedia – Social and Behavioral Sciences*, *31*(1), 473–479.

Mruck, K., Puebla, C., César, A., & Faux, R. (2005). Editorial: About qualitative research centers and peripheries. *Forum: Qualitative Social Research*, *6*(3). DOI:10.17169/fqs-6.3.2.

National Commission for the Protection of Human Participants of Biomedical and Behavioral Research. (1978). *The Belmont Report: Ethical principles and guidelines for the protection of human subjects of research*. Retrieved from https://www.hhs.gov/ohrp/regulations-and-policy/belmont-report/index.html

Nolen, A. L., & Puten, J. V. (2007). Action research in education: Addressing gaps in educational principles and practices. *Educational Researcher*, *36*(7), 401–407.

Office of Human Research Protections. (2009). *Informed consent checklist – Basic and additional elements*. Retrieved from https://www.hhs.gov/ohrp/regulations-and-policy/guidance/checklists/index.html

Pardhan, A. (2007). Methodological issues and tensions: Reflections of conducting ethnographic research with women in Booni Valley, Chitral District, Pakistan. In J. Rareiya & R. Qureshi (Eds.), *Gender and education in Pakistan* (pp. 237–256). Karachi, Pakistan: Oxford University Press.

Qureshi, R. (2010). Ethical standards and ethical environment: Tensions and a way forward. In F. Shamim & R. Qureshi (Eds.), *Perils, pitfalls and reflexivity in qualitative research in education* (pp. 78–100). Karachi, Pakistan: Oxford University Press.

Qureshi, R. (2011). Who pays the price: The ethics of vulnerability in research. In A. Halai & D. Wiliam (Eds.), *Research methodologies in the 'south'*. Karachi, Pakistan: Oxford University Press.

Rarieya, J. (2010). The complexity of researching the lives of women school leaders in Kenya. In F. Shamim & R. Qureshi (Eds.), *Perils, pitfalls and reflexivity in qualitative research in education* (pp. 127–147). Karachi, Pakistan: Oxford University Press.

Regmi, K., Naidoo, J., & Pilkington, P. (2010). Understanding the processes of translation and transliteration in qualitative research. *International Journal of Qualitative Methods, 9*(1), 16–26.

Roberts, C. (2005, August). Gatekeeping theory: An evolution. Paper presented at the meeting of the Association for Education in Journalism and Mass Communication, San Antonio, USA.

Shamim, F. (1993). The process of qualitative research: A socio-cultural experience. Paper presented at a doctoral seminar, School of Education, University of Leeds, UK.

Shamim, F. (2005, April). *Building communities of practice in Pakistani schools*. Paper presented at the IATEFL Conference, Brighton, UK.

Shamim, F. (2006). *Case studies of organization of English language teaching in public-sector universities in Pakistan*. Islamabad, Pakistan: National Committee on English, Higher Education Commission.

Shamim, F. (2013). Teaching-learning of English in the Arab world: Experiences and perceptions. Paper present at the English Language Centre, Taibah University, Saudi Arabia.

Shamim, F., & Farah, I. (2005). Building communities of practice in schools in Pakistan. In J. Retallick & I. Farah (Eds.), *Transforming schools in Pakistan: Towards the learning community* (pp. 199–214). Karachi, Pakistan: Oxford University Press.

Shamim, F., & Qureshi, R. (Eds.). (2010). *Perils, pitfalls and reflexivity in qualitative research in education*. Karachi, Pakistan: Oxford University Press.

Sikes, P. (2006). On dodgy grounds? Problematics and ethics in educational research. *International Journal of Research and Method in Education, 29*(1), 105–117.

Simon, H., & Usher, R. (Eds.). (2000). *Situated ethics in educational research*. London, England: Routledge.

Small, R. (2002). Codes are not enough: What philosophy can contribute to the ethics of educational research. In M. McName & D. Bridges (Eds.), *The ethics of educational research* (pp. 89–110). Oxford, England: Blackwell.

Taylor, J., Plaice, E., & Perley, I. (2010). Culture and ethics in first nations educational research. *Collected Essays on Teaching and Learning, 3*, 94–99.

Wanat, C. L. (2008). Getting past the gatekeepers: Differences between access and cooperation in public school research. *Field Methods, 20*(2), 191–208.

Welland, T. (2002). Research and the fate of idealism: Ethical tales and ethnography in a theological college. In T. Welland & L. Pugsley (Eds.), *Ethical dilemmas in qualitative research* (pp. 135–148). Ashford, England: Ashgate.

Welland, T., & Pugsley, L. (Eds.). (2002). *Ethical dilemmas in qualitative research*. Ashford, England: Ashgate.

PART III

Reimagining educational research approaches for emancipation

12

INDIGENOUS DATA, INDIGENOUS METHODOLOGIES AND INDIGENOUS DATA SOVEREIGNTY

Maggie Walter and Michele Suina

Within the social research landscape Indigenous methodologies were established by Linda Tuhiwai Smith's groundbreaking 1999 publication *Decolonizing Methodologies*. Smith's book did not specify a particular research method or even type of research method as synonymous with Indigenous research. Rather, the book's delineation of the set of principles and broad-based philosophy of Kaupapa Maori is an approach to any research, qualitative, quantitative, or mixed methods that relates to Maori. In the two decades since Smith's work, however, the growing field of Indigenous methodological scholarship has been primarily aligned with qualitative research. Largely to the exclusion of quantitative research.

This quantitative avoidance can be linked to Indigenous peoples' longstanding (and largely justified) suspicions around research using positivist methodologies. Such research has frequently positioned Indigenous peoples within a deficit discourse under the guise of 'objectivity'. Yet, this critique, in its valid emphasis of the harm wrought by positivism, tends to scoop up all quantitative research as methodologically similar. The result is a type of orthodoxy: a presumption that qualitative methodologies and Indigenous methodologies are natural partners and that quantitative methodologies, by nature, are Western (Walter, 2005; Walter & Andersen, 2013). This is not so. Indigenous peoples are, and have always been, highly numerate in how we understand our worlds. Complex formulas and calculations underpin/ned Indigenous cropping, hunting, and navigation to name just a few traditional daily activities.

Quantitative avoidance also has serious consequences. Being non-active in the quantitative research space equates to lived consequences for Indigenous peoples at the individual and collective level. Quantitative research methods are powerful analytical techniques and the statistics they produce form the

DOI: 10.4324/9781003355397-15

primary evidence base for Indigenous policy in first world colonising nation states such as the United States, Australia, Canada, and Aotearoa/New Zealand. An Indigenous absence from the field of Indigenous data and quantitative analysis, therefore, risks the absence of Indigenous participation in the framing of the policy directions that flow from those data (Lovett, 2016; Walter & Andersen, 2013).

To our knowledge only one major publication has directly addressed Indigenous quantitative methodologies by Walter and Andersen (2013). Their book's central argument is that the Western logic of statistical data are so pervasive, and the tropes of these logics in relation to Indigenous statistics so embedded, that these must be fundamentally disturbed before an Indigenous quantitative methodology can emerge. This chapter reiterates Walter and Andersen's (2013) core premises, but extends these using the concept of Indigenous LifeWorlds as its key theoretical frame. The chapter also draws on recent Indigenous quantitative methodological developments, including the Indigenous Data Sovereignty movement, to demonstrate the growing interest, primarily by Indigenous scholars, in Indigenous statistical data and in Indigenous quantitative methodologies. In the second half of the chapter, we explore Indigenous quantitative methodologies in practice, using a case study of the introduction of Indigenous quantitative methodologies within a Tribal Epidemiology Centre in New Mexico as our primary example.

Indigenous LifeWorlds and Indigenous methodologies

As Indigenous scholars (palawa, Tasmania; Cochiti Pueblo, New Mexico), we have been aware since graduate days of a lack of fit between Western methodology and Indigenous research. Within Indigenous scholarship this incongruity is articulated through the notion that Indigenous methodologies make visible within the research process what is meaningful and logical in Indigenous understanding of ourselves and the world (Porsanger, 2004). An Indigenous methodology, therefore, is a methodology where the approach to, and undertaking of, research process and practices take Indigenous worldviews, perspectives, values, and lived experience as their central axis. As such, Indigenous methodologies are a separate methodological paradigm; not the opposite or a derivative of Western methodologies (Tuhiwai Smith, 1999; Walter & Andersen, 2013).

We develop Porsanger's (2004) insight of Indigenous methodologies as grounded in Indigenous ways of knowing, being, and doing via the concept of the Indigenous LifeWorld. The lifeworld, in the Western canon, is linked to phenomenology. Its research contribution is its emphasis on the subjectivity of lived reality. As per Husserl (1970) the lifeworld is the taken-for-grantedness of our embodied realities. But this seeming fixedness is a reflection of the social and cultural conditions of those experiences, not verifiable truths. As human beings our existence is always contextual. Our lived experience is inseparable from the social, cultural, and physical world in which we exist and our experiences of this world are shaped by our relational positioning within it (Harrington, 2006). Thus, we interpret and make meaning through embodied phenomena such as touch, memory, imagination, and social interactions, which in turn are shaped by our cultural and social background and the established social practices of our society (Stanford Encyclopedia of Philosophy, 2013).

The 'we' in the writings of the phenomenological philosophers was largely unquestioned as male, White, middle class, 20th-century European. This intersubjectivity is not translatable to Indigenous lived realities. Rather, the Indigenous lifeworld, as defined here, has as its base the dual intersubjectivities of first world dispossessed Indigenous peoples. That is, peoples who meet Dyck's (1985) 4th world definition as those who are Indigenous but have had their sovereignty appropriated, are now minorities within their traditional lands, are culturally stigmatised, economically and politically marginalised, and struggling for social justice. The Indigenous lifeworld, therefore, encompasses the relational positioning inherent in the social, political, historical, and cultural embodied realities of Indigenous lives framed through:

- intersubjectivity within peoplehood and the ways of being and doing of those peoples; inclusive of traditional and ongoing culture, belief and systems, practices, identity, and ways of understanding the world and their own place, as a people, within it and
- intersubjectivity as colonised, dispossessed marginalised peoples whose everyday life is framed through and directly impacted by their historical and ongoing relationship and interactions with the colonising nation state.

The intersections/intertwining of these two inter-subjectivities define the lifeworld similarities and differences between dispossessed Indigenous peoples. Thus, for palawa Aboriginal Tasmanian and Pueblo Native American peoples, our identity, traditions, belief systems, and everyday practices come from very different places geographically and culturally. But the embodied lived experience of that intersubjectivity exists within our shared positioning as dispossessed, politically marginalised Indigenous peoples, experiencing intergenerational and embedded socio-economic and health disparities. We both also share a historically and contemporaneously conflicted relationship with the nation state who now govern our traditional lands. This dual positioning encompasses what Tuhiwai Smith (1999) posits as the shared key tenets and underpinning philosophies of Indigenous methodological frames.

Indigenous statistics

Across first world colonising settler nation states, Indigenous data largely conform to what Walter (2016, 2018) describes as 5D data. That is, mainstream Indigenous statistics focus almost exclusively on items related to Indigenous difference, disparity, disadvantage, dysfunction, and deprivation. Magnifying the impact of this discursive frame, 5D data are produced within a set of research practices that tend to the aggregate, are decontextualised from their social and cultural context and simplistically analysed with the problematic Indigene compared pejoratively to the non-Indigenous norm (Kukutai & Taylor, 2016; Walter, 2018; Walter & Andersen, 2013). Evidence to support this claim is easily found through a Google search of the term 'Indigenous statistics' or by inserting the name of a 4th World Indigenous people into the search, i.e., Native American, Aboriginal and Torres Strait Islander, Maori, Native Hawaiian, First Nations, Alaskan Native. What comes up, invariably, is a sad list detailing Indigenous over-representation in negative health and education data, in incarceration rates and in embedded material disadvantage. Such 5D topics continue to dominate both official statistics and academic quantitative research on Indigenous peoples.

The lifeworld explains the marked similarity of the Indigenous statistical narrative across these diverse and geographically separate nation states. The underlying belief and value systems, epistemological approach and ontological assumptions of such data are largely drawn from a non-Indigenous relational positioning. From this intersubjective position a presumption of Indigenous deficit is entirely predictable. This problematic is magnified by the established practice of rendering these approach factors invisible. Those using Western methodologies frequently confuse methodology with method. Research papers detail in great depth how data were collected and the statistical techniques used. But they tend to prioritise muteness on their methodological approach as if it is inconsequential. It is not. As argued by Walter and Andersen (2013) who we are, the values that underpin our concept of self and our concept of others, our perspective on how the world operates and our own place within it and our understandings of how knowledge is construed and who the knowers are, fundamentally impact our research practices and presumptions.

This assertion of the centrality of methodology is as true for quantitative research as it is for other research practices. Accepting the premise that numbers exist as per Quine (1948) differs from accepting that numbers have a fixed reality. Numbers are not neutral entities. Statistics are human artefacts and in colonising nation states such numbers applied to Indigenous peoples have a raced reality (Walter, 2010; Walter & Andersen, 2013). Their reality emerges not from mathematically supported analytical techniques but the social, racial and cultural standpoint of their creators who make assumptive determinations to collect some data and not others, to interrogate some objects over others, and to investigate some variable relationships over others. As Zuberi and Bonilla-Silva (2008) assert, it is dominant settler society questions that are hidden behind the cover of claims of objective methodology. Within this, the Indigene remains the object, caught in a numbered bind, viewed through the straitjacketing lens of deficit (Walter & Andersen, 2013).

For dispossessed Indigenous peoples, the more critical ontological questions are how are such numbers deployed and whom do they serve? Statistically supported narratives, framed by Euro defined definitions of civilisation, were (and are) used to demonstrate our unfitness, to rationalise our dispossession, marginalisation and to question even our right to be Indigenous (Tuhiwai Smith, 1999). These discourses ripple into contemporary racially differentiating statistics. Positioned as objective descriptors these numbers operate now, as they have always done, as mechanisms of unequal power relations. They define who and what Indigenous people are according to the terms of their non-Indigenous producers and consumers. They also define what we cannot be. This impact is heightened by quantitative research use of numbers not just as counts, but as representatives of subjective items. Their form also conceals what is excluded; the lifeworld of those they purport to represent; Indigenous peoples (Walter, 2016; Walter & Andersen, 2013).

Big Data and Open Data, operate to further distance lived social and cultural realities from their database embodiment. With Big Data, understanding that dominant norms and social understandings, not statistical methods, determine social data meanings is even further concealed. Linking multiple 5D data sets (health, schooling, justice system, welfare, etc.) and/or mining other data will provide a bigger ball of data, but not necessarily a more informative one. No matter how sophisticated the linking or the analytical techniques used, if only deficit-related items (i.e., educational comparisons) are included then obtaining 'results' outside of the tired existing trope of Indigenous statistics is dim (Walter, 2018). Open Data, without specific Indigenous data protocols, just expands the number of Indigenous statistical analyses that are conceived and executed from non-Indigenous worldviews.

Indigenous data and Indigenous data sovereignty

Indigenous quantitative research, as currently construed, is missing data framed through the Indigenous Lifeworld and/or which prioritise Indigenous data requirements. This lacuna is not just a methodological imperative. There is a link between Indigenous development agendas and data as a resource. Indigenous self-determination relies on data self-determination. This connection is a recurring theme at the United Nations Permanent Forum on Indigenous Issues where concerns about the relevance of existing statistical frameworks and the lack of Indigenous participation in data processes have long been raised (Davis, 2016). Specific data needs vary across Indigenous peoples and geographies, but there is broad agreement on the need for data, which meet Indigenous data needs and aspirations. These include, but are not limited to, data that disrupt deficit narratives, data that are disaggregated, data that reflect the embodied social, political, historical, and cultural realities of Indigenous people's lives, as Indigenous peoples, and data that address Indigenous nation re-building agendas (Rainie, Rodriguez Lonebear, & Martinez, 2017; Walter, 2018).

These issues cohere within the Indigenous Data Sovereignty movement. Indigenous Data Sovereignty centres on Indigenous collective rights to data about our peoples, territories, lifeways, and natural resources and is supported by Indigenous peoples' inherent rights of self-determination and governance over their peoples, country, and resources as described in the United Nations Declaration on the Rights of Indigenous Peoples (UNDRIP) (Taylor & Kukutai, 2015). The concept is defined as the right of Indigenous peoples to determine the means of collection, access, analysis, interpretation, management, dissemination, and reuse of data pertaining to the Indigenous peoples from whom it has been derived, or to whom it relates (Kukutai & Taylor, 2016; Snipp, 2016). Data in this sense are not restricted to statistical data, but such data are a primary concern of the Indigenous Data Sovereignty movement and its advocacy. Data sovereignty is practiced through Indigenous data governance, which assert Indigenous interests in relation to data. The primary vehicle is Indigenous decision-making across the data ecosystem; from data conception to control of access to and usage of data. Indigenous decision-making is a prerequisite for ensuring Indigenous data reflects Indigenous priorities, values, culture, LifeWorlds, and diversity.

An early response to the problematic of the alienation of Indigenous peoples from their own data are the OCAP© (Ownership, Control, Access, Possession) principles from Canada. In 1995, tired of non-Indigenous data users assuming the mantle of unbiased experts to speak with authority about First Nations realities, data control was demanded as a prerequisite for participation in a government health survey. A new model of how statistical data were done, OCAP©, was developed by First Nations. Trademarking the acronym to prevent its misuse, these principles provide First Nations with collective and broad-based control of their own data, its collection, and its use (FNIGC, 2016). National bodies such as the Institute for Clinical Evaluative Sciences have adjusted their Indigenous data practices through the enactment of a set of data principles aligned to OCAP (Walker, Lovett, Kukutai, Jones, & Henry, 2017).

The reclaiming of Indigenous data rights is now occurring across colonising nation states. In Australia, the *Maiam nayri Wingara* Indigenous Data Sovereignty Collective seeks to change data practices in relation to Aboriginal and Torres Strait Islander peoples. A 2018 meeting determined that Indigenous peoples in Australia had the right to exercise control of the Indigenous data ecosystem inclusive of data creation, development, stewardship, analysis, dissemination, and infrastructure to ensure that such data are: contextual and disaggregated; relevant and empowering of sustainable self-determination and effective self-governance; accountable to Indigenous peoples; protective of Indigenous individual and collective interests (Indigenous Data Sovereignty Summit Communique, 2018). In Aotearoa/New Zealand the *Te Mana Raraunga* Indigenous Data Sovereignty Network's Charter (2018) states its purpose as enabling Māori Data Sovereignty and to advance Māori aspirations for collective and individual well-being by: asserting Māori rights and interests in relation to data; ensuring data for and about Māori can be safeguarded and protected; requiring the quality and integrity of Māori data and its collection; advocating for Māori involvement in the governance of data repositories; supporting the development of Māori data infrastructure and security systems; and supporting the development of sustainable Māori digital businesses and innovations. The United States Indigenous Data Sovereignty Network (The University of Arizona, 2018) is working to ensure that data for and about Indigenous nations and peoples in the United States (American Indians, Alaska Natives, and Native Hawaiians) are utilised to advance Indigenous aspirations for collective and individual well-being. The Network's primary function is to provide research information and policy advocacy to safeguard the rights and promote the interests of Indigenous nations and peoples in relation to data.

Indigenous quantitative methodologies in practice: Albuquerque Area Southwest Tribal Epidemiology Centre

A pertinent example of the adoption of Indigenous quantitative methodologies aligned with Indigenous Data Sovereignty principles is the work of the Albuquerque Area Southwest Tribal Epidemiology Centre (AASTEC). AASTEC is based at the Albuquerque Area Indian Health Board (AAIHB) and serves tribal communities in New Mexico, Southern Colorado, and West Texas. Established in 2006, the mission of AASTEC is to collaborate with the 27 Tribes in the Indian Health Service (IHS) Albuquerque Administrative Area to provide high quality, culturally congruent epidemiology/surveillance, capacity development, programme evaluation, and health promotion/disease prevention services.

AASTEC is one of 12 Tribal Epidemiology Centres serving American Indians and Alaska Natives throughout the United States. As a Tribal Epidemiology Centre, AASTEC has public health authority status as mandated in the US Indian Health Care Improvement Act (IHCIA), permanently reauthorised under the Patient Protection and Affordable Care Act (PL 111–148). The IHCIA also allows Tribal Epidemiology Centres to access health data from the US Secretary of the Department of Health and Human Services (DHHS) about American Indians and Alaska Natives and tribal nations in their regions (Hoss, 2015).

Even though federally recognised tribes also have public health authority status, challenges remain in accessing their own data from federal and state entities. It is also challenging for AASTEC to access tribal data on behalf of tribes at their request. However, AASTEC is situated in a unique position to serve as an intermediary between federal and state government to provide tribal specific data directly to tribes through the establishment of data sharing agreements between tribal nations and AASTEC. AASTEC is also positioned to be more responsive to the unique data needs of tribes in the Albuquerque Area based on tribal self-determined data priorities. This can help to alleviate data access issues and to move towards higher quality and representative data by working directly with tribes to analyse and interpret data to inform tribal decision making and move towards action.

AASTEC has been committed, since its inception, to honouring tribal sovereignty and working side-by-side with tribes to provide meaningful data. In recent times the work of Walter and Andersen (2013) on quantitative methodologies and the Indigenous Data Sovereignty movement has further highlighted the problematics of dominant epidemiological quantitative data practices and the resultant data based on western constructions of the world and numbers. In response, since 2017, AASTEC has adopted an active Indigenous quantitative methodological approach within its own work. The purpose is to move beyond superficial consultation and mere adaptation of survey instruments based on western understandings of the world. Rather, this approach recognises tribal self-determination to decide what health means based on their own Indigenous LifeWorlds as the driver of what data are collected.

For Indigenous peoples, health is not just about maintaining physical health, such as through exercise or taking medications to prevent and manage diseases, it is connected to their ways of being and doing that are unique to their identity and understanding of the world. For example, Pueblo health is connected to a total Pueblo way of life that supports wellness and includes Pueblo spirituality and ceremonies, traditional medicine, heritage languages, family and community connectedness, agricultural way of life, and physical wellness (Suina, 2016). This holistic perspective is largely absent in current public health surveillance and epidemiology processes and practices. A search of validated survey instruments, typical of public health practice, finds a body of literature driven by western constructions of life that define health. But it is not possible to validly add tribal related health concepts to survey instruments that have at their base western ideations of health. What are required are instruments that are conceived and validated by tribes from the very beginning. Tribes must be in the driver's seat and maintain control of what questions are asked and who gets to ask the questions about health based on their Indigenous LifeWorlds, as well as who can access this information to protect their Indigenous knowledge and to ensure that it is not misrepresented.

Both intersubjectivities, Indigenous and public health epidemiology, drive our work. These dual subjectivities necessitate the need to find balance between both to not reproduce a system that constructs narrow deficient-based Indigenous statistical narratives and 5D data that are driven by the non-Indigenous relational positioning. This is the problematic that AASTEC has to address. It is not enough to include data that reflect health concepts connected to Indigenous LifeWorlds, but it is imperative to make visible the methodology that drives epidemiology in its current state so that an Indigenous quantitative methodology becomes clearer to transform epidemiological practice. This methodology must also consider the role of colonialism in the health conditions experienced today by Indigenous peoples.

A key aim of AASTEC's adoption of Indigenous quantitative methodologies and the principles of Indigenous Data Sovereignty is to strengthen existing tribal public health data systems and reporting to produce the highest quality, tribe-specific data available to the American Indian population throughout our area. Furthermore, this adoption provides AASTEC with the opportunity to better understand how to more effectively serve the tribes in the region by assessing our current practices so as not to replicate harmful colonial data practices that continue today in public health and epidemiology practice (Poudrier, 2003; Walter & Andersen, 2013). Indigenous Data Sovereignty and governance frameworks also provide a strong foundation based on the rights of Tribal nations for approaching Tribal related data issues such as appropriate presentation of race and ethnicity in health-related data and the inclusion of tribal-specific questions in state-wide public health surveillance instruments.

In April 2017, AASTEC's Good Health and Wellness in Indian Country Program convened a '*Native think tank*' in collaboration with a well-respected tribal community entity, the Santa Fe Indian School Leadership Institute. The aim was to better understand the role of a tribal serving organisation such as AAIHB/AASTEC in the practical enactment of Indigenous quantitative methodologies and Indigenous Data Sovereignty. Understanding the role of tribal serving entities is critical because the inherent power to control data lies within the sovereign tribal nations and not external organisations. This important point must be underscored to disrupt the traditional paternalistic orientation of state and federal governmental entities towards tribes and to support sovereign tribal nations to realise their own vision for health and wellness instead of one that is imposed by outside standards. The think tank resulted in the establishment of a road map for AASTEC to strengthen our current efforts to provide the highest quality of data to the Tribal nations and bands we serve. The think tank also sought to equip AASTEC to support Indigenous Data Sovereignty and promote the use of Indigenous quantitative methodologies within our own area, as well as to inform efforts to advance data sovereignty by others. This process led to three think tank recommendations that could immediately be acted upon:

1 To cultivate technical skills among community members related to survey development, data collection, analysis, and reporting;
2 To build comfort and understanding regarding research methodologies and methods among tribal partners; and
3 To advocate for Indigenous research methodologies and Indigenous Data Sovereignty.

Each of these recommendations is discussed in the following section alongside an outline of the work that has occurred since April 2017 to address each.

Recommendation 1: cultivate technical skills among community members related to survey development, data collection, analysis and reporting

An initial step for working with tribes is to foster technical skills that lead to the development and validation of tribal driven health surveys. Such skills allow tribes to develop instruments that are built on their own Indigenous LifeWorlds definitions and explanations of health to generate Indigenous data. This includes providing support and coaching related to data collection, analysis, and report writing where data analysis and interpretation are tribally driven by our tribal partners. It is important to note that ownership of the methodological and Indigenous Data Sovereignty processes and resulting outcomes belongs to the tribes and AASTEC would play a supportive role.

Much of AASTEC's work is already to provide technical assistance, training, and resources to the tribes we serve. However, this recommendation pointed to the need for rethinking how we deliver technical assistance and epidemiological training so that an Indigenous centred approach is foundational to what we offer. This includes incorporating Indigenous Data Sovereignty and Indigenous research/evaluation methodologies and methods into our training programme. Since April 2017, we have developed and piloted a training module that teaches about these concepts and utilises experiential group activities to reinforce understanding of content. For example, we used an interactive team building activity to identify Native determinants of health at the beginning of the training to theorise what health means to Native people. This conceptualisation was then used as the basis for determining evaluation questions and approaches. This module will be incorporated into future trainings related to data collection, analysis and reporting and will be incorporated into an epidemiology 101 course at a local tribal college that is currently being planned.

Recommendation 2: build comfort and understanding regarding research methods among tribal partners

The harmful research by outsiders and the resulting deficit based data generated makes discomfort and distrust towards western research a reality when working with tribes. Shifting the power back to tribes to decide what they determine are relevant data and for what purposes they deem appropriate is fundamental for rebuilding trust. Demystifying western scientific research methodologies and methods is critical to disrupt the academic institutional monopoly on research/evaluation and to create a local understanding of research and data for tribal-driven approaches to quantitative data to truly emerge. Deconstructing how research methodologies are informed by Euro-American values and notions about the world and health is key to demystifying western science and research to move towards Indigenous centred quantitative methodologies to drive the tribal health data in our area.

In our pilot training module described in the previous section, we incorporated a case study related to federal health data to demonstrate how western quantitative methodologies construct a broken picture of American Indian/ Alaska Native people. We have also recently incorporated an experiential activity that utilises the Barnga simulation game on cultural clashes (Thiagarajan & Thiagarajan, 2011) to generate dialogue about how one's worldview drives one's perceptions and understandings related to data. This game creates conflict due to different understandings of the game rules at the individual and group level that is intentionally built into the game. Furthermore, participants are silenced after a few practice rounds and are not allowed to ask questions. These game characteristics contribute to a dynamic where some individuals become empowered and others become disempowered, even though words are not exchanged among participants once silence is imposed. Participants still communicate with their body language and use of symbols while the game is in play. The lessons emerge during the debriefing period after participants are no longer silenced where they reflect on their experience playing the game and apply lessons learned to their future work with data. These activities are important for both Indigenous and non-Indigenous people alike to understand how the spoken and unspoken 'rules' that drive western research methodologies are not neutral or objective and are made up by a non-Indigenous relational positionality to be better able to confront and call out harmful quantitative data practices.

Recommendation 3: advocate for Indigenous research methodologies and Indigenous data sovereignty

Speaking for the legitimacy of Indigenous research methodologies and Indigenous Data Sovereignty is a critical strategy in influencing how western data systems interact with Indigenous data. Tribal control over data about them is the aim and AASTEC operates to advance this aim through its service as an intermediary with governmental entities, universities, and other non-tribal serving organisations that produce data about American Indians/Alaska Natives. This intermediary role is a means to facilitate the production of higher quality and more credible data to be used by tribes. After the April 2017 think tank we have received numerous requests to present on Indigenous Data Sovereignty directly to tribes and tribal leaders as well as to non-Indigenous audiences that produce data about the tribes in our area. We have also been fortunate to host thought leaders involved in the global Indigenous Data Sovereignty movement from Australia, Aotearoa/New Zealand and the United States. These visits allow AASTEC to continue to learn from and exchange ideas on how to be better stewards of Indigenous data while at the same time making the case to non-tribal serving organisations for change in Indigenous data practices.

Continuing Indigenous data sovereignty and methodological engagement

Linking AASTEC into the global Indigenous Data Sovereignty movement is a positive response to dealing with challenging data issues and advocating for more tribal involvement in the data held about them by governmental entities. This engagement has led to a critical examination of how we as an Indigenous organisation support tribal efforts. It has also allowed us to be conscious of not doing unintentional data harm. The aforementioned think tank led to a better understanding of the role and benefits of AASTEC being an active data sovereignty partner and how to move forward by hearing directly from our tribal partners. It has also opened the door to possibility and creativity in advocating for meaningful tribal health data driven by tribal sovereignty and interests. This engagement also validates the need for further development of Indigenous quantitative methodologies as per Walter and Andersen (2013).

AASTEC quantitative data-related training already supports health numeracy and data literacy by teaching skills related to quantitative data collection, analysis, and reporting (Peters, Hibbard, Slovic, & Dieckmann, 2007). But it is also imperative to think about what this means to tribes. As an organisation we are also working to articulate a theoretical base to drive our work and incorporate this base into our practices and training. We have tasked ourselves with asking what more do we need to consider. For example, Brayboy's (2005) Tribal Critical Race Theory asserts that colonisation is endemic to society and that Indigenous ways of knowing are critical for tribal sovereignty and self-determination. Also useful is Tygel and Kirsch's (2015) work on *critical data literacy* informed by the work of Paulo Freire which examines skills needed to allow an individual 'to use and produce data in a critical way'. New theoretical frames are also being developed. For example, author Suina proposes *Critical Indigenous Data Literacy* as a way of thinking about Indigenous data skills (i.e., collection, analysis, reporting, etc.) from an Indigenous LifeWorld perspective. The key emphasis is to assess that the data are reliable, valid, and useful. What these descriptors mean is determined by tribal nations drawing from their own knowledge systems that support tribal sovereignty and recognises that colonialism is embedded in standard epidemiological practice and data production. More work is needed to advance this way of approaching epidemiology training as a tribal epidemiology centre. We expect to learn more while working in partnership with the tribes in our area to inform how best to meet their data needs and how to transform colonial systems that permeate public health.

Conclusion

Indigenous centred approach to tribal health data, inclusive of Indigenous quantitative methodologies and Indigenous Data Sovereignty demonstrate how these central concepts can change the way, for the better, that Indigenous data are done.

References

Brayboy, B. M. (2005). Toward a tribal critical race theory in education. *The Urban Review, 37*(5), 425–446.

Davis, M. (2016). Data and the United Nations declarations on the rights of Indigenous peoples. In T. Kukutai & J. Taylor (Eds.), *Indigenous data sovereignty: Toward an agenda* (pp. 25–38). Canberra, Australia: ANU Press.

Dyck, N. (1985). *Indigenous peoples and the nation-state: 'fourth world' politics in Canada, Australia, and Norway*. St. Johns, Canada: Institute of Social and Economic Research.

FNIGC. (2016). Pathways to First Nations' data and information sovereignty. In T. Kukutai & J. Taylor (Eds.), *Indigenous data sovereignty: Toward an agenda* (pp. 139–156). Canberra, Australia: ANU Press.

Harrington, A. (2006). Lifeworld. *Theory, Culture & Society, 23*(2–3), 341–343.

Hoss, A. (2015). *Tribal epidemiology centers designated as public health authorities under the Health Insurance Portability and Accountability Act*. Retrieved from https://www.cdc.gov/phlp/docs/tec-issuebrief.pdf

Husserl, E. (1970). *The crisis of European sciences and transcendental phenomenology*. Evanston, IL: Northwestern University Press.

Indigenous Data Sovereignty Summit Communique. (2018, June). *Indigenous data sovereignty data for governance: Governance of data*. Retrieved from https://static1.squarespace.com/static/5b3043afb40b9d20411f3512/t/5b70e7742b6a28f3a0e14683/1534125946810/Indigenous+Data+Sovereignty+Summit+June+2018+Briefing+Paper.pdf

Kukutai, T., & Taylor, J. (2016). Data sovereignty for indigenous peoples: Current practice and future needs. In T. Kukutai & J. Taylor (Eds.), *Indigenous data sovereignty: Toward an agenda* (pp. 1–24). Canberra, Australia: ANU Press.

Lovett, R. (2016). Aboriginal and Torres Strait Islander community wellbeing: Identified needs for statistical capacity. In T. Kukutai & J. Taylor (Eds.), *Indigenous data sovereignty: Toward an agenda* (pp. 213–232). Canberra, Australia: ANU Press.

Peters, E., Hibbard, J., Slovic, P., & Dieckmann, N. (2007). Numeracy skill and the communication, comprehension, and use of risk-benefit information. *Health Affairs, 26*(3), 741–748.

Porsanger, J. (2004). An essay about Indigenous methodology. *Nordlit, 8*, 105–120.

Poudrier, J. (2003). Racial" categories and health risks: Epidemiological surveillance among Canadian First Nations. In D. Lyon (Ed.), *Surveillance as social sorting: Privacy, risk and digital discrimination* (pp. 125–148). London, England: Routledge.

Quine, W. V. O. (1948). On what there is. *The Review of Metaphysics*, *2*(5), 21–38.

Rainie, S. C., Rodriguez-Lonebear, D., & Martinez, A. (2017). *Policy brief: Data governance for native nation rebuilding – Version 2*. Retrieved from https://nnigovernance.arizona.edu/policy-brief-data-governance-native-nation-rebuilding

Snipp, M. (2016). What does data sovereignty imply: What does it look like. In T. Kukutai & J. Taylor (Eds.), *Indigenous data sovereignty: Toward an agenda* (pp. 39–56). Canberra, Australia: ANU Press.

Stanford Encyclopedia of Philosophy. (2013). Phenomenology. Retrieved from https://plato.stanford.edu/entries/phenomenology/

Suina, M. (2016). Reflections of a Pueblo Indian health educator: Weaving Pueblo worldview into health education. *Journal of American Indian Education*, *55*(3), 72–90.

Taylor, J., & Kukutai, T. (2015, October). *Indigenous data sovereignty and indicators: Reflections from Australia and Aotearoa New Zealand*. Paper presented at the UNPFII Expert Group Meeting on Indigenous Peoples and the 2030 Agenda for Sustainable Development, United Nations, New York, USA.

Te Mana Raraunga Maori Data Sovereignty Network. (2018). *About us*. Retrieved from https://www.temanararaunga.maori.nz/

The University of Arizona. (2018, May). *Indigenous data sovereignty: Global progression*. Retrieved from https://nnigovernance.arizona.edu/indigenous-data-sovereignty-global-progression

Thiagarajan, S., & Thiagarajan, R. (2011). *Barnga: A simulation game on cultural clashes – 25th anniversary edition*. Boston, MA: Nicholas Brealey Publishing.

Tuhiwai Smith, L. (1999). *Decolonizing methodologies*. London, England: Zed Books.

Tygel, A. F., & Kirsch, R. (2015). Contributions of Paulo Freire to a critical data literacy: A popular education approach. *The Journal of Community Informatics*, *12*(3), 108–121.

Walker, J., Lovett, R., Kukutai, T., Jones, C., & Henry, D. (2017). Indigenous health data and the path to healing. *The Lancet*, *390*(10107).

Walter, M. (2005). Using the 'power of the data' in indigenous research. *Australian Aboriginal Studies*, *2*, 27–34.

Walter, M. (2010). The politics of the data: How the Australian statistical indigene is constructed. *International Journal of Critical Indigenous Studies*, *3*(2), 45–56.

Walter, M. (2016). Data politics and Indigenous representation in Australian statistics. In T. Kukutai & J. Taylor (Eds.), *Indigenous data sovereignty: Toward an agenda* (pp. 79–98). Canberra, Australia: ANU Press.

Walter, M. (2018). The voice of Indigenous data: Beyond the markers of disadvantage. *Griffith Review*. Retrieved from https://www.griffithreview.com/articles/voice-indigenous-data-beyond-disadvantage/

Walter, M., & Andersen, C. (2013). *Indigenous statistics: A quantitative methodology*. New York, USA: Routledge.

Zuberi, T., & Bonilla-Silva, E. (2008). Towards a definition of white logic and white methods. In T. Zuberi & E. Bonilla-Silva (Eds.), *White logic, white methods: Racism and methodology* (pp. 3–30). Lanham, MD: Rowman and Littlefield.

13
FOCUS GROUPS AND METHODOLOGICAL RIGOUR OUTSIDE THE MINORITY WORLD

Making the method work to its strengths in Tanzania

Hilde Jakobsen

Focus group discussions (FGDs) have become a widely used data generation method in the majority world, also known as the 'third world', 'developing world' or 'Global South'. In the wake of their initial surge in the *minority* world, an Anglo-American literature of "sceptical enthusiasm" (Barbour & Kitzinger, 2001, p. 3) emerged, clarifying what the method was good for and how to use it to its strengths (Bloor, Frankland, & Thomas, 2001; Parker & Tritter, 2006; Wilkinson, 2006). However, this critical awareness had less influence on FGD practice in the majority world. Most of the published knowledge on how to conduct FGDs to achieve these strengths is specific to minority world contexts (Amoakohene, 2005; Bloor et al., 2001; Greenbaum, 2000; Hennink, 2007).

How can FGDs be made to work to their strengths in a majority-world context? This chapter relates my attempts to address this question in Tanzania, in the face of challenges to rigour endemic to researching across difference in the majority world. I was only able to tackle these once I achieved the interaction that gives FGDs their unique advantages. Achieving this interaction required the type of "imaginative experimentation with facilitator styles and group exercises" (Barbour & Kitzinger, 2001, p. 201) that the 'sceptical enthusiasts' call for (Barbour, 2009). My experience also shows that whereas *carrying out* FGDs – the goal of existing FGD methods texts in the region – was easy, *generating high-quality data* through FGDs requires the researcher to move through more difficult, and largely unmapped, terrain.

The distinction between majority- and minority-world contexts demands some caveats. First, it is not meant as a reified division of the world into two categories, but rather as an imagined continuum. Many of the concerns raised in this chapter will also be relevant, to a lesser degree, to minority-world contexts. Second, the distinction is not synonymous with 'cultural differences',

DOI: 10.4324/9781003355397-16

despite the common association of 'non-western' with 'culture' (Narayan, 1997). The chapter focuses on majority-world contexts in general, not culture specifically, and illustrates that 'cultural sensitivity' alone does not overcome steep power gradients and different discursive dispositions, neither of which are absent from minority-world research. Nevertheless, the minority-majority distinction is a useful heuristic device in allowing us to see the following. First, that what passes as 'general' knowledge about FGDs, actually draws almost exclusively on knowledge from Europe, North America, Australia, and New Zealand, thus raising the question 'what does this actually tell us about FGDs in countries like Tanzania?' Second, this terminology, rather than North-South, developed-developing, overturns the assumptions made in this status quo about what is 'normal' and what is 'other', by suggesting that this is not 'general knowledge' at all, given that the contexts on which it is built, are actually in a global minority. It thus shows knowledge about how focus groups work in Tanzania as something more than a charitable special interest; although not generalisable to one homogenous 'majority world', it is one step towards a more truly general knowledge about how focus groups work: knowledge that is not limited to a minority of the world.

This chapter begins with an overview of the FGD method. This overview includes discussions of the types of data the method can reliably generate and the interaction by which it does so, and the method's potential to address challenges to rigour related to positionality, power, and alterity. It then describes how these challenges are pinpointed in the literature on methodology in majority-world research as in special need of being addressed there. It identifies a gap on how to work the method to address such challenges outside the minority world in the little methods literature that exists on majority-world FGDs. It explains how the study was carried out in accordance with the existing literature on this, and depicts the type of data this generated. The chapter then describes how positionality in particular was central to the 'failure' of the first FGDs, and how even successful manoeuvring between multiple identities did not address this threat to data quality. Finally, the chapter describes the modifications that finally *did* make the method work to its strengths, and contrasts the data generated by the modified discussions with those from the initial discussions.

Focus group discussions: uses, misuses and opportunities

FGDs are discussions among five to ten people on a given topic. A moderator keeps the discussion as focused, non-threatening, and 'natural-feeling' as possible with minimal self-involvement. In summary, the method is useful for *group-level data on perceptions and norms as performed though inter-respondent interaction*. Methodologists concerned with sub-optimal or sloppy uses of FGDs ascribe these to an inadequate understanding of the distinguishing features of the method and the data it generates (Barbour, 2009; Barbour & Kitzinger, 2001; Kitzinger, 1994; Puchta & Potter, 2004; Stewart, Rook, & Shamdasani, 2007; Wilkinson, 1998, 2006).

One common mistake is to use FGDs as group interviews. Group interviews simply replicate interactions between researcher and interviewee on a group scale (Kitzinger, 1994; Morgan, 1997; Parker & Tritter, 2006; Wilkinson, 2006). In FGDs, the goal is that participants converse among themselves, questioning, challenging, and answering one another.[1] What is said reflects participants' judgments of what is appropriate to say in the group, generating data of dubious *individual* value, and uniquely useful for exploring predominant *social* norms and values (Krueger & Casey, 2009; Lloyd-Evans, 2006; Smithson, 2000). Critics of 'faddish' uses of the method see group norms as the *only* topic for which it is not inferior to others (Bloor et al., 2001). FGDs show attitudes as socially *per*formed instead of individually *pre*formed (Puchta & Potter, 2004).

However, the method's ability to generate such data, the very data it is good for, hinges on inter-respondent interaction. In many studies using FGDs, inter-respondent interaction is neither ensured, acknowledged, nor even understood (Kitzinger, 1994; Smithson, 2000; Wilkinson, 2006).

Group interaction is also what has caused researchers concerned with researcher-researched power relations to appreciate the method as a way of changing these. As interaction is shifted from researcher-participant to participant-participant, so are control and reference. This addresses some of the concerns raised by feminist social scientists regarding the exploitative potential of interviews (Wilkinson, 2006). As participants discuss and interpret the questions, re-phrase them and ask their own, not only are they less the subject of the researcher's 'imposition of meaning', but views and opinions emerge in greater complexity than they do from surveys and one-on-one interviews (Kotchetkova, Evans, & Langer, 2008). Another concern in researching across boundaries of difference is that of 'otherness' and the danger that what participants say will be largely a function of the impression they want to give to an outsider. To a certain extent, the opinions expressed in FGDs, as in any research encounter, will be coloured by participants' self-presentation to an outsider. However, as respondents speak to one another, rather than to the external researcher, inter-participant dynamics supersede self-presentation vis-à-vis the researcher, moving the discussion to "somewhere between an explanation to the Other – the researcher – and a group debating a topic of relevance to their lives" (Smithson, 2000, p. 111). Participants' numerical advantage and the researcher's self-effacing facilitator role make it more likely that any 'othering' is done by the respondents rather than by the researcher (Poso, Honkatukia, & Nyqvist, 2008; Smithson, 2000; Wilkinson, 2006).

It is this potential of FGDs to decentre the role of the researcher and increase participants' ownership of the research process that makes it "rife with multiple affordances for (moving) through ... the triple crisis of representation, legitimation and praxis that has haunted qualitative work for the past two decades" argues Kamberlis and Dimitriadis (2005, p. 903). They refer to Fine's (1994) work on othering in qualitative research. Fine (1994) reminds qualitative researchers of post-colonial critiques of othering to underline the importance of enabling resistance to it, which we can do, she reassures, "when we construct texts collaboratively" (p. 74). Kamberlis and Dimitriadis see FGDs as one form of such collaboration. Using the method strategically to inhibit the authority of researchers and to allow participants to take over and own the interview space, they argue, can help researchers avoid both othering and navel-gazing, as well as Haraway's (1991) twin "god-tricks" of "relativism" and "totalization", so called because they "deny the stakes in location, embodiment and partial perspective" (cited in Kamberlis & Dimitriadis, 2005, pp. 903–905).

Researching across difference in the majority world

The opportunities the method offers to tackle issues of othering, power relations and the role of the researcher seem especially promising when used in majority-world contexts. Efforts to address the crises of legitimacy and representation identified in development research (Scheyvens & Storey, 2003) over the past two decades have found these same three issues to be more central to methodological rigour for researchers in the majority world, than in social science in general (Bell, Caplan, & Karim, 1993; Staeheli & Lawson, 1994).

"Who are we for them? Who are they for us?" This is how Caplan summarises positionality. She sees it as one of the most important determining factors in the kind of data researchers generate in developing countries[2] (Bell et al., 1993, p. 178). With several fieldwork analyses confirming the impact of positionality on data generation, the debate has since moved beyond reflexive confessions of this impact, and on to questions of *how* it plays out in the research setting, how multiple positionalities can be navigated, and to building said awareness of positionality effects into research design (Henry, 2003; Madge, 1994; Rose, 1997; Srivastava, 2006).

Henry's (2003) struggles with self-representation in India show respondents rather than the researcher deciding who the latter would be in their eyes, and how this decision determines the data that could emerge from the research encounter. Srivistava (2006) similarly describes how she mediated 'multiple positionalities' to achieve 'temporary shared positionalities' with respondents, arguing that "field identities are multiple and continually mediated constructs in response to the anticipated or experienced perceptions of how participants receive, accept or reject the researcher's positionalities vis-à-vis their own" (p. 214).

It is accumulated field-based analyses, such as these that Apentiik and Parpart (2006) draw on when they highlight two issues as particularly important for quality in majority-world data generation: power gradients and "the identities assigned to researchers on the basis of more fixed positions" (p. 41).[3] The power differential between researcher and respondents intertwines with who the researcher is to the researched. How respondents perceive power relations between them and the researcher flows from who they perceive the researcher to be, and it is their perceptions of both that determine their perceived stake in presenting themselves and the topic in a certain way. In communities where foreigners are associated with aid, respondents are more likely to give a foreign researcher whatever answer they think will attract external assistance (Apentiik & Parpart, 2006).

Thus, FGD methods are primed to address issues that the literature on research in the majority world marks as needing to be addressed. This literature also indicates areas where the method would need to adapt. Desai and Potter (2006) stress the cultural contingency of conversation norms, and how in many rural African contexts, respondents' abilities to voice disagreement or independent opinions are subject to social etiquette, which again depends on who is speaking to whom, and their relative positions in the social hierarchy. Momsen (2006) points to how in post-socialist and centrally planned countries, such as Tanzania, detailed 'factual' information is readily given, but "requests for personal opinions or ideas are seen as threatening" (p. 45). Moreover, many respondents from lower status groups are unaccustomed to being asked for their opinion, and so may find researchers' insistence that they share their own ideas on a topic bewildering.

Focus groups in the majority world: working to the strengths of the method?

Given the method's potential to address fundamental challenges to majority-world research, and the cultural contingency of the interaction on which the potential hinges on, it seems reasonable to look to methods texts on majority-world FGDs for how to make the method work to its strengths in majority-world contexts. How can FGDs generate data on opinions where respondents are loath to voice opinions? How do issues of positionality, alterity, conversation norms, and power gradients impact efforts to achieve a discussion where respondents interact with one another, challenging, questioning, supporting and expanding on one another's responses? For instance, how does the tendency for respondents to tell the researcher what they think (s)he wants to hear, as deduced from how they see the researcher, and his/her power in relation to them, play out in discussions in rural African communities? And how can FGDs' distinguishing features be mobilised to reduce this 'foreigner effect' on the data?

Unfortunately, the first and only methods text on FGDs in majority-world research, Hennink's *International Focus Group Research,* throws little light on such questions (Jakobsen, 2010). Its main contribution is advice on practicalities, as if these cover the difference in using the method in majority-world contexts: meeting outdoors, dealing with uninvited respondents, and translating questions. It says little about how the interactive processes on which the method hinges may play out differently in majority-world contexts, and how to handle this. Thus, it leaves the need for advice on conducting discussions in a way that both considers and addresses the aforementioned challenges in majority-world research, largely unmet.

Vissandjee, Abdool, and Dupere go further in filling the gap on how "to make focus groups culturally sensitive and competent" (2002, p. 840). However, their adaptation of the method to rural India is limited to how respecting local etiquette wins the trust of respondents, making them "comfortable opening up and sharing" (p. 838). It treats opinions as internal data that are either divulged or not, rather than socially performed according to the audience, influenced by the speaker's perception of whom (s)he is speaking to. They address power relations only between respondents, and only as influencing *whether* individuals 'share'. The influence of these power relations, as well as those of the researcher's positionality,[4] on the nature of the responses given, is not addressed. Asking of the data 'to what extent is this merely what they say to me, based on who I am to them?', and adjusting the FGDs accordingly, requires cultural competence beyond simply conforming to social norms.

Thus, a gap can be seen in the literature. Positionality, alterity, and steep researcher-researched power gradients are identified both as particularly threatening to data quality in majority-world research, and as potential strengths of the FGDs method (Lloyd-Evans, 2006). However, while *general* FGD literature points to how achieving the method's strengths hinges on *how* the discussions are conducted, considering especially context and conversational norms (Hollander, 2004; Smithson, 2000), *majority-world* FGD texts say little about how to actualise these strengths when context and conversational norms are very different. The prevalence of sub-optimal uses of majority-world FGDs is a result of this gap (Ellsberg & Heise, 2005; Hennink, 2007; Hennink, Rana, & Iqbal, 2005; Walraven, 1996).

The study: focus grouping for opinions in Tanzania

The focus group study recounted here forms part of a larger research project on attitudes to violence against women and corruption, aimed at exploring the norms and values people refer to when voicing opinions on these two issues. The groups were held in two disparate districts in Tanzania, in villages surrounding Kigoma and Arusha towns. Respondents were village residents, and sampling reflected each district's diversity regarding age, sex, socio-economic and educational levels, religion, and ethnicity. I was white, female, from a recognised donor country, and had grown up and worked in this and other

African countries for over 20 years. All groups were segmented by age and sex, and some by ethnicity, socio-economic status, and acquaintance levels: friends, neighbours, cooperatives, and strangers (Morgan, 1997). Each group consisted of eight to ten respondents. Three pilot and eight 'real' discussions were planned; eventually 40 were held in 20 villages.

Why the method was chosen

While working with corruption and violence in the region, I had found dominant village discourse both pivotal in case outcomes, and different from what people might think privately, or say to outsiders. I wanted data about what people might say to one another in public: which viewpoints could be voiced, and how they could be presented. Also, 'white-in-Africa' experience in discussing politically correct topics made me concerned about social desirability: I hoped the group context might counteract this. I imagined that while interviews would give me what people say *to me*, FGDs would yield data on what people say *to one another*. I also anticipated respondents feeling more 'in the spotlight', anxious about being singled out, in one-on-one interviews than in group discussions.[5]

I, therefore, chose the method for its group context and interactive nature, to generate the type of data for which it is the most reliable: group norms and understandings (Bloor et al., 2001). I wanted data on attitudes in a social context, not as individually *pre*formed, but as *per*formed to others in the group: precisely the type FGDs generate (Puchta & Potter, 2004). My hope that they would generate data beyond the standard responses to foreigners was also supported by the literature (Barbour & Kitzinger, 2001; Lloyd-Evans, 2006). Nevertheless, despite this support, the first eight discussions failed to exhibit the characteristics for which I had chosen the method. 'Tweaking' the method until it finally addressed these issues of positionality, alterity, and power gradients was to take 20 more discussions.

How the method was used

The process behind the first 'failed' FGDs was no less adapted to local norms than Vissandjee et al. (2002) recommends. Sampling decisions were based on contextual knowledge gleaned not only from the literature but also from my own experience and a network of local experts. I chose two disparate districts to cover two 'extremes', and peri-urban villages within these as sites that could not be written off as purely 'urban' or 'rural'. Arumeru district represented one of the most well-connected, developed, educated, touristified, and researched districts, while the less developed Kigoma Rural district is popularly described as a 'backwater'.

I recruited respondents through village councillors, in deference to bureaucratic procedure. Having followed procedure unquestioningly from capital to village level, I found every village officer equally unquestioning vis-a-vis his superiors' request to introduce me to whomever I needed for my 'state-approved research'. Vissandjee et al. (2002) found that soliciting permission from local leaders showed respect towards the community. I found that it put leaders and my respondents at ease. Since I neither needed a random sample, nor believed he could skew the sample, I deferred to the village leader's expectation that he recruits respondents according to my criteria. This assured both the leader and the respondents they were inculpable in cooperating with me.

In each village, I asked to meet with one group of men and one of women according to varying criteria of age and social standing. I invited participants to choose the time and place. At the beginning of each session, I introduced myself and my assistant and explained the purpose of the discussion. On explaining that participation was voluntary, I stressed that I kept no record of who stayed and who left. After the discussion, I paid for refreshments and debriefed with the participants.[6]

FGDs are often seen as an easy way of getting many people to talk (Bloor et al., 2001; Parker & Tritter, 2006). I found the process of getting the respondents to talk – from access to recruitment to actually meeting with them and asking questions – easy. After responding in culturally appropriate ways throughout the process – from bowing to reprimands at government offices to responding to social cues in village conversations – I found unquestioning goodwill and cooperation among respondents when we finally met. While western FGD literature recommends factoring no-shows into recruitment, I encountered requests to join. While other white researchers in the area complained of having to 'pay per interview', only once in 40 interviews did I have payment set as a condition for participation.[7] While many of my questions were about violence against women and corrupt leadership, responses did not indicate that these were taboo or even sensitive issues, or even that respondents were hesitant to discredit the leaders who had recruited them.

The clearest suggestion of how effortless it all was, however, was the way the talk flowed. Respondents talked. For an anxious researcher, this was a comforting sign of success. Despite my uncertainties and theirs, when gathered in a group, someone always spoke. Eventually. About something. This confirms the idea of FGDs as deceptively simple.

Problems with the type of data generated

Conducting FGDs in a culturally sensitive way, following existing technical advice, did get respondents talking. However, the first ten discussions left me entirely unconvinced they were generating the type of data for which I chose the method, or the type that could reliably say anything at all about my research questions. Making the method work to its strengths and the study's purposes in the Tanzanian context required more modifications than respecting local culture.

Rather than discussing informally with one another, respondents answered formally in turn, gradually choosing one 'representative' to speak for them. Rather than sharing their views and opinions, they recounted what actually happened. This was problematic because what people say in a group is not a reliable source of such 'factual information', nor was it easy to discern viewpoints and opinions in these accounts. Also, I found the ethical implications of discussing real local cases of violence and corruption so serious that I stressed before each session that I was there to hear what they thought of the issues, not what actually happened. The following extract from one of the discussions exemplifies these tendencies:

Researcher: So, in such a conflict, can a man be right to discipline his wife?

Juma: Many times, a man can beat his wife, if they disagree. They can disagree to such an extent that he beats her. One might say, disagree until he beats her. There are some places here where this happens a lot. So –

Assistant: Is it right then? What do you say?

Juma: Ah ... Yes, ok ... Well, then ... here, in our African community, we have our African traditions. So, if a man is not right, the woman will go to the council of elders. She will tell her story. They will listen. Then they will call the man. He will tell his story. They will do what? – Listen. Then they will decide. This is our African tradition.

Researcher: Thank you ... So, what do you think? In your eyes, is it right sometimes, for a man to discipline his wife? Someone else?

Bakari: Me, I agree with the previous speaker. He spoke well. It is true. There is disagreement, there is conflict. Especially when times are difficult. Then in a disagreement, it happens. According to our custom, it is not a foot or a hoe, but a hand only. The whip also is used. These are our customs.

Ezekiel: My turn? I also agree. This is how it is.

Paul: And me.

Peter: Me too. I agree. It's true. It's our tradition. Now maybe in Europe it's different, but here in Africa, it can happen that a man beats his wife. It happens a lot. Now my addition is, it is because of poverty. When there is no food and no money, what can you do. And here, where there is no good education. Where there is no good education, there are no opportunities. And then, when the disagreement comes – what is there? Nothing. There is nothing. You are here, you can see: this is the state of us here.

Musa: I agree. It is true. – Ah!

Both I and the goals of the research were frustrated by this discussion. The encounter resembled more a formal panel interview than a group discussion.

There seemed to be an understanding among respondents that any differences of opinion should be taken outside: this was the place to present a united, co-operative, orderly, and respectable front. As some said, they were, after all, the ones selected to speak. This underlying norm seemed impervious to any verbal attempts by me to set a different tone.

This was problematic since opinions were what I wanted data on. When asked for a normative judgement on wife-beating, respondents gave 'factual' accounts about beating (it happens a lot, it happens when people disagree) and what happened afterwards (the elders) as well as one cause of why it happened (poverty). I could later have analysed these as reflecting the speakers' opinions about beatings ('all beatings are legitimate, or the elders would say otherwise', or 'men cannot be blamed for beating their wives, because they're poor', or 'whatever tradition says, is right'), but I had no reason to assume they reflected opinions. Rather, they seemed to be a deflection of the question by speakers who did not experience the FGD context as one that legitimated the airing of, and disagreeing on opinions. This matches Momsen's (2006) observation from similar settings that 'factual' reports are much more easily elicited than respondents' opinions (p. 46). Regarding Peter's response in particular, it would be a mistake to interpret this as an opinion of poverty justifying beating. It seemed to reflect how he saw me, and the purpose of a conversation with me (to gain sympathy and thereby funding), more than how he saw wife-beating. Thus, the issue of positionality was central to the method's initial malfunctioning in Tanzania. What also seemed to be happening was that participants would watch to see if I 'accepted' an answer, and then, relieved, would quickly support that answer, as Ezekiel, Paul, and Musa did in this exchange.

While this extract is from a men's group, women seemed even less used to being asked their opinion than men – as found in similar contexts (Momsen, 2006). There were some differences in how men and women understood their roles in the FGDs. Many women seemed nonplussed that there was no 'task' for them, expecting to follow instructions or to give me practical information I needed. Men had several familiar roles they could step into to expound on social issues, referring to one another as 'speaker', 'representative', 'councillor', and 'comrade'. When I tried to shift the conversation to a more informal tone, one man exclaimed 'I see! Like in the evenings when we brothers go to the coffee place, to drink and talk!' While sitting and talking was a role men had some experience in, women debriefed that 'we never do this: just sit and talk'.

What I found the most problematic, however, was how I seemed to be inducing respondents to present themselves and their communities to me as 'We Africans'. My question of what individuals thought about certain social issues somehow solicited representations of what *the* tradition of a homogenous mass of 'Africans' said, as opposed to 'you Europeans'. Despite having chosen a method whose collaborative nature could 'enable resistance to othering', I had initiated a process that did just the opposite, that produced precisely the target of postcolonial critiques of othering (Fine, 1994; Kamberlis & Dimitriadis, 2005). Instead of participants challenging, adjusting, questioning, and re-developing each other's responses, as described in the FGD literature (Barbour & Kitzinger, 2001; Morgan, 1997; Wilkinson, 2006), my groups were producing what Homi Bhabha has unravelled as "discourses that weave ideologies of 'common culture', ... made coherent by the repression of social divisions" (1990, cited in Fine, 1994, p. 74). I seemed to be inviting the respondents to present themselves as the African 'other' to my white self (or perhaps their African selves to the white 'other'), and to do so as representatives of the entire community.

I thus faced questions raised by previous researchers concerned with postcolonial representation across difference: How can we incorporate the voices of others without colonising them by replicating the same imperialist discourses? (England, 1994). While 'cultural sensitivity' (Vissandjee et al., 2002) had helped simply to get people together and get them talking, ensuring data quality required engaging with alterity, positionality, and power. Doing so yielded entirely converse data – as will be seen in the very last focus group, conducted in the same community and on the same topic as the one cited above.

The power dimension of positionality

I came to see positionality as central to the 'failure' of the initial FGDs, and conventional advice that this can be solved by a skilful deployment of the self – for example, by staying long enough to 'blend in' or by emphasising commonalities with the researched – as requiring a blithe disregard for how a steep power gradient may over-ride any such efforts by the researcher.[8] The aforementioned 'International Focus Group Handbook' claims that:

> The deference effect ... (where participants say what they think a moderator wants to hear rather than their own opinion about an issue) ... can be avoided by clearly reinforcing to participants at the outset of the discussion that all views are valued and it is participants' own views that are being sought.
>
> *Hennink (2007, p. 184)*

My experience confuted the belief that positionality is dealt with through self-deployment, because I *did* succeed in changing the way the respondents saw me – and the problem remained. Throughout the conversations, I did what would supposedly take care of the 'deference effect'. Long-term residence afforded me more positionalities, and more experience of deploying them, than most western researchers in Tanzania. I sought a balance between being forthcoming and sociable, and not revealing my own opinions. I stressed aspects of my identity that would not only provide a shared positionality with the respondents, but also complicate the presentation of the African other to the white self. Respondents' de-briefing questions revealed a success in this self-deployment that sometimes-exceeded intentions: a group of women who had spoken extensively on how to avoid beatings asked me if I had gathered enough advice to get married now.

Significantly, the most successful self-deployment could not prevent respondents from trying to guess what the 'right' response was, based on who they thought I was, and adjusting what they said accordingly. As my positionality changed, so did their answers. Much of the talk said more about their thoughts on *who I was and how to relate to me*, than about their opinions on the topic, as seen in a group who assigned me a different position:

Researcher: So, in such a conflict, can a man be right to discipline his wife?
Ali: It's true, a man is never right to discipline his wife. Our problem here, as you know, is that many women don't know this. If only we could convince them!
John: What? What's he saying?
Yosefu: (interrupting, tapping John on the knee) He's right.

What is Ali's 'It's true' agreeing with? No-one had said 'a man is wrong to discipline'. I had withheld my opinion, stressing that there were no right or wrong answers. Nevertheless, his perception of who I was convinced him this was the thing to say. Visual observations confirmed this sense that what people told me said more about who they thought I was than about my research questions. Respondents would seek eye contact with me as they spoke, even when addressing one another. This seemed either to refer to me – to gauge my reactions to what they were saying as they were saying it – or to defer to me – using facial expressions to excuse themselves if they were wrong. No matter how much I marginalised myself in the room, what was said and how it was said revolved around me and my imagined position. My positionality and opinions – real or imagined, held by me or assigned to me – dominated the discussion and determined the data it generated.

Conventional advice on the 'deference effect' proved inadequate because positionality owes most of its impact to the power gradient between researcher and researched, which in my case was especially and unavoidably steep. No culturally adept self-deployment or opinion-hiding could prevent respondents from *trying* to guess my opinion, or tailoring theirs to who they thought I was. Had my undeniable whiteness not communicated power and privilege, Yusuf and Ali's presumption of the researcher's anti-violence stance would not necessarily lead them to mirror it. FGD respondents in western contexts with less steep power gradients have responded to that same stance with derision and abuse (Green, Barbour, Bernard, & Kitzinger, 1993). It is, therefore, the power dimension of positionality that makes respondents scan the researcher's identity for 'the answer'. Whether they find it is irrelevant; my positionality still determines the discussion.

In summary, I found that while I used FGDs to generate inter-participant opinion exchanges, power dynamics endemic to researching across the minority-world/majority-world boundary produced a very different type of talk: accounts of events, procedures, and behaviour as presented to me on behalf of the community. While a researcher usually influences the data, respondents' deferring and referring to my perceived position made me the centre of the discussion. This did not yield the sort of data that FGDs can reliably generate or that answered my research questions.

Tweaking the method to decentre positionality

My main concern in trying to get the FGDs to 'work', therefore, was to decentre myself: to shift the respondents' attention away from *me*, who *I* was, and how to relate to *me*, and over to co-respondents and the discussion topic. I improvised with group exercises and facilitator styles.[9] The aim was not so much to change the 'western' method to fit 'local culture' as it was to find ways within the Tanzanian context to achieve the defining characteristics of the method. Four improvisations were particularly effective.

The first of these was asking respondents to share responses with their neighbour first, and then to the group. This had several advantages. First, it made half the respondents commit themselves to a stance before having heard other responses and having watched my reactions to those: it complicated attempts to 'find the answer'. Second, it meant that even if respondents did refer to me in plenary, they would mostly be repeating a response that had initially been formulated not to me, but to a peer. Also, it seemed to increase participants' engagement with others' responses, and lower the threshold for the reticent. I discovered a second effective adjustment as a pair of women in one group spontaneously acted as a team when responding in plenary. I started asking participants to form teams according to their opinion on an issue, and then presenting the arguments for that standpoint, and challenging other teams' arguments. The contrast between respondents' ways of talking during these exercises and during the first FGDs was striking. In this artificial situation, participants who in a more naturalistic discussion were cautious about revealing opinions, self-consciously focusing on the white researcher, could openly challenge each other's opinions. Having a role imposed on one provided a legitimate space for difference, dissent, and general deviance from normal rules of behaviour, a space that was filled with creative rhetoric. This confirmed my impression that the 'malfunction' of FGDs was partly due to the trouble respondents – especially women – had fitting the exchange of personal opinions on right and wrong into who they should be and how to behave in relation to me.

These role-plays were so successful both in the fun they infused and the interaction they induced, that I incorporated them into all discussions. However, the interaction was clearly contrived: were respondents voicing their 'real' opinions? In the following exchange, participants had responded individually to a vignette about a leader accused of corruption, and teamed up with others of similar opinions. Each team then argued for their position, and was challenged in turn by each of the other teams. Sometimes respondents spoke more out of their commitment to a stance than from personal conviction:

Zakarias: So, in this way, even if the leader truly did those things, the man who accuses him should be chased! Yes. Questions?
Daudi: (grinning) what can I say? (laughter)
Bakari: It's your turn, you have to question.
Daudi: Ok ... Ah-hah ... So. This man who is accusing the leader, maybe he also has money, maybe he can also help people. Then, if you villagers chase him, don't you also chase away that money?

Daudi at first admitted that he found Zakarias' argument convincing and had no issue with it. It was only when Bakari reminded him it was his role to question it, that he did so. Surely this shows that what people said in my 'new and improved' discussions was not necessarily their 'true opinions', but what the situation – albeit a different situation now – seemed to require of them?

This question illustrates how easily the whole purpose in using FGDs may slip from view. Since it is socially performed and not individually internally held opinions that FGDs generate data on in the first place, then the crux is not whether opinions are 'real', but *whom* they are performed *to* (Puchta & Potter, 2004). Daudi seemed clear that his audience was his co-respondents, and was perfectly 'in tune' with them. As a result, what he eventually chose to say to that audience is critically relevant data, regardless of how it relates to his own internal convictions. The way I interpreted his body language, his 'what can I say?' was a humorous appeal for sympathy, as he sensed it was obvious not only to him but also to others that Zakarias' point was incontestable. The response to his comment – general laughter – confirmed this. When he finally found a counter-argument, it is clear that he was 'performing' it, but it is also clear that it was the 'best shot' of a perspicacious performer, following an evaluation of what counts as a good argument among participants, an evaluation validated by his audience's laughter. Thus, the performance yields valuable data on what is socially acceptable or appropriate to say in defence of the given stances.

A third element that helped respondents forget about me and instead exchange opinions with one another was various 'evaluative exercises'.[10] Using cards and drawings, I asked people to rank social problems, vote on moral dilemmas, and choose between scenarios. The women who expected to be set a task, and appeared self-conscious when asked just to sit and talk, said they enjoyed this. Also, men's groups said they felt they were being consulted on serious issues when the exercises came out. While I specified that I would leave the tape recorder running, having a task to tackle together meant that respondents mostly ignored me, focused on the task, and spoke to one another in a more straightforward manner. For example, in sorting social issues into 'good for society' and 'bad for society', the following exchange accompanied a card on 'leaders favouring their own':

Maria: Read it.
Miriam: 'Leaders favouring their own'.
Bahati: Is good. Goes here.
Teresia: Put it with the happy face.
Hadija: It's bad-
Maria: No, it's good-
Hadija: No, it's here. It's bad! It's not like they're from here-
Bahati: Yes, they are from here!
Hadija: The country's leaders? Who?
Maria: Not them-
Hadija: This is the country's leaders-
Teresia: Of the whole country, the ministers?
Bahati: We need to know *whose* people.
Maria: I thought it was *our* people-

This is a very different discussion from an earlier one on the same topic. There, each response was directed at me, and often implied some case for assistance.

Such exercises generated data on how people evaluated the issues in talk to one another, rather than on how they presented the issues to me. In addition to these very contrived interactions, I tried to decentre myself also from the 'normal' discussions, where participants responded to vignettes and questions. Since the usual self-effacing moderator behaviour did not work, I tried a fourth modification to see what would happen if I removed myself altogether. I interspersed the discussions with *unmoderated* questions:

Researcher: So, let's – yes. I want to start with a question. I want to ask you a question, and leave it with you to discuss. Then when you're done, please could you call me in, and then someone summarises the discussion ... is this ok?
Women: It's ok.
Researcher: I will leave you to discuss without me. So, the question is this: What kinds of things can cause a conflict between husband and wife? What are the things that can cause a conflict?

Assistant:	You understand? What is it that can cause a conflict?
Hanna:	That's ok. What causes conflict?
Researcher:	So, we are leaving, but this thing stays here. It keeps taping your voices.
Elisa:	Ok, we'll call you.
	(Researcher and assistant leave)
Naomi:	So, we start. What things?
Bahati:	What was the question?
Elisa:	Me too, I didn't understand.
Sara:	Conflict.
Hadija:	What brings conflict between husband and wife?
Fatoma:	Ah. We should stop it?
Sara:	No, we say what brings it. The different things.
Bahati:	Ah, it's just this – (laughter)
Fatoma:	It's just this!
Gloria:	I can answer this.

This exchange shows participants tense and self-conscious in my presence, and speaking more freely in my absence. I interpreted the laughter as one of relief, laughing at how nervous they had been, and how simple it really was. As I stepped out, participants could step into the discussion, and take ownership of it. While in the first moderated discussions participants looked to me for cues or for the next question, in discussing the unmoderated questions, participants themselves decided when to wrap up and call me back in. This gave them a feel of the type of interactive discussion the questions called for. When I conducted the first question of a session in this manner, for the rest of the session, while I was present, participants seemed more relaxed, interacted more, and paid less attention to me.

With all this tweaking, were these still FGDs? Each choice came with costs. During the unmoderated question, the discussion often went off-track, as I was not there to probe or rein it back in. Nor could I encourage equal participation, although the range of voices recorded suggests the group self-managed this aspect. The sharing in pairs limited the development of opinions as the discussion went on. The evaluative exercises limited the range of opinions that could be expressed, and the role-play format may have exaggerated some stances. However, neither unmoderated questions nor group exercises form a departure from FGD literature (Barbour & Kitzinger, 2001; Bloor et al., 2001; Morgan, 1996; Ritchie & Lewis, 2003). On the contrary, this type of innovation is where 'sceptical enthusiasts' see the most promise for higher quality FGDs (Barbour & Kitzinger, 2001).

Thus, after 20 sessions of experimenting, I arrived at an adaptation of the method that avoided the worst of the problems that plagued the first focus groups. What then did these 'successful' discussions look like, and how were the data they generated different from the 'failed' ones?

Bringing out the strengths of the method

First, the groups appeared more heterogeneous. As I was decentred and participants felt more at ease to engage with the questions and one another, differences emerged within the group. For example, in discussing bribes to traffic authorities, one man who was a truck driver surprised the rest of the group by having the opposite opinion to theirs. This resulted in an in-depth discussion of work-place dilemmas he faced. Such earnest minority disagreement seemed impossible in the first FGD, where most participants seemed to understand their role as presenting a united and respectable front to me.

Engaging earnestly in the discussion led some participants to change their stance. For example, towards the end of a discussion of justifications for wife-beating, one woman who had first provided several examples of this, and then fallen silent for a while, said "I'm thinking a little. We're saying the man has the right to beat us if we do these things. We always say this. But when we all say that don't we support them?"

Another feature that fits with descriptions of the strengths of FGDs is how participants challenged one another. For example, while the first FGDs had left me silently wondering whether respondents were just taking their cue from whoever seemed to have given the 'right' answer, in the final FGDs I found respondents calling one another on precisely this:

Sikujua: Me too, I say it depends.
Mohamed: Depends on what?
Sikujua: Huh?
Mohamed: When you say 'it depends', you mean it depends on something.
Sikujua: Oh? ... so then – 'it depends' ...?
Mohamed: So just because he said it depends, you also say it depends? (laughter)
Sikujua: (laughing) In fact, for me, I think this man did wrong. You cannot treat your own relatives like that. It's wrong.
Mohamed: So, it does not depend on anything.
Sikujua: No! It's totally wrong! A man like that-!
Mohamed: So then don't say it depends.
Sikujua: Ah ... you know-! *He* said 'it depends'-! (laughter)
Thomas: We cannot hide!

Respondents also challenged one another on expressed viewpoints, although the tone remained politely conciliatory:

Bakari: For this reason, it is not correct at all for a leader to accept gifts from people.
Ezekiel: If I may be allowed to enter the conversation a little. I ask for permission to oppose you. You see, we're the ones who said

something that's a little different from you. Now let's try to understand one another. What if the leader has done so much for your village, and you give not even one egg? And the other village, they thank him? He'll say why am I getting tired for people who don't want it? Then when the other village gets development, what will you do? That is my question.

Differences of opinion were often couched in such assuaging preambles. In this sense, the modified FGDs respected local etiquette. However, what was different from the first groups was that participants did actually find roles within these general norms of politeness in which it was possible to argue different viewpoints.

Increasing inter-participant interaction and addressing positionality achieved very different conversations from the initial presentation of the 'African other' to the 'White self'. Rather than representing a homogenous group, participants discovered aloud differences among themselves, and within themselves, as they were able to relax and reflect on the topics, pace the discussion, and challenge one another. The opinions they expressed were performed not to me but to one another. Consequently, in the last FGD, when I asked about the 'African traditions' related in the first discussion, in the same community, the conversation was very different. The difference is a useful warning against using FGD data as evidence on actual events, and of underestimating the effect of positionality, power gradients, and social desirability:

Researcher: So, what about this tradition of elders, where a woman can go and complain if she has been beaten and it's wrong, like the examples you've been giving?
Musa: What?
Steven: The council of elders.
Ezekiel: Heh-! (laughter)
Steven: Who does that?
Musa: They cannot.
Ezekiel: I think it is not they cannot. They can complain. But for what?
Patrick: You're disciplining your wife, and the elders tell you to stop?
Peter: But let's think. What if your wife has a lover who is an elder? (laughter)

Conclusions

FGDs' minority-world origins do not preclude the method from being useful elsewhere. On the contrary, when deployed rigorously, it can address threats to data quality common in majority-world research. The fieldwork recounted here illustrates this as follows.

First, it points to the implications of *not* paying attention to the extent to which the method actually is generating the type of data it is reliable for, namely interactive data on group norms. The way the chapter's last excerpt says almost the opposite of the first one epitomises this. The initial FGDs more than matched prevailing majority-world FGD standards, yet failed to yield interactive data on social norms. If I had assumed that they were 'working' simply because people were talking, as many do assume when conducting FGDs, I would have generated data saying the direct opposite of what the data produced by a rigorous use of the method could tell me.

Second, the chapter shows the unique – but not automatically realised – potential of FGDs to deal with issues of positionality and power difference. In the fieldwork recounted here, FGDs were used to counter the deference effect of positionality when a steep power gradient rendered any self-deployment futile. Much majority-world research is undertaken across steep power gradients. Unlike one-on-one methods, FGDs allow participants to generate data to one another. Without this group element, the 'decentring' of the researcher that all my tweaking aimed for would not have been feasible: the impetus and audience for the responses would have been removed with the researcher. It was achieving this inter-respondent interaction within local conversational norms that unleashed the method's strengths.

Third, the fieldwork illustrates how FGD interaction can counter another challenge in majority-world research: alterity. The first FGDs, strongly coloured by respondents' concerns about how to relate to me, invited representations of the African 'other'. The tweaked groups produced the hallmarks of the method, such as capturing the complexity and fluidity of opinion, compared to surveys' 'false certainty' (Kotchetkova et al., 2008). As participants questioned their own and others' responses, the FGDs no longer produced Bhabha's deceptively and coercively coherent "ideologies of common culture" (Fine, 1994, p. 74).

Methodological rigour and attention to data quality is absolutely doable in FGD studies in the majority world. Specifically, rigour involved addressing positionality, alterity, and power gradients, and simply ensuring the FGDs displayed the method's defining characteristic: participants discussing among themselves. This required an understanding of the structures and conditions that regulate what can be said and how, and knowing how and when to neutralise or work within these constraints – as well as the sheer tenacity to make interaction happen.

Acknowledgements

Thanks to Julia Brannen, Jannike Seward, and Liz Spencer as well as participants at the ECAS3 conference for their advice.

Notes

1 I use the terms 'respondent' and 'participant' interchangeably.
2 Caplan, like most writers on positionality, sees it as determining not only data generation but also data analysis (Bell et al., 1993). However, since the focus of this chapter is on a data generation method, the importance of positionality in other parts of the research process are not dealt with here.
3 Apentiik and Parpart's (2006) term 'gradient' is useful here in its implication that the difference between two adjoining fields determines the dynamics where the two meet.
4 Their study is not a case of a minority-world moderator from the majority world, in that they employed Indian moderators. Nonetheless, the moderator is still researching across difference, and subject to the very power differentials the authors problematises in relation to group composition.
5 This was confirmed by three attempts at individual interviews, where respondents were visibly distressed and gave short, incoherent, and haphazard answers. The same respondents participated with ease in discussions.
6 Most decided to keep the money. Debriefing included their questions for me, and brochures on the topics discussed that I had received from local non-profits.
7 I paid 200 shillings (20 cents) to each after the interview, ostensibly for refreshments, without having promised this. Twice this was bargained up to 500. In some places where the respondents seemed poorer than others in their community, I gave assistance. Significantly, this was neither an expectation nor a condition for talking. There are regional traditions for giving from empathy rather than for services rendered.
8 Henry has made a similar point from her experience of how conventional advice on self-representation may exaggerate the researcher's agency in the research encounter.
9 As called for by Barbour and Kitzinger (2001, p. 201).
10 Also known as "enabling and projective techniques" (Ritchie & Lewis, 2003, p. 126), "collective tasks" (Barbour & Kitzinger, 2001, p. 12) and "focusing exercises" (Bloor et al., 2001, p. 43).

References

Amoakohene, M. I. (2005). Focus group research: Towards an applicable model for Africa. In K. Kwansah-Aidoo (Ed.), *Topical issues in communications and media research* (pp. 167–190). New York, NY: Nova Science Publishers.

Apentiik, C. R. A., & Parpart, J. (2006). Working in different cultures: Issues of race, ethnicity and identity. In V. Desai & R. B. Potter (Eds.), *Doing development research* (pp. 34–43). London, England: Sage.

Barbour, R. (2009). *Doing focus groups*. London, England: Sage.

Barbour, R., & Kitzinger, J. (2001). Afterword. In R. Barbour & J. Kitzinger (Eds.), *Developing focus group research: Politics, theory and practice* (pp. 201–202). London, England: Sage.

Bell, D., Caplan, P., & Karim, W. J. (1993). *Gendered fields: Women, men and ethnography*. London, England: Routledge.

Bloor, M., Frankland, J., & Thomas, M. (2001). *Focus groups in social research*. London, England: Sage.

Desai, V., & Potter, R. B. (Eds.). (2006). *Doing development research*. London, England: Sage.

Ellsberg, M., & Heise, L. (2005). *Researching violence against women*. Geneva, Switzerland: WHO.

England, K. V. L. (1994). Getting personal: Reflexivity, positionality and feminist research. *The Professional Geographer*, 46(1), 80–89.

Fine, M. (1994). Working the hyphens: Reinventing the self and other in qualitative research. In N. K. Denzin & Y. S. Lincoln (Eds.), *Handbook of qualitative research* (pp. 70–82). Thousand Oaks, CA: Sage.

Green, G., Barbour, R., Bernard, M., & Kitzinger, J. (1993). 'Who wears the trousers?' Sexual harassment in research settings. *Women's Studies International Forum*, 16(6), 627–637.

Greenbaum, T. L. (2000). *Moderating focus groups: A practical guide for group facilitation*. Thousand Oaks, CA: Sage.

Hennink, M. (2007). *International focus group research: A handbook for the health and social sciences*. Cambridge, England: Cambridge University Press.

Hennink, M., Rana, I., & Iqbal, R. (2005). Knowledge of personal and sexual development amongst young people in Pakistan. *Culture, Health & Sexuality*, 7(4), 319–332.

Henry, M. G. (2003). 'Where are you really from?': Representation, identity and power in the fieldwork experiences of a South Asian diasporic. *Qualitative Research*, 3(2), 229–242.

Hollander, J. (2004). The social contexts of focus groups. *Journal of Contemporary Ethnography*, 33(5), 602–637.

Jakobsen, H. (2010). Review: International focus group research: A handbook for the health and social sciences by Monique M. Hennink. *Graduate Journal of Social Science*, 7(1), 73–77.

Kamberlis, G., & Dimitriadis, G. (2005). Focus groups: Strategic articulations of pedagogy, politics and inquiry. In N. K. Denzin & Y. S. Lincoln (Eds.), *The Sage handbook of qualitative research* (pp. 887–908). London, England: Sage.

Kitzinger, J. (1994). The methodology of focus groups: The importance of interaction between research participants. *Sociology of Health and Illness*, 16(1), 103–121.

Kotchetkova, I., Evans, R., & Langer, S. (2008). Articulating contextualized knowledge: Focus groups and/as public participation? *Science as Culture*, 17(1), 71–84.

Krueger, R. A., & Casey, M. A. (2009). *Focus groups: A practical guide for applied research*. Thousand Oaks, CA: Sage.

Lloyd-Evans, S. (2006). Focus groups. In V. Desai & R. B. Potter (Eds.), *Doing development research* (pp. 153–162). London, England: Sage.

Madge, C. (1994). The ethics of research in the 'Third World'. In Robson, E., & Willis, K. (Eds.), *Post-graduate fieldwork in developing areas: A rough guide* (pp. 91–102). London, UK: Royal Geographical Society.

Momsen, J. H. (2006). Women, men and fieldwork: Gender relations and power structures. In V. Desai & R. B. Potter (Eds.), *Doing development research* (pp. 44–51). London, England: Sage.

Morgan, D. L. (1996). Focus groups. *Annual Review of Sociology*, 22, 129–152.

Morgan, D. L. (1997). *Focus groups as qualitative research*. Thousand Oaks, CA: Sage.

Narayan, U. (1997). *Dislocating cultures: Identities, traditions, and third-world feminism*. New York, NY: Routledge.

Parker, A., & Tritter, J. (2006). Focus group method and methodology: Current practice and recent debate. *International Journal of Research & Method in Education*, 29(1), 23–37.

Poso, T., Honkatukia, P., & Nyqvist, L. (2008). Focus groups and the study of violence. *Qualitative Research*, 8(1), 73–89.
Puchta, C., & Potter, J. (2004). *Focus group practice*. London, England: Sage.
Ritchie, J., & Lewis, J. (2003). *Qualitative research practice: A guide for social science students and researchers*. London, England: Sage.
Rose, G. (1997). Situating knowledges: Positionality, reflexivities and other tactics. *Progress in Human Geography*, 21(3), 305–320.
Scheyvens, R., & Storey, D. (Eds.). (2003). *Development fieldwork: A practical guide*. London, England: Sage.
Smithson, J. (2000). Using and analysing focus groups: Limitations and possibilities. *International Journal of Social Research Methodology*, 3(2), 103–119.
Srivastava, P. (2006). Reconciling multiple researcher positionalities and languages in international research. *Research in Comparative and International Education*, 1(3), 210–222.
Staeheli, L. A., & Lawson, V. A. (1994). A discussion of 'women in the field': The politics of feminist fieldwork. *The Professional Geographer*, 46(1), 96–102.
Stewart, D. W., Rook, D. W., & Shamdasani, P. N. (2007). *Focus groups: Theory and practice*. Thousand Oaks, CA: Sage.
Vissandjee, B., Abdool, S. N., & Dupere, S. (2002). Focus groups in rural Gujarat, India: A modified approach. *Qualitative Health Research*, 12(6), 826–843.
Walraven, G. (1996). Willingness to pay for district hospital services in rural Tanzania. *Health Policy and Planning*, 11(4), 428–437.
Wilkinson, S. (1998). Focus groups in feminist research: Power, interaction, and the co-construction of meaning. *Women's Studies International Forum*, 21(1), 111–125.
Wilkinson, S. (2006). Analysing interaction in focus groups. In P. Drew, G. Raymond, & D. Weinberg (Eds.), *Talk and interaction in social research methods* (pp. 50–62). London, England: Sage.

14
SOCIAL NETWORK INTERVIEWING AS AN EMANCIPATORY SOUTHERN METHODOLOGICAL INNOVATION

Sharlene Swartz and Alude Mahali

Social Network Interviewing/Interviews (SNI/SNIs) is an emancipatory methodological research and intervention innovation. It is a way to enhance traditional qualitative research methodologies through interviews conducted by research participants (participant-researchers) with members of their community and networks without the presence of the formally trained researcher. It aims to recruit participant-researchers and train them, in order to conduct research that has as its goal some form of social change, intervention or emancipation for those who are participating. It is a reaction to extractive, non-collaborative, and objectifying research. It is a Southern methodology, not only because it originates in the South, but also because it aims to follow the tenets of 'decolonising methodologies' (Tuhiwai Smith, 1999, p. 1), resisting,

> the ways in which scientific research is implicated in the worst excesses of colonialism ... [research that] can assume to know all that it is possible to know of us, on the basis of their brief encounters with some of us. It appals us that the West can desire, extract and claim ownership of our ways of knowing, our imagery, the things we create and produce, and then simultaneously reject the people who created and developed those ideas.

In qualitative research the interview technique is commonly utilised as one of the key methods for data collection. Much has been written about its usefulness as well as its shortfalls, for example regarding unequal power dynamics, lack of interpersonal skills on the researcher's part and lack of rapport, and its inability to enrol hard-to-reach groups into the research process (Gill, Stewart, Treasure, & Chadwick, 2008). Less has been said about its potential as an emancipatory methodology, one that helps the interviewer and interviewee

DOI: 10.4324/9781003355397-17

gain new insight and potentially change their understanding of a phenomenon, especially as a form of intervention. This chapter presents SNI as an alternative that addresses some of the mentioned shortfalls, and holds emancipatory and decolonising possibilities.

Drawing on important social science theories, including that of intersectionality (Collins, 1993), forms of social capital (Bourdieu, 1997), and conscientisation (Freire, 2000), SNI integrates how social locations (race, class, gender, and geography), social norms, and social practices of individual and collective agency all combine in an interview process to help two parties in dialogue develop strategies to overcome social problems. The aim of these interviews is to create unique opportunities for participant-researchers to discuss a subject with their social networks (friends, family, peers, authority figures and community members) in order to provide a rich and nuanced understanding of the topic both for themselves (as a participatory and emancipatory exercise) and for the research project (as knowledge production).

SNI ascribes to a constructivist framework. Knowledge can and is co-constructed by people in interaction, and their meaning-making of phenomena is related to the varied contexts in which they find themselves (Bryman, 2012; Creswell, 2009). Or as Bourdieu puts it, "the objects of knowledge are constructed, not passively recorded, and ... the principle of this construction is the system of structured, structuring dispositions, the *habitus* which is constituted in practice" (Bourdieu, 1990, p. 52 emphasis in original). SNI helps to understand behaviour by focussing attention on the relationships between individuals and society, what Bourdieu refers to as the habitus. Rather than exclusively studying the particular context of an individual, such as demographic and socioeconomic traits, individuals' social location as raced, classed, or gendered, is considered in relation to social norms produced by religious and educational institutions, traditional and street cultures, and prevailing attitudes towards issues of recognition and respect, among others.

SNI, in considering research participants agents or knowers-in-context (and engaging them as participant-researchers), provides an opportunity for discussions of the effects of culture, poverty, and inequality on opportunity and behaviour, creating openings for the participants to engage in self-evaluation, in relation to those impacted by their choices and actions (Swartz, 2011). Such participant-researchers are likely to access and interpret the realities of members within their networks in a way that exceeds that of the traditional researcher-researched dyad. Furthermore, due to research participants' intricate links with the communities under study, SNI spreads the benefits that participant-researchers accrue from their involvement in the formal research process to the larger community. This is emancipatory because the participant-researchers (and those who compose their social networks) are seen as knowledgeable collaborators who involve themselves in difficult conversations, find value in each other's feelings or perspectives, establish areas of common interest and may as a result be willing to work – separately or together – towards social justice in their shared communities (Mahali & Swartz, 2018; Swartz, 2011).

SNIs can be used as part of a larger study, and aid triangulation, or it can be a standalone methodology. SNI has as its aims: (1) to help participant-researchers marshal their thoughts about a particular issue, converting those thoughts into critical responses; (2) to expose participant-researcher to existing and wider networks as they engage on a particular topic of importance to themselves and the formal researcher; (3) to facilitate elucidatory exchange between participant-researchers and relevant community members; (4) to develop participant-researcher capitals through this exchange; (5) to promote identification and information sharing among marginalised or disadvantaged people; and (6) to stimulate reflection for the purpose of individual or collective action by participants. SNI also involves an element of capacity development because it requires that participant-researchers be adequately trained to effectively engage in SNIs, which last between 20 and 30 minutes. It is useful to understand more deeply the theoretical influences of SNI in order to position it conceptually.

Theoretical footprint and emergent influences of SNI

Paulo Freire outlines the relationship between knowledge and emancipation. Freire posited that the only way the poor and oppressed could control the naming of their world was if they were conscientised and engaged in dialogue about the conditions of their oppression with the view to transform it (Freire, 2000). SNI is as much concerned with changing relationships and behaviours of individuals as it is about changing or at least facilitating understandings of conditions of oppression.

SNI strongly draws on the tenets of social network analysis (Vera & Schupp, 2006; Wasserman & Faust, 1994); participatory action research (PAR) (Hawkins, 2015; Kaukko & Fertig, 2016); public health's motivational interviewing (Miller & Rollnick, 2002); and nudge theory from the world of behavioural economics (Bradbury, McGimpsey, & Santori, 2013; Kosters & Van der Heijden, 2015; Thaler & Sunstein, 2009).

Social network analysis is a sociological method that has been operational since the 1960s (Vera & Schupp, 2006), and is based on the belief that individuals are connected by linkages through which information, cultural norms and other social resources pass. Analysis within this method uses descriptions of webs of connections to examine how behaviour is both constrained and facilitated (Wasserman & Faust, 1994). The extrapolation from research to action rests on the assumption that intervening in the flow of social resources within networks will potentially shift behaviours. Social networks enhance the ability of communities as collective and cooperative entities to develop strategies for resisting poverty, gender inequality, xenophobia, and marginal economic participation. It does so through asking questions that ensure that participant-researchers reflect on how these social identities intersect to form "interlocking systems of oppression" (Collins, 1993, p. 67) that affect the ways in which people see the world around them, as well as individual and group life chances (Meer & Muller, 2017).

SNI attempts to widen the networks of participant-researchers so that they might also begin to acquire what Pierre Bourdieu (1997) calls social, symbolic, and cultural capital – knowledge about the structuring of society, the rules of the game, and social allies and networks who might help introduce them to future opportunities, including being accorded respect and honour in going about their lives. Social network analysis is of importance here because understanding the extent and nature of connections and relations between individuals, organisations, and communities aids in understanding social worlds (Marin & Wellman, 2011), including the characteristics or nature of those relational ties.

PAR similarly maintains that people within communities or specific populations under study possess knowledge of their communities and should be included in research efforts affecting their communities. In PAR, issues of concern are identified collaboratively by researchers and stakeholders, and action plans are developed based on research findings. The strengths and assets of community participants are drawn on to various degrees throughout the research process (Kaukko & Fertig, 2016). Additionally, the process is geared towards problem-solving (Hawkins, 2015). Particularly related to participatory studies with vulnerable populations, it is believed that action to address the vulnerability should necessarily be the focus of the research (Kaukko & Fertig, 2016). SNI can be considered to be a kind of PAR because it is interactive with the aim of drawing on the knowledge of participants and their social networks, co-developing research questions of concern, and including participants in generating an understanding of the issues under study. This is done with the purpose of facilitating the flow of resources and to influence change.

Although SNI is a qualitative tool that has been used primarily in social science research, it draws some inspiration from the clinical method of motivational interviewing, often used to help people change their addictive and adherence behaviours (to say taking medication for a chronic condition) (Miller & Rollnick, 2002). Motivational interviewing, much like PAR is interactive in nature with a view to influencing change. Typically, motivation is understood as internal, residing within the individual as a personal state or trait. Motivational interviewing departs from this notion in that it is an interpersonal process, the product of an interaction between people. Miller and Rollnick argue that "motivation for change can not only be influenced by but in a very real sense arises from an interpersonal context" (2002, p. 22). This point is critical because SNI is not individually driven. Put differently, contrary to simply asking a participant to reflect on an issue either verbally or in writing, SNIs place value on the interpersonal exchange between the participant-interviewer and the community-interviewee.

The dialogue supported by a purposefully structured guide is precisely what is expected to galvanise change. Miller and Rollnick go on to explain that interpersonal interaction inspires collaboration which involves being attuned to and monitoring one's own aspirations (i.e., reflecting on your own goals, hopes, or obstacles). In general, young adults are often ambivalent and this ambivalence extends beyond risk behaviour to quite general issues of identity and roles. Motivational interviewing is salient here because it is "about helping to free people from the ambivalence that entraps them in repetitive cycles of self-defeating or self-destructive behaviour" (Miller & Rollnick, 2002, p. 41). For young people, motivational interviewing tends to support personal change goals, which naturally supports explorations of worldviews and continued efforts towards autonomy.

While SNI and motivational interviewing encourage positive and agential interaction with the view to influence change, these aims are not always made obvious to the participant. This is how SNI takes some inspiration from nudge theory. A nudge is any aspect of "choice architecture that alters people's behaviour in a predictable way without forbidding any options or significantly changing their economic incentives" (Thaler & Sunstein, 2009, p. 6). "Nudges seek to change behaviour through a wide range of interventions ... through a financial incentive ... through providing relevant information ... or even by actively blocking an inappropriate choice" (Kosters & Van der Heijden, 2015, p. 279). For Bradbury et al. (2013, p. 247) nudge theory,

> suggests that individuals do not always make the choices that would benefit them most, that failures to choose well are the result of common cognitive flaws or limitations and are thus predictable and that therefore everyday decision making can and should be framed in particular ways to encourage ('nudge') people to choose in advantageous ways.

Nudging is influential in its efforts to "understand how to promote desired behavioural changes amongst young people" (Bradbury et al., 2013, p. 251). This is a "soft ... nonintrusive type of paternalism" (Thaler & Sunstein, 2009, p. 6), that aims to nudge people towards healthier, safer, wiser choices without telling them what to do (Bradbury et al., 2013). SNI nudges participant-researchers by helping to facilitate a reflective discussion that allows insights, choices, and options for behaviour to emerge. SNIs nudge participant-researchers to develop a network by facilitating and encouraging them to interact with people who they might otherwise not seek out and from whom they can potentially gain knowledge, a resource, economic opportunity, or key information. What is particularly transformative about

SNIs is the idea that catalytic conversation with community members has the potential to promote positive behaviour change. The formal researcher acts as both the catalyst and the mediator of this process.

Furthermore, SNI offers the opportunity to bridge the gap between social networks and social capital. The notion of social capital works through mechanisms such as "positive feelings from joint association or shared values ... and social identity" (Moody & Paxton, 2009, p. 1494). Social capital offers people the confidence to pursue opportunities, find information, and carry themselves in the world in different ways compared to feeling as if they are isolated or alone in the situation (Bourdieu, 1997). It is the combination of real networks and social capital that has the potential to inspire action in concrete settings. Research on social capital can help contextualise network models by highlighting how contexts shape relations. What these theories and methods have in common is that they move us closer to an interactive, and over time, an emancipatory outcome; one that creates change despite contexts of marginality and oppression. Emancipatory research aims to engage with and address issues of concern within communities (Ledwith, 2007; Robinson & Meerkotter, 2003), and does so through a commitment to "mutual and sustainable learning, self-reflection, the co-construction of knowledge and the empowerment of research participants" (Swartz & Nyamnjoh, 2018, p. 3). Central to SNI is the belief that people in communities have knowledge about their communities; they are 'transcultural knowers' (Butz & Besio, 2004), linking researchers, research participants, and community actors. The importance of the voices of participant-researchers and those in their contexts, in this type of research cannot be overstated.

Three research studies through which Social Network Interviewing was developed

Before describing the stages of Social Network Interviewing, it is important to describe the three studies that have helped to shape the methodology. Table 14.1 summarises these studies that focus on contemporary youth-related topics of importance and relevance in South Africa: young fatherhood, youth sexual risk behaviour and young people's struggles and strategies to succeed in university. All names used in the extended descriptions below are pseudonyms or generic labels for participant-researchers.

Young fathers

Fatherhood and masculinities have in the past 20 years become an increasing focus of researchers, funders, and development practitioners. Often controversial, the amount of resources expended on work with men and boys results from two main perceptions about gender and human development. First, that

TABLE 14.1 A summary of the three research studies through which Social Network Interviewing was developed

	Young fatherhood	*Youth risk behaviour*	*Success in higher education*
Aims of the study	• To understand how young men living in poverty, and those involved with them, experience fatherhood; • To understand the factors that help or hinder young men's engagement in the parenting of their children.	• To understand the value that young people associate with loveLife (a youth focused HIV prevention initiative in South Africa); • The factors that impact their life choices; • Young people's engagement with risk.	• To understand the social factors that aid or hinder students' success; • How race, class, and gender impact on students' perceptions and experiences of success; • How students use personal and social agency to create opportunities and success.
Study participants	27 young men who were aged between 14 and 20 at the time they first became fathers.	61 youth aged between 18 and 23 who were involved in a loveLife programme.	80 first year students enrolled in university.
Main study output	Teenage Tata (Swartz & Bhana, 2009)	*Evaluating the value that young people attach to loveLife and investigating factors impacting the life choices and risk tolerance of youth* (Peltzer et al., 2012).	*Studying while black* (Swartz et al., 2018)

attention to the experiences of women and girls in development has seen significant success in terms of poverty alleviation, health, and economic growth (Nussbaum, 2001). Second, that issues such as unemployment, gender-based violence, parenting, and alcohol dependency would improve if similar attention were paid to the challenges of men's lives (White, 1997). Research and intervention efforts based on these perceptions tend to address men or groups of men as individuals without taking account of their day-to-day lives and those who share it with them – in other words, their social networks.

The study *Teenage Tata* [Teenage Father] employed SNI as a means of studying young fathers within an impoverished community. Research participants – young fathers – carried out interviews with members of their social networks, including parents, extended family, and family members of the mother of their child, along with teachers, friends, and religious leaders, based on questions collaboratively developed. Questions the young fathers asked in these interviews included, "What kind of father do you think I have been since my baby was born?" and "What advice do you have for me about being a young father?" As well as providing rich qualitative data about the lives of young fathers – a frequently invisible group – interviews presented an opportunity for these young fathers to engage with people who share their lives with them to talk about their feelings and thoughts related to fatherhood. SNI also created space for the young men to engage in self-evaluation in relation to those impacted by their choices and actions.

Furthermore, SNI allowed for challenging messages to be relayed about their behaviour and practices in a manner to which young men were more likely to be receptive than standard educational sessions, workshops, and media messages. For example, Vuyo (age 17, father of a 2-year-old child) interviewed a male friend, who candidly said:

> As your closest friend, uh, because I've been spending a lot of time with you – [I can see that] you don't take care of your baby. You're very – Sometimes you become irresponsible – you're [with your new girlfriend] instead of doing what you must do to keep contact with your baby.

Commenting on sensitive cultural issues, Lwandile's (age 17, father of a 2-year-old child) grandfather commented:

> The culture forced us to stand for you at the beginning when the family had to tell you that you make their child [pregnant]. So, they could not talk with you because of your age. That's how the culture made you a good father. But it also made you a bad father because of excluding you in many things.

Both examples show how social network interviews can provide messages that challenge current practices, whether individual or cultural. These messages were well received by the young father in question. Compare how differently they might have been received in the context of a workshop or admonishment from a parent. Too often research and support programmes interact with men either as individuals with personal challenges, restraints, and opportunities or as groups of men with shared obstacles and experiences. Through interventions such as educational programmes and workshops, focus groups, and counselling, productive gains may be made at the level of individual men's lives but a gap persists between these improvements and wider social change and benefits to the communities in which men live.

SNI has the potential of spreading the benefits men accrue from their interaction with these activities to the larger community. The function of SNI is well illustrated by Lwandile who said that the experience gave his community a chance to express their criticisms of his behaviour and allowed him to "hear some of the other things" members of his network had to say, including "what they could have done, and [what] they never did do to help". Community involvement is a priority of both research and intervention projects but is notoriously difficult to achieve. SNI represents an opportunity to make meaningful advances towards positive change at the community and wider societal level.

Youth sexual risk taking

Although there is evidence of decreased rates of HIV incidence among youth in South Africa, there is still scope to reduce the baseline prevalence among young adults, as well as to decrease their continued tolerance of high-risk sexual behaviours. Over the past two decades, loveLife – a South African national HIV prevention initiative for young people – has intensified efforts to lower HIV prevalence rates among young people by addressing the socioeconomic factors that exacerbate the spread of HIV. These include helping young people think through sexual risk-taking behaviours and offer guidance on healthy relationships, as well as linking young people to diversionary opportunities. A large study evaluating the effectiveness of their intervention, and young people's risk behaviours and experience with regard to opportunities, included as a component, social network interviews.

Ultimately SNIs, individual interviews and a survey produced much of the same data: the influence of alcohol on unprotected sex; risky sexual behaviours with multiple partners as compensations for feeling deprived in other ways (possessions, respect, recognition); and young people tending to live only in the present, "not thinking about what happens next". However, inviting youth who have been through loveLife's programmes to use SNIs in order to spend time in their communities asking a set of deeply reflective questions, was key to prompting further conversations and social connection.

Of the myriad of insights gleaned from SNIs in this study two stand out. The first concerned the level of openness participants encountered about culture, especially from older family members. Johannes (male, age 21) was told by his 19-year-old female friend that risk taking arises because "parents can't tell their children the truth". This is not an unusual sentiment from young people. But it's the corroboration from older family members that makes it noteworthy. "*As Africans* in the household, the communication is poor, parents don't talk to their kids" (Youth worker, male, age 38, interviewed by Zoleka, female, age 22, emphasis added). A 66-year-old father, reflected on the reason why this communication does not happen: "I guess it is due to [their] own ignorance" (interviewed by Mbalenhle, female, age 23). Many more adults spoke of the cultural taboos that keep them from speaking to their children about sexual decision making, and that perpetuates sexual risk taking.

Phelo (male, age 22), experienced further openness from his 45-year-old aunt who told him that "stress is the cause of risk behaviours ... sometimes you need a beer to cheer you up ... from my side I need one tap of dagga [marijuana] for me when stressed". A second insight concerned peer pressure. Here there were numerous conversations, as might be expected, about the pressure from peers. But in a SNI, Petunia (female, age 19) heard the following from her 25-year-old boyfriend: risk taking comes "because as young people we tend to listen to what people say about our lives and start doing what we don't really want to do".

SNIs therefore acted as a means of triangulating data, an important consideration for qualitative research. It also produced a depth of insight into many of the common themes produced in the study, that might not otherwise have been obtained. It allowed us to explain youth risk behaviour, in candid (the role of culture and parents' ignorance), and surprising ways (societal pressure rather than peer pressure).

Struggles and strategies for student success

Studying while black was a five-year longitudinal, qualitative study of agency and obstacles to success amongst higher education students. Set in a sample of South African universities, the study asked, 'who succeeds, who does not?' and was intentionally student-centred. It followed a cohort of 80 first year students from eight universities, over five years, noting obstacles along the way and strategies they used to stay the course, amid high dropout rates amongst black students (50% completion rate). Given South Africa's history, the study was framed within theory that recognised students' ability to succeed at university remains mediated by the legacies of colonialism and apartheid. The study's key research questions asked: (1) What structural and social factors do 'historically disadvantaged' students identify as helping and/or hindering success; (2) What role do intersecting identities (race, class, gender, and language) play in students' perception and experiences of, and access to success; and (3) How do students use agency to create opportunities and attain success?

In the first three years of the study, all 80 participants were asked to conduct 5–7 SNIs with community members, peers, university faculty, and people from university support services. Here, the idea was to get them to broaden their own networks, this time beyond family and friends and in so doing to extend what Bourdieu (1997) terms the multiple 'forms of capital': the acquisition of social, symbolic, and cultural capitals, creating a network that produces confidence, engenders respect, and potentially offers future opportunities alongside insights for success in their current studies. Cultural capital was built by providing students with wider access to human resources that could aid in generating knowledge and the capacity to understand institutional requirements, information and structures. Students were given insight into the function of symbolic capital – the notion that one's race, class, and gender, creates differential privilege and benefits at university – through SNIs, especially in interacting with other students (Mahali & Swartz, 2018).

Participants reported that SNIs were a helpful exercise for different reasons. Some felt a sense of responsibility and expertise because of the training provided which made them feel like researchers, saying that "conducting the interviews ... gave them a sense of purpose and professionalism" (Swartz et al., 2018, p. 105). Others were able to gain insight or new information – especially pertinent when that insight involved aspects of academic development or the information encouraged help-seeking behaviour. For example, students reported that hearing other's stories of struggle helped them put their own finances in perspective and spoke of coming to the realisation that poor backgrounds do not define you, as many students suffer from financial difficulties, and still manage to succeed. Another student, in the second year of the study, became aware of how the social network interviews inspired moments of self-directed action: "A lot of people were just talking about discipline, studying hard and stuff and I actually realised that wow, I don't do all that, like I'm not that disciplined" (Student 8, female, age 22, University of Johannesburg).

Another student spoke of how she gained a different perspective concerning student counselling services when she heard one of the university counsellors she interviewed express frustration and sadness about how little students access these services despite the high rates of depression and trauma. Yet another spoke of being forewarned of the racism to expect from lecturers as classes got smaller, and so felt better equipped to deal with it.

Students as SNI participant-researchers reported being both challenged by their own behaviour and empowered by others' stories:

> The participants' engagement with interviewees (especially other students) was, in many ways, an exercise of holding up a mirror to themselves. It is not enough to hear the stories, but we hoped that through the social network interviews, participants would be encouraged to think or do things differently; a change that can be as significant as accessing a particular service on campus to finding the courage to ask a lecturer a question in class, for example.
>
> *Swartz et al. (2018, p. 105)*

Of course, many were as frustrated in trying to conduct interviews with university administrators. They experienced reluctance and roadblocks in the process not dissimilar to what they experienced in trying to obtain everyday information from them during their studies. The difference with conducting interviews concerned the confidence and perseverance they learnt in pushing though the barriers. In addition, students were offered small reimbursements (data, airtime, transport money) for conducting SNIs which no doubt contributed to their perseverance. Because this study, unlike the others described above, was conducted over five years, students were able to convincingly demonstrate the gains that participating in SNIs brought to them. The research study also benefitted from this additional data and the knowledge that intervention and research can be closely aligned.

The eight stages in a social network interview

Since its initial use in the study on young fathers in 2009, SNI has gone through an evolution. From inception, the method has aimed to ask about gendered and community norms, invite constructive internal and external evaluation from participants as well as help the two parties in dialogue develop strategies to overcome problems. Over time however, SNI has been developed into a framework that can be reprised across different circumstances, evidenced by the three distinct case studies presented in this chapter. These case studies illustrate SNI's ability to provide participants with a road map within which community messages and existing resources from social networks may be accessed. Regardless of the subject, the conceptually underpinned formula provides participants with an opportunity to expand their network with the view to increase capitals, self-reflect, gain insight and information, question their biases and critique their current contexts and actions.

Over time, and the studies described above, eight stages (see Figure 14.1) have emerged in the process of Social Network Interviewing.

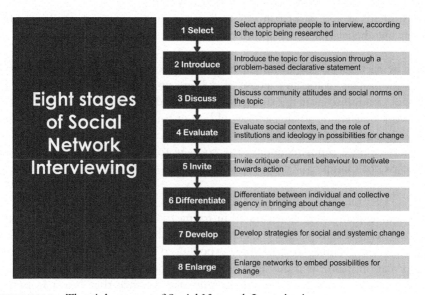

FIGURE 14.1 The eight stages of Social Network Interviewing.

Source: Authors.

This deliberate structuring aims to help others to use the methodology. The stages also support the novice participant-researcher through a series of questions (Stages 1–3) that focus first on formulating the topic for discussion, selecting appropriate members of their networks to interview and introducing an opening declarative statement that sets the scene for the interview, and situates the interviewee. What follows is a discussion of current scripts and norms circulating within communities, societies and sub-culture groups.

The next part of the template (Stages 4–8) elevates the discussion by prompting an evaluation of the participants' social context and environment, followed by an invitation to both parties to develop individual and collective strategies for action, and ends with questions that attempt to create linkages and social connections that extends the usefulness of interviewing beyond data collection to social benefit. While the questions, contexts, and subject may change across studies, the conceptual organisation by which questions are structured should not change. Each stage is described below, along with its specific conceptual inspiration (although these frequently overlap), and examples of the specific interview questions that were asked in the three studies already described.

Stage 1: Select appropriate people to interview

Formulating the topic for investigation together with participant-researchers is a pre-step to selecting individuals relevant to the topic being researched. Both can be done together. The aim in selecting appropriate people is to include a range of people at different social levels in order to expose participant-researchers to a wide network from whom they can potentially learn or find support. Ask *Who can contribute meaningfully to the topic?* Participant-researchers need, however, to feel comfortable in being able to access and engage potential interviews in the project. Selecting 5–7 people to be interviewed is usually adequate. In a study that runs over multiple years this number can be extended, or interviews repeated (Table 14.2).

Stage 2: Introduce the topic for discussion through a problem-based declarative statement

This opening declarative statement makes clear the specific issue the study is concerned with and sets the tone for the interview. It asks *What is the problem?* and offers a rationale for why it is important to have a discussion on the topic rather than merely introducing a subject, for example, just saying this study is on 'young fathers' or 'youth risk behaviour' or 'university failure rates'. Setting up this problem statement carefully and in collaboration with participant-researchers ensures a thorough understanding of the

TABLE 14.2 Stage 1 of Social Network Interviewing – selecting appropriate people to interview

Who Can Contribute Meaningfully to the Topic?

	Young fatherhood	Youth risk behaviour	Success in higher education
Stage 1 Select appropriate people to interview, according to the topic being researched [Specific conceptual influence: social network analysis; participation action research]	• Male family members (e.g., father, grandfather, uncle, brother, cousin) • Male friends • Female friends • Female family members (e.g., mother, grandmother, aunt, sister, cousin) • Current romantic partner • Former romantic partner • Family members of mother of child • Former/current teacher • Community or youth leader	• Male family members (e.g., father, grandfather, uncle, brother, cousin) • Male friends • Female friends • Female family members (e.g., mother, grandmother, aunt, sister, cousin) • Current romantic partner • Former romantic partner • Family members of current romantic partner • Former/current teacher • Community or youth leader	• A person from your hometown who never went to university • A student like you • A student you consider more/less privileged than you • A teacher from your previous school • A person in university leadership • A recent graduate • A person working in student support services • A student who dropped out of university • A person who helped you get to varsity • A person who has helped you this past year • A family member who has been to university

topic and confidence in being able to conduct the interview. It also sets the interviewee at ease from the outset with a clear understanding of the topic (Table 14.3).

Stage 3: Discuss community attitudes and social norms on the topic

The first question in a Social Network Interview should be designed to be easy to answer and put both the participant-researcher and the interviewee at ease. The question or questions asked are: *What do people believe about this subject?* The purpose is to build rapport, open the discussion with a wide range of opinions and in so doing establish the context in which the phenomenon operates. By asking a broad open-ended question here, multiple community norms and values can be placed on the table for further discussion, including current scripts circulating within communities, families, cultural traditions and youth sub-culture groups (Table 14.4).

TABLE 14.3 Stage 2 of Social Network Interviewing – introducing the topic through a problem-based declarative statement

What Is the Problem?

	Young fatherhood	Youth risk behaviour	Success in higher education
Stage 2 Introduce the topic for discussion through a problem-based declarative statement [Specific conceptual influence: emancipatory research]	Young fathers are frequently accused of not participating in the upbringing of their children. This research study aims to find out why this might be so and what can be done to help them stay in touch.	Young people living in townships have high rates of HIV/AIDS and STIs, experience early and unplanned parenting and experience high levels of violence. This research study aims to find out how young people can better protect themselves from these risks.	Many students struggle to both enrol at and successfully complete university. This research study aims to find out why this is so and what could be done about it.

TABLE 14.4 Stage 3 of Social Network Interviewing – discussing community norms and social attitudes

What Do People Believe about this Subject?

	Young fatherhood	Youth risk behaviour	Success in higher education
Stage 3 Discuss community attitudes and social norms on the topic [Specific conceptual influence: habitus]	1 Do you remember how you responded when I told you that I was going to be a father? What did you say at the time? What did you think at the time? 2 What advice did you give me at the time?	1 What behaviours pose a risk to our community? To young people in our community? 2 What is it about South Africa that pushes young people to take risks with their health and safety?	1 Why is it important for young South Africans to succeed at university? 2 In your opinion, what are some of the struggles facing university students in South Africa, and what are some of the reasons for these struggles?

Stage 4: Evaluate social contexts, and the role of institutions and ideology in possibilities for change

These questions elevate the discussion by prompting an evaluation of the participant-researchers social context. Questions here ask: *How does (our) context affect the problem?* The goal of this group of questions is to highlight and

TABLE 14.5 Stage 4 of Social Network Interviewing – evaluating how contexts affects the issue

How Does Context Affect the Problem?

	Young fatherhood	Youth risk behaviour	Success in higher education
Stage 4 Evaluate social contexts, and the role of institutions and ideology in possibilities for change [Specific conceptual influence: cultural and symbolic capital]	3 What role do you think a young father should play in the life of their children – if they are not married to the mother? Should this role change over time, for example when the child is newly born, when s/he is 10, when she is 18 years old? 4 Who should decide about this role?	3 What places in our community encourage young people to take risks? Why? 4 How do young people make the community safer or less safe?	3 In your opinion, what affects someone's success at university? 4 Who is responsible for students succeeding at university?

evaluate the enablers and barriers in the environment that contributes to the problem or contributes to finding solutions for the problem. The discussion here should consider intersectional social locations (race, class, gender, and their interactions) as well as the way churches, families, schools, and other institution help or hinder young people with regard to this problem (Table 14.5).

TABLE 14.6 Stage 5 of Social Network Interviewing – critiquing current behaviour

What Must I Do Differently to Bring about Change?

	Young fatherhood	Youth risk behaviour	Success in higher education
Stage 5 Invite critique of current behaviour to motivate towards action [Specific conceptual influence: nudge theory; motivational interviewing]	5 What kind of father do you think I have been since the time my baby was born? 6 How do you think I should have behaved differently – since hearing I was going to become a father?	5 What do I do that makes you worry about me? 6 What do I do that puts other people in danger?	5 From what you know of me (or students in general), what do I do that stops (sabotages) me from succeeding at university? 6 What should I be doing?

Stage 5: Invite critique of current behaviour to motivate towards action

This stage calls for constructive analysis and critique from both the participant-researcher and the interviewee. The aim here is for the participant-researcher to ask: *What must I do differently to bring about change?* What can 'we do' comes in the next stage – for now the focus is on individual and internal agency. A level of discomfort and reflection is expected as the participant-researcher is invited to question their (sometimes risky) behaviours. This should be addressed in training (Table 14.6).

Stage 6: Differentiate between individual and collective agency in bringing about change

This stage gets at the heart of Freire's idea of conscientisation, being able to differentiate between individual agency in order to bring about personal change, and the collective agency needed to address systemic and structural problems. Here interview questions ask: *What must we do together to bring about change?* This is a difficult undertaking, and it is likely that the participant-researcher and the interviewee will only begin to address this large topic in such a short encounter as the SNI is, but the potential insights outweigh the difficulty (Table 14.7).

TABLE 14.7 Stage 6 of Social Network Interviewing – differentiating between individual and collective agency

What Must We Do Together to Bring about Change?

	Young fatherhood	Youth risk behaviour	Success in higher education
Stage 6 Differentiate between individual and collective agency in bringing about change [Specific conceptual influence: conscientisation]	7 In what way do you think our culture has helped me to be a good father? 8 In what way do you think our culture has stopped me from being a good father? (Probe: damages, respect, bride price, status as a man or a 'boy'.	7 What is it about our community and culture that contributes to young people taking risks with their health? How is risk taking different for young men and young women? 8 How does our community help young people avoid danger and HIV/AIDS?	7 How does racism and gender discrimination affect student's lives? 8 How is success at university affected by people's backgrounds? (Prompt: gender, education, race, social class).

TABLE 14.8 Stage 7 of Social Network Interviewing – differentiating between individual and collective agency – developing strategies for change

What Practical Steps Can Be Taken?

	Young fatherhood	Youth risk behaviour	Success in higher education
Stage 7 Develop strategies for social and systemic change [Specific conceptual influence: intersectionality, emancipation, justice]	9 Why do you think young men often lose contact with their children over the years? 10 What advice do you have for me about being a young father for the future?	9 How would you like someone who you care about to look after themselves? 10 What advice do you have for me about taking risks?	9 In your opinion, who should be helping students succeed at university, and what should they be doing to help? 10 What steps have you taken (or are you taking) in order to be successful in your life?

Stage 7: Develop strategies for social and systemic change

This stage invites the participant-researcher and interviewee to develop strategies to recognise and overcome barriers (and behaviours) identified in previous sections. It asks *What practical steps can be taken?* This is what makes SNI not only a potential intervention but also a tool that inspires individual and collective action through guided dialogue. Here, as with all the other stages, only modest steps for action are expected, and should be applauded. The conceptual underpinning here of intersectionality (Collins & Bilge, 2016) is cited because of the social justice bias towards action that is inherent to intersectionality's theory of change (Table 14.8).

Stage 8: Enlarge networks to embed possibilities for change

The final stage in SNI consists of a series of referral and advice-seeking questions that aims to enlarge networks and develop participant-researchers' social capital. Questions here ask: *Who else would it be valuable to talk to?* The intention is, following the recognition of what is and what is not possible, to point the participant-researcher to social networks or practices that are valuable. The aim is not only motivational but also promotes information sharing with the view to develop confidence and further agency (or collective co-agency). Frequently these referrals will create advantageous linkages and promote help-seeking in transferable contexts for the participant-researcher (Table 14.9).

TABLE 14.9 Stage 8 of Social Network Interviewing – enlarging networks to embed change

Who Else Would It Be Valuable to Talk To?

	Young fatherhood	*Youth risk behaviour*	*Success in higher education*
Stage 8 Enlarge networks to embed possibilities for change [Specific conceptual influence: social capital, nudge theory]	11 Who else should I talk to, who would have helpful advice for me, about being involved in the life of my child?	11 Who else should I talk to about protecting myself and others from risks?	11 Who else should I talk to that might be able to help me to be successful at university?

Opportunities and challenges of Social Network Interviewing

Social Network Interviewing has the potential to influence culture, norms, and beliefs in communities and individuals. It also has the potential to reach hard-to-reach groups, triangulate data, address stereotypes, encourage change and help-seeking behaviours, and recognise where systemic change is needed. There are however various processes that need to be in place for SNIs to realise its full potential, and to succeed in being an emancipatory research tool that makes visible critical issues related to oppression and marginalisation, as well as enabling transformative intentions that places the researcher-participant at the centre. These include the training that participant-researchers require; ensuring that participant-researchers are at the centre of the process; and paying attention to various ethical concerns.

Training is needed in multiple areas. Novice participant-researchers, like all qualitative researchers, need basic training in how to approach and build rapport with potential interviewees, obtain informed consent, ask open-ended questions and use a voice recorder. For SNIs to fully realise its emancipatory potential, not only as a tool for intervention, but also as a methodology that allows participants to investigate areas of concern to themselves, participant-researchers need to be at the centre of the process. Formulating the topic for investigation and co-creating interview schedules are ways to achieve this outcome. However, to ensure that questions are aligned with the conceptual framework on which SNI is built, participant-researchers must be helped to understand this underlying rationale. Co-creation thus also requires further training. The eight stages described above are meant to facilitate this training and to make crafting questions easier. Besides co-creating questions, another way to ensure that participant-researchers are always at the centre of the SNI activity is to debrief and have a feedback session with them after the SNI exercise about their experience.

There are minimal risks to SNI but there are a few limitations to be considered by researchers looking to adopt the methodology. The first is the reliability of data. It is critical to remember that participant-researchers, although trained, conduct SNIs unsupervised. This poses a potential risk for both the participant-researcher and the person being interviewed, particularly when a sensitive (or reportable) issue arises and neither are equipped to resolve the issue.

While formal consent should be obtained when conducting SNIs, confidentiality/anonymity is not paramount. This is because SNI aims to build dialogue and social links. However, participants must be reminded not to disclose any personally sensitive information in the exchange. A final consideration regards offering compensation to participant-researchers for every SNI completed. In Global South contexts especially, the mobility and economic capacity of young people cannot be taken for granted. Compensation for time, travel, and tools is essential. Incentives, when provided, should motivate but not coerce participation. This is a fine line to traverse, but one which should be thoroughly considered, along with the foregoing, each time SNI is employed.

Conclusion

Although this chapter deals with SNI as a method of research and intervention to support positive change in the lives of particular groups of people (disadvantaged young people including students and young fathers), it is a framework that can be extended to work with other marginalised groups around issues such as work, displacement, mental health, and even civic engagement. SNIs work best when integrated with other methods for research and for facilitating change. Ultimately SNIs bring together research and intervention and form part of a Southern approach to knowledge production (Breakey, Nyamnjoh, & Swartz, 2021) that benefits not just the researcher, or the intended audience of the research, but those who participate in the study too.

In the difficult and disjointed social context of the Global South, rebuilding communities around positive action is essential to producing meaningful and lasting social change. Support of social networks enhances the ability of communities as cooperative entities to develop individual and collective agency in the context of poverty, inequality, and unemployment. SNI is part of a growing pool of research tools that puts participants at the centre, shifting their marginality. By encouraging open and reflective communication about difficult topics, especially issues of power and oppression, SNI, helps participant-researchers build skills for developing and maintaining relationships with people who may not be 'like them'.

In doing so it allows young people (and others) to offer suggestions on how the policies and practices which affect their lives are analysed and understood – SNI innocuously excavates such suggestions. This is empowering for young people and ensures that young people do not blame themselves for many of the constraints they experience which in turn can lead to hopelessness, anti-social behaviour and avolition – the loss of will to act. SNI as a participatory methodological tool is a rich addition to existing research and intervention methods. It is offered as an evolving contribution towards the emancipation of both those researching and being researched in the Global South and beyond.

References

Bourdieu, P. (1990). *The logic of practice*. Cambridge, England: Polity Press.

Bourdieu, P. (1997). The forms of capital. In A. H. Halsey, H. Lauder, P. Brown, & A. S. Wells (Eds.), *Education: Culture, economy, society* (pp. 46–58). Oxford, England: Oxford University Press.

Bradbury, A., McGimpsey, I., & Santori, D. (2013). Revising rationality: The use of 'nudge' approaches in neoliberal education policy. *Journal of Education Policy*, 28(2), 247–267.

Bryman, A. (2012). *Social research methods* (4th ed.). Oxford, England: Oxford University Press.

Breakey, J., Nyamnjoh, A., & Swartz, S. (2021). Researching the South from the South. In S. Swartz, A. Cooper, C. Batan, & L. Kropff Causa (Eds.), *The Oxford handbook of Global South youth studies* (pp. 539–552). New York, NY: Oxford University Press.

Butz, D., & Besio, K. (2004). The value of autoethnography for field research in transcultural settings. *The Professional Geographer*, 56(3), 350–360.

Creswell, J. W. (2009). *Research design: Qualitative, quantitative, and mixed methods approaches* (3rd ed.). Los Angeles, CA: Sage.

Collins, P. H. (1993). Black feminist thought in the matrix of domination. In C. C. Lemert (Ed.), *Social theory: The multicultural and classic readings* (pp. 615–625). Boulder, CO: Westview Press.

Collins, P. H., & Bilge, S. (2016). *Intersectionality*. Cambridge, England: Polity Press.

Freire, P. (2000). *Pedagogy of the oppressed*. New York, NY: Bloomsbury.

Gill, P., Stewart, K., Treasure, E., & Chadwick, B. (2008). Methods of data collection in qualitative research: Interviews and focus groups. *British Dental Journal*, 204(6), 291–295.

Hawkins, K. A. (2015). The complexities of participatory action research and the problems of power, identity and influence. *Educational Action Research*, 23(4), 464–478.

Kaukko, M., & Fertig, M. (2016). Linking participatory action research, global education, and social justice: Emerging issues from practice. *International Journal of Development Education and Global Learning*, 7(3), 24–46.

Kosters, M., & Van der Heijden, J. (2015). From mechanism to virtue: Evaluating nudge theory. *Evaluation*, 21(3), 276–291.

Ledwith, M. (2007). On being critical: Uniting theory and practice through emancipatory action research. *Educational Action Research*, 15(4), 597–611.

Mahali, A., & Swartz, S. (2018). Using qualitative tools as interventionist research strategies for emancipation. *International Journal of Qualitative Methods*, 17(1), 1–10.

Marin, A., & Wellman, B. (2011). Social network analysis: An introduction. In J. Scott & P. J. Carrington (Eds.), *The Sage handbook of social network analysis* (pp. 11–25). London, England: Sage.

Meer, T., & Muller, A. (2017). Considering intersectionality in Africa. *Agenda, 31*(1), 3–4.

Miller, W. R., & Rollnick, S. (2002). *Motivational interviewing: Preparing people for change* (2nd ed.). New York, NY: The Guilford Press.

Moody, J., & Paxton, P. (2009). Building bridges linking social capital and social networks to improve theory and research. *American Behavioral Scientist, 52*(11), 1491–1506.

Nussbaum, M. C. (2001). *Women and human development: The capabilities approach* (Vol. 3). Cambridge, England: Cambridge University Press.

Peltzer, P., Swartz, S., Naidoo, P., Ramlagan, S., Mlambo, M., Sanger, N., Bray, R., Louw, J. S., Mchunu, G., Garzouzie, G., Zuma, K., Seutlwadi, L., Tutshana, B., Matseke, G., Chirinda, W., Njuho, P., Satekge, M., & Scott, D. (2012). *Evaluating the value that young people attach to loveLife and investigating factors impacting the life choices and risk tolerance of youth*. Cape Town, South Africa: HSRC Press.

Robinson, M., & Meerkotter, D. (2003). Fifteen years of action research for political and educational emancipation at a South African University. *Educational Action Research, 11*(3), 447–466.

Swartz, S. (2011). Going deep and giving back: Exceeding ethical expectations when working amongst vulnerable youth. *Qualitative Research, 11*(1), 47–68.

Swartz, S., & Bhana, A. (2009). *Teenage tata: Voices of young fathers in South Africa*. Cape Town, South Africa: HSRC Press.

Swartz, S., Mahali, A., Moletsane, R., Arogundade, E., Khalema, E., Rule, C., & Cooper, A. (2018). *Studying while black: Race, education and emancipation in South African universities*. Cape Town, South Africa: HSRC Press.

Swartz, S., & Nyamnjoh, A. (2018). Research as freedom: A continuum of interactive, participatory and emancipatory methods to understand youth marginality. *HTS Theological Studies, 74*(3), 1–11. DOI: 10.4102/hts.v74i3.5063.

Tuhiwai Smith, L. (1999). *Decolonizing methodologies: Research and indigenous peoples*. London, England: Zed Books.

Thaler, R. H., & Sunstei, C. R. (2009). *Nudge: Improving decisions about health, wealth and happiness*. London, England: Penguin Books.

Vera, E., & Schupp, T. (2006). Network analysis in comparative social sciences. *Comparative Education, 42*(3), 405–429.

Wasserman, S., & Faust, K. (1994). *Social network analysis: Methods and applications*. Cambridge, England: Cambridge University Press.

White, S. C. (1997). Men, masculinities, and the politics of development. *Gender and Development, 5*(2), 14–22.

15
GETTING THE PICTURE AND CHANGING THE PICTURE

Visual methodologies and educational research in South Africa

Claudia Mitchell

This chapter exposes key elements of working with the visual as a set of methodologies and practices at a time when questions about the social responsibility of researchers are critical for educational research. The term 'visual methodologies' should not simply be reduced to one practice or to one set of tools in order to ensure that the full complexity of these methodologies is appreciated. In this chapter, I focus on doing research through drawings, photo-voice, photo-elicitation, researcher as photographer, working with family photos, cinematic texts, video production, material culture, and advertising campaigns.

Some years ago, there was a study of adults caring for their elderly parents who were suffering from Alzheimer's disease (McIntyre & Cole, 1999). The findings were presented in an exhibition that included several installations, including *Lifeline*, which was made up of a clothes line from which were hung undergarments, up to and including adult-sized diapers. Another part of the installation, *Alzheimer's Still Life 1*, included a series of refrigerator doors, each covered with fridge magnets holding various artefacts: a school photo of a child, reminders about medication, and so on. In another exhibition, there was a voice-activated tape recorder with which viewers could record their own 'caring for' stories. Yet another installation, *Alzheimer's Still Life 2*, contained visual images taken from the two artist-researchers own family photograph albums, both of whom looked after their mothers who were suffering from Alzheimer's.

This work demonstrates the complexities of visual methodologies and the multiple forms of visual data. The work also shows the multiple ways of working with the visual: representation (transforming interviews into visual representations, through the use of material culture), dissemination (creating a

DOI: 10.4324/9781003355397-18

visual exhibition that drew attention from the public, health care researchers, and health care policy-makers), and, as in the second level of interviews with the participants, a mode of inquiry (a type of data elicitation).

There are two other critical aspects of the visual. One relates to epistemology and how we come to know what we know (and how to account for subjectivity and validity). The researchers are inside their own experience as caregivers, as much as they are studying the experiences of other caregivers interviewed and met through their exhibitions. The other aspect relates to broader questions: Why engage in social science inquiry in the first place? and, What difference does this make anyway?

The idea that data collection can in, and of, itself be an intervention is crucial in that it can be transformative for the participants. These installations provoke people with a personal connection to the topic to tell their own stories (Knowles & Cole, 2007). If visual data can mobilise individuals or communities to act, it may be possible for research to effect social change.

Participatory and other visual approaches

Consider these prompts: draw a scientist; take pictures of where you feel safe and not so safe; produce a video documentary on an issue in your life; and find pictures from your family photographs that you can construct into a narrative about gender and identity. Each of these prompts speaks to the range of tools that might be used to engage participants (learners, teachers, parents, pre-service teachers) in visual research (a drawing, simple point-and-shoot cameras, video cameras, family photographs), and suggests some of the types of emerging data: drawings, photographic images, and captions produced in the photo-voice project, video texts produced in a community video project, and the newly created album or visual text produced by the participants in an album project.

In each case there is the immediate visual text or primary text, as Fiske (1989) terms it, the drawing, photo image, collage, photo-story, video documentary or narrative, or album, which can include captions and more extensive curatorial statements or interpretive writings that reflect what the participants have to say about the visual texts. In essence, participation is not limited to 'take a picture' or 'draw a picture', though the level of participation will depend on the time available, the age and ability of the participants, and their willingness to be involved. A set of drawings or photos produced in isolation of their full participatory context (or follow-up) does not mean that they should be discarded, particularly in large-scale collections.

These examples can also include Fiske's (1989) so-called 'production texts' – or how participants engaged in the process describe the project, regardless of whether they are producing drawings, photographic images, video narratives, or 'reconstructing' a set of photographs into a new text, and indeed what they make of the texts. These production texts are often elicited during follow-up interviews and can include secondary visual data based on the researcher taking pictures that show levels of engagement. Pithouse and Mitchell (2007) called this 'looking at looking' to describe the visual representations of children looking at their own photographs.

Each of these visual practices has its own methods, traditions, and procedures. The approaches range from those that are relatively 'low tech' and require no expensive equipment, to those requiring more expensive cameras; from those that are camera-based to those that focus on things and objects (including archival photographs); from those where participants are respondents to those which engage participants as producers; from where researcher and participants collaborate to those in which it is the researcher who is the producer and interpreter. The constant is some aspect of the visual.

Drawings

The use of drawings to study emotional and cognitive development, trauma and fears, and, more recently, issues of identity, has a rich history. Using drawings in participatory research with children and young people, and beginning teachers, is a well-established methodology. Drawings allow children to express themselves regardless of linguistic ability (Chong, Hallman, & Brady, 2005) and this methodology is economical since all it requires is paper and a writing instrument. Drawings have been used with pre-service teachers to study their metaphors for teaching mathematics in the context of HIV and AIDS (van Laren, 2007); with children and pre-service teachers to study images of teachers (Mitchell & Weber, 1999); with children to study their perceptions of illness (Williams, 1998); and to explore children's perceptions of living on the street (Swart, 1988); on violence in refugee situations (Clacherty, 2005), and on girl, young woman and gender violence (Mitchell & Umurungi, 2007).

Photo-voice

Made popular by the award-winning documentary, *Born into Brothels*, photo-voice – as Wang (1999) terms the use of simple point-and-shoot cameras in community photography projects – has increasingly become a useful tool in educational research in South Africa. Building on Wang's work, which looks at women and health issues in rural China, Lykes's (2001) work with women in post-conflict settings in Guatemala, Ewald's (2000) photography work with children in a variety of settings, including Nepal, the Appalachian region of the United States and Soweto, and Hubbard's (1994) work with children on reservations in the United States, researchers in South Africa have worked with rural teachers and community health care workers to address numerous challenges and solutions when looking at HIV and AIDS (de Lange, Mitchell, & Stuart, 2007; Mitchell, de Lange, Moletsane, Stuart, & Buthelezi, 2005).

Photo-elicitation

Using photographs to elicit data offers educational researchers access to the views, perspectives, and experiences of participants. Collier and Collier (1986, p. 105) suggest that "images invite[d] people to take the lead in inquiry, making full use of their expertise". They also suggest that using photographs allows interviewing to continue through subsequent interviews, in ways in which using verbal interviews do not.

> Psychologically, the photographs on the table performed as a third party in the interview session. We were asking questions of the photographs and the informants [sic] became our assistants in discovering the answers to these questions in the realities of the photographs. We were exploring the photographs *together*.
>
> Collier and Collier (1986, p. 105)

While the range of topics and issues addressed through photo-elicitation is vast, a particularly fascinating set of images within educational research can be found in work with the school photograph. Mitchell and Weber (1999) wrote about 'picture day' at school and the resulting portraits. Drawing on interviews with children and beginning teachers, they explored the conventions of this genre of photography: the 'sitting', often in front of a staged backdrop, forces poses with the child holding a pen or some other school-related artefact, and the subject is often required to dress up. Subjects are usually required to smile, regardless of how they are feeling. What is produced is what a parent will want to purchase: a package of school photographs. What is absent is what the child feels about the moment and perhaps some sense of the child's autonomy. Years later, as was evident in the interviews, subjects still look back on some of these sittings with dismay. Added to this dismay is that their photos are sometimes still displayed years later by an aunt or grandparent. These 'lasting impression' images are usually out of the control of the child (Rose, 2001).

Family photographs

Much has been written on family albums, particularly in the area of the visual arts and art history. These studies range from work on one's own family album(s) (Kuhn, 1995; Mitchell & Weber, 1999; Spence, 1988; Spence & Holland, 1991; Weiser, 1993), to the work of Arbus (Lee & Pultz, 2004), Chalfen (1991), Hirsch (1997), Langford (2021), and Willis (1994) to name only some of the scholars who examine 'other people's albums'. These projects highlighted the personal aspect in working with one's own photographs, but there is also the idea of explicitly looking at other people's photo albums through a socio-cultural lens (Langford, 2021). The issues range from questions of cultural identity and memory, through to what Spence (1988) has described as 'reconfiguring' the family album. Faber's (2003) work on family albums in South Africa points to the rich possibilities for this work in exploring apartheid and post-apartheid realities. Mitchell and Allnutt (2008) and Allnutt, Mitchell, and Stuart (2007) have used family albums in participatory work with teachers.

In one study a young South African male teacher, T. (also documented in a video *Our Photos, Our Videos, Our Stories*, Mak, Mitchell, & Stuart, 2005), used the album project to explore life in rural KwaZulu-Natal in the age of AIDS – death and dying, silences, and 'the afterlife' (as in how the survivors deal with all of this). In this case, he documented the story of his sister who, in her early 20s, died unexpectedly and mysteriously, leaving behind her six-year-old son to be raised by T. and the grandmother. T. used the project to explore the silences, not just about the cause of his sister's death, and the importance of naming the disease, but also the position of AIDS orphans. When T. presented the album to his Honours class, he showed his mother falling asleep with the album under her arm. It is a poignant representation of what the album project meant to his family in terms of breaking silences.

Also described in Mitchell and Allnutt (2008), is a black teacher in her late 20s who is more-or-less adopted into the white family for whom her mother works. As Grace goes through the family photos, she observes that she is dressed the same as the little white girl in the family and that they were sometimes given identical toys. The culminating event, ostensibly, is her graduation photo – or is it? Grace's documentary is an interrogation of privilege – her own to a certain extent, but this is not done unquestioningly.

Researcher as photographer/visual ethnographer

A less participatory though no less rich area of visual research using photographs, is when researchers work as visual ethnographers and visual artists, as in Harper's 15-year study of a dairy farming community (Harper, 2001). Another study produced what the authors call 'environmental portraits' (du Toit & Gordon, 2007). In this photo work looking at the effects of oil refineries on people living nearby, they used a collection of photos of smoke stacks belching out pollutants, chained fences, landscape photos that position the residential area against the backdrop of the refineries, and so on. The photos are devoid of people, though the impact of person-created pollution is everywhere.

du Toit and Gordon's (2007) photos sit alongside photos produced by the participants who live in the area, and their family photographs which, as part of photo-elicitation, may talk to their lives 'before pollution' (including images of when they may have felt healthier or when a loved one was still alive). In the case of the research team photographing participants engaged in taking

FIGURE 15.1 Dividing fence (Photo: Naydene de Lange)

photographs (Pithouse & Mitchell, 2007), the process photos become visual data in and of themselves.

The significance of the 'photographic participant-observer eye' is highlighted, particularly within school-based research. de Lange, Mitchell, and Bhana (2008) included an image taken by a member of the research team of the fence dividing the school girls on one side (and apparently in the safety of the school) and a young man on the other (Figure 15.1). This speaks to the ways in which schools remain sites of violence, and becomes part of a collection of photos over time from the view of the researchers. Such photographs serve as visual data (different from the types of images produced within a photo-voice or video project), and can themselves become part of an exhibition of visual representations.

Video

The use of video in educational research (beyond video-taping classrooms or video-taping interviews) may be framed as collaborative video, participatory video, Indigenous video, or community video. Pink (2001) argues that video within ethnographic research can break down traditional hierarchies between visual and textual data. She maintains that these hierarchies are irrelevant to a reflexive approach to research that acknowledges the details, subjectivities, and power dynamics at play in any ethnographic project. A common theme is the idea of participants engaged in producing their own videos across several genres, including video documentaries, video narratives (melodramas or other stories) and public service narratives. As with the photo-voice work, both the processes and the products lend themselves to data analysis within visual studies.

In terms of process and video-making, several authors (Mitchell & de Lange, 2020; Mitchell, Walsh, & Weber, 2007; Moletsane et al., 2009) write about how young people might participate in this work, noting its particular relevance to addressing gender violence, and HIV and AIDS. Equally, work with adults, teachers, parents, and community health care workers is critical (Moletsane et al., 2009; Olivier, Wood, & de Lange, 2007). Building on the work of Ruby (2000) and others in relation to ethnographic video as text, Mitchell and de Lange (2020), propose a meta-narrative on working with community-based video through the researcher-generated production of a composite video of each project. These composite videos become an interpretive part of the process for the research team and are tools of both dissemination and inquiry when community participants view them.

Working with cinematic texts

Educational researchers can also use commercial film narratives and documentaries within visual research. This can include close readings of school or education-related texts in the vast array of teacher films such as *Kindergarten Cop*, *To Sir with Love*, and *Dangerous Minds* (Mitchell & Weber, 1999). Several films are particularly relevant to studying education in South Africa: *Sarafina* in exploring education under apartheid education (Butler, 2000) and *Yesterday* in looking at rurality and HIV and AIDS.

Alongside the use of textual analysis to read social practices, researchers might also use film texts in more participatory work with audiences. As an intervention involving boys and the study of gender violence in South Asia, Seshradi and Chandran (2006) used documentaries that address masculinities and themes such as friendship, violence, and bullying, to provoke reflection and discussion within focus groups. They investigated how boys' attitudes changed as a result of the viewings and discussions. In studies on HIV and AIDS and sex education in South Africa, Mitchell (2006) and Buthelezi et al. (2007) refer to the use of the video documentary *Fire+Hope* to provoke discussion among young people in relation to addressing youth activism.

Material culture

How objects, things, and spaces can be used within visual research in education draws on work in socio-semiotics, art history, and consumer research. Objects (including fridge magnets and adult-sized diapers) have connotative or personal meanings (and stories), which draw on autobiography and memory, along with their denotative histories, which may be more social and factual. Riggins' (1994) critical essay on studying his parents' living room offers a systematic approach to engaging in a denotative and connotative reading of the objects and things in one physical space. This method can be applied to various texts, ranging from clothing and identity, bedrooms, documents and letters, and even desks and bulletin boards as material culture.

As Mitchell et al. (2005) highlight, some of the 'photo subjects' mentioned in the interviews within a photo-voice project with teachers and community health care workers on HIV and AIDS are actually objects: a school bus, empty chairs and hair dryers in a beauty salon, or a shrivelled tree. Weber and Mitchell (2004) offer a series of essays on the connotative meanings of various items of (mostly women's) clothing and issues of identity, associated with dress, across the lifespan.

Ralfe's (2004) narrative on the *isishweshwe*, focuses on ethnic dress in South Africa. She interrogates the ways in which this type of fabric, first associated with Dutch traders and later with Zulu women, has become 'common currency' for fashion more generally. And yet this fabric still carries with it remnants as a signifier of a border-crossing identity, something Ralfe takes up as a white woman (Ralfe, 2004). She talks about what it meant to appear at her workplace in a skirt made of this fabric, noting the reactions of black staff members. Similarly, Grossi's (2007) auto-ethnographic work on her life as an early childhood educator in Durban shows the ways in which life-documents as material culture – circulars, report cards, letters, and photographs – can serve as the raw material for engaging in self-study.

Working with visual images within popular culture

Work on semiotics and visual images, particularly in advertising campaigns and public service announcements, draws on many of the techniques used in studying material culture, as well as some issues relating to working with a single photograph (Frith, 1997). This is a promising area within educational research in South Africa, applied, for example, to the work around HIV and AIDS, and in relation to gender violence in schools. The area includes Johnny and Mitchell's (2006) work on deconstructing UNESCO's 'Live and Let Live', Stuart's (2004) analysis of media posters produced by pre-service teachers in Life Skills, and Mitchell and Smith's (2001) work on the ABC campaign in schools.

"Help! What do I do with the visual images?" Interpretive processes and visual research

There is no easy way to map out the interpretive processes involved in working with visual research any more than there is a quick and easy way to map out the interpretive processes for any type of research data, though Prosser (1998), Banks (2001), Rose (2001), Pink (2001), and others, offer useful suggestions which include the following:

1 At the heart of visual work is its facilitation of reflexivity in the research process, as theorists on seeing and looking, such as Berger (1982) and Sontag (1977), have so eloquently discussed. Indeed, as Denzin (2003) and others have noted, situating one's self in the research texts is critical to engaging in the interpretive process.
2 Close reading strategies (drawn from literary studies, film studies, and socio-semiotics) are particularly appropriate to working with visual images. These strategies can apply to a single photograph (Moletsane & Mitchell, 2007), a video documentary text (Mitchell et al., 2008), or a cinematic text (Mitchell & Weber, 1999).
3 Visual images are particularly appropriate to making the participants themselves central to the interpretive process. In work with photo-voice, participants can be engaged with their own analytic procedures with the photos: Which ones are the most compelling? How are your photos the same or different from others in your group? What narrative do your photos evoke? (de Lange, Mitchell, Moletsane, Stuart, & Buthelezi, 2006). Similarly, with video documentaries produced as part of community video, participants can be engaged in a reflective process, which also becomes an analytic process: What did you like best about the video? What would you change if you could? Who should see this video? The interpretive process is not limited to the participants and the researcher – communities may also decide what a text means. Because visual texts are very accessible, the possibilities for other interpretations are critical to this issue (Mitchell, 2006).
4 The process of interpreting visual data can benefit from drawing on new technologies. *Transana* is a software application that is particularly appropriate for working with video data (Cohen, 2007). Digitising and creating meta-data schemes can be applied to working with photo-voice data (Park, Mitchell, & de Lange, 2007).
5 The process of working with the data can draw on a range of practices that may be applied to other types of transcripts and data sets, including content analysis, and engaging in coding and developing thematic categories.
6 Archival photos bring their own materiality with them and may be read as objects or things. Where are they stored? Who looks after them?
7 Visual data (especially photos produced by participants), because it is so accessible, is often subjected to more rigorous scrutiny by ethics boards than most other data. There are many ways of working with the visual and the choice of which type of visual approach to take should be guided by, among other things, the research questions, the feasibility of the study, the experience of the researcher, and the acceptability to the community under study.

8 Working with the visual to create artistic texts (for example, installations, photo albums, photo exhibitions, video narratives) should be regarded as an interpretive process in itself. This point is critical for understanding the relationship between visual studies and arts-based research (Bagley & Cancienne, 2002; Denzin, 1997; Knowles & Cole, 2007).

On the limitations and challenges

Although many of the scholars whose work has been described in this chapter normally work in visual sociology and anthropology, cultural studies, and film and photography, a growing body of interdisciplinary scholarship is incorporating image-based techniques into its research methodology. But research designs which use the visual raise many new questions and suggest blurring of boundaries: Is it research or is it art? Is it truth? Does the camera lie? Is it just a 'quick fix' on doing research? How do you overcome the subjective stance? The emergence of visual and arts-based research as a viable approach is putting pressure on the traditional structures and expectations of the academy. Space, time, and equipment requirements, for example, often make it difficult for researchers to present their work in the conventional venues and formats of research conferences.

Yet, there are other questions which further interrogate the relationship between the researched and the researcher. Do we as researchers conduct ourselves differently when the participants in our studies are 'right there', either in relation to the photos or videos they have produced, or in their performance pieces? How can visual interventions be used to educate community groups and point to ways to empower and reform institutional practices? What ethical issues come to the fore in these action-oriented studies? How do we work with 'confidentiality' and 'anonymity' within this kind of work, especially where stigma is a major issue?

Emmison and Smith (2000) state that one of the issues in visual research is the methodological adequacy of the method, but we must also challenge the adequacy of the questionnaire, the interview, and the photograph/drawing/video. That does not mean that we exclude the visual, but that we examine its function, use, and limitations, and continue with the process, taking these aspects into account. They are equally concerned with the partiality of the photograph: a photograph "must always be considered a selective account of reality" (Emmison & Smith, 2000, p. 40). As Goldstein (2007, p. 61) writes, "All photos lie". At the same time, there remains the emotional impact of the image, which can overwhelm the researcher and the viewer and even preclude a proper analysis of content.

Clearly some studies lend themselves to one type of visual data more than another, and not *all* questions are best answered using the visual. While there are few research questions that could not be addressed through visual methodologies, this does not mean that this is the only approach, or that all audiences or recipients of research (funders, policy-makers, review boards) are equally open to qualitative research, generally, or visual research, specifically. And as Karlsson (2007) points out, the time and effort required may be problematic. At the same time, the preparation of new researchers in this area relies on access to methodology textbooks and course material that offers support for making informed choices about methods.

All students should be exposed to a variety of approaches, and even if they do not choose to work with the visual, they should be able to critically evaluate studies using visual methodologies in the same way that they can critically evaluate more conventional approaches. Concomitantly, it is critical that those using visual methodologies contribute to debates about the support that is needed along with paying attention to critiques. Significantly, we need to provide training to research students and, where possible, bring forward our expertise in working with the visual to review boards, research committees, and so on. Technically, we need to recognise the limitations of working with large electronic files, and become attuned to new ways of working with digitising and other techniques that are critical to the success of working with the visual (Park et al., 2007).

And finally, what about reaching the public?

"Why are there no white people in the film?"
"Why did you choose this talking head genre? Wouldn't it be more effective to create a story line or a drama?"
"Where did you get the statistics about boys being at risk? Are those numbers true?"
"Could you help us do research?"
"Why can't we produce something like this right here in KwaZulu-Natal where the problems are even greater than in the Western Cape?"

These questions may sound like the questions that would be raised by an external reviewer of a journal article or research proposal, or a film critic. They were questions posed at a Youth Day event by members of the audience, young people from the area who had just viewed the video documentary *Fire+Hope*. These are tough questions and I wished I had had better answers, and I wished that the audience did not have to ask the question in the first place (Walsh & Mitchell, 2004).

As has been noted by Schratz and Walker (1995) and Tuhiwai Smith (1999), among others, the issue of research accessibility is a critical topic within institutional practices. It becomes especially so when the topics of the research are as vital a part of the social situation as education and health care, and where issues of power, control, regulation, and access are ones that are central to policy development.

What this event highlights is that what starts as research (a project interrogating youth activism and HIV and AIDS) and becomes a visual text (a 16-minute video documentary *Fire+Hope*) evolves into an intervention (a screening and discussion at a Youth Day event) and then yields more research questions, both for the research team and the audience (who in turn also want to make their own video documentary). The example of the transfer of knowledge and engagement from a group of young people in the Western Cape to a group of young people in KwaZulu-Natal, through the medium of a video documentary, highlights a type of peer education and social networking that, while predating Facebook and My Space, is no less striking for what it can inspire.

Conclusion

Though the description of visual methodologies may seem both ridiculously simple and ridiculously complex, this paradox can resolve itself in the doing of the research. In this chapter, I have focused on the doing, and in particular the various approaches to doing through the visual (drawings, photo-voice, photo-elicitation, researcher as photographer/visual ethnographer, working with family photos, cinematic texts, video production, material culture, advertising campaigns). There are, of course, other visual approaches, including archival work, collage, and performance. While the chapter offers some comments on the interpretive process, the types of issues that might be addressed, some limitations to visual research, and finally some notion of the ways in which the visual can serve recursively as a mode of inquiry, as a mode of representation, and as a mode of dissemination, it is far from being a comprehensive 'primer' on visual methodologies. It suggests, rather, that visual studies have a great deal to offer educational research.

Acknowledgements

Much of the work for this chapter came out of my work with the research teams at the University of KwaZulu-Natal, working out of the Centre for Visual Methodologies for Social Change (www.cvm.org), Naydene De Lange, Jean Stuart, Relebohile Moletsane, Thabisile Buthelizi, and Myra Taylor. I also acknowledge the contributions of Susann Allnutt, Shannon Walsh, Sandra Weber Ann Smith, and Katie MacEntee.

References

Allnutt, S., Mitchell, C., & Stuart, J. (2007). The visual family archive: Uses and interruptions. In N. de Lange, C. Mitchell, & J. Stuart (Eds.), *Putting people in the picture: Visual methodologies for social change* (pp. 89–99). Rotterdam, Netherlands: Sense.

Bagley, C., & Cancienne, M. B. (Eds.). (2002). *Dancing the data*. New York, NY: Peter Lang.
Banks, M. (2001). *Visual methods in social research*. London, England: Sage.
Berger, J. (1982). *Ways of seeing*. London, England: Penguin Books.
Buthelezi, T., Mitchell, C., Moletsane, R., de Lange, N., Taylor, M., & Stuart, J. (2007). Youth voices about sex and AIDS: Implications for life skills education through the "Learning Together" project in KwaZulu-Natal, South Africa. *International Journal of Inclusive Education, 11*, 445–459.
Butler, F. J. (2000). *Hollywood films, reflective practice, and social change in teacher education: A Bahamian illustration* (Doctoral dissertation, McGill University, Montreal, Quebec, Canada). Retrieved from https://central.bac-lac.gc.ca/.item?id=NQ69976&op=pdf&app=Library&oclc_number=1007118662
Chalfen, R. (1991). *Turning leaves: Exploring identity in Japanese American photograph albums*. Albuquerque, NM: University of New Mexico Press.
Chong, E., Hallman, K., & Brady, M. (2005). *Generating the evidence base for HIV/AIDS policies and programs*. New York, NY: Population Council.
Clacherty, G. (2005). *Refugee and returnee children in Southern Africa: Perceptions and experiences of children*. Pretoria, South Africa: UNHCR.
Cohen, L. (2007). Transana: Qualitative analysis for audio and visual data. In N. de Lange, C. Mitchell, & J. Stuart (Eds.), *Putting people in the picture: Visual methodologies for social change* (pp. 173–183). Rotterdam, Netherlands: Sense.
Collier, J., & Collier, M. (Eds.). (1986). *Visual anthropology: Photography as a research method*. Albuquerque, NM: University of New Mexico Press.
de Lange, N., Mitchell, C., Moletsane, R., Stuart, J., & Buthelezi, T. (2006). Seeing through the body: Educators' representations of HIV and AIDS. *Journal of Education, 38*, 45–66.
de Lange, N., Mitchell, C., & Stuart, J. (Eds.) (2007). *Putting people in the picture: Visual methodologies for social change*. Rotterdam, Netherlands: Sense.
de Lange, N., Mitchell, C., & Bhana, D. (2008, March). *'If we can all work together' in the age of AIDS*. Poster presentation at the American Education Research Association, New York, USA.
Denzin, N. K. (1997). Performance texts. In W. G. Tierney & Y. S. Lincoln (Eds.), *Representation and the text: Re-framing the narrative voice* (pp. 179–218). Albany, NY: State University of New York Press.
Denzin, N. K. (2003). The cinematic society and the reflexive interview. In J. Gubrium & J. Holstein (Eds.), *Postmodern interviewing* (pp. 141–156). Thousand Oaks, CA: Sage.
du Toit, M., & Gordon, J. (2007). The means to turn the key: The South Durban photography project's workshops for first time photographers (2002–2005). In N. de Lange, C. Mitchell, & J. Stuart (Eds.), *Putting people in the picture: Visual methodologies for social change* (pp. 257–273). Rotterdam, Netherlands: Sense.
Emmison, M., & Smith, P. (2000). *Researching the visual: Images, objects, contexts and interactions in social and cultural inquiry*. London, England: Sage.
Ewald, W. (2000). *Secret games: Collaborative works with children, 1969–99*. Berlin, Germany: Scalo.
Faber, P. (2003). *Group portrait South Africa: Nine family histories*. Cape Town, South Africa: Kwela Books.
Fiske, J. (1989). *Understanding popular culture*. Boston, MA: Allen & Unwin.

Frith, K. T. (1997). *Undressing the ad: Reading culture in advertising*. New York, NY: Peter Lang.

Goldstein, B. (2007). All photos lie: Images as data. In G. S. Stanczak (Ed.), *Visual research methods: Image, society and representation*. London, England: Sage.

Grossi, E. (2007). The 'I' through the eye: Using the visual in arts-based autoethnography. In N. de Lange, C. Mitchell, & J. Stuart (Eds.), *Putting people in the picture: Visual methodologies for social change* (pp. 71–88). Rotterdam, Netherlands: Sense.

Harper, D. (2001). *Changing work: Visions of a lost agriculture*. Chicago, IL: University of Chicago Press.

Hirsch, M. (1997). *Family frames: Photography, narrative and postmemory*. Cambridge, MA: Harvard University Press.

Hubbard, J. (1994). *Shooting back from the reservation*. New York, NY: New Press.

Johnny, L., & Mitchell, C. (2006). "Live and let live" An analysis of HIV/AIDS related stigma and discrimination in international campaign posters. *Journal of Health Communication, 11*, 755–767.

Karlsson, J. (2007). The novice researcher. In N. de Lange, C. Mitchell, & J. Stuart (Eds.), *Putting people in the picture: Visual methodologies for social change* (pp. 185–201). Rotterdam, Netherlands: Sense.

Knowles, G., & Cole, A. (Eds.). (2007). *Handbook of the arts in qualitative research: Perspectives, methodologies, examples and issues*. London, England: Sage.

Kuhn, A. (1995). *Family secrets: Acts of memory and imagination*. London, England: Verso.

Langford, M. (2021). *Suspended conversations: The afterlife of memory in photographic albums* (2nd ed.). Montreal, Canada: McGill-Queen's Press.

Lee, A., & Pultz, J. (2004). *Diane Arbus: Family albums*. New Haven, CT: Yale University Press.

Lykes, M. B. (2001). Creative arts and photography in participatory action research in Guatemala. In P. Reason & H. Bradbury (Eds.), *Handbook of action research: Participative inquiry and practice* (pp. 363–371). Thousand Oaks, CA: Sage.

Mak, M. (Director), Mitchell, C., & Stuart, J. (Producers). (2005). *Our photos, our videos, our stories* [Motion picture]. Canada: Taffeta Production.

McIntyre, M., & Cole, A. L. (1999). *Still life with Alzheimer's. From in illness and in health: Daughters storying mothers' lives*. [Multi-media]. Presented at the Third Annual International Conference on Mothers and Education, Brock University, St. Catharines, Canada.

Mitchell, C. (2006). Visual arts-based methodologies in research as social change. In T. Marcus & A. Hofmaenner (Eds.), *Shifting the boundaries of knowledge* (pp. 227–241). Pietermaritzburg, South Africa: UKZN Press.

Mitchell, C., & Allnutt, S. (2008). Photographs and/as social documentary. In G. Knowles & A. Cole (Eds.), *Handbook of the arts in qualitative research: Perspectives, methodologies, examples and issues* (pp. 251–262). London, England: Sage.

Mitchell, C., & de Lange, N. (2020). Community-based participatory video and social action. In L. Pauwels & D. Mannay (Eds.), *The Sage handbook on visual research methods* (pp. 254–266). London, England: Sage.

Mitchell, C., de Lange, N., Moletsane, R., Stuart, J., & Buthelezi, T. (2005). The face of HIV and AIDS in rural South Africa: A case for photo-voice. *Qualitative Research in Psychology, 3*, 257–270.

Mitchell, C., de Lange, N., Moletsane, R., Stuart, J., Taylor, M., & Buthelezi, T. (2008). Trust no one at school": Participatory video with young people in addressing gender violence in and around South African schools. In F. Ogunleye (Ed.), *African Video Film Today 2* (pp. 1573–9090). Matsapha, Swaziland: Academic Publishers Swaziland.

Mitchell, C., Moletsane, R., Stuart, J., Buthelezi, T., & de Lange, N. (2005). Taking pictures/taking action! Using photo-voice techniques with children. *Children-FIRST, 60,* 27–31.

Mitchell, C., & Smith, A. (2001). Changing the picture: Youth, gender and HIV/AIDS prevention campaigns in South Africa. *Canadian Woman Studies, 21*(2), 56–61.

Mitchell, C., & Umurungi, J. P. (2007). What happens to girls who are raped in Rwanda. *ChildrenFIRST, 65,* 13–18.

Mitchell, C., Walsh, S., & Weber, S. (2007). Behind the lens: Reflexivity and video documentary. In G. Knowles & A. Cole (Eds.), *The art of visual inquiry* (pp. 97–108). Halifax, Canada: Backalong Books.

Mitchell, C., & Weber, S. (1999). *Reinventing ourselves as teachers: Beyond nostalgia.* London, England: Falmer Press.

Moletsane, R., & Mitchell, C. (2007). On working with a single photograph. In N. de Lange, C. Mitchell, & J. Stuart (Eds.), *Putting people in the picture: Visual methodologies for social change* (pp. 131–140). Rotterdam, Netherlands: Sense.

Moletsane, R., Mitchell, C., de Lange, N., Stuart, J., Buthelezi, T., & Taylor, M. (2009). What can a woman do with a camera? Turning the female gaze on poverty and HIV and AIDS in rural South Africa. *International Journal of Qualitative Studies in Education, 22*(3), 315–331.

Olivier, M. A. J., Wood, L., & de Lange, N. (2007). Changing our eyes': Seeing hope. In N. de Lange, C. Mitchell, & J. Stuart (Eds.), *Putting people in the picture: Visual methodologies for social change* (pp. 10–29). Rotterdam, Netherlands: Sense.

Park, E., Mitchell, C., & de Lange, N. (2007). Working with digital archives: Photovoice and meta-analysis in the context of HIV & AIDS. In N. de Lange, C. Mitchell, & J. Stuart (Eds.), *Putting people in the picture: Visual methodologies for social change* (pp. 162–172). Rotterdam, Netherlands: Sense.

Pithouse, K., & Mitchell, C. (2007). Looking into change: Studying participant engagement in photovoice projects. In N. de Lange, C. Mitchell, & J. Stuart (Eds.), *Putting people in the picture: Visual methodologies for social change* (pp. 141–151). Rotterdam, Netherlands: Sense.

Pink, S. (2001). *Doing visual ethnography.* London, England: Sage.

Prosser, J. (Ed.). (1998). *Image-based research: A sourcebook for qualitative research.* London, UK: Falmer Press.

Ralfe, E. (2004). Love affair with my isishweshwe. In S. Weber & C. Mitchell (Eds.), *Not just any dress: Narratives of memory, body, and identity* (pp. 211–218). New York, NY: Peter Lang.

Riggins, S. H. (1994). Fieldwork in the living room: An autoethnographic essay. In S. H. Riggins (Ed.), *The socialness of things: Essays on the socio-semiotics of objects* (pp. 101–148). Berlin, Germany: Mouton de Gruyter.

Rose, G. (2001). *Visual methodologies.* London, England: Sage.

Ruby, J. (2000). *Picturing culture: Explorations of film and anthropology.* Chicago, IL: University of Chicago Press.

Schratz, M., & Walker, R. (1995). *Research as social change: New opportunities for qualitative research.* London, England: Routledge.

Seshradi, S., & Chandran, V. (2006). Reframing masculinities: Using films with adolescent boys. In F. Leach & C. Mitchell (Eds.), *Combating gender violence in and around schools* (pp. 135–142). Staffordshire, England: Trentham Books.

Sontag, S. (1977). *On photography*. New York, NY: Doubleday.

Spence, J. (1988). *Putting myself in the picture: A political, personal and photographic autobiography*. Seattle, WA: The Real Comet Press.

Spence, J., & Holland, P. (1991). *Family snaps: The meaning of domestic photograph*. London, England: Virago.

Stuart, J. (2004). Media matters: Producing a culture of compassion in the age of AIDS. *English Quarterly, 36*(2), 3–5.

Swart, J. (1988). *Malunde: The street children of Hillbrow*. Johannesburg, South Africa: Wits University Press.

Tuhiwai Smith, L. (1999). *Decolonizing methodologies: Research and indigenous peoples*. London, England: Zed Books.

van Laren, L. (2007). Using metaphors for integrating HIV & AIDS education in mathematics curriculum in pre-service teacher education: An exploratory classroom study. *International Journal of Inclusive Education, 11*(4), 461–479.

Walsh, S., & Mitchell, C. (2004). Artfully engaged: Arts activism and HIV/AIDS work with youth in South Africa. In G. Knowles, L. Neilsen, A. Cole, & T. Luciani (Eds.), *Provoked by art: Theorizing arts-informed inquiry*. Halifax, Canada: Backalong Books.

Wang, C. (1999). Photovoice: A participatory action research strategy applied to women's health. *Journal of Women's Health, 8*(2), 185–192.

Weber, S. J., & Mitchell, C. (Eds.). (2004). *Not just any dress: Narratives of memory, autobiography, and identity*. New York, NY: Peter Lang.

Weiser, J. (1993). *PhotoTherapy techniques. Exploring the secrets of personal snapshots and family albums*. San Francisco, CA: Jossey-Bass.

Williams, S. J. (1998). Malignant bodies: Children's beliefs about health, cancer and risk. In S. W. Nettleton (Ed.), *The body in everyday life* (pp. 103–123). London, England: Routledge.

Willis, D. (Ed.). (1994). *Picturing us: African American identity in photography*. New York, NY: New Press.

16

ENTERING AN AMBIGUOUS SPACE

Evoking polyvocality in educational research through collective poetic inquiry

Kathleen Pithouse-Morgan, Inbanathan Naicker, Vitallis Chikoko, Daisy Pillay, Pholoho Morojele and Teboho Hlao

As academic researchers, we refer to published work to acknowledge the roles that others have played in our thinking. Thus, we value conventions of academic citations and referencing in distinguishing and bringing into dialogue our voices and the voices of diverse scholars in our research texts. A conversation metaphor has been used to describe this polyvocal research dimension. For example, Clandinin and Connelly (2000, p. 136) advise researchers preparing for a new study to "ask questions about what scholarly conversations we want to engage in". Similarly, Badley (2009a, p. 107) explains academic writing "as a process of reflecting upon our experience and on the experience of others in an attempt to make useful suggestions for change and growth as part of a conversation in progress".

Polyvocality, voice, and voicelessness have been the focus of scholarly conversations in which educational researchers have sought to address a perceived absence of the voices of those most directly affected by the research: learners or students (and their families and communities) and teachers or educators. Regarding teachers' voices, Gitlin (1990, p. 443) argued for "educative research [as] a dialogical approach that attempts to develop … teachers' voices" as producers of research knowledge. Subsequently, Hargreaves (1996, pp. 12–13) acknowledged that teachers' voices have "frequently been silenced … and suppressed or distorted within educational research", but cautioned that diverse teachers' voices are too often reduced to "*the* teacher's voice" and that certain teachers' voices tend to be "represented and sponsored in isolation from or to the exclusion of other voices".

Mitchell, de Lange, Moletsane, Stuart, and Buthelezi (2005, p. 258) proposed that educational researchers should aim not only to elicit and communicate teachers' voices, but also to assist "groups such as teachers and community health workers, ... [to] hear each other". In response to concerns about voice, voicelessness, and polyvocality, an increasing number of educational researchers are turning to participatory (often arts-based) methodologies to engage learners, teachers, and community members as vocal partners in studies that aim to address educational and social challenges (Mitchell et al., 2005; Theron, 2012).

However, tensions concerning polyvocality, voice, and voicelessness are also apparent in debates on participatory research, particularly forms of participatory research where "community members, or stakeholders in communities, collaborate with researchers in addressing needs and enhancing resilience and well-being in societies" (Ferreira, 2012, p. 512). On the one hand, the principal intention of such participatory research is to give community members a voice in public research conversations (Bergold & Thomas, 2012). On the other hand, concerns are raised about whose voices are present, how diverse voices are re-presented, and which voices dominate in participatory research analysis and research texts (Borg, Karlsson, Kim, & McCormack, 2012; Riecken, Strong-Wilson, Conibear, Michel, & Riecken, 2005). Hence Riecken et al. (2005, unnumbered) argue for paying specific attention to "an ethic of voice and voicing" in participatory research.

Polyvocality is thus a central and challenging issue in scholarly conversations that seek to understand how educational and participatory research can make a qualitative difference to the lives of 'the researched'. As Mitchell (2008, pp. 257–258) explains, in these conversations, "questions of the social responsibility of the academic researcher (including postgraduate students as new researchers, along with experienced researchers expanding their repertoire of being and doing) are critical".

From another perspective, Smith (1997) considers the social responsibility of the academic researcher concerning how researchers within the broad educational research community engage each other in conversation. Smith argues that, within this community, "different vocabularies ... are being used to tell different stories to ourselves and to others about research and about who we are as educational researchers" (p. 10). Smith (1997, p. 11) raises concerns about educational researchers dividing into warring factions that appear unwilling to participate in polyvocal conversations "to cultivate and maintain a pluralism of vocabularies and stories".

Sparkes (1991, p. 103) is similarly concerned "to enhance the possibilities of critical dialogue [across factions] within the [educational] research community so that understanding might prevail". He suggests that factionalism might be mitigated by researchers developing "critical and reflective self-awareness" of the "taken-for-granted" ways in which we construct research texts. Sparkes argues that a heightened consciousness of research texts as "literary enterprises" could be a "vital first [step] in opening up the possibilities for entertaining alternative views and exploring the intellectual landscape of others".

Likewise, Vasudevan (2011, pp. 1155–1156) proposes that "at a time when evidence of human diversity is in abundance and accessible like no time before", educational researchers should participate in self-reflexive conversations in which we inquire into "how our [diverse] ways of knowing come to be established". In this chapter, we take up this challenge of making our ways of knowing visible as we explore the potential of collective poetic inquiry for evoking polyvocality in educational research. Our conceptualisation of polyvocality is dialogic, as we focus on what emerges through the "interillumination" or "interanimation" (Holquist, 1981, pp. 429–430) of diverse voices.

Poetry as research

Increasingly, qualitative researchers within and beyond the domain of educational research have been exploring poetry as a literary arts-based research medium. Poetry is understood as a way of representing the uniqueness, complexity, and plurality of research participants' and researchers' voices (Kennedy, 2009; Richardson, 2000). In addition, poetry is acknowledged as a mode of research analysis that can heighten creativity and reflexivity (Lahman et al., 2010; Richardson, 2003).

There is also a growing awareness of the participatory potential of poetry as research. For instance, MacKenzie (2012) engaged participants in creating individual and collective poems during a participatory research process. Hopper and Sanford (2008) used their poetic representations of participants' responses to involve them in data analysis. Co-researchers Lahman et al. (2010, p. 45) offered a reflexive account of how their participatory methodological journey as a research poetry group enabled them to "create meaning from one another and to construct their individual and shared meanings of this creative and thought-provoking process".

Researchers who focus on the performative dimensions of poetry have proposed that notions of research participation should include the live or virtual performance of poems and engagement with audience or reader responses to contextualise, deepen, and rethink research learning and knowing (Lapum, 2008; Wiebe, 2008). Scholarly conversations about poetry and research have also considered debates on polyvocality, voice, and voicelessness in participatory research. In particular, researchers have paid attention to ethics concerning the voices of participants whose words serve as 'raw material' for poems created by researchers or who contribute their poems to the research (Kennedy, 2009; Richardson, 2000).

We aim to contribute to methodological conversations about poetry as research, focusing on understanding the potential of collective poetic inquiry for evoking polyvocality in educational research. This chapter is written as a poetic performance to bring into conversation our diverse researcher voices and perspectives and those of our research participants and audiences. We encourage readers to read the poems aloud, to engage with them through multiple senses, and to be aware of thoughts and feelings that they might evoke (Lapum, 2008; Leggo, 2008). While we do not make any claims about our poems' inherent artistic or literary merit, we offer them as demonstrations of our "knowing in the making" (Badley, 2009a, p. 108) and invitations to join us in continuing participatory inquiry.

The poems are interwoven with research discussions in which we take a reflexive stance to make visible how we are coming to know as educational researchers (Badley, 2009a; Vasudevan, 2011; Vinz, 1997). Through these discussions, we endeavour to open up our research knowing for ongoing questioning and meaning-making.

Setting the scene

We are a research team of five academics and one postgraduate student, all located in a School of Education at one university. We teach, study, and research within the disciplines of Educational Psychology, Teacher Development Studies, Social Justice Education, and Education Leadership, Management and Policy Studies. Accordingly, we participate in varied theoretical and methodological conversations within the broad educational research community. While we are all currently situated in KwaZulu-Natal, South Africa, we grew up in diverse social and linguistic contexts in Lesotho, South Africa, and Zimbabwe.

Over the past two years, we have been working together to research the phenomenon of internationalisation and related possibilities for knowledge-making and knowledge interchange within our university community. Our shared interest in this topic stems from experiences of being international students and studying, teaching, and researching within international university communities. Student enrolment records at our University indicate a strong representation of international students in various undergraduate and postgraduate programmes. We have been asking questions about what lies beyond the statistics to understand better what we can learn from international and local postgraduate students' stories of social and academic experiences.

We obtained full ethical approval from our institution before conducting our research. The first phase of our research project focused on stories told by African international postgraduate students (students from African countries outside of South Africa). Part of this research was communicated in a publication (Pithouse-Morgan et al., 2012) in which we took a narrative inquiry stance to explore what we could learn from one student's stories (Clandinin & Connelly, 2000). We used narrative vignettes – brief evocative scenes or accounts – to represent data generated through unstructured interviews and collage-making. The vignettes portrayed how this student's daily life on campus was constrained by anxiety about xenophobic harassment and violence. Hence, we argued that the pedagogic setting was educationally unsound, even when effective teaching and learning activities might occur in designated spaces. To conclude, we deliberated on possibilities for cultivating pedagogic environments that are favourable and safe for all those who learn and teach within them.

After writing the chapter, we decided to explore the concept of 'pedagogic settings' in more depth for a conference presentation. As discussed in Pithouse-Morgan et al. (2012), we were working with an understanding of *setting* as a literary or narrative element (Coulter & Smith, 2009). From a narrative perspective, a setting is more than a backdrop for stories of experience; it is an intrinsic and influential (yet often intangible) element in these stories. Our view of pedagogy was influenced by humanist and phenomenological perspectives emphasising experiential, formative and relational aspects of learning and teaching processes (Allender, 2004; Van Manen, 1990).

Deciding to try collective poetic inquiry

We scheduled a three-day writing retreat to prepare for our upcoming presentation. Beforehand, Kathleen e-mailed other team members to suggest poetic inquiry as a literary arts-based methodology that would resonate with the concept of setting as a literary element. Kathleen explained how she had used found poetry (extracts from data sources re-presented in poetic form) in her PhD research (Pithouse-Morgan, 2007). She also sent team members an article on poetic inquiry by Butler-Kisber (2002).

We began the retreat with an animated and robust conversation about poetry as research, using the Butler-Kisber (2002) article to orientate us. Some team members, unfamiliar with poetic inquiry, expressed reservations about using this 'non-traditional' methodology. Kathleen explained that she had not previously been involved in *collective* poetic inquiry, so this would be a new experience for her. We realised that poetic inquiry would require each of us to take "a non-expert stance", which is risky for educational researchers who are "called upon more often to demonstrate expertise than to render visible the 'unexpected' in their stances of inquiry" (Vasudevan, 2011, p. 1156).

We audio-recorded and transcribed this initial conversation. At a subsequent writing retreat, we returned to the recording and transcript to construct found poems to capture our discussion's polyvocal content and tone (Pithouse-Morgan, 2007). In co-creating these poems, we listened to the recording and viewed the transcript projected onto a screen. We found that listening to the recording enabled us to re-experience the discussion more directly and vividly (Pithouse-Morgan, 2007). It was also helpful to view the transcript to pay close attention to each word. We used the highlighting function in MS Word to colour-code sections of the transcript that seemed significant and resonated with each other. We then reworked these extracts into found poems. This process involved repeating or removing words and phrases that seemed more or less important, constructing lines and stanzas by rearranging words and phrases, inserting breaks and spaces, noting visual patterns, and listening to rhythms (Leggo, 2008). Thus, we had to pay close and sustained attention to the idea that "rhythm is the relation of part to part and parts to the whole" (Leggo, 2008, p. 167). In keeping with the conventions of found poetry, we did not add any words or phrases that did not appear in the transcript (Butler-Kisber, 2002).

The poetry-making process required continual reading and re-reading (both silent and aloud) of the transcript and the emerging poems. It also involved bringing into dialogue our individual memories of the discussion and our retrospective responses to the recording and transcript. Commonalities and differences in what we remembered revealed diverse ways we had made meaning of the discussion and pointed to its most significant aspects. The poetry-making process demanded that we explain our understandings and reach a consensus on what to portray and how to do so through the found poems. This required what Leggo (2008, p. 167) expresses as "poet's commitment [which] entails a zeal for attending, and questioning, and perceiving".

Poetic performance

The found poem, 'What's traditional and non-traditional?', portrays our deliberations about 'traditional' and 'alternative' modes of research, while 'Not just presenting data' conveys our musings about the possibilities and limitations of poetry as research. 'Shakespeare???' re-presents our discovery that, despite our diverse schooling contexts, we all had vivid

---

What's traditional and non-traditional?

What do we mean by traditional?
Which are traditional methods?
We often make assumptions ...

In the traditional way
You code
Report categories
And you move on
And on ...

Presenting it
In traditional form
Wouldn't capture the richness
We have to go beyond ...

Not just presenting data

Poetry
As *re*-presenting
data Also
As analysis

We want to
Participate
Shift
Open it up
Capture
Emotion, empathy
Embodied understanding

Use with caution
Never a neutral process
Ways in which we re-present
Influence meaning

Whatever we do
We can't get away from
Ambiguities
Subjectivities
Positioning

Shakespeare???

Using poetic inquiry
To understand
The concept
Pedagogic settings

Everybody did
Shakespeare
No way you could avoid
Shakespeare ...

If you remember ...
Words
Carefully used
This way

Rather than
That word
To create feeling
To create setting
We are talking about
Atmospheric conditions
We are talking about
Environment

It all comes together
In creating a feeling
A mood
It's intangible

Creating usable poems

Answering research questions
Requires creative thought
Create found poems
Use haikus
To respond

Looking at data
As potential poetry
How does that
Create change?

Start to see
Beautiful
Profound
Rather than
"So and so said X"

How do we
Know *what* words?
Be aware of
Bias?
Position?

Playing with words:
This way
What will emerge?
That way
What will emerge?

Text jump out
How can you
Arrange?
Present?
See what emerges

Leave critical self
For the moment
Bring up imaginative self
Engaging
In a different way

memories of studying Shakespeare's plays in English classes. (Kathleen suggested Shakespeare to stimulate discussion about setting as a literary element and how particular words and arrangements of words can evoke mood and tone.) 'Creating usable poems' conveys our thinking about how we might re-present data in the form of found poems and analyse data through creating haiku poems (brief, three-line poems that follow a pattern of a number of syllables per line).

Constructing found poems to re-present stories of experience

Having agreed to try poetry to explore the concept of pedagogic settings, we began by observing a photographic collage made by an African international postgraduate student to portray his experiences of campus life. (Not the same student whose collage and interview data we had drawn upon for our previous publication.) The student was asked to create a collage of photographs that he had either taken or found to depict significant aspects of his campus life, giving each photograph "a caption … that [reflected] what [he had] to say about the visual texts" (Mitchell, 2008, p. 367). In an unstructured interview, he explained his choice of photographs and elaborated on what each meant. A postgraduate student research assistant facilitated the collage-making and interview process because we anticipated that student participants might feel more comfortable sharing their stories of campus life with fellow students. The project team members mentored the student researcher.

We decided to try to create a found poem for each of the six photographs, using extracts from the interview transcript to build them and developing titles for the poems based on the photograph captions. We each chose one photograph to work with. The student team member worked together with an academic. The remaining two photographs were set aside for us to work with collectively.

As explained in the previous discussion, we discovered that constructing poetry to re-present data was a non-linear process. We started by highlighting keywords and phrases in the transcript and then deconstructed and reconstructed the transcript by electronically 'cutting and pasting' selected words and phrases. We experimented with word combinations to create rhythm, pauses and emphasis (Leggo, 2008). This required returning to the photographs and transcript many times to create a 'mental kaleidoscope' of sights, sounds and silences in the data.

Once we had constructed the first draft of each poem, we projected these and read them aloud. Because poetry has integral auditory and performance dimensions (Leggo, 2008), this helped us 'hear' our poems and interact with others' responses. We then collectively reshaped the poems to enhance flow, tone, and coherence. After finalising the first four poems, we created poems for the remaining two photographs.

Each of the six found poems displays "knowing in the making" (Badley, 2009a, p. 108), provoked by using poetic inquiry to engage with data.

Significantly, we did not know who the student participant was because, as per the confidentiality agreement, the collage and transcript were given to us without his real name. Our African international student participants were very concerned about remaining anonymous. This heightened sense of the need for identity protection could be linked to anxiety about xenophobia (as discussed in Pithouse-Morgan et al., 2012).

Our only means of connecting with our participant was through his 'voice' as conveyed by the photographs, captions, and transcript. Constructing and reconstructing the poems engendered a sense of empathetic participation in his lived stories (Eisner, 1997). However, while we felt that we were coming to 'know' our participant in a complex way, we also became aware that we were making our own meanings through the found poems, individually, and collectively. We realised how data re-presented as poetry could allow us to communicate an evolving, provisional, polyvocal understanding of a university campus (and of educational experience, more generally) as a pedagogic setting, evoked through interacting poetically with one person's voice (Van Manen, 1990).

Poetic performance

'Creating the poems' offers a polyvocal account of our knowing in the making through collective poetic inquiry. We co-constructed this found poem from individual written reflections and audio-recorded conversations about our poetry-making.

Creating the poems

Collaboratively
Putting things together
Sharing ideas

Spark off each other
Things start to move
On their own momentum

Read and re-read
Immerse
Extract meaning

Live the experiences
Words and pictures entangled
In most unexpected ways

We created the following found poems to re-present different dimensions of what we were coming to know through engaging with our participant's stories through a poetic inquiry lens: 'Lecture theatre', 'Snakes on campus', 'Strikes and violence', 'My brother, stabbed to death', 'My family', and 'I miss my wife'. (Our student participant worked part-time as a contract lecturer, and the 'Lecture theatre' poem relates particularly to his lecturing experience.)

Using a poetic format allowed us to re-present data in a way that "[did] not aim at closure so much as raising further doubts and questions" (Badley, 2009a, p. 108).

Snakes on campus

Snakes
Not friendly
I don't even want to see them

Places
You don't like
I don't even want to see them

Run away
Switch it off
I don't even want to see them

A picture
Or life
I become worried

I don't even want to see them

Lecture theatre

I have a fear
About the lecture theatre

I go to the lecture theatre
And it is extreme

It is big
And they are many there

They will be scattered all over
I always perform badly there

A lecture room
Is a nightmare

Strikes and violence

Demonstrations I see in South Africa
I don't normally understand
I don't know why you find people burning, breaking

Breaking and being violent is another thing
I don't like them

It's like a norm since I arrived here in this university
These people are not actually striking for good reason
I don't normally understand

They just look for anything that can make them strike
I don't like them

My brother, stabbed to death

My younger brother was killed here in Durban
Is *this* the one who killed my brother?
We didn't know who killed him for what
Is this the *one* who killed my brother?
It took time to know that actually he was killed
Is this the one who *killed* my brother?
Better if I knew who killed him
Is this the one who killed *my brother?*

My family

My family, actually we are seven
My brother and sisters
Three sisters and three brothers
My brother and sisters
All in all, we are seven
My brother and sisters
Four boys and three girls
My brother and sisters
So I am the sixth in the family
My brother and sisters
There is only one after me
My brother and sisters
Mother and the father have passed away
My brother and sisters
They have gone
My brother and sisters
The middle ones are remaining

I miss my wife

They make me miss my wife
I miss my wife so much
I miss my wife always

There is a space here

I am here alone
My wife alone there
She is alone

There is a space here

Collective poetry-making as analysis

After we had created found poems based on the interview transcript and photographic collage, Daisy and Kathleen explained to the research team how they had recently adapted an activity by Samaras (2010) to use haiku poetry-writing in a Masters' student research workshop. A participatory process of creating, sharing and responding to haiku poems written to express research topics generated dialogic re-thinking among students and staff. It evoked new ideas and questions about ways of knowing in educational research (Pillay & Pithouse-Morgan, 2012). Consequently, we decided to experiment with creating a haiku poem to respond to the six found poems we had constructed as data re-presentation.

Haiku poetry is a "structured poetic form" (Lahman et al., 2010, p. 40) with the following pattern: line 1–5 syllables; line 2–7 syllables; line 3–5 syllables. Samaras (2010) explains that creating haiku poetry can assist researchers with the concise expression of ideas. Janesick (2001) demonstrates how she composed haiku poems to reflect on her research learning and knowing.

Using a haiku format to offer a collective understanding was a complex and iterative process. We spent time viewing and reading out the six poems to see and hear recurring narrative patterns and tensions (Clandinin & Connelly, 2000). After much discussion and some contestation, we reached a negotiated understanding of these patterns and tensions. Together (with one of us as a scribe, in a Word document projected on a screen), we wrote down words and phrases to capture this emerging understanding. We consulted a thesaurus to find alternative words to reflect our sense-making best. We then tried to select and regroup words and phrases to create a coherent interpretation within the structure of a three-line haiku poem.

Using the haiku format for analysis often felt 'messy' and discomforting as we grappled with finding words to "[shape] and [re-shape] our limited knowing and understanding of where we currently [were]" (Badley, 2009b, p. 218). Significantly, we debated whether to use the word 'ambiguous' in the poem. During this heated discussion, we discovered that 'ambiguous' had different connotations for us – probably because of our diverse theoretical, methodological and linguistic backgrounds. Some of us interpreted 'ambiguous' to mean 'vague' or even 'misleading', while others read it as 'open to more than one interpretation' or 'subject to change'. Recourse to the thesaurus revealed that, indeed, 'ambiguous' could convey all or any of these meanings. This contestation (as with our initial heated conversation about poetry as research) could have led to us dividing into warring factions that refused to engage with "a pluralism of vocabularies" (Smith, 1997, p. 11). However, perhaps because of our growing trust in each other and our participatory process, we took the time to explain and listen to our diverse understandings and to acknowledge that each of us was working with a "taken-for-granted" definition (Sparkes, 1991, p. 103). This critical conversation allowed us to realise that while we had to come to some agreement about what we regarded as the function of this word in this particular poem, we also had to acknowledge that potential audiences would bring new perspectives. We had to accept that we could not direct how others should make meaning from our poem and that we could rather look forward to engaging with multiple perspectives to extend our own knowledge (Leggo, 2008). In this instance, we recalled Eisner's (1997, p. 8) concept of "productive ambiguity", which we had come across in our preliminary reading on poetry as research (Butler-Kisber, 2002). Reference to Eisner's thinking helped us to appreciate how "the open texture of the [poetic] form increases the probability that multiple perspectives will emerge [to] make our engagement with the phenomena more complex" (Eisner, 1997, p. 8).

Poetic performance

The haiku poem 'Pedagogic settings' reveals our evolving knowing about pedagogic settings and poetry as analysis. In limiting ourselves to the concise haiku format, we had to choose what we believed was most important to express; therefore, the understandings we offer in this instance are necessarily incomplete. Using this particular form, we acknowledge that other modes could offer different insights (Eisner, 1997). However, we are emboldened by Richardson's (2003, p. 515) reminder that "when we read or hear poetry, we are continually nudged into recognising that the text has been constructed. But all texts are constructed – prose ones, too".

Pedagogic settings

Ambiguous space
Scattered dreams and feelings
Moving amidst time

Collective poetic performance as polyvocal inquiry

We originally planned to engage with several students' photographic collages and interview transcripts to develop our conference presentation. However, after constructing the six found poems and the haiku poem, we realised that our interaction with one student's stories had given us sufficient material for a 30-minute conference presentation. As we became more aware of poetry's performative and polyvocal potential as research, we deliberated on how to provoke our audience to participate in our collective poetic inquiry.

We began our presentation by performing the six found poems, without any introduction or prior explanation. We stood in a row at the front of the room, and each of us performed a poem one after the other. As we had anticipated, this surprised the audience, and we could see from their faces that it elicited a direct and powerful interaction with the poems.

We then offered a brief overview of our process of developing the found poems to re-present data and explained how we had used the haiku format as analysis. To end, we read our haiku poem and invited discussion. During the ensuing vigorous and challenging conversation, it became evident that poetic inquiry was, to a large extent, an unfamiliar research genre for this audience of educational researchers (who mainly appeared to be working or studying in South African universities). Some audience members showed great enthusiasm for research as poetry, whereas others (as expected) expressed doubts about its validity.

Because this conversation had prompted us to deepen our thinking, we agreed that, immediately after the conference, each of us would email a page of written reflections on the performance and resultant discussion to the other team members. A month later, we held another writing retreat where we discussed our considerations and viewed a transcript of our audio-recorded conversation with the audience. Our written reflections and the transcript highlighted how the poetic performance evoked emotional and intellectual engagement among the performers and audience (Lapum, 2008). We decided to portray the reflections and audience discussion in the form of found poems.

Poetic performance

'Research as performance' represents our collective multifaceted experience of the conference session. The poem reveals apprehensions about moving away from more familiar and comfortable forms of research presentation to the 'risky' mode of poetic performance. It also portrays how the emotionality and intensity of the shared performance experience evoked dynamic, embodied ways of research knowing. 'Where are we coming from?' re-presents the complexity of the multiperspective audience response that provoked us to acknowledge the tentativeness of our knowing about or through poetry as research. The poem also makes public our growing appreciation of the promise of collective poetic inquiry as a participatory educational research methodology.

Research as performance

They saw us standing there
Everyone wanted to know
What's happening here?
What's going to happen?

We were nervous
We didn't know
What's happening here?
What's going to happen?

The poem:
Human experiences
And emotions
Insight into inner life
Personal and intimate

Performing the poem
I felt the 'air' change
The performance moved me
To become one
With the experience
I struggled
Not to become tearful

I was not only one
Listening to the others
Inserting themselves
The poems come alive

The audience connecting
Forgetting who they are
In this entanglement
The poems come alive

Us and *them* and *those* merged
Swirled around
Rousing emotion
In the body
And the mind

We all felt different
We connected
Together performing

Audience connecting
Provoked
Jolted
Nobody neutral

Connected
In a new way
We came together
We responded

Where are we coming from?

Whatever the data
You bring analysis to life
You are actually seeing
Getting that feeling
There is a bit of you

It's human experience
In our different worlds
They actually talk to me
Where we are coming from
The human aspect

I have a problem
Not talking me
Reliability?
How will they look at this?
Those in different cultural
setting?
How do you measure?
What do you lose?

We should be doing more
We need to go this way
You must invent
You must experiment
Take changes
Break the rules
Have fun

Conceptualising our collective poetic inquiry process as polyvocal

We began our journey of collective poetic inquiry to explore the concept of pedagogic settings. While reflecting on the experience of performing our poems at the conference, we realised that our poetic exploration of this concept had been a catalyst for an inquiry that took us in the divergent, unexpected direction of deconstructing and re-constructing our ways of knowing and being as educational researchers. We, individually and collectively, are not the same as when we started. We have changed how we think about who we are, what we know and how we feel about what we know and do not know.

Looking back, we recognise a shifting that began when we, as researchers and educators whose job it is to know and tell others what we know, ventured into an unsettling space of what Vinz (1997, pp. 139–140, italics in the original) describes as "*un-knowing*" and "*not-knowing*". Vinz explains "*un-knowing*" as "giving up present understandings (*positions*) ... to make gaps and spaces through which to ... discover a multiplicity of meanings" and "*not-knowing*" as "[acknowledging] ambiguity and uncertainty – dis-positioning from the belief that [researchers and] teachers should know or be able to lead or construct unambiguous journeys toward knowledge".

Far from constructing an unambiguous journey towards knowledge, our collective poetic inquiry pushed us to the precarious point of confronting and publicly revealing ambiguities in what and how we come to know. Eisner (1997, p. 8) describes this as a "productive ambiguity" generated through arts-based forms of research, in which "the material presented is more evocative than denotative, and in its evocation, it generates insight and invites attention to complexity ... [and results] in less closure". While another participatory arts-based research methodology might have had similar consequences, our exploration of poetry as research suggests that this literary arts-based medium has particular qualities that facilitate a *polyvocal* engagement with and immersion in research knowing, un-knowing and not-knowing.

Poetic performance

We co-constructed the poem, 'Ambiguous space' to portray our evolving understanding of the polyvocal promise of collective poetic inquiry. This poem is a hybrid of the found poem and haiku poem forms. The six lines are made of 'poetic fragments' from our collection of research poems, which were shaped into a 'double-layer' haiku pattern of lines 1 and 2 (5 syllables), lines 3 and 4 (7 syllables), and lines 5 and 6 (5 syllables).

> *Ambiguous space*
>
> Ambiguous space
> This entanglement
>
> Scattered dreams and feelings
> Live the experiences
>
> Moving amidst time
> Us, *them* and *those* merge

Concluding thoughts

As educational researchers, we have a critical social responsibility to keep returning to this question: "What difference could this make to learners or students (and their families and communities) and teachers or educators?" Thus we ask why it should matter to anyone else if we are "expanding our repertoire of being and [knowing]" (Mitchell, 2008, p. 258). We have experienced through our process of collective poetic inquiry that how we research shapes and reshapes what we come to know and un-know and how we share that knowledge with others. If we genuinely seek to use participatory methodologies to become "partners in knowledge generation and sharing" (Ferreira, 2012, p. 512) rather than to establish and demonstrate our expertise, then we need to take risks and open ourselves to ways of researching that provoke ongoing, complex, polyvocal conversations.

Suppose we acknowledge that our understanding is always partial, contingent and subject to change? In that case, we can affirm that we always have something to learn from and with others in our quest to make a qualitative difference in our lived educational experience.

References

Allender, J. S. (2004). Humanistic research in self-study: A history of transformation. In J. J. Loughran, M. L. Hamilton, V. K. LaBoskey, & T. Russell (Eds.), *International handbook of self-study of teaching and teacher education practices* (pp. 483–515). Dordrecht, Netherlands: Kluwer Academic Publishers.

Badley, G. (2009a). Academic writing: Contested knowledge in the making? *Quality Assurance in Education, 14*(2), 104–117.

Badley, G. (2009b). Academic writing as shaping and re-shaping. *Teaching in Higher Education, 14*(2), 209–219.

Bergold, J., & Thomas, S. (2012). Participatory research methods: A methodological approach in motion. *Forum: Qualitative Social Research, 13*(1). DOI: 10.17169/fqs-13.1.1801.

Borg, M., Karlsson, B., Kim, H., & McCormack, B. (2012). Opening up for many voices in knowledge construction. *Forum: Qualitative Social Research, 13*(1). DOI: 10.17169/fqs-13.1.1793.

Butler-Kisber, L. (2002). Artful portrayals in qualitative inquiry: The road to found poetry and beyond. *Alberta Journal of Educational Research, 48*(3), 229–239.

Clandinin, D. J., & Connelly, F. M. (2000). *Narrative inquiry: Experience and story in qualitative research*. San Francisco, CA: Jossey-Bass.

Coulter, C. A., & Smith, M. L. (2009). The construction zone: Literary elements in narrative research. *Educational Researcher, 38*(8), 577–590.

Eisner, E. W. (1997). The promise and perils of alternative forms of data representation. *Educational Researcher, 26*(6), 4–10.

Ferreira, R. (2012). Call for papers: Special issue on participatory methodologies and educational research. *South African Journal of Education, 32*(4), 512.

Gitlin, A. D. (1990). Educative research, voice, and school change. *Harvard Educational Review, 60*(4), 443–466.

Hargreaves, A. (1996). Revisiting voice. *Educational Researcher, 25*(1), 12–19.

Holquist, M. (1981). Glossary. In M. Holquist (Ed.), *The dialogic imagination: Four essays by M. M. Bakhtin* (pp. 423–434). Austin, TX: University of Texas Press.

Hopper, T., & Sanford, K. (2008). Using poetic representation to support the development of teachers' knowledge. *Studying Teacher Education, 4*(1), 29–45.

Janesick, V. J. (2001). Intuition and creativity: A pas de deux for qualitative researchers. *Qualitative Inquiry, 7*(5), 531–540.

Kennedy, B. L. (2009). Infusing participants' voices into grounded theory research: A poetic anthology. *Qualitative Inquiry, 15*(8), 1416–1433.

Lahman, M. K. E., Geist, M. R., Rodriguez, K. L., Graglia, P. E., Richard, V. M., & Schendel, R. K. (2010). Poking around poetically: Research, poetry, and trustworthiness. *Qualitative Inquiry, 16*(1), 39–48.

Lapum, J. (2008). The performative manifestation of a research identity: Storying the journey through poetry. *Forum: Qualitative Social Research, 9*(2). DOI: 10.17169/fqs-9.2.397.

Leggo, C. (2008). Astonishing silence: Knowing in poetry. In J. G. Knowles & A. L. Cole (Eds.), *Handbook of the arts in qualitative research* (pp. 165–184). Thousand Oaks, CA: Sage.

MacKenzie, S. K. (2012). Circles of (im)perfection: A story of student teachers' poetic (re)encounters with self and pedagogy. *International Journal of Education & the Arts, 12*(7), 1–17.

Mitchell, C. (2008). Getting the picture and changing the picture: Visual methodologies and educational research in South Africa. *South African Journal of Education, 28*(3), 365–383.

Mitchell, C., de Lange, N., Moletsane, R., Stuart, J., & Buthelezi, T. (2005). Giving a face to HIV and AIDS: On the uses of photo-voice by teachers and community health care workers working with youth in rural South Africa. *Qualitative Research in Psychology, 2*(3), 257–270.

Pillay, D., & Pithouse-Morgan, K. (2012, November). *Teaching research in aesthetic ways to cultivate dendritic learning*. Paper presented at The Higher Education Learning and Teaching Association of South Africa (HELTASA) Conference, Stellenbosch, South Africa.

Pithouse-Morgan, K. (2007). *Learning through teaching: A narrative self-study of a novice teacher educator*. Doctoral dissertation, University of KwaZulu-Natal, Durban, South Africa. Retrieved from https://researchspace.ukzn.ac.za/xmlui/handle/10413/482

Pithouse-Morgan, K., Morojele, P., Pillay, D., Naicker, I., Chikoko, V., Ramkelawan, R., & Rajpal, R. (2012). "The air is hostile ...": Learning from an African international postgraduate student's stories of fear and isolation within a South African university campus. *Alternation*, *19*(2), 73–93.

Richardson, L. (2000). New writing practices in qualitative research. *Sociology of Sport Journal*, *17*(1), 5–20.

Richardson, L. (2003). Writing: A method of inquiry. In N. K. Denzin & Y. S. Lincoln (Eds.), *Collecting and interpreting qualitative materials* (pp. 473–500). Thousand Oaks, USA: Sage.

Riecken, T., Strong-Wilson, T., Conibear, F., Michel, C., & Riecken, J. (2005). Connecting, speaking, listening: Toward an ethics of voice with/in participatory action research. *Forum: Qualitative Social Research*, *6*(1). DOI: 10.17169/fqs-6.1.533.

Samaras, A. P. (2010). Explorations in using arts-based self-study methods. *International Journal of Qualitative Methods*, *23*(6), 719–736.

Smith, J. K. (1997). The stories educational researchers tell about themselves. *Educational Researcher*, *26*(5), 4–11.

Sparkes, A. (1991). Toward understanding, dialogue, and polyvocality in the research community: Extending the boundaries of the paradigms debate. *Journal of Teaching in Physical Education*, *10*(2), 103–133.

Theron, L. (2012). Does visual participatory research have resilience-promoting value? Teacher experiences of generating and interpreting drawings. *South African Journal of Education*, *32*(4), 381–392.

Van Manen, M. (1990). *Researching lived experience: Human science for an action sensitive pedagogy*. Albany, NY: State University of New York Press.

Vasudevan, L. (2011). An invitation to unknowing. *Teachers College Record*, *113*(6), 1154–1174.

Vinz, R. (1997). Capturing a moving form: 'Becoming' as teachers. *English Education*, *29*(2), 137–146.

Wiebe, N. G. (2008). Mennocostal musings: Poetic inquiry and performance in narrative research. *Forum: Qualitative Social Research*, *9*(2). DOI: 10.17169/fqs-9.2.413.

17
RESEARCHING FAMILY LIVES, SCHOOLING AND STRUCTURAL INEQUALITY IN RURAL PUNJAB

The power of a *Habitus Listening Guide*

Arif Naveed

Within the intimate relational environment of the home there is not one family voice, nor just one person's view. Families and their individual members are polyphonic, variably speaking the languages of their class, caste, culture, religion, gender, and as able and disabled bodies. Employing a range of discourses, families make sense of the economic and social change associated, for example, with the rise of mass schooling and its uptake in traditional communities. Formal schooling is 'read' by families in different ways, depending on their opportunities to exploit this institutionalised space (Arnot & Naveed, 2014).

Using a postcolonial approach, this chapter aims to demonstrate how family-focused data collection and a richer analysis of the voices of those living in rural communities in the Global South can help shift the homogenised, individualised, and often urban-derived models implicated in many metropolitan social scientific methodologies (Gyekye, 2003). This methodological shift makes audible the domestic, inner, deeper-seated workings of social inequality that challenge, and are challenged by, educational expansion in the push to Education for All (Naveed, 2021). Although researching poverty in Southern contexts through voice-based methods is valued because it challenges the artificial homogenising of the rural poor (World Bank, 2000), Hulme (2004) argued that researchers still need to address the complex family dynamics *within* households. For example, the dynamics surrounding age, gender, and disability create diverse understandings and experiences. Similarly, a postcolonial approach necessitates a relational methodological way of situating, rather than extracting, young people from their family relations where their social identities, subjectivities, and futures are shaped.

DOI: 10.4324/9781003355397-20
This chapter has been made available under an open access CC-BY-NC-ND 4.0 license.

A postcolonial approach also requires, according to Spivak (1988), speaking to and listening to the 'Subaltern' thus escaping what Foucault (cited in Kay, 2006, unnumbered) called the "indignity of speaking for others". Rather than looking for a family 'representative', a relational research design needs to hear first-hand the views of a range of different family members. However, this creates methodological challenges since it involves hearing individual and collective narratives simultaneously and equally recognising what Brown and Gilligan (1991, p. 44) usefully called the "harmonics of voice", the tempos, contrapuntal rhythms, and acoustics, and the cultural influences on these voices (Haste, 2014). Brown and Gilligan's *Listening Guide*, although designed to explore urban youth identity in the United States, if sensitively adapted to Southern rural contexts offers a powerful methodological tool with which to 'hear' the complex polyvocal voices of families. But critical too is the application of Bourdieu's (1979) theory of social reproduction which moves Brown and Gilligan's *Listening Guide* away from its individualistic emphasis towards an analysis of the social structural relations of cultural and economic power, the social and educational inequalities and the relational worlds of age, gender, and generation, so significant, for example, within rural Muslim families in Pakistan such as those in the study I describe below.

The development of a *Habitus Listening Guide* with four 'listenings' provided an opportunity to hear the many voices of rural family members in a village in the Punjab (Naveed & Arnot, 2019). The aim of the current chapter is to show how using a relational method and the *Habitus Listening Guide* to analyse family narratives allows a better understanding of what it means to participate and/or succeed, in this case, in an educational system based initially on British colonial structures, reshaped later by Islamic ideals and appropriated by national elites (see Naveed, 2019, for further details). It shows how family members living in poverty, each not only in their own way but also in relation to each other, negotiate the education system, the hierarchical socio-structural scape of the village and its elites, and the experience of social exclusion.

The *Habitus Listening Guide*: from theory to practice

The *Habitus Listening Guide* distinguishes between four distinctive rounds of listening described in Table 17.1 (Naveed & Arnot, 2019). By working on the same interview transcripts, the *Guide* encourages us to listen to each of four family members on a range of themes. Together they create a collage of information about where schooling sits in a family's life and social location, illustrating the challenge of using education as a transformative tool to confirm their values, or even to better their lives.

An empirical study in a Punjab village, 30 km from a main city was conducted in 2010 with the intention of employing a culturally relevant, sensitive approach to the study of traditional rural communities in a Muslim country.

TABLE 17.1 Listenings, methods, and objectives

Listenings	Objectives
1 Social Structural Listening	Here we seek to understand the historical and contemporary structures and objective conditions that surround family members' lives in their community, and their relation to the education system. The four interlinked cross-generational educational biographies are brought together to construct a family biography situated in the rural social order.
2 Horizontal Intergenerational Listening	A closer listening to the narratives uncovers the dialogical relationship between social disadvantage and educational aspirations, successes, and defeats to shed light on the place of schooling within the culturally shaped family dynamics. *Inter-narrativity* is generated through the repeated paired intergenerational listenings of father-mother and son-daughter narratives. We hear how the parental and children's accounts are differentially enabled and constrained in different eras, conditions, and place.
3 Vertical Gender Listening	A deeper listening to the intra-family masculine and feminine narratives reveals the potentially tacit acceptance of family and social gender controls by youth, their submissive and transformative agentic tendencies, and the material conditions producing both tendencies which impact on their educational trajectories. *Inter-narrativity* is generated through the paired gendered listenings of father-son and mother-daughter narratives. Comparisons within and across the paired narratives reveal the impact of the gender order over generations on educational aspirations, strategies, and outcomes.
4 Mythic-ritual Listening	The final listening makes audible how religious beliefs are called into play, either contributing to the maintenance of poverty and social inequality, or inspiring strategies to disrupt power structures through education as a religious duty. By identifying a 'spiritual poem' in the transcripts, we hear generational shifts in the use of mythic-ritual beliefs (in comparison with secular legitimations) to explain, for example, their notions of luck, duty, fate, and prospects, and how these beliefs affect poverty and/or progress.

Source: Developed from Naveed and Arnot (2019).

The village is one of many 'Canal Colonies' set up by the British colonial government in the late 19th to early 20th century to boost agricultural production in Punjab's newly irrigated areas. Agricultural land was granted to those migrating from India based on the prior family background and social status (Douie, 1914). Whilst cross-border migration at independence in 1947 altered the demographic, the village continued to reflect the colonial normalisation of the class-caste hierarchy. The village now included a few large landowners, small farmers landless agricultural workers, small businessmen and traders, and a few government employees. Girls could study up to Grade 12 within the village whereas boys had to travel elsewhere to study after Grade 10. A small number of seminaries provided religious education. This study involved tape recorded semi-structured 90-minute interviews with the father, mother, and one son and one daughter (aged between 15 and 25) in 10 village families. The interviews were conducted in Punjabi, transcribed and translated into English. For a deeper understanding and to respect cultural expressions and idioms, both Punjabi and translated English transcripts were used in the analysis.

The following section describes how the *Habitus Listening Guide* was used in the analysis of the transcripts of four members of Munawar Hussain's (pseudonym) family, and its value for such Southern contexts.

Listening to the social structure: educational biographies in a field of power

The *social structural listening* aims to understand the structure of relative social positions – what Bourdieu (1979) calls 'a field of power' – within which families are situated. This critical listening hears the overlapping, yet distinctly different, descriptions of local educational provision and community life, political and educational events, and the relationship of such events to narrators' values and experiences. It uncovers family members' discursive narratives about the plots connecting their biographies, offering a temporal sequence of family life events (Horsdal, 2011). They reveal the (in)formal institutions, material pressures, the socio-political/cultural organisation of the community and the economic power of local elites' control over poor families. These shape the family's social and educational trajectory, its insecurity and eventually the choices it makes to stabilise itself.

In the case of Munawar, the local field of power is his village and the social structure within which family members take relative positions by virtue of the forms and volume of their economic, social, and cultural capital (Hilgers & Manges, 2015). The constellation of landlessness, poverty, and caste identity formed a social-scape with implications for what was achievable *in* and *through* education. These objective conditions and material realities are embodied in the family's own *symbolic order* which can be heard in the subsequent listenings (Bourdieu, 1979).

This first listening of 52-year-old Munawar revealed that, like his parents, he had never been to school; he had been a brick-kiln worker for 30 years yet three decades of such hard labour had not earned him economic security in old age. His 50-year-old wife Tabinda had been the first girl in her extended family to attend school. To survive poverty and to *protect the honour* of her kinship, her widowed mother married her off to her cousin Munawar at the age of 12, ending her schooling after Grade 4. The couple had six daughters and five sons.

A close listening uncovered the critical working of the local social hierarchy. The family had been allocated residential land in a public housing scheme. But being nervous, Munawar took possession sooner than others providing rival factions an opportunity to register a formal complaint. Munawar was arrested but later released, having had his right over the land recognised. However, he had to pay huge bribes and legal expenses that far exceeded the land's market value. The family borrowed from his employer, a rich brick-kiln owner, falling into the same trap as millions of bonded labourers in the country. This experience had a deep effect on the family's educational and economic trajectory.

Despite such experience, Munawar and Tabinda were predisposed to believe in education as a route out of their poverty. Their sons were intelligent and performed well at school but sadly, because of poverty, the first two sons left school to work as labourers just before obtaining their secondary school certificate. The teenage sons studying in Grade 6 and 7 were taken out of school when the family became indebted due to the land dispute and were sent to work. The youngest son completed primary schooling and planned to continue his studies. Munawar's daughters were better schooled than their brothers with two daughters managing to complete Grade 12 – the highest level available in the village – and one later teaching at a private school. Laiba, the daughter we interviewed, left school when she had just started Grade 6 – three other daughters left school at Grades 7 and 8. Despite such educational ambitions and several years of schooling, none of Munawar's 11 children succeeded in securing any salaried employment. Getting jobs required "political connections" or "paying bribes" that they did not have.

Revealing strong political views, Munawar voiced great interest in village politics and mobilised people of his *biradree* (kinship), the majority of whom were poor like him, to have their own representative in the village council against the wishes of the dominant groups. This political participation had provoked a personal vendetta against him:

> We took part in politics, but it caused us losses because *we do not have the feathers to take the political flight*. The landlords try to keep people suppressed ... Even if we take part in politics, a political leader from the top would ask us not to contest against him or his people. Then what will happen to our politics? It is finished there.

Munawar saw no end to his hardship and continued to work as a labourer because his sons' earnings were irregular. The persistence of these intergenerational occupational hazards demonstrates how, for the young, the past survives the present and perpetuates the future (Bourdieu, 1979). The economic possibilities determined by social locations meant that he understood there were no jobs or business prospects for "people like them", no matter how much education they gained. Munawar recognised the limits imposed by the oppressive social conditions, noting that "the poor rarely succeed". Using the language of rights and social justice, Munawar articulated the nexus between power, schooling, employment, and poverty:

> The son of the poor does not get job even when he is highly educated. Therefore, the poor question the usefulness of such education. They begin learning some skills at the earliest. The political parties are bound to do injustice to the poor.

The structuring of the family's collective biography makes explicit the educational interruptions and employment vulnerabilities, and uncovered the consequences of how low social status deprives families of rights, trapping them in poverty. Yet, paradoxically, it also revealed the continued 'capacity to aspire' that Munawar and Tabinda encouraged in their children (Naveed, 2021) – a theme revealed in the second listening.

Horizontal intergenerational listening: chronological educational narratives

Next, the *Habitus Listening Guide* recommends a *horizontal intergenerational listening* which examines how parents and children use education to engage with the inequalities in the local social structure and talk about it. It exhibits the social conditioning of aspirations and everyday practices in ways that reproduce and, at times, subtly transform these very conditions of production (Bourdieu, 1979). Here, the discursive frames that each generation uses to make sense of their educational trajectories – the commonalities *within* and *across* the paired interviews of (a) husband and wife and (b) son and daughter give us access to generational shifts about family life, education, and inequality/poverty.

Pairing the narratives of the father/mother and of the sons/daughters generates *inter-narrativity*. At a practical level, the content of the parents' and their children's speech, the events they describe, and the educational motifs embedded in their values, perceptions, aspirations, and strategies are compared. Treating these data as temporally situated interpretations of life and experience, we hear attitudes to the persistence or change in generational cultures and the outcomes of education for life chances. Some of these paired generational narratives are given below.

Voicing parental aspirations: Munawar (father) and Tabinda (mother)

This listening exposed how Munawar's greatest regret about being uneducated and Tabinda's high sense of accomplishment for being the first educated women in her extended family came together to shape their aspirations to school their children. Munawar saw himself as dependent, vulnerable to exploitation, and at the disposal of others, "like an animal in the herd, at the mercy of the shepherd" – voicing as it were the 'symbolic violence' (Bourdieu & Passeron, 1990) caused by the massification of a schooling system that made the unschooled discredit themselves and feel worthless. In contrast, Tabinda's small amount of schooling helped her become self-confident and consider herself a life-long learner. Despite such differences, together they assumed that education was a meritocratic route for social mobility, albeit with gender-differentiated pathways. Both realised that parental education represented economic, social, and cultural capital, central to children's education. Munawar thought "If I were educated, I would have pushed my children to study further … and secured them a proper job". Meanwhile, Tabinda had an appreciation of the importance of education: "by educating my children, I have multiplied the light of *ilm* [knowledge] … helped them how to read, write, and count".

Both parents saw a son's schooling as linked to economic gain. Tabinda thought her sons could have achieved better employment only if they were "more educated" whilst Munawar believed that the lack of salaried jobs was a product of the wider structures of inequality, since sons of the poor did not find jobs even when highly educated. Knowing the 'rules of the game' enabled him to 'penetrate', to use Willis' (1977) term, the illusory meritocratic promise of schooling in an unequal social order and recognise injustice in the distribution of scarce economic opportunities through patronage-based local networks. Educational transitions and investments over two generations, despite being significant, had not yielded any economic gain in these parents' view, as all their sons were doing manual labour and "barely surviving".

This listening revealed that the daughters' schooling was talked about primarily in relation to the "increased prospects for the future generation" – metaphorically and instrumentally situating female schooling at the core of long-term intergenerational transitions. Linked to motherhood and domesticity, daughters' educational gains were seen in terms of achieving the right dispositions to boost their marriageability. Overwhelmed by the sense of duty, Munawar hoped for a 'matrimonial dividend' that would bring better lives for their daughters (Arnot & Naveed, 2014): "I am trying to marry them off … they will go to their homes … with the blessing of Allah, their future generation will also be good". Educating daughters could "create a good environment at home", and they would also be disposed to "give good advice". Further, "education would give children *tameez*", a notion encompassing moral behaviour, respectful bodily manners, and the ability to judge, classify, and distinguish between good and bad, and the worthy and unworthy.

This second listening also uncovered the ways parents talked about the physical embodiment of cultural values and capital – the 'body hexis' (Bourdieu,

1979) – which they wanted youth to acquire through their schooling. In Tabinda's view, educated people had a "distinct style", and Munawar observed "when an educated [person] is walking, he [sic] can be recognised"; "an educated person, when [he] speaks, his [sic] manners reveal that he is educated". Educated could do *achee baat*, representing a set of conversational dispositions and manners, including reasoning, articulation, communication and convincing others. Tabinda linked educational dispositions to speaking the 'superior' language of the public sphere, Urdu, instead of Punjabi.

Voicing agency: Najam (son) and Laiba (daughter)

In comparison to their parents, Najam and Laiba's narratives offered glimpses into important other spaces in which schooling offers cultural capital including the internalisation and personalisation of failure. Najam, for example, saw social privilege in schools' use of academic ability and its violent consequences: "those who were *laaik* (capable) used to study [better]". But this capability depended on having prior cultural capital; "those children whose parents are educated are also *laaik* in the classrooms". This was an implicit recognition of rural schools' built-in processes of exclusion which selectively facilitated some, and pushed away the 'undesirable': "teachers used to beat only those students who made mistakes ... some children would make a plan and run away together". Such daily classifications, allied discourses, and abusive practices within classrooms had an adverse impact on the motivation of socially disadvantaged students. Personal favours were demanded by teachers who "used to ask pupils to do their personal stuff; sometimes they would ask you to fetch water to their cattle and sometimes to get their fodder". Laiba observed: "teachers used to ask students to wash [the teacher's] dishes". The burden of such practices fell heavily on poorer children. In such crude ways, schools socialised pupils into the social order, deepening hierarchy, and potentially producing resigned personality types that matched the stratification of society.

This generational listening demonstrates how, despite her parents' aspirations, Laiba could not cope with the change in social relations from the primary to the high school and dropped out: "I was very intelligent. Had a great interest in studies ... when I moved to high school, the environment was changed, I lost interest. I just could not understand what happened to me. I couldn't study at this new school". She described the systematic processes in which even smart students with little cultural capital, felt like fish out of water, and this tightly circumscribed their autonomous choices: "my parents asked me to continue my studies but I had lost interest so left the school". Laiba regretted giving up: "it was a wrong decision ... Now I don't make any decisions". But she wanted to help her siblings' study by doing "their share of household chores". She had recently got engaged and was looking forward to her wedding in a year or so.

Her brother, Najam had left school after Grade 5 and had worked with his father at the brick-kiln for 14 years. He was married and had a daughter. His decision to drop out revealed the code of honour and gendered expectations for sons to undertake economic responsibilities in the wake of poverty: "I had grown-up sisters, and my father was the only one working in the family. I didn't consider it appropriate to study further". The parents "insisted upon continuation of my studies. But I felt embarrassed that father is the only one working in the family". Najam saw poverty and a lack of parental cultural capital as inter-locking, shaping the reproduction of generational occupations: "I am spending my life like my father … I am doing the same labour like him". With five years of schooling, he internalised his failure and considered himself responsible for this intergenerational pattern "since I did not get enough education, there is no change".

Listening to this generation's accounts revealed the role of 'respect' and agency. For Najam as a man, education was a means to *get* respect, whereas for Laiba, it taught her to *give* respect – an attribute for a marriageable daughter. But girls' schooling also induced subtle changes in this gender order. Laiba's description of the need to hold conversations demonstrated a great sense of agency about what girls could acquire through education – the ability to judge, courage to stand for what was right, and the dispositions to articulate and convince others:

> One has to raise voice against something which is wrong. Educated girls raise voice often because they have learnt the ways to speak as compared to the uneducated girls. Also, if they have to say anything, they can make the other person understand them.

Najam and Laiba's parents and their schooling had taught them the need to educate their own children "as much as they wanted". However, when asked whose education would be preferred if they faced any economic crisis, their voices diverged. Najam saw there were no jobs for men anyway, so sons' schooling had little economic value but "if a girl is educated her future will be better … her future generation will be better off … I'll provide education to my daughter". In contrast, and like her mother, Laiba's response reflected her agency and ability to strategise for all her children: "If I ran short of money in the meanwhile, even then I shall educate [sons and daughters] by all means, like, by stitching clothes".

The generational continuities around the value of education and realisation of its power were tempered with suggestions of conserving strategic traditional gender divisions. The third reading explores this complex story in more depth.

Vertical gendered listenings: the internalisation of male domination

By pairing father/son interviews and mother/daughter interviews, the *vertical gender listening* offers a deeper structural and dialogic analysis of the intra-family gender power relations as embodied, enacted, reproduced, and/or transformed over generations. It involves hearing (a) male identities and duties as parents or siblings; (b) women's position, duties, and their negotiating power *vis-a-vis* husbands and brothers; and (c) gendered boundaries and differential goals for sons and daughters within the family.

The negotiations between the gendered pairs uncover the deep cognitive structures of the men and women in this family which shape their values, perceptions, and practices. They also expose forms of symbolic violence through the structure of speech and contextual information. The internalisation of 'masculine domination' (Bourdieu, 2001) shapes understandings, and an acceptance of gender power relations using duty and devotion, as well as love, admiration, and respect. But such close gender listenings also reveal emergent forms of women's agency around schooling.

Father and son: reworking male honour

Although Munawar and his son Najam seemed initially to agree on how the socio-political structure works, their place within these power relations, and the importance of education, key differences around male honour emerged. Munawar's experience and *practical knowledge* led him, as a father, to *adjust* his high aspirations for social mobility for both his sons and daughters to what was normal for *people like him*. He saw the *reproductive* nature of education at the community level through the growing inequality caused by education itself:

> If you give balance in the hands [of the educated], they will favour the heavier side. If there is any decision against the poor, everyone says rich is right. Educated people don't support the truth. They also favour the rich, who are politically strong.

Najam seemed to accept the status quo but did not see structural inequality as being so extreme: "I have never understood/recognised richness or poverty ... *Jaat, Gujjar* or *Kumhiyar*, no [caste] is above or below ... whether one is rich or poor, everyone works for oneself, none gives to others". He saw education as neutral in relation to social hierarchies: "there was no inequality before education, neither is there now". His perception of political organisation also appeared to be inclusive and egalitarian. Since he 'escaped' from the structure of inequality by misrecognising its effects, his level of contentment and his faith depended on destiny and luck: "the *rizq* (sustenance) that Allah has written in your fate, will reach you anyway". Najam surrendered his aspirations – as a man, all he needed was a "menial job", an "obedient wife" and "obedient relationship" with his father, trading his agency in favour of strong masculine tendencies.

Hence, when it came to their educational biographies, both father and son interpreted the event of Najam leaving school differently. Munawar spoke it only in light of the economic crisis: "my son left his school due to my indebtedness. He put his school bag at home and said, 'I shall also work at brick-kiln and pay back the debt'". Whereas, for Najam, it was a matter of his male honour to take up economic responsibilities with "grown-up sisters" at home, and his father being the "only one working in the family", he "felt embarrassed", and "didn't consider it appropriate to study further". These divergent voices pointed towards gendered dispositions differentiated by age, generation, and schooling, where masculine strategies justified an early transition from school into male manual work.

Further, as a young man, Najam's commitment to a stringent code of honour meant he downplayed female educational attainments: "We don't let the adult girls go outside home and keep her in the veil … girls' study only up to 8th [Grade] … girls are not allowed to go outside home … it is not due to poverty, they already studied under poverty". Whilst his parents took pride in a daughter completing Grade 12, Najam insisted that girls in his family were not allowed to study beyond Grade 8. He spoke of girls' early transition into adulthood at the age of 10 implying the need for early marriage and offering religious authority in support: "Girls' [marriage] should not be delayed. *Maulvi Sb* [a cleric] decreed that the prayers of those who have adult daughters at home are not accepted".

One might expect the unschooled father to hold conservative gender values, and the young and schooled son to hold more democratic values. However, as we saw earlier, sounding like a *father*, Munawar took pride in the accomplishments of his daughters, considering them as contributing to his own social mobility. Najam spoke as a *man* with a traditional patriarchal set of values, attitudes, and responsibilities. The honour of the brother sounded stronger and louder than the father's pride. Bourdieu (2001) associates this phenomenon with the ways in which male domination persists and perpetuates in the internalisation of the "sexually ordered social order" through "schemes of perceptions and appreciation" which are internalised subconsciously, accepting this social order to be "normal or even natural" (p. 95).

Negotiating a gendered habitus: mother and daughter

In contrast, the listening of mother-daughter voices not only offered support for the patriarchal structure but also revealed a tentative modern femininity. At one level, mother's and daughter's female identities differed greatly. Tabinda, the mother, was the trend-setter, the first-ever girl in her generation in her extended family to be schooled, whereas Laiba was the least educated amongst her sisters. Embodied in her style, articulation, and conversational manners, Tabinda possessed a strong sense of self-confidence which helped her make family decisions when strategising under difficult circumstances: "It was because of [my schooling] that I have educated [my daughters] until Grade 12 ... I myself make family decisions".

However, Tabinda's freedom to study was "conditional" upon her "appropriate behaviour", such as not taking too much interest in others, and "covering her head properly". Consequently, her sense of equality was not strong enough to question male dominance: "in my view, men have a higher status. Wife should not interfere in the matters of husband. Wife is lower. Women have to accept whatever men say. Women are lower than men". An unconditional submission to male authority lies at the core of Tabinda's conception of a good life. Whilst schooling her 11 children she was not allowed to interfere with these power relations – thus, whilst taking pride in her daughters' education, their schooling must "not [have] spoiled" them. Her interview transcript revealed that conformity to family values needed to be demonstrated if her schooling decisions were not to be threatened: "when we sent girls to school, we made sure they were observing veil".

Yet within these paired narratives, Tabinda voiced the art of negotiation. She described how her schooling experience widened her "set of possibilities" beyond her economic means. Thus, when Laiba's sister wanted to study further, Tabinda approached the schoolteacher and convinced her to help: "This is how we educated our children". She avoided early marriages for her children: "children can take family responsibilities only if they are *sianay* (wise)". She saw daughters' education beyond its marital gains: "I wish my daughters get some job. But who will give job ... they can't become schoolteachers either as that involves bribes".

In Laiba's voice, we can hear a similar emergent sense of self-hood, demonstrating her cognitive development, and self-confidence. This third listening uncovered the story about how leaving school had placed Laiba at the bottom of the rank amongst her siblings: "I lack confidence because I left school ... It was a wrong decision to quit the school. Now I don't make any decisions". Nevertheless, schooling gave Laiba the ability to communicate and the courage to take a stand, "to raise [her] voice against something which is wrong... because educated girls raise their voices often because they have learned the ways to speak ... to make the other person understand" as quoted earlier.

Such transformative views challenged any unconditional submission to the social order. Education would provide girls with an opportunity for economic participation "when one faces any hardship". Laiba argued that "if the girls are educated, they should work like men", implying that work allowed them to claim equality with men.

Yet this listening also revealed a somewhat contradictory contrapuntal voice. Laiba was very optimistic about her future. In a context where girls are seen to be wedded off as a 'responsibility', a 'burden', and a 'duty' by their families and where their education is meant primarily to raise their marital prospects, the fact that she was engaged to be married brought Laiba a sense of reaching her destination. Plans to marry into a relatively better off family added to her satisfaction. "In my view, our life would be easy. One should keep good hopes. In my opinion, I shall not need to work that hard in my life because the person I am engaged with is the only son, has no sister either". She was largely content with her current circumstances: "I am spending a good life. I am satisfied. I don't lack anything … I see myself after 5 years … in good circumstances. I shall be a housewife then".

By dropping out of school, Laiba and Najam, driven by their gendered dispositions of honour and sacrifice, limited their 'free will' by 'voluntarily' making educational choices against their individual interests. They illustrated what Bourdieu (2001, p. 39) calls "the passion of the dominated habitus". In the final listening, we hear another underlying contrapuntal voice.

Mythic-ritual listening: a spiritual poem of fate and duty

This fourth unique listening offers a way of exploring the religious shaping of the family's understanding of inequality, schooling, and its outcomes (Naveed & Arnot, 2019) – an element that is often absent in educational research, yet which is so vital in theocratically shaped countries in Southern contexts. The assumption that all research subjects are secular agents is damaging to religious postcolonial cultures not least since they ignore the complex conditionalities of living. It is vital to explore whether, and if so how, religion and religious identity shape individuals' understanding of their world and the contribution that education can make to that. Social scientific research in Southern contexts needs to attend methodologically to the instances when religious beliefs are called into play, supporting a particular form of structuration of the perception and thinking of the world (Bourdieu, 1979). Such beliefs can contribute to, maintain, or challenge the maintenance of poverty and social inequality, or inspire strategies to disrupt power structures as a religious duty (Naveed & Arnot, 2019).

Schooling in religious values can inculcate the relations of the social order (Bourdieu, 1991) but mass schooling with its expectations of individual academic success can have an impact on the different explanatory/legitimatory frameworks used by the poor. The challenge for social scientists is to hear the voices of the family members which, even if not religiously active, may position themselves in relation to a socially and spiritually ordered world. This could help differentiate between those who explain the possibilities and the limitations they face in their lives using the moral-spiritual order, and those who seek explanations in individualised secularised agency and practice. This listening uncovers the existence of another, this time religious, contrapuntal voice underlying the family narratives.

A spiritual poem

The method used in this fourth listening involves extracting each interviewee's 'spiritual poem' – in other words all the sentences that refer to religious identities, spiritual beliefs, symbols, and arguments that refer to the 'divine', 'fate', and 'duty'. These poems include the mythic discourses that shape family explanations of their position in the social order, their perceived successes and failures and the intergenerational shifts in the dispositional worlds of parents and their children. The poems also reveal the socio-psychological/emotional subjectivities and outcomes of schooling which religion is drawn upon to legitimise or question.

For example, a feeling of resignation and renouncement can immediately be heard in Munawar and Tabinda's poems. As we have seen, Munawar aspired for his children, albeit with little control over their future: "I have tried to give education to my children … May Allah help and [if my youngest son] gets admission in Grade 6 … By the will of Allah, we shall do some business … But the thing is, the poor rarely succeed".

The implication in Munawar's reference to Allah's will is that it determines the fulfilment of aspirations, but it also offers hope that, amidst the unfavourable conditions faced by the poor in his community, it could lead to some opportunities. The success of all his strategies around daughters' schooling depended upon Allah's will that also obligated prioritising their marriage:

> Allah will do good … We have educated our daughters up to Grade 12 and got them engaged. Allah will improve our earnings and we shall marry them off. We hear that it is in the Quran that you shouldn't keep the girls at home [unmarried] for long. My children have received Quranic education as well as the Urdu [formal] education. Whoever we discuss with, they say to marry off the girls very soon. This is Allah's discretion.

Further listening to Munawar's account shows that religion's sphere of influence appeared very wide – covering all aspects of Munawar's life. He voiced a great deal of helplessness against oppressive power structures with a dwindling faith in his own agency: "at the higher level, nobody listens to us. Here,

Chauhdary (village elites) doesn't let us rise. Nobody takes care of us at the top. Then why shouldn't we be beaten up?" Munawar believed there was little that the government would do for his family. Their survival and security required them to be "physically well" to be self-sufficient, but this depended on the will of Allah rather than a healthcare system. Divine intervention might turn things around and address all the wider political problems:

> May Allah do something better in the election. This system can improve if Allah brings a good ruler ... We just pray to Allah to do good for us. May Allah give us a ruler who brings in peace and stability ... There should come Allah's man who improves things ... government has its own problems, and the poor are getting worse further.

The strategy for political change was to pray, as there was little else to do. Munawar described how unequal access to education was playing into increasing inequalities: "if the situation remains the same ... the rich will get education, but the poor will not. We can only pray that Allah gives progress to the village ... We pray that this government goes today instead of tomorrow".

Tabinda, in contrast, saw participating in the political process as a religious obligation, irrespective of its role in preserving elite structures and poverty: "We never wasted our votes. Vote is *amanah* (trust/obligation) ... This is also the order of Allah". She admitted there were dangers that the family would be neglected, but considered poverty to be justifiable, given the experience of the Prophet (Peace Be Upon Him):

> I read that Allah's Prophet slept on the carpet made of date leaves which left imprints on his back and his companion Omar asked, 'You sleep on this carpet being Allah's Prophet whereas infidels sleep on soft beds?' The Prophet replied, 'You don't know we shall be rewarded in the life hereafter' ... Thanks to Allah, whatever he has given is enough.

This religious orientation offered Tabinda contentment with the adverse conditions of her existence which could, after all, be worse and inspired her to adopt a strong commitment to educate her daughters. "Only Allah knows we had nothing to get my daughter admitted ... Education is like a light fragrance, it spreads if you open it and vanishes if you close it. Allah has elevated the status of the teacher".

This mythic-ritual listening exposed the bonding associated with religious consent intergenerationally. Making fewer references to religion in their narratives, Laiba and Najam felt equally blessed. Laiba commented: "I always thank Allah that I am in better circumstances than many people". Whilst Najam commented on the harsh life and their strata in the village: "Thanks to Allah I spend my day by doing labour". With gratitude for life not being worse, he yet had hopes for his own children: "Allah will help and if I and my daughter have the life, I'll give her education up to Grade 10". Accepting fate helped Najam overlook deprivation and discrimination: "I shall get the *rizk* (sustenance) that Allah has written for me. We are neither too rich nor too poor, we are in the middle ... People don't discriminate against us, thanks to Allah ... because we are poor, nor because of our caste". This symbolic interpretation of the political world and the predominant ethos of resignation and renouncement is noteworthy. Of significance too is the family's fate – its association with the unequal social relations within rural communities, legitimised less through schooling and more through the socially differentiated functions fulfilled by religion (Bourdieu, 1991). Differently located within the social structure, such families are also variously positioned within "the division of religious labour" (Bourdieu, 1991, p. 17). Religious representations and practices bore down on educational dispositions which, whilst aspirational, potentially, can also contribute to the acceptance and the reproduction of an unequal social order.

Bourdieu warned that systems of religious representations and practices, when invisible and official, can justify the existence of the dominance of certain classes and practices, and representations that impose a legitimacy on the dominated – they can imply that the power of the elite is not arbitrary. Such narratives require us to recognise, particularly in theocratic countries, this complex symbolic shaping of aspirations.

The power of the *Habitus Listening Guide*

The relational family-centred method and the methodological power of the *Habitus Listening Guide*, when used in postcolonial contexts such as rural Pakistan, brings to light the subtly different reproductive and socially transformative roles of education in society. First, it enables hearing the socially conditioned meanings, aspirations, and strategies of Munawar's family as they struggled to achieve education, social mobility, and a valued life. It makes audible the effects of age and, importantly, social change occasioned by the rise of schooling in the community. Further, its use reveals the play of masculinity and femininity, and age and religion, in family members' lives, uncovering how deeper cognitive structures influence educational aspirations. The four listenings reveal how the local gender culture strengthens mother-daughter relations and selfhood, and how gender values can divide father and son, with the latter even keener to reproduce patriarchal relations than his father. The cultural domain (in the form of manners, language, self-confidence, and agency) appeared to be as important a form of capital as employment. Politically, there are nuanced divisions between family members about what is possible for families like theirs, where change can enter, and what role education can play. These tensions between reproductive *and* transformative dispositions can also be heard in individual subjectivity about duty, fate, and acceptance, albeit peppered with the hope that luck will change. In Munawar's family, social mobility through education simultaneously appears possible but doubtful, and impossible but understood.

Second, in Southern postcolonial contexts, such as rural Pakistan where family relations are pivotal, the *Guide* offers a methodological tool with which to identify social change and not just continuity (Bourdieu is often accused of the latter). Conventional social scientific methodologies proffer a somewhat linear, *factual* collective biography narrative usually gleaned from the household head. These risk continuing to see the poor as captured in a prison of deprivation and disadvantage, without agency, capital or resilience. Deconstructing family voices and listening to them through a relational, dialogic method validates rather than denigrates such collective cultures. The methodological approach operationalised in this case study attempts to do justice to families by capturing the durable dispositions of individuals, and their complex 'practical knowledge' – it challenges their assumed homogeneity and submissive passivity. By listening with compassion to the voices of the poor in such a Southern context, it is possible to avoid 'readmitting the Subaltern through the backdoor' or what O'Hanlon (1988) described as a "self-originating, self-determining individual, who is at once a subject in his possession of a sovereign consciousness whose defining quality is reason, and an agent in his power of freedom" (p. 191). In contrast, the approach offered here enables us to hear the localised social structuring of individual and collective subjectivities, rationalities, values, and meanings, and the agentic strategies which the disadvantaged use to better their lives (Naveed, 2021).

Third, as an innovative method of data analysis, the *Habitus Listening Guide* offers a new way of 'hearing' the impact of mass schooling when embedded in colonialist structures and situated within an unequal religious and caste system. It illustrates the erratic, resisted, and negotiated social changes associated with schooling which are both internalised and embodied within poor families progressing without disrupting the social order (Naveed & Arnot, 2019). By reworking Brown and Gilligan's listening guidance to address both the structures of poverty and the realities of a different cultural/religious environment such as the Punjab, it was possible to challenge the assumptions of individualism and secularity, and to deconstruct the universal notions of family homogeneity amongst the poor, especially in Southern contexts.

Fourth, a deeper listening of family narratives also challenges the stereotypes about how negatively girls' schooling is thought to be viewed by families living in rural poverty, particularly by fathers. It therefore challenges simplistic explanations for the low take up of girls' schooling which fail to locate schooling within local gender and social structural inequalities. The conditions in which families find themselves economically poor are characterised by their internal collaborative strength – a collectivity that can generate conditions for its members to progress socially or be held back.

From a postcolonial perspective, young people living in rural Southern cultures need to be represented methodologically – they need to participate in research that works with intergenerational relations. This relational polyvocal case study demonstrates how, as social scientists, we can move closer to uncovering and understanding the ways poverty controls lives and is internalised by members of the community, and to reveal the legitimatory discourses used by families to explain their inability to exploit the educational opportunities provided by schooling or their success in so doing. This methodological approach generates insights which suggest that the expectations around mass schooling can only be met, if such nuanced elements are addressed.

Acknowledgements

This chapter has benefitted greatly from discussions with Madeleine Arnot. I am grateful to Munawar Hussain and his family for sharing their life histories. My thanks also go to the research team at the Mahbub-ul-Haq Human Development Centre, Islamabad, and especially to Fareeha Ali, Tauseef Ahmad, Noorulain Ali, and Ghulam Mustafa for conducting the fieldwork.

References

Arnot, M., & Naveed, A. (2014). Educational outcomes across the generational and gender divide: The rural family habitus of Pakistani families living in poverty. *Gender and Education*, 26(5), 505–523.
Bourdieu, P. (1979). *Outline of a theory of practice*. Cambridge, England: Cambridge University Press.
Bourdieu, P. (1991). Genesis and structure of the religious field. *Comparative Social Research*, 13, 1–44.
Bourdieu, P. (2001). *Masculine domination*. Cambridge, England: Polity Press.
Bourdieu, P., & Passeron, J. C. (1990). *Reproduction in education, society and culture*. London, England: Sage.
Brown, L. M., & Gilligan, C. (1991). Listening for voice in narratives of relationship. *New Directions for Child Development*, 54, 43–61.
Douie, J. M. (1914). The Punjab Canal Colonies. *Journal of the Royal Society of Arts*, 62(3210), 611–623.
Gyekye, K. (2003). Person and community in African thought. In P. H. Coetzee & A. P. J. Roux (Eds.), *The African philosophy reader* (pp. 348–366). London, England: Routledge.
Haste, H. (2014). Culture, tools, and subjectivity: The (re)construction of self. In T. Magioglou (Ed.), *Culture and political psychology: A societal perspective* (pp. 27–48). Charlotte, NC: Information Age Publishing.
Hilgers, M., & Manges, E. (Eds.). (2015). *Bourdieu's theory of social fields: Concepts and applications*. New York, NY: Routledge.
Horsdal, M. (2011). *Telling lives: Exploring dimensions of narratives*. New York, NY: Routledge.

Hulme, D. (2004). Thinking 'small' and the understanding of poverty: Maymana and Mofizul's story. *Journal of Human Development, 5*(2), 161–176.

Kay, J. (2006, September 9). Intellectuals and power: A conversation between Michel Foucault and Gilles Deleuze. *Libcom.org*. Retrieved from https://libcom.org/library/intellectuals-power-a-conversation-between-michel-foucault-and-gilles-deleuze

Naveed, A., & Arnot, M. (2019). Exploring educational and social inequality through the polyphonic voices of the poor: A habitus listening guide for the analysis of family-schooling relations. *Comparative Education, 55*(2), 175–196.

Naveed, A. (2021). Overriding social inequality? Educational aspirations versus the material realities of the rural families in Pakistan. In P. Rose, M. Arnot, R. Jeffery, & N. Singal (Eds.), *Reforming education and challenging inequalities in Southern contexts: Research and policy in international development* (pp. 123–143). London, England: Routledge.

Naveed, M. A. (2019). *Reconceptualising the role of schooling in intergenerational social mobility: Patterns, perspectives and experiences from rural Pakistan*. Doctoral dissertation, University of Cambridge, Cambridge, UK. Retrieved from https://doi.org/10.17863/CAM.41890

O'Hanlon, R. (1988). Recovering the subject Subaltern studies and histories of resistance in colonial South Asia. *Modern Asian Studies, 22*(1), 189–224.

Spivak, G. (1988). Can the subaltern speak. In C. Nelson & L. Grossberg (Eds.), *Marxism and interpretation of culture* (pp. 271–316). London, England: Macmillan.

Willis, P. (1977). *Learning to labour: How working class kids get working class jobs*. Westmead, England: Saxon House.

World Bank. (2000). *Voices of the poor: Can anyone hear us?* Washington, DC: Oxford University Press.

18
PEDAGOGY OF ABSENCE, CONFLICT AND EMERGENCE

Contributions to the decolonisation of education from the Native American, Afro-Portuguese and Romani experiences

Miye Nadya Tom, Julia Suárez-Krabbe and Trinidad Caballero Castro

What might Native American[1] communities in the United States, communities of Cape Verdean origin in Portugal, and Romani[2] communities (*gitanos*) in Spain have in common? This chapter offers insights on the decolonisation of education, often only marginally addressed in fields like comparative and international education, global citizenship education, and scholarship on public pedagogy. These fields remain anchored in the Western paradigm, which is the unquestioned perspective from which 'particularities' are also addressed (Grande, 2004). In this sense, there is often a "reading from the centre" (Connell, 2007, p. 44). Education, however, can challenge Eurocentric models that have been imposed on Indigenous peoples and the Global South as a consequence of imperial and neo-colonial domination (Hickling-Hudson, 2011; Hickling-Hudson & Ahlquist, 2003).

This chapter focuses on pedagogies and educational practices that preceded, endured, or challenged modern schooling. Other work in this field has concentrated on the Anglophone world in the Global South (Hickling-Hudson, 2014) but this contribution uses studies in the US settler-colonial context, Spain, and Portugal. By focusing on Native Americans, Roma peoples in Europe, and legacies of hip-hop culture, we surpass the Global North/South binaries commonly reproduced in mainstream postcolonial and anticolonial approaches (Tom, 2013).

Our work differs from mainstream approaches: instead of employing a nationalist or postnationalist approach to education, we propose the Pedagogy of Absence, Conflict, and Emergence (PACE) as a method that works from the pedagogies and educational projects of communities marginalised through coloniality and as a pedagogy that can help change dominant education practices in colonial and postcolonial contexts. PACE seeks to transcend Eurocentric

DOI: 10.4324/9781003355397-21

knowledge construction. One of its fundamental efforts is to think from and for places, experiences, temporalities, and life projects otherwise rendered absent or negated in dominant education models.

PACE articulates the conditions shaping who and what we are, and involves taking responsibility for thoughts and ideas (Suárez-Krabbe, 2015). Coloniality continues to socially produce what Fanon (1963) called *le damné de la terre*; people whose humanity has been negated. Being human entails civil, political, epistemological, and social access, participation, and impact on the world and society (cf. Davis, 2012; Gilmore, 2007). The social production of nonbeing – an ontological process – is what Fanon (1986) called sociogenesis. The cases analysed in this chapter offer an empirically based understanding of how different groups may share the condition of being *damné* while displaying how the process of damnation has also made them different in sociogenic terms. Because these groups have distinct knowledges and onto-epistemic groundings, their work towards 'a new humanity' is different, attesting precisely to the need to take plurality seriously. Indeed, PACE relates to difference not as something to be "merely tolerated but as a fund of necessary polarities between which our creativity can spark like a dialectic" (Lorde, 1984, p. 110).

We employ PACE to study the decolonisation of knowledge and education in the following case studies: digital media in the Native American community of San Francisco, United States; efforts to 'standardise' education among Romani/Gypsy communities in Córdoba, Spain; and, hip-hop culture/rap music and social intervention in Lisbon, Portugal. These cases help to understand coloniality and decoloniality in the 'South inside the North'.

Most of the material in this chapter was produced during Tom's doctoral research (2013). Tom is a researcher of mixed Native American (Paiute and Pomo) and Russian descent. Her doctoral research, conducted for the University of Coimbra in Portugal, included black Portuguese youth (predominately of Cape Verdean descent) in Lisbon and Native American youth in the United States, with an emphasis on the urban context of San Francisco–Oakland Bay Area in California. San Francisco was selected because of a youth-centred media project developed by an Indigenous hip-hop artist of Pomo and African American descent. In Portugal, Tom sought to examine how the colonial question applied to the country where she was studying. Lisbon was selected because of its concentration of communities of African origin in the aftermath of Portugal's colonial endeavours in Africa.

The discussion of these case studies starts with Native American perspectives forged by different chapters of colonialism in California history – from Catholic Spanish missionaries up until the present. Drawing from California history, we then look towards two 'postcolonial' metropoles to broadly address global dimensions of coloniality and decoloniality. We have focused on Roma communities in Córdoba, Spain, to examine how similar historical experiences of genocide and resistance frame similar issues in education today.

Information here was collected while Tom was a visiting scholar at a nearby university. While researching, she also volunteered as an English tutor for a local nongovernmental organisation (NGO). Further information was collected and co-analysed by Caballero Castro, a Roma university student and teacher who is currently developing culturally relevant curriculum for children and youth from her community. Finally, we return to Tom's doctoral research in Lisbon, where we cross languages and historical legacies to examine how Black Portuguese youth of Cape Verdean descent use hip-hop culture/rap music to create alternative modes of education. While rap music is commonly regarded as an emblem of American cultural imperialism and globalisation, its spread to Lisbon and pedagogical uses are based on transnational histories of black and anticolonial resistance.

The methods involved participatory observation and semi-structured interviews, and dialogue with members of the communities. The selected cases involve processes in which groups take responsibility for thoughts and ideas and articulate the conditions that have made them who and what they are, while also building grounds for changing these conditions through action. In each context, education is a means of transformation; it endeavours to break from Eurocentricity both in terms of knowledge and in terms of forging ideas and practices that can undergird radical social change. As such, groups' sociogenic efforts are carried out through PACE.

Pedagogy of Absence, Conflict and Emergence (PACE)

PACE includes articulating the conditions shaping who and what we are. It involves taking responsibility for thought and ideas, making it part of a decolonising process. This effort includes scrutinising sociohistorical and economic-political experiences shaped by coloniality and considering the intellectual contributions that have emerged from diverse struggles for decolonisation. PACE involves a decolonial historical realist approach that rejects the relativism embedded in the idea that history will always be partial as it is always told by the winner (Suárez-Krabbe, 2015).

A decolonial realist approach argues that one cannot deal with contemporary problems without considering the historically constituted structures within which they continue to be produced. For example, understanding the struggles of Native Americans, Romani in Spain, and Afro-Portuguese requires taking account of how coloniality shaped them in different but relational ways and manifests at global, regional, and national levels (Quijano, 2000). Hence, the making of the Americas (Mignolo, 2005) and the invention of Africa (Ndlovu-Gatsheni, 2013) both involved the work of explorers, cartographers, missionaries, travellers, colonial anthropologists, slave masters, enslaved Africans, conquerors, Indigenous peoples, historians, imperialists, communists, socialists, Catholics, and so on. And the making of

Europe correspondingly involved actors overlapping with those mentioned. But race ranked and ordered people and places into power relations and in the institutional functions from which this hierarchy is articulated, such as the modern nation-state or in social categories of difference, and what constitutes hegemonic Western knowledge. Additionally, these processes happened at the expense of something and someone else who was sociogenically produced as absent.

PACE is consequently divided into three fundamental steps. First, the pedagogy of absence implicates the conceptualisation and location of how colonised subjects have been produced as absent in history, in knowledge production, and within the confines of public schooling. This production of absences (Santos, 2014) is part of what Fanon (1963) conceptualised as the 'zone of nonbeing' – a zone created through the countless negations on which colonial rationality, knowledge, and education are constructed.

Second, the pedagogy of conflict:

> seeks to provoke epistemological conflict in order to make vulnerable the arguments of hegemonic thinking and of the application of science … Human experience and the historical understanding at the basis of the knowledge linked to that sort of educational project will destabilise the instrumental rationality of mono-logic thinking that sustains imperialisms in order to recover 'our capacity of bewilderment and indignation', pushing forth emancipatory educational projects.
>
> *Fontella Santiago (2012, pp. 2–3)*

Finally, the pedagogy of emergence, often a result of or dependent on the pedagogy of absence and conflict, relates to the social, political, historical, and existential affirmation of the existence of marginalised or historically dispossessed groups: an emergence as historical subjects and as agents of history and social change. The pedagogy of emergence corresponds to the sociogenic production of a new humanity and is framed by the imperative to "transgress, displace and influence the ontological, epistemic and cosmogonic spiritual negation which has been and is – strategy, end, and result of the power of coloniality" (Walsh, 2009, p. 13).

PACE involves addressing and redressing privileges that are otherwise hidden in knowledge and education. Indeed:

> Although the white body is regarded as Presence, it lives the mode of Absence, and it offers, instead, its perspective as Presence. In other words, the white body is expected to be seen by others without seeing itself being seen. Its presence is therefore its perspectivity. Its mode of being, being self-justified, is never superfluous.
>
> *Gordon (1999, p. 103)*

The white perspectivity is what we are taught in schools. It includes three primary privileges and several derivative ones. Teleological privilege is concerned with time and with the future. It implies that those who hold it determine the future of all, monopolising politics, economic organisation, and social change. In the case of epistemic racism, the problem involves the addition of some selected 'other' scholars, histories, or events into Eurocentric scholarship without engaging with their conceptualisations, critiques, and consequences. Many of the scholars and educators who pretend to have transcended the problems of racism and coloniality in their scientific or educational practices continue to enjoy and defend the privilege of epistemic perspective.

The privilege of epistemic perspective is inseparable from the privilege to define what is and what is not, based on ideas about validity, scientificity, and method. These primary privileges carry with them the privilege to choose and define subject matter in schools, the privilege to define the context from and in which it is taught, and the privilege to define what is relevant and irrelevant. Any attempt at working towards decolonial social change from within education must address these privileges. We argue that the cases presented in this chapter take a necessary step in the direction of decolonisation by displaying how white perspectivity upholds itself as self-justified educational practice.

Urban Native American youth

Settler colonialism is a structure involving the continued appropriation of Indigenous lands (Wolfe, 2006). What we learn from Indigenous peoples around the world is how the continued existence of settler colonialist structures and legacies is a problem that cannot be resolved by disregarding the ways in which different racial or ethnic groups are also products of and instrumental to its violent perpetuation (Tuck & Yang, 2012). If decolonisation has become a metaphor to address social justice rather than the restitution of Indigenous land rights, how may we honour these distinct sociohistorical experiences and ongoing struggles while also using the concept to challenge coloniality at large? Bearing these contexts in mind, this section illustrates how the conquest of the Americas and the ongoing reality of settler colonialism shape the context within which the Native American community in San Francisco operates.

The diverse and multi-layered Native community of the San Francisco–Oakland Bay Area remains invisible, mostly because of the dominant imaginary of Native peoples being isolated to reservation life, far away from mainstream society, hence produced as absent. In public schools, Native students rarely see themselves reflected in school curricula. Students typically learn about the early civilising efforts of imperial Spain that soon gave way to the superiority of the United States. However, since the Native American and Mexican American (*Chicano*) uprisings of the 1960s and 1970s, the reality of genocide under colonial regimes has been shown from the perspectives of these populations. As Weber (1992) observed, both the Spanish or Latin and Indigenous presences fold into the same ideology, wherein the former is celebrated for its earlier efforts of civilising the latter, and each would succumb, eventually, to the superiority of the Anglo-American national project. Indeed, "[recent] education reformers have sought a middle ground by offering a consensus curriculum that includes evidence from both the fantasy and victimisation narratives and encourages students to interpret the past for themselves" (Gutfreund, 2010, p. 163). Nevertheless, these pedagogies of conflict remain invisible efforts that are delegitimised in Gutfreund's text when referred to as undertaken by "militants".

These continued denigrations have a vast impact on how Native Peoples are perceived as well as the significance of their voices, which, alongside settler colonialism, go widely unacknowledged by the general public in the United States. Tuck and Yang (2012) note how such invisibility manifests in mainstream educational research:

> Indigenous peoples are included only as asterisks, as footnotes into dominant paradigms of educational inequality in the U.S. This can be observed in the progressive literature on school discipline, on 'under-represented minorities' in higher education, and in the literature of reparation, i.e., redressing 'past' wrongs against non-white Others.
> *Tuck and Yang (2012, p. 22)*

Additionally, they note that, amid decolonial approaches in educational research, "'Urban education' ... is a code word for the schooling of black, brown, and ghettoised youth who form the numerical majority in divested public schools" (p. 23). In this sense, the production of Native American populations as absent is strengthened through dominant imaginaries pertaining to not only Native Americans but also other racialised groups in the United States.

The *Seventh Native American Generation* (*SNAG*) magazine can be seen as a pedagogy of absence in its aims to address "modern day and historical grievances" that go against the grain of the above-mentioned dominant imaginaries (SNAG, n.d.). *SNAG* was cofounded in 2002 by Ras K'dee, a musician of mixed Pomo (a tribe from northern California) and African American origins. Ras K'dee held workshops where young people shared their experiences with broader audiences; one of these included brainstorming on what kinds of projects could bring their desires to fruition. *SNAG* not only brought arts education to generations of Native youth but also provided internships in areas such as journalism.

SNAG has publicised Californian Native peoples' histories and has sought to create open-access curricula based on past editions of the magazine using content produced by youth themselves. Additionally, community farming and basket-making workshops contribute to the decolonising urban education endeavour. The pedagogy of absence turns into a pedagogy of conflict when the dominant imaginary of Native American people is challenged by *SNAG*'s projects. For example, in 2016, a Pomo master weaver taught Native and non-Native participants how to make traditional Native baskets. The practice of weaving and applying techniques represents the pedagogy of emergence, where other ways of doing and knowing gain centrality.

SNAG uses public events to allow non-Native inhabitants of the Bay Area to learn about contemporary Indigenous peoples, especially in an urban dynamic. As a reclaiming of voices, they involve PACE by shedding light, addressing and elaborating on the otherwise invisible issues confronting Native American peoples (Tom, 2013). As Ras K'dee elaborates:

> We're creating media and making it available to the public on a large scale so we're in effect changing the perception of how Natives are viewed and what we're capable of ... It's a school. It's like anything involving education and liberation. We're talking about respecting young Native voices, viewing the value of young Native voices, those things.
>
> Ras K'dee (personal communication, March 23, 2010)

In a city where contact with other Native American youth is sparse, bi-weekly *SNAG* events complement after-school programmes, counselling, and weekly powwow dance classes.

Not only has *SNAG* brought diversity to urban Native education, but it also veers towards an indigenised education project that teaches about the land and its peoples and challenges historical narratives that commit Indigenous people to some distant, primordial past. Given that American Indian education was one of several tools used by the US Government for assimilation, *SNAG*'s extracurricular activities increase young people's awareness of the absences created by this history and their understanding of the traumas derived from its violence – they also embody the pedagogy of absence and conflict. The involvement of youth and the communities they come from is at the heart of continuing tradition while offering youth tools to construct self-knowledge through their surroundings and to represent themselves. The magazine and public events (including rap shows) enrich youths' interest in learning their culture and are seen as fundamental by the participating youth. It is not merely a question of becoming active members within Native American communities, or claiming a place in contemporary US society, using knowledge achieved largely outside of the educational system, but also challenges normative notions on indigeneity, history, and territory. In other words, as a representation of PACE, *SNAG* offers young people the tools necessary to speak out, self-represent, and make interventions in the world they have inherited. In acknowledging the legacies of these struggles, the magazine also helps make visible the reality of settler colonialism, as it pertains to Indigenous peoples and other groups who are part of it. Native Americans are not silenced but rather shown as contemporary peoples.

Roma and the 'standardisation' of education

Romani communities (or *gitanos*) in Andalusia, Spain, have vastly influenced regional culture (e.g., flamenco music), language (Caló), and national literature (e.g., Lorca). The Spanish Roma have persevered despite state-sanctioned efforts to forcibly assimilate, expel, or eradicate this population. In 1978, the illiteracy rate of Spanish Roma over the age of 10 was 68%, and the level of compulsory education only reached 55% (Instituto de Sociología Aplicada de Madrid, 1982). These rates were the result of historical segregation of Romani populations and of the legally sanctioned denial of education to the Romani populations amid the outlawing of language and cultural practice under the Franco regime (Gómez García, 2009). Gómez Garcia noted that when democracy arrived in Spain, Gypsy communities created organisations to live as free citizens and sought to challenge illiteracy without compromising the ethnic community's unique cultural attributes.

While almost all Romani children are now educated in public schools and illiteracy is almost non-existent, it is difficult for social integration not to be assimilatory because normative models of education do not integrate minority cultures (Gómez García, 2009). Indeed, Fernández Enguita (2000) observes how the problematic fashioning of the modern nation-state reproduces the notion that culture and ethnic differences impede Roma students' successful schooling. Another enduring challenge highlighted by scholars is the reproduction of such common prejudices at the level of research and knowledge production (Macías & Redondo, 2012). Romani students in Spain have poorer educational success rates when compared to their peers from the majority populations and continued high absentee and dropout rates (Fundación Secretariado Gitano, 2014), while only 5% reach higher education (Fernández Garcés, Jiménez González, & Motos Pérez, 2015).

Over the years, local Romani associations and NGOs have undertaken several initiatives to address dispiriting in education through a culturally based lens. We focus here on the implementation of a project started by a pan-Romani NGO in 2009 in Córdoba, which we shall call *Elevate*, for the sake of anonymity. The programme aims to help young Romani students complete compulsory schooling and continue their studies afterwards. These efforts aim to improve access to the labour market by changing practices in formal education that contribute to Roma segregation. *Elevate* raises awareness of how research and school materials reproduce negative stereotypes of the Roma, as do the media, teachers, parents, and children – both within and outside the Roma communities.

As a Roma university student and teacher in *Elevate*, Caballero Castro has personally experienced and observed the extent to which mainstream school curriculum marginalises, devalues, or excludes children and youth from her community. On many occasions Caballero Castro has had to work extensively with students on a given school subject that their teachers had not explained. In Caballero Castro's experience, students also identify absences, as when they ask her why they learn French or English and not Caló. In addressing this type of question from a Roma critical perspective, PACE takes place. Pedagogy of absence includes explaining to the students how the hierarchies of language work as part of larger sociohistorical constituted racial relations. Pedagogy of conflict and pedagogy of emergence take place to the extent that pedagogy of absence requires addressing historical and current events in ways that radically differ from and challenge dominant accounts and highlighting the ways in which formal schooling is often decontextualised from the realities of Roma students.

Within formal schooling, some teachers discriminate against Romani students because of the widespread stereotype that Gypsies are susceptible to failure and dropping out. Young women in compulsory secondary education may quit attending classes, only going to school to take exams or to turn in homework, because traditionally girls marry young and have children. In other cases, both boys and girls go to work with their parents to help secure household income. Thus, high absentee rates leading to academic failure may be due to socioeconomic circumstances rather than cultural differences alone (Fernández Enguita, 2000). Education may sometimes be regarded as a waste of time in the face of severely disadvantaged material conditions. As Miguel explains:

> There is a tremendous mixture and uncertainty of identity. Is it good or bad? I don't know, but I would like for [our young people] to have more knowledge of the identities they want ... If they could study [students would have] the opportunity of consciously selecting. Often, we find that elders don't connect with youth ... [saying] I didn't have this education [or form of socialisation]. I have always sat with elders and listened to their stories and this has always enabled me to connect better ... If there is not a link between generations it is difficult to understand where your identity comes from and where you are going.
>
> *Miguel (personal communication, August 8, 2014)*

Elevate addresses the main absences in relation to education and access to work. Keeping students within the educational system simultaneously increases pressure towards structural societal changes while also addressing racism and coloniality from the bottom-up perspective of Roma communities, therein enacting PACE. The programme intervenes in the reproduction of coloniality and racism at the level of research and knowledge production, as well. It closely monitors whether research reproduces social exclusion or works towards transformation by including perspectives and realities from members of Romani communities (Macías & Redondo, 2012). *Elevate* provides a range of activities designed to facilitate the engagement of Romani parents and family in their children's learning. One could argue that PACE manifests through public gatherings and activities during the celebration of key Romani days. The International Romani Peoples Day, for example, is a day of remembrance of Porajmos, the often-ignored Romani holocaust that took place during World War II. Extra-institutional activities also include speech contests whereby Romani children are invited to present their own account of what being *gitana* or *gitano* entails. In spite of these efforts, the rejection of Roma remains widespread.

The educational system continues to serve the dominant society and, as such, is structured in a way that produces absenteeism, high dropout rates, and resultant low academic achievement of minority communities. These challenges may be resolved when there is a policy that fights against exclusion and applies affective critical pedagogy and when there is both greater teacher training and greater educational resources to support such work (Abajo, 1997). A law mandating the inclusion of Roma culture and history in schools was recently passed in the region of Castilla y León. Such policy – if implemented nationally, and especially in regions such as Andalusia, with its large Gypsy population – would significantly challenge school curricula that continue to formulate the Roma absent as historical agents.

Rap Kriolu: contesting coloniality in Lisbon, Portugal

The influxes of people of African (predominately Cape Verdean) descent into Portugal are tightly knit to the Portuguese imperial endeavour. The 1980s and 1990s saw increased immigration from former colonies due to Portugal's entrance into the European Economic Community/European Union and the consequent demand for civil construction. Against this background, Rap Kriolu offers a counter-narrative. Kriolu, on the one hand, and rap/hip-hop, on the other, both express key processes in neglected histories of globalisation. Their combination in Rap Kriolu speaks of globalised resistances. Kriolu, a creole language that emerged with the Portuguese colonial endeavour and investment in the transatlantic slave trade, "combines primarily Portuguese vocabulary with structural elements of Mandingo, Wolof, Fulani, and other West African languages" (Pardue, 2012, p. 47).

Hip-hop originally comprised four elements: graffiti, break dancing, DJing (*deejaying*), and rapping (*emceeing/MCing*). Spread by globalised entertainment in the final decades of the twentieth century, hip-hop impressed many as a cultural manifestation of decadence, criminality, misogyny, and materialism. While it is true that American culture has been disproportionately projected across the globe, subtler insidious and revolutionary aspects of hip-hop culture have transgressed such clichéd and reductionist notions of American cultural imperialism. The culture and its elements, especially rap music, "identified with lower social classes and minority and marginalised groups throughout the world" (Morgan, 2009, p. 14) and society at large has been reluctant to hear and engage with the analyses, critiques, and stories that resonate from these musical expressions. The forefathers of the hip-hop generation were those living in the US post–civil rights era when the gains made from this historical era were revoked by subsequent administrations (Lusane, 2004). Hip-hop was about navigating the ambiguous binaries of inclusion/exclusion from European or white American society. These movements have fought in arenas that include education, social advancement, the fight to end legal and socioeconomic segregation, repression, and the demand for reparations of historical wrongs – all of which spoke of access and inclusion.

As a 'language of the periphery' in Lisbon, where not only youth of Cape Verdean descent but also youth of other African-Portuguese origins (e.g., Angolan) speak Kriolu, "Rap in Kriolu articulates various subjective positions framed by the experience of growing up in racialised and marginalised urban communities while supplying a sense of the daily drama of life on the margins within and beyond Portugal" (Tom, 2013, p. 88). Rap Kriolu is a means to convey knowledge of and from racially marginalised positions, histories, and experiences not provided in schools. To use Kriolu in rap is a way of reclaiming identity and expressing pride in their Cape Verdean origins in the face of Portuguese racism and maintaining historical memory of anticolonial struggles (Pardue, 2012; Tom, 2013).

While the language is a product of the imperial endeavour, and can be considered a part of the epistemicides inherent in Portuguese imperialism, to rap in Kriolu is prioritising Africa inside Portugal. This may suggest that Kriolu is an alternative epistemological platform: a locus of enunciation that, by its mere existence, inhibits the forgetting of the imperial project, as well as being the place from which counter-narratives emerge. The MCs and educators who contributed to Tom's study emphasised that their project is to contest the existing structures of inequality and racism, as well as to offer alternative forms of education – to help the youth learn about rights in relation to police violence, African or African diasporic histories of anticolonial and antiracist struggles, and about racism. Some of the younger MCs affirmed that it was not just producing lyrics and having performances but screening documentaries, having sit-ins, or engaging in protest. One of Lisbon's prominent MCs, LBC (a moniker that stands for Learning Black Conception and, more recently,

Luta Bu Consigi, Kriolu for "you can fight") has used rap to produce music with youth in the neighbourhood of Cova da Moura. As he explains:

> I teach them that the ghetto is like a prison, a social prison. I teach them that they got to see what they got before, what they got after the ghetto, what they got as opportunities in this country – all those things. What is the word African? What is the meaning of Conception – Black Conception? They don't use that. Because I teach them about the colours, why sometimes they project ... a fight, like you fight against your colour. I teach them about that. And it works. It works because you can see the self-esteem of the kids. Now when they speak they say: 'Yo, I'm not what they say' because I tell them, 'Yo, you got to know that we used to have queens and kings, you know, we created mathematics'. Like other people, too, we have culture. I don't believe that the Ministry of Education will let us teach our history. I don't believe that. I think that we got to create our own centre. We gotta get close together, the community, and find a way, independently, with no money from the government. We can do that and create a re-education centre. It's not education, it's a re-education centre.
>
> *LBC (personal communication, November 6, 2010)*

By addressing the ghetto as a social prison, LBC refers to how racism organises spatially, creating places of exclusion and confinement that reflect how the larger society is organised through structural neglect (El-Tayeb, 2011). Police brutality is the norm in these places, as is the deprivation and lack of quality public services. Within these spaces of confinement, or social prisons, the larger society often finds grounds to confirm the image of the people living there as being violent, uneducated, and aggressive, lacking integration, and displaying a culture of poverty, thus obscuring the fact that the problems in the ghettos are socioeconomic and political (Hajjat, 2006).

LBC and other MC educators in Lisbon aim to help the youth see this reality and provide them with tools to break away from it through an African-centred, or Black, Conception, which we may call a pedagogy of conflict. The pedagogy of absence appears to be the first step: it takes place by teaching the youth how the same segregationist system makes black populations be at war with themselves – what Du Bois (2006) called double consciousness – and how to recognise the conditions of oppression and to transcend oppression by learning about the different social levels that it works on. As a part of this approach, Black Conception is a pedagogy of emergences that includes the rejection of the dominant frameworks imposed on these youth to think of and about themselves and a recentring of their own history, of Africa's legacy in terms of knowledge, and of the anticolonial and antiracist struggles led by Africans and African diasporic peoples.

Concluding remarks

The alternative education projects examined in this chapter counter the historically constituted power relations of coloniality, as different communities struggle to create space for their epistemologies, histories, and ways of being and living in the world. Using PACE as an analytical framework, we have demonstrated how these initiatives urge us to consider education as part of a broader decolonial project that can align our knowledge of the world with the realities excluded.

Although the histories, languages, and cultures of these populations are produced as absent in the Spanish, United States, and Portuguese national education systems, access to formal schooling is essential to realising equal citizenship rights – without renouncing the right to difference. The case of *Elevate* illustrates how community-based interventions that challenge barriers between schools, students, and families help to promote scholastic achievement of Romani youth and processes of resistance against the disintegration of Romani communities. As noted, there is a further need to address the current generational rifts. As we surmised, the nonformal educational processes call for structural and societal change addressing racism from the bottom up. At the same time, recent incentives are also attempting to change school curricula. In the case of San Francisco, *SNAG* aims to teach the diverse cultures, histories, and contemporary realities of Native Peoples, with an emphasis on California. The fact that the US Government historically used education – alongside policies such as relocation – to assimilate this population is underdiscussed. As a pedagogy of conflict, the project contests the drawing and redrawing of settler colonial territories alongside racist logics of displacement that continue today. The pedagogical efforts of Romani communities in Córdoba and the Native American community of San Francisco go beyond formal schooling. In both cases, the pedagogy of absence attests to the involvement of youth within their communities and as a part of communities that continue to be invisibilised. These efforts also touch on the importance of intergenerational learning as a way to counter community dismemberment. Hip-hop/rap Kriolu in Portugal further exhibits how young people may be protagonists of these efforts. Hip-hop and music – born of historical marginalisation – is used in different social, material, historical, and cultural contexts where producers of hip-hop/rap appropriate the medium as an alternative approach to education.

Rap Kriolu in Portugal reflects the problem of the relationship between language, epistemology, and the political hierarchies between different languages and, of course, the people who speak them. Language is inseparable from culture, from how we understand the world and how we interact with it and in it (wa Thiong'o, 1987). Kriolu emerges from imperial processes of imposition, hierarchisation, and violence. Rap Kriolu, however, attempts to articulate alternatives beyond the horizon of possibilities offered by dominant colonial thinking in relation to the African experience, as it is configured globally – but distinctively localised – throughout the world. As such, Kriolu MCs use rap music as a medium of nonformal education that decolonises or transforms monocultures of knowledge reproduced within formal schooling to promote inclusion and community sustenance from the marginalised angles of Portugal's colonial legacy and, sometimes, in dialogue with marginalised experiences resonating from the US settler-colonial contexts and beyond. Challenging coloniality unique to the contemporary Portuguese context, youth confound the depoliticising discourses of mixity and challenge historically wrought and static notions of Portugueseness through their demands for another knowledge and affirmations of being Portuguese and living in Portugal without renouncing their differences.

The counterhegemonic use of language in Rap Kriolu is not a singular case. Indeed, even though the work of *SNAG* with Native American youth and the standardisation of education projects involving Romani communities do not centre on language, and function in the imperial languages (English and Spanish, respectively), it is important to understand that precisely because language is inseparable from culture, dominant language can also change through alternative interaction in and with the world, alternative modes of understanding it, and alternative political aims. In this way, 'standardisation' from a Romani perspective cannot be confounded with what is meant and implied by the same term from a dominant Spanish perspective on education, nor can *SNAG* be understood from within the grammar of dominant language. Yet even the name requires us to place ourselves in the margins of empire and to think of ourselves not only as heirs of colonialism but also as ancestors of future generations. We affirm that challenges to the manifestation of coloniality in national school systems worldwide is a feat that can be undertaken by approaches such as PACE that engage the perspectives and practices of communities historically subjected to repression. There is much to be learned from these communities if we seek to transform education.

From the remnants of empires to the continued existence of settler colonialism, the cases studied here suggest that decolonisation of education passes through the centralisation of the knowledges and realities that are produced as absent as part of the Eurocentricity in coloniality. As such, one can say that the Native American case centralises the Native realities, points of view, and histories, while the Romani and the Afro-Portuguese do the same from these distinct vantage points. Therefore, these projects can be seen as necessary methodological recentralisations: Africanisation (Kriolusation), Indigenisation, and Romanisation, respectively. The question of identity remains significant, as none of these populations are static or 'pure'. Indeed, the process of sociogenesis in formulation of a new humanity entails abandoning the colonial imaginaries of purity and authenticity without a priori rejecting notions of purity and authenticity stemming from 'other' onto-epistemological groundings. A process involving taking responsibility for thought and ideas and articulating the conditions that make us who and what we are, applying a decolonial approach to education does not reject identity. Instead, it involves a process of articulation that respects identity and difference between peoples, knowledges, and histories, and that also recognises how past and present hierarchical difference created through coloniality continues today. For example, it includes taking seriously that being Native American is not the same as being what the wider US society understands as Native American. In other words, being Native American needs to take account of the specific tribe or nation, with its own historical trajectory; its ontological, spiritual, and epistemic groundings; and its current processes of sociogenesis. Decolonial historical realism allows navigating through the seeming contradictions that otherwise emerge when we address groups through the rationality imposed on them – and our understanding of them – through coloniality. It requires that we understand difference, taking outset in plurality without ignoring coloniality. In doing so, we simultaneously work towards understanding our shared histories without ignoring how these, as well as our presents and our futures, are different. We contend that these analytical moves contribute to a solid basis on which "our creativity can spark like a dialectic" (Lorde, 1984, p. 110).

Acknowledging difference implies acknowledging the continued existence of colonial hierarchies and structures that support those hierarchies. The cases studied illustrate interconnected struggles that challenge the colonial master narrative and history while they also exhibit applicability of PACE in different contexts. For while decolonisation is not a metaphor, it is a philosophical process that may consider the relationship between the European colonial endeavour, settler colonialism, the administration of diversity, and the processes of resistance, to coloniality in contemporary societies (Suárez-Krabbe, 2015). The official histories that are taught in public schools have concrete (sociogenetic) repercussions in relation to the current inability of formal educational institutions to accept plurality and diversity in a consequential manner. The nonformal education projects studied here seem not only to affirm difference and underscore plurality but, by challenging received practices of education, and contributing to thinking of diversity from frameworks beyond dominant Eurocentric understandings, they also make a difference: they are engaged in the necessarily multifaceted and manifold process of decolonisation, including the construction of a new humanity.

Notes

1 We use 'Indigenous' or 'Native American' in reference to First Peoples, which are diverse communities in and of themselves. We also refer to specific tribes/nations when applicable.
2 While the terms 'Roma' and 'Romani' are politically correct in English, it is common to refer to oneself as 'Gypsy' in Spain (*gitano* as the masculine term for Gypsy and *gitana* as feminine). In the cases in which we use these last terms, we do so to allude to the definitions or perceptions of each of these respective communities.

References

Abajo, J. E. (1997). *La escolarización de los niños gitanos*. Madrid, Spain: Ministerio de Trabajo y Asuntos Sociales.

Connell, R. (2007). *Southern theory: The global dynamics of knowledge in social science*. Cambridge, England: Polity Press.

Davis, A. (2012). *The meaning of freedom: And other difficult dialogues*. San Francisco, CA: City Lights.

Du Bois, W. E. B. (2006). *The souls of black folk*. State College, PA: Pennsylvania State University.

El-Tayeb, F. (2011). *European others: Queering ethnicity in postnational Europe*. Minneapolis, MN: University of Minnesota Press.

Fanon, F. (1963). *The wretched of the earth*. New York, NY: Grove Press.

Fanon, F. (1986). *Black skins, white masks*. London, England: Pluto Press.

Fernández Enguita, M. (2000, December). Escuela y etnicidad: El caso de los gitanos. *Revista Bimestral de la Asociación Secretariado General Gitano, 7*(8), 66–73.

Fernández Garcés, H., Jiménez González, N., & Motos Pérez, I. (2015). *Guía de recursos contra el antigitanismo*. Alicante, Spain: Federación Autónoma de Asociaciones Gitanas de la Comunidad Valenciana.

Fontella Santiago, A. R. (2012, July–August). *Pedagogia crítica e educacão emancipatória na escola pública: Um diálogo entre Paulo Freire e Boaventura Santos*. Paper presented at the IX ANPED Sul Seminar, UCS Campus in Caxias do Sul, Rio Grande do Sul, Brazil.

Fundación Secretariado Gitano. (2014). *Executive summary: Roma students in secondary education in Spain: A comparative study*. Retrieved from https://www.gitanos.org/upload/28/78/Roma_Students_in_Secondary_Education_in_Spain__Executive_Summary_.pdf

Gilmore, R. (2007). *Golden gulag: Prisons, surplus, crisis and opposition in globalizing California*. Los Angeles, CA: University of California Press.

Gómez García, M. N. (2009). La educación del pueblo gitano en España: Parámetros históricos. In M. R. Berruezo Albéniz & S. Conejero López (Eds.), *El largo camino hacia una educación inclusiva: La educación especial y social del siglo XIX a nuestros días – XV coloquio de historia de la educación* (Vol. 2, pp. 89–100). Pamplona, Spain: UPNA.

Gordon, L. (1999). *Bad faith and anti-black racism*. New York, NY: Humanity.

Grande, S. (2004). *Red pedagogy: Native American social and political thought*. New York, NY: Rowman & Littlefield.

Gutfreund, Z. (2010). Standing up to sugar cubes: The contest over ethnic identity in California's fourth-grade mission curriculum. *Southern California Quarterly, 92*(2), 161-197.

Hajjat, A. (2006). El levantamiento de las barriadas tiene un historia. *Viento Sur, 84*, 27–34.

Hickling-Hudson, A. R. (2011). Teaching to disrupt preconceptions: Education for social justice in the imperial aftermath. *Compare, 41*(4), 453–465.

Hickling-Hudson, A. R. (2014). Striving for a better world: Lessons from Freire in Grenada, Jamaica and Australia. *International Review of Education, 60*(4), 523–543.

Hickling-Hudson, A. R., & Ahlquist, R. (2003). Contesting the curriculum in the schooling of Indigenous children in Australia and the USA: From Eurocentrism to culturally powerful pedagogies. *Comparative Education Review, 47*(1), 64–89.

Instituto de Sociología Aplicada de Madrid (1982). *El libro blanco de los gitanos Españoles*. Madrid, Spain: Secretariado Nacional Gitano.

Lorde, A. (1984). The master's tools will never dismantle the master's house. In A. Lorde (Ed.), *Sister outsider: Essays and speeches* (pp. 110–113). Berkeley, CA: Crossing Press.

Lusane, C. (2004). Rap, race, and politics. In M. A. Neal & M. Forman (Eds.), *That's the joint! The hip-hop studies reader* (pp. 351–362). New York, NY: Routledge.

Macías, F., & Redondo, G. S. (2012). Pueblo gitano, género y educación: Investigar para excluir o investigar para transformar. *RISE*, *1*(1), 1–92.

Mignolo, W. D. (2005). *The idea of Latin America*. Oxford, England: Blackwell.

Morgan, M. H. (2009). *The real hip hop: Battling for knowledge, power and respect in the L.A. underground*. Durham, NC: Duke University Press.

Ndlovu-Gatsheni, S. J. (2013). *Coloniality of power in postcolonial Africa: Myths of decolonization*. Dakar, Senegal: CODESRIA.

Pardue, D. (2012). Cape Verdean creole and the politics of scene-making in Lisbon, Portugal. *Journal of Linguistic Anthropology*, *22*(2), 42–60.

Quijano, A. (2000). Coloniality of power, eurocentrism, and Latin America. *Nepantla: Views from South*, *1*(3), 533–580.

Santos, B. (2014). *Epistemologies of the south: Justice against epistemicide*. London, England: Paradigm.

SNAG. (n.d.). About. Retrieved from https://www.snagmagazine.com/about

Suárez-Krabbe, J. (2015). *Race, rights and rebels: Alternatives beyond human rights and development*. London, England: Rowman & Littlefield.

Tom, M. N. (2013). *Hip-hop culture, community and education: Postcolonial learning*. Doctoral dissertation, University of Coimbra, Coimbra, Portugal. Retrieved from https://ces.uc.pt/en/doutoramentos/programas-de-doutoramento/poscolonialismos-e-cidadania-global/teses/hip-hop-culture-community-and-education

Tuck, E., & Yang, W. K. (2012). Decolonization is not a metaphor. *Decolonization, Indigeneity, Education and Society*, *1*(1), 1–40.

wa Thiong'o, N. (1987). *Decolonizing the mind: The politics of language in African literature*. Harare, Zimbabwe: Zimbabwe Publishing House.

Walsh, C. (2009). Interculturaldad crítica y pedagogía de-colonial: Apuestas (des)de el in-surgir, re-existir y re-vivir. In V. M. Candau (Ed.), *Educação intercultural hoje en América Latina: Concepções, tensões e propostas* (pp. 12–42). Rio de Janeiro, Brazil: Departamento de Educacão PUC-Rio.

Weber, D. J. (1992). *The Spanish frontier in North America*. New Haven, CT: Yale University Press.

Wolfe, P. (2006). Settler colonialism and the elimination of the native. *Journal of Genocide Research*, *8*(4), 387–409.

CONTRIBUTORS

Madeleine Arnot is Emerita Professor in Sociology of Education at the University of Cambridge, UK. She has published extensively on gender, race, and social class inequalities in education and strategies to promote social justice. In collaboration with colleagues in Ghana, Kenya, India, and Pakistan, she has researched the impact of education, gender, poverty, and citizenship on rural and urban youth. She edits the Routledge series *Education, Poverty and International Development* and co-edited *Gender Education and Equality in a Global Context (2008); Youth Citizenship and the Politics of Belonging (2013); and Reforming Education and Challenging Inequalities in Southern Contexts (2022)*.

Tim Bond is an Emeritus Professor at the University of Bristol and a former Visiting Professor at the University of Malta. He has had a longstanding commitment to researching and writing about professional ethics for talking therapies and promoting mental well-being. He has consulted to the British Association for Counselling and Psychotherapy on professional ethics and standards, has been a member of the Ethics Committee for the British Psychological Society and has served on the Executive Council of the International Association for Counselling.

María Trinidad Caballero Castro is an Early Childhood Education teacher, whose passion is to contribute to the improvement of education for children in a situation of social disadvantage. As a Gypsy/Roma woman from the Córdoba province, Andalusia (Spain), she has worked to favour the educational promotion of Roma students, seeking their academic and social improvement and mobility. Currently, she works as an interim official for the Junta de Andalucía.

Vitallis Chikoko, PhD, is Professor of Educational Leadership at the University of KwaZulu-Natal. He has experience of teaching in three Southern African Development Community countries: Zimbabwe, Botswana, and South Africa. He is passionate about researching international trends in educational leadership, particularly on the African continent. In 2019 he edited the book: *Africa Handbook for School Leadership*, published by Nova Science Publishers, which includes chapters from 14 African countries. In 2022, he co-edited the book: *Critical Issues in Professional Development: Situated Knowledges from South Africa*, published by Unisa Press. He has extensive postgraduate research supervision experience.

George Sefa Dei is a Ghanaian-born Professor of Social Justice Education and Director of the Centre for Integrative Anti-Racism Studies at the Ontario Institute for Studies in Education of the University of Toronto. His research interests focus on race and anti-racism studies, inclusive schooling, the advancement of human rights in education, equity and diversity to champion an African-centred application of educational philosophies in schools in Canada. Professor Dei has been the Carnegie African Diaspora Fellow over multiple years. In 2012, he was awarded the honorary title of 'Professor Extraordinaire' from the Department of Inclusive Education at the University of South Africa.

María del Mar del Pozo Andrés is a Lecturer in Theory and History of Education at the University of Alcalá and Director of the Antonio Molero Museum of Education. Her research concentrates on the history of urban education, the reception and transfer of international educational currents (especially the New Education movement), the role of education in the construction of national identities, visual studies in education, the history of women's education, and the history of school culture. In 2021 she was elected as President of the Spanish Society for the History of Education. Since 2022 she is the managing editor of *Paedagogica Historica: International Journal of the History of Education*.

Shailaja Fennell is Professor of Regional Transformation and Economic Security, the Department of Land Economy, University of Cambridge, and a Fellow of Jesus College. She currently holds the office of Director, Centre of South Asian Studies within the Consortium of the Global South (comprising the Centres of African Studies, South Asian Studies, Latin American Studies, Gender Studies, and Development Studies) at Cambridge. Her research interests include rural-urban transitions and sustainable land use; institutional reform and economic (particularly food) security; and the case for the provision of public goods and has researched in Asian and African contexts over the past three decades.

M. Obaidul Hamid, PhD, is a Senior Lecturer in TESOL Education at the University of Queensland, Australia. He researches TESOL policy and practice in developing societies. He was born and educated in Bangladesh, where he also worked at the University of Dhaka. His most recent publication includes an article in *Language in Society* entitled "English as a Southern language". He co-edited *Language planning for medium of instruction in Asia* (Routledge, 2014). He is on the editorial boards of *Discourse, Current Issues in Language Planning, English Teaching: Practice & Critique, Journal of Asia TEFL,* and *Asiatic*.

Teboho Hlao is based at the University KwaZulu-Natal's School of Education. His scholarship is in inclusivity, understanding and supporting international students and understanding students' life in residences. In 2011 he graduated with a Bachelor of Education Honours in Educational Psychology. In 2013, Teboho graduated with a Master's in Educational Psychology. Teboho presented at the Poetic Inquiry Symposium 2013, and the UTLO Conference in 2015 and 2016. He lectured in curriculum studies 2017–2021. Teboho is the Residence Life Officer at the University of KwaZulu-Natal. He started a food security project for students without funding.

Hilde Jakobsen, PhD (Bergen), MPhil (Cantab), is an independent consultant based in Dakar, Senegal. She advises the UN and other intergovernmental organisations on gender and human rights dimensions of disaster risk reduction and humanitarian response. She is passionate about feminist and qualitative research in the majority world, especially in Tanzania, Burundi, and Kenya. Her passport country is Norway.

Kokila Roy Katyal is an educational researcher and consultant and serves as a Senior Consultant to Consultants International for Human Capital Development with expertise in United States, East Asia, and South Asia educational systems. Her doctoral work focused on teacher leadership and its impact on student engagement in schools. She was an academic faculty member at the University of Hong Kong and at the Education University of Hong Kong as well as a high school English teacher in India. Her current research program includes ongoing theorisation of educational leadership and cross-cultural research methodologies focused on training and education for teacher leadership, teacher's roles, and barriers and facilitators to teacher leadership. She is also investigating autonomous student learning and learning in schools, home-school interactions and the effects of family educational values on student learning across a range of educational contexts.

Mark Edward King (retired) has been professor at RMIT University, Australia and Academic Director, Singapore. He has held academic and executive positions at UNSW Sydney, the University of Melbourne, and The University of Hong Kong. Mark researches in the areas of human interactivity and learning and has pioneered Multimodal Event Analysis as a methodology for studying human learning within distributed cognitive systems, including an eye-tracking technique for investigating the co-synchronisation of language behaviours and visual perception between persons in learning events. Mark has executed over AUD $60 million in strategic educational grants, and has been engaged as a higher education consultant in Uganda, Saudi Arabia, Kazakhstan, China, Vietnam, and Australia. Prior to his academic career, Mark conducted field research spanning two decades and 77 countries.

Alude Mahali is Chief Research Specialist in the Equitable Education and Economies research division at the Human Sciences Research Council in South Africa. She currently works mainly in the areas of transforming higher education. Alude's research expertise and experiences range from youth social justice work to innovative visual and participatory methodologies in the sociology of education. Her most recent publications look at the domestic worker trope and youth activism. Alude holds an honorary lecturer position in the Department of Drama and Performance Studies at the University of KwaZulu-Natal. She is currently a board member of the Uyinene Mrwetyane Foundation.

Claudia Mitchell is the Distinguished James McGill Professor, McGill University, Montreal Canada and an Honorary Professor at the University of KwaZulu-Natal. She is the founder and director of the Participatory Cultures Lab at McGill, a funded unit that focuses on training and research in the area of participatory visual methodologies and is home to the annual McGill International Cellphilm Festival. She is the co-founder and Editor-in-Chief of *Girlhood Studies: An Interdisciplinary Journal*

Pholoho Justice Morojele is Dean of Research: College of Humanities and former Academic Leader: Research & Higher Degrees in the School of Education, University of KwaZulu-Natal, South Africa. He is a Commonwealth scholar and studied as part of his PhD at the Institute of Education, University of London. His research interests and publications are in gender, children's geographies and social justice in education.

Christina S. Morton, PhD, is Associate Director of the Program on Intergroup Relations at the University of Michigan. Her research explores diverse students' experiences with and meaning-making of social justice education as well as how cultural resources, such as spirituality, contribute to the success of Students of Color in STEM fields. Christina creatively blends art and science as she disseminates her work through poetry and storytelling. Christina earned her doctorate in Higher Education from the University of Michigan and completed training as a National Center for Institutional Diversity Postdoctoral Research Fellow at the University of Michigan.

Rahul Mukhopadhyay is visiting faculty at the School of Education, Azim Premji University, Bengaluru, and a guest faculty for the Masters in Elementary Education programme, the Masters in Education programme, and the BEd-MEd. Integrated Innovative programme at Tata Institute of Social Sciences, Mumbai, India. He is also involved with the Field Research team of the Azim Premji Foundation and with the work of the Wipro Foundation in education in East and North-East India. Rahul has also been actively involved in initiating a Community of Practice for organisations working in the space of libraries for children in the East and North-East under the aegis of the Wipro Foundation.

Inbanathan Naicker is Associate Professor and an NRF-rated researcher in Educational Leadership at the University of KwaZulu-Natal. His research interests include leadership development, leadership and context, arts-based research methods, and self-reflexive research methodologies. He has published numerous journal articles, book chapters, and edited books; has presented papers at several national and international conferences and has guest-edited several journal special issues. He co-edited a special edition of the journal *Alternation* titled, "Academic Identities as Epicentres for Social Cohesiveness in Higher Education" and has recently completed co-editing a book titled, *Working between the folds: School leaders re-imagining school life*.

Arif Naveed is a Lecturer in Education and International Development at the University of Bath. His research examines the social, cultural and economic consequences of the uptake of mass schooling in rural Southern contexts. From 2008 to 2014, he led major strands of research in Pakistan on improving educational outcomes for the poor, on the representation of religious diversity in school textbooks and on the role of South Asian think tanks in promoting international development agendas. His work employs statistical analyses of longitudinal data sets on economic returns to education and social mobility and encourages deep qualitative analysis of the voices of the poor using a Habitus Listening Guide. In 2019, he was engaged by the British Academy to synthesise the findings and policy implications of the GCRF-DFID-funded research programme on early childhood development in low-and-middle-income countries.

Gabriela Ossenbach Sauter is a graduate in pedagogy and Latin American history (Universidad Complutense de Madrid) with a PhD in Educational Sciences (Universidad Nacional de Educación a Distancia – UNED). She is

Professor of History of Education at UNED and the Director of the MANES School Textbook Research Centre also at UNED. Her research focuses on the origin and evolution of national education systems in the nineteenth and twentieth centuries from a comparative perspective, with a special emphasis on Latin America. She has devoted a good part of her research to the history of school culture (school textbooks; study and conservation of the historical heritage of educational institutions).

Daisy Pillay is a teacher educator and researcher in Teacher Development Studies at the University of KwaZulu-Natal, South Africa. Her scholarship is in Identity Studies and focuses on teacher's personal-professional lives as the source and site for their learning, revising, and self-transformation. Her creative methodological approaches for studying lives include critical narrative inquiry, autoethnography, and other self-reflexive methodologies. Her most recent publications include autoethnography in higher education and life writing with objects.

Kathleen Pithouse-Morgan is Professor of Education at the University of Nottingham and an honorary professor at the University of KwaZulu-Natal. Her professional learning scholarship motivates educators and other professionals to see themselves as curious, resourceful learners with the power to effect practitioner-led change. Her work centres on self-reflexive methodologies such as self-study, poetic inquiry, memory-work, autoethnography, and narrative inquiry. Kathleen is passionate about arts-informed inquiry and pedagogy and collaborates with researchers and educators worldwide to promote creativity in research and education. A recent publication is *Memory Mosaics: Researching Teacher Professional Learning Through Artful Memory-Work* (Pithouse-Morgan, Pillay, & Mitchell, Eds., 2019).

Rashida Qureshi is an Associate Professor at the Department of Social Sciences of Shaheed Zulfikar Ali Bhutto Institute of Science and Technology in Pakistan. She has a PhD in Sociology from Kansas State University, USA. As a researcher, she has worked with public and private research institutions. She has extensive field research experience, especially in remote rural areas. As a trainer, she has conducted workshops on gender and research for public and private institutions. She has edited two books as an editor and one as a co-editor. Her research interests include teaching and learning of research, ethics in research and issues of research supervision.

Nidhi Singal is Professor of Disability and Inclusive Education at the Faculty of Education, University of Cambridge. Her work focuses on addressing the educational exclusion of marginalised groups, with a specific focus on persons with disabilities across Southern contexts. She is committed to developing culturally sensitive approaches in educational research, particularly in relation to critically examining power relations in North-South research partnerships and the ethics of research dissemination. She works extensively with international organisations, such as the World Bank and UNESCO. In 2022, Nidhi was elected Fellow of the Academy of Social Sciences (FAcSS) and is also the President of the British Association for International and Comparative Education (BAICE).

Fauzia Shamim works as the Chief Academic Officer at Durbeen, an NGO working towards improving the quality of teachers in Pakistan. Earlier, she has served as Professor and founder Dean of the Faculty of Liberal Arts and Human Sciences, Ziauddin University, Karachi, Pakistan. Dr. Shamim has vast experience as a teacher/researcher, and leader at various universities in the public and private sector in Pakistan and internationally. She is a regular presenter at national and international conferences. Her current research interests include context-appropriate pedagogy, teaching English in difficult circumstances, program and curriculum development and evaluation, and Language-in-Education policy including English as a medium of instruction.

Linda Tuhiwai Smith is Distinguished Professor at Te Whare Wānanga o Awanuiārangi in Whakatane, Aotearoa New Zealand. Her current research is in the field of Indigenous knowledge, Inter-generational historic trauma and Kaupapa Māori strategies for preventing and healing from family violence. She has recently written a series of children's books published in English and Māori languages that address trauma. She is a Fellow of the Royal Society of New Zealand, a Fellow of the American Education Research Association and an Honorary International Member of the American Academy of Arts and Sciences, and is best known for her work on *Decolonizing Methodologies: Research and Indigenous Peoples* first published in 1999 by Zed Books and recently published in a third edition by Bloomsbury.

Arathi Sriprakash is Professor of Sociology and Education, University of Oxford, UK. Over a number of years, she has been examining the politics of education reform in the Indian and Australian contexts as well as the global governance of childhood and the family. Underlying this work has been an abiding interest in the politics of knowledge, not least questions about the relationship between epistemic justice and racial justice. She is co-author of *Learning Whiteness: Education and the Settler Colonial State* (2022).

Julia Suárez-Krabbe is a Colombian-Danish scholar, activist, and Associate Professor in Cultural Encounters, Roskilde University, Denmark. Her work focuses on race and (anti)racism, 'other' knowledges/epistemologies from the South and the ontological, epistemological, material and existential dimensions of decolonisation. Julia is the author of *Race, Rights and Rebels: Alternatives to Human Rights and Development from the Global South* (2016), co-editor of *Transdisciplinary Thinking from the Global South: Whose Problems, Whose Solutions?* (2022) and *Coloniality of Power and Decolonization in the Nordic Countries* (forthcoming).

Michele Suina, PhD, is a tribal member of Cochiti Pueblo located in New Mexico, USA. She currently is a Program Director at the Albuquerque Area Southwest Tribal Epidemiology Center. Michele is a health educator and chose this pathway to contribute to the vitality of Indigenous peoples and to influence Western approaches to public health so tribes can realise their own self-defined health goals. In 2015, Michele graduated from Arizona State University School of Social Transformation with the first Pueblo PhD Justice Studies cohort. Her scholarly interests include research ethics and health education approaches grounded in Indigenous Knowledge Systems.

Sharlene Swartz is the executive head of the Equitable Education and Economies research division at the Human Sciences Research Council in South Africa. She researches and writes extensively on transformative education, reimagined inclusive economic development for young people, and decolonising and emancipatory practices in research across the African continent. She is currently the Principal Investigator of a ten-year longitudinal research study *The Imprint of Education*, funded by the Mastercard Foundation, that investigates the ways in which higher education impacts on the lives of first-generation students, and how they in turn affect their worlds.

Leon Tikly is UNESCO Chair on Inclusive and Good Quality Education for All at the University of Bristol. He currently directs a UKRI-funded network on *Transforming Education for Sustainable Futures* with partners in India, Rwanda, Somalia/Somaliland and South Africa. His scholarship over many years has focused on initiatives to improve the quality of education for disadvantaged learners, particularly in sub-Saharan Africa and on issues of race, ethnicity and education in the UK. His work draws on critical realism, postcolonial, and decolonial perspectives and is underpinned by a commitment to social, environmental and epistemic justice.

Miye Nadya Tom (citizen of the Walker River Paiute Tribe) has researched, published, and lectured on race/ethnicity in education nationally and internationally. She has devoted the past decade to working with students and youth from various communities in the United States, Spain, and Portugal. She lectures in Native American Studies at the University of Nebraska and also teaches elementary school on her reservation in Schurz, Nevada. She is also an aspiring creative nonfiction writer. In 2022, she concluded her MFA at the Institution of American Indian Arts, Santa Fe, New Mexico.

Maggie Walter (PhD, FASSA) is palawa and Distinguished Professor of Sociology (Emerita) at the University of Tasmania. Her research interests encompass inequality, race relations and Indigenous Data Sovereignty. She is a founding member of the Indigenous Data Sovereignty group in Australia (Maiam nayri Wingara) and an executive member of the Global Indigenous Data Alliance. Recent books include *Indigenous Children Growing Up Strong* (with Martin and Bodkin-Andrews, Palgrave McMillan: 2017), *Indigenous Data Sovereignty and Social Policy* (with Kukutai, Carroll and Rodriguez Lonebear, Routledge, 2020), and *The Oxford Handbook of Indigenous Sociology* (with Kukutai, Gonzales, and Henry, 2022).

INDEX

Note: Page references in *italics* denote figures, in **bold** tables and with "n" endnotes.

Abdool, S. N. 226
Aboshiha, P. 200
Abraham, A. 83–84, 92
abstraction 71
accepted culture 99–100
accommodations 187–188, 192–200
acculturation 98
Acker, S. 9
action: collective 69, 260; critique of current behaviour to motivate towards 258; individual 29, 83, 260; political 82, 86, 97; self-directed 253; social 69, 81
action research 4, 11, 200; participatory 11, 200, 245
activist and scholarly gaze 1
actor–network theory (ANT) 116, 120
acts of citizenship 66
Addlakha, R. 49
Africa 73; classic European-style colonialism 31; feminist standpoints 63–64; gender relations 68–69; women's roles and identities 66–67
African Americans 155, 167, 320, 324; *see also* Black/African education
African-centred paradigm 90
African feminists 66, 68
African humanism 25, 154

African Indigenous knowledge: as heritage knowledge 87–90
African other/White self 232, 238
African socialism 25
Africa Today 62
Afro-Portuguese 321, 332
agency: collective 258–259, **259**; and gender education 68–72; horizontal intergenerational listening 307–308; individual 258–259, **259**
Albert, B. 54
Albuquerque Area Indian Health Board (AAIHB) 213, 215
Albuquerque Area Southwest Tribal Epidemiology Centre (AASTEC) 213–218
Alexander, M. 73–74
Allnutt, S. 269
alterity 222, 225–227, 231, 239
Alzheimer's disease 265
American Educational Research Association (AERA) 91–92, 187, 189, 191
American feminism 64
Andersen, C. 208, 210, 214
Andrews, J. 179, 181
Anglo-American core principles 189
Aniekwe, C. C. 54

Annual Status of Education Report (ASER) 52
anonymity 176, 190, 193, 197, 199, 262, 274, 326
anticipatory consciousness 25
anti-colonial: discursive framework 88; intellectuality 82–83, 87; *see also* postcolonial
anti-foundationalist approach 116
anti-textuality 83
Apentiik, C. R. A. 224
Armstrong, A. C. 50
Armstrong, D. 50
Asante, M. 81, 90
Ashraf, D. 197–198
Asia literate 136
Asif, S. 194, 197
asymmetry of ignorance 6
auditory senses 68
AusAID 46
Australia 173, 176, 208, 212, 218, 222
authentic 187, 197; data 197; dialogue 169; knowledge 9; selves 82, 90
autonomy 190–191, 194–196, 198, 247, 268
avoidance: quantitative 207; of political controversy 136

Badley, G. 281
Baldwin, K. 144
Bangladesh: avoiding harm 182–184; ethical dilemmas 176–178; home setting 179–180; implications 184–185; informed consent 178–179; language education research in 172–185; Nadiranga 173–174; PhD research and its setting 173–174; politeness/ hospitality/obligation issues 179–180; privacy and confidentiality 180–182; researching English language education 174–176; right to withdrawal 178–179; Western research ethics 176–178
Banks, M. 273
Barnes, C. 45
Batan, C. M. 3
Batra, P. 124, 128
behavioural norms 172
Bell, D. 139
Berger, J. 273
Berghs, M. 48

Bevan-Brown, J. 145
Bhabha, H. 3, 231
Bhana, D. 270
Bhola, H. S. 61–62
Biklen, S. K. 193
Biko, S. 24–25
bio-psycho-social approach 51
Black/African education 83, 84–87, 89–90; Canadian 84; in Diasporic context 87; local cultural knowings 89
Black/African ontology 86
Black Conception 329–330
Black feminists: analysis 157–158; conceptual frameworks 153–156; data collection process *157*; endarkened feminist epistemology 154–156, 158–160; implications for academic practice 169–170; implications for research 169; implications for student affairs practice 169–170; insights 158–164; positionality statement 152–153; spiritual 151–170; study 156–157; thought 153–154, 164–168
Bloch, E. 25
Bogdan, R. C. 193
Bond, T. 119
bonded labour 195, 304
Bonilla-Silva, E. 210
Born into Brothels (film) 267
Botswana 50
Bourdieu, P. 119, 244, 246, 252, 301, 303, 310, 312
Braunholtz, T. 42
Brayboy, B. M. 218
Brazil 96, 99–100, 105–106
Breakey, J. 9
British Educational Research Association (BERA) 187, 189, 191
Brokeback Mountain 142
broker 116, 120–123
Brown, A. M. B. 47
Brown, L. M. 301, 316
Buthelezi, T. 271, 282

Canadian school system 84
Canagarajah, A. S. 119
Cannella, G. 31, 35
capacity to aspire 305
Carspecken, L. 155
Cartographies of Struggle (Mohanty) 64

Caruso, M. 106
centre 99, 101, 105–106
Chalfen, R. 268
Chandran, V. 271
change: ideology and possibilities for 257–258, **258**; individual and collective agency 258–259, **259**; institutions and possibilities for 257–258, **258**
Chappell, P. 52
Chataika, T. 48
Chattopadhyaya Commission 123
Chia, R. 118, 120, 122–123
Chinese culture 134–148
choice biographies 61
Choudhuri, M. A. 52
Christian ethics 25
Christians, C. G. 191
chronic poverty 46
Chronic Poverty Research Centre 46
chronological educational narratives 305–308
cinematic texts 265, 271, 273, 276
Clandinin, D. J. 281
class-caste hierarchy 303
classical imperialism 22–23
Clifford, J. 80
cognitive justice 4, 26
collective poetic inquiry 285–288; collective agency 258–259, 259; collective co-agency 260; collective poetic performance 293–295; collective poetry-making 291–293; poetic performance 286–288; and polyvocality in educational research 281–297; process as polyvocal 296–297
collective uniformity 135
Collier, J. 268
Collier, M. 268
Collins, P. H. 153–154, 164, 166–167, 169
colonial 86; anthropologists 321; colonial encounter 86; colonising experience 86; cultural heritage 65; culture 24; defined 88; economy 31; education 31–32, 79–80, 83, 322; forms of pedagogy 3; identities 24; knowledge 322; legacies 13, 33, 99, 101, 124, 332; mappings/cartographies 82; mentality 96; mimicry 86; politics 24; power relations 79; rationality 322; regimes 323; relations 88; schooling 31; systems of power 3; theory 7
colonialism 24; European-style 22, 31; is narrativised 23; Western 24
coloniality in Lisbon, Portugal 328–330
common culture 231, 239
common sense 189
community 83; academic 54, 188; community-based organisations 189; Indigenous 73; mapping 11; Native American 320, 323; photography projects 267
community attitudes 256, **257**
community dismemberment 331
comparative and international education (CIE) 119–120; postcolonial research ethics in 21–37; postcolonial scholarship for 22; research 29–30
compassion 160–162
confidentiality 176, 180–182
Confucian cultures 134–136; *see also* Confucian Heritage Cultures (CHCs)
Confucian Heritage Cultures (CHCs) 134, 136, 146–148
Connell, R. 60, 62
Connelly, F. M. 281
conscientisation 244, 258
conversation norms 225
Cooper, A. 3
cosmopolitanism 28–29, 97
credibility 152–153
critical awareness 3, 5
critical data literacy 218
critical idiom 22
critical race theory 5
criticised/disputed culture 100
Cross-Cultural Perspectives in Educational Research (Robinson-Pant) 6
Crossley, M. 119
cultural: capital 180, 246, 252, 303, 306–308; cognition 137–138, 147; crisis 85; differences 221; engagement 80; essentialism 3–4; estrangement 8, 78, 80; exchange 97–98, 104, 107; knowledge 80–84, 90–92, 147; mediation 81; realities 172, 211; sensitivity 222, 231; spaces 98; transfers 98

Dangerous Minds (film) 271
Das, V. 49
data: interpretation challenges 144–146; visual 265–267, 270, 273–274
De, A. 44
de Boer, A. 51
debrief 261
de-canonization 4
decentring 239; of European thought 23; hegemonic gender theory 60–74; of hegemonic power 71; of modernist metanarratives 24; positionality 233–236
decolonial historical realist approach 321
decolonising research praxis 6
Decolonizing Methodologies: Research and Indigenous Peoples (Tuhiwai Smith) 5, 33, 207
deconstructive aspect, postcolonial theory 25
deference 135, 139, 227, 231–232, 239
definitional power: of anti-textuality 83; of idealism 83
de Lange, N. 270–271, 282
Dennett, D. C. 146
Denzin, N. K. 273
Department of Health and Human Services (DHHS) 213
dependency theory 101
Desai, V. 225
de-secularization 4
development actors/researchers 121
dharma 27
diachronic contexts 127
dialogic ethics 27, 35–36
Diasporic contexts: African 82; African/Black education in 78, 87; education of youth in 86
diatopical hermeneutics 26, 35
Dillard, C. B. 152–153, 155, 158, 160, 162–164, 169–170
Dimitriadis, G. 224
Dinges, N. 144
Directorate of Secondary and Higher Education (DSHE) 178
disability: children with, educational status of 43–45; Indigenous knowledge and research on 49; researching 42–56
disabled people *see* people with disabilities
Disabled People's Organisations (DPOs) 53–54
disabled sexualities 52
dislocation 68–72; discrepant 70
displaced reflexivity 117
Disrupting Preconceptions: Postcolonial and Education (Hickling-Hudson, Matthews and Woods) 71
Dlamini, M. 52
double consciousness 330
drawings 12, 234, 265–267
Du Bois, W. E. B. 84–87, 330
Duflo, E. 126
Dupere, S. 226
Dussel, E. 101
du Toit, M. 269
Dyck, N. 209
Dyer, C. 124

ecology of knowledges 8, 26
economic capital 180, 303, 306
eco-specific 188
eco-transferable 188
education: African-centred 90; anti-colonial 86, 89; Black 84–87; Black/African (*see* Black/African education); colonial 31–32, 79–80, 83, 322; defined 91; gender (*see* gender education); gender scholarship 61; human capital theory 32; inclusive 46, 49–50; Indigenous 91; Indigenous African 85–86; moral imperative of 32; national gender agendas in 61; as practice of freedom 102; researching 42–56; Roma and 'standardisation' of 326–328; site 91; spiritual in 88; *see also* gender education
educational biographies in field of power 303–305
educational development 115–131; second-order engagement with reflexivity in 115
educational research: in Bangladesh 172–185; canons of 1–13; and collective poetic inquiry 281–297; decolonising 3–5; ethical dilemmas in 192; evoking polyvocality in 281–297; feminist 63–64, 74; gender 61, 68, 71–74; implications for 60–74; informed consent in 187–201; language 172–185; in

Nadiranga 174–176; normative methodological discourse in 117; in Pakistan 187–201; polyvocality in 281–297; postcolonial condition 31–33; reframing codes, rules and rituals of 7–10; in South Africa 265–276
Education Commissions 123
Education for All (EFA) 61, 62–64
Education for Self-reliance (Nyerere) 31
Eisenhart, M. 137
Eisner, E. W. 293, 296
emancipation 243, 245; of Indigenous people 100; political 99; research approaches for 10–12; semantic 106; spiritual 99
emancipatory approach 54–55
emancipatory ethics 25
Emmison, M. 274
emotions 154, 167–168
empathy 154, 168
encounters 102, 105
enculturation 98
endarkened feminist epistemology 154–156, 158–160
England 32
enlightenment ethics 23
environmental portraits 269
epistemicide 2, 329
epistemic justice 4; reflexivity 119; relation 118
epistemological imperialism 80
epistepraxis 3
equality of opportunities 8
Escobar, A. 102
essentialism 4, 90
ethical codes 172, 176, 187, 198; dilemmas 172–185, 192; issues 172–185; space 201
ethics: of care 152; Christian 25; dialogic 27, 35–36; in educational research 31–33; emancipatory 25; enlightenment 23; postcolonial research, in education 29; and postcolonial theory 21–29; situated 34–35; and social justice 21–29; universal 23; Western 23; Western research 29, 31, 176–178
Euro-American school system 86
Eurocentric curriculum 32
Euro-colonial modernity 86
Euromodernity 78
European colonialism 22, 31
European enlightenment 23
European feminism 64
evaluate social contexts 257–258, **258**; *see also* Social Network Interviewing/Interviews (SNI/SNIs)
Evans, P. 44
Evers, C. W. 147
Ewald, W. 267
extraverted gaze 9

Faber, P. 269
Facebook 276
factionalism 282
faith 162, 164, 310; filled research 152, 155; in integration 85
family lives: chronological educational narratives 305–308; *Habitus Listening Guide* 301–303, **302**, 315–317; horizontal intergenerational listening 305–308; internalisation of male domination 309–312; mythic-ritual listening 312–315; overview 300–301; in rural Punjab 300–317; social structural listening 303–305; vertical gender listening 309–312
family of 'relational' approaches 98
family photographs 268–269
Fanon, F. 3, 83–87, 320, 322
Farooqui, A. 194, 196
fatherhood 248–250
feminism/feminists 6; African 66, 68; American 64; Black (*see* Black feminists); development 63; European 64; Indian 68, 72; Indigenous 69; Nego-feminism 69; postcolonial 68, 71; transnational multicultural 66; Western 66–67; Western European 64
feminist epistemology 151; endarkened 154–156
feminist researchers: globalised 63–64; on universalising agendas 62–64
Fernández Enguita, M. 326
Ferris, L. E. 198
field of power 303–305
fieldwork: in developing countries 184; for education research in rural Bangladesh 172–185; in home setting 179–181; in Nadiranga 176

Fine, G. A. 198, 224
Fire+Hope (film) 271, 275
Fiske, J. 266
Focus group discussions (FGDs) 221–239; misuses 222–224; opportunities 222–224; uses 222–224
foreigner effect 225
Foucault, M. 23, 28, 37n5, 69, 71, 301
found poems 285–286, 291–294; constructing to re-present stories of experience 288–291; "knowing in the making" 288–289
Freire, P. 102, 218, 245

Galtung, J. 97
Gandhi, M. 24
gate-keeping 146
Geertz, C. 80
Gender and Development (GAD) approach 63
gendered habitus, negotiating 310–312
gender education 60; and agency 68–72; and dislocation 68–72; and positionalities 68–72; research in other regions 72–74; scholarship 61; *see also* education
gender theory: hegemonic 60–74; metropolitan 63–64; Southern 63
'Genealogies of Community, Home, and Nation' (Mohanty) 70
geographies of feminist knowledge formation 62
A Geopolitics of Academic Writing (Canagarajah) 119
Gilligan, C. 301, 316
Gilroy, P. 28
girl child 64–66; Southern countries 65
Gitlin, A. D. 281
global citizenry/global good 83
global inclusionism 50
Global Monitoring Report (GMR) 42
Global South 2–4, 6, 8–9, 221, 262–263, 300, 319
Goble, C. 48
Goldstein, B. 274
Gómez García, M. N. 326
Goodman, J. 103
Gordon, J. 269
Grande, S. 152
Grande, S. 33–34
Gronn, P. 138

Grossi, E. 272
grounded inclusionism 50
guanxi ('networks of assistance') 139
Guenther, K. M. 10

habitus 173, 244, 310–312
Habitus Listening Guide 300–317; family lives 301–303, **302**; listenings, methods, and objectives **302**; power of 315–317; from theory to practice 301–303; vertical gendered listenings 309–312
Halai, A. 4, 199
Hall, S. 35
Handbook of Critical and Indigenous Methodologies (Denzin, Lincoln and Tuhiwai Smith) 5–6
The Handbook of Critical Theoretical Research Methods in Education (Matias) 4
Haraway, D. 224
Hargreaves, A. 281
Harrison, M. 54
Hasan, R. 52
Hennink, M. M. 225
Henry, M. G. 224
heritage knowledge 87–90
Hèung Góng Yàhn ('Hong Kong People') 135
Higher Education Commission (HEC) 188
hip-hop culture 319–321, 328–329, 331
Hirsch, M. 268
histoire croisée (entangled history) 98
Historia de la Educación 103
historiographic: analysis 103; perspectives 96; production 104
HIV/AIDS 251, 267, 269, 271–272
Ho, D. Y. F. 135
Holliday, A. R. 200
Holloway, I. 192
homo economicus 23
Hong Kong 134–136
Hoogeveen, J. G. 49
hooks, b. 3
Hopper, T. 283
horizontal intergenerational listening 305–308; voicing agency 307–308; voicing parental aspirations 305–307
Howe, K. 187
Howgego, C. 46
Hsiung, P. 189

Hubbard, J. 267
Hue, M.-T. 139
Huer, M. B. 145
Hulme, D. 300
human capital theory 32
human diversity 282
humanism 28; African 25; planetary 28; Western 23, 25, 28
Husserl, E. 208
hybridity 105, 107, 200, 201n1

Iberian: metropolis 99; postcolonial studies in 102–107; *see also* Spain
ideology 86, 98; political 89; and possibilities for change 257–258, **258**
ilm ('knowledge') 306, 311
implementers of education policy 125
implementing agency 124
imposed culture 99
inclusionism: global 50; grounded 50
inclusive education 46, 49–50
India: children with disabilities and education 44; national feminists in 72; politics of knowledge production 123–129; teachers' work in 123–129; women empowerment 66
Indian feminism 68, 72
Indian Health Care Improvement Act (IHCIA) 213
Indian Health Service (IHS) 213
Indigenous: African education 85–86; data 207–219; data sovereignty 207–219; education 91, 106; epistemologies 79–80; indigene 210; indigenism 100; knowledge 61–62, 72, 87–88; lifeworlds 208–209; methodological engagement 218–219; methodologies 207–219; quantitative methodologies in practice 213–218; reality 82; statistical narratives 210, 214; statistics 209–211
Indigenous anti-colonial framework 89–90; see also *anti-colonial*
Indigenous anti-colonial knowledge 78–92; African 87–90; and Black education 84–87; cultural knowledge challenge 80–84; as heritage knowledge 87–90; intellectual and political challenge 78–79; see also *anti-colonial*

Indigenous Research Methodologies (Chilisa) 5
individual agency 258–259, **259**
individualism 67–68
individual/personhood 49
inferiority complex syndrome 87
informed consent (IC) 2, 10, 140, 146, 187–201; in educational research in south 187–201; in practice in Pakistan 192–198; principles of 176, 189; right to withdrawal 178–179; and right to withdrawal 178–179; voluntary 191
infra-reflexivity 121
insider/outsider 172, 176
installations 265–266, 274
institutionalised space 300
institutions, and possibilities for change 257–258, **258**
intellectual imposters 78, 80
interanimation 283
interculturality 102
interdependence 26, 69, 83, 86, 89, 91
intergenerational: learning 331; occupational hazards 304; relations 317; transfer of economic deprivation 49
interillumination 283
internalisation of male domination 309–312
inter-narrativity 305; see also *Habitus Listening Guide*
International Classification of Functioning, Disability and Health 51
International Focus Group Research (Hennink) 225, 231
internationalism 97
international treaties on human rights 26
inter-participant 223, 233, 238
interpretations 162, 170; of American developments 101; of contact between cultures 98; data 144–146; of Latin American 101; ontological primacy of 87
interpretive processes and visual research 272–274
interrogating policy 85
intersubjectivity 69, 209
intervention innovation 243
The Invention of Women (Oyewumi) 67, 68

Jafarey, A. M. 194, 196
Janesick, V. J. 292
John, M. E. 70–71, 72
Johnny, L. 272
just research practice 3–5

Kamberlis, G. 224
Karenga, M. 85
Karlsson, J. 275
K'dee, R. 324–325
Kelly, M. 136
Kember, D. 139
Kembhavi, G. 52
Khandake, A. J. 52
Khanna-Bhutani, S. 44
Kindergarten Cop (film) 271
King, J. E. 135
Kingdon, G. G. 125
Kirsch, R. 218
Kitchener, K. 29
Kitchener, R. 29
knowers 115
knowing 115, 117, 135, 145
knowing in the making 283, 288–289
knowledge: authentic 9; colonial 322; cultural 80–84, 90–92, 147; ecology of 8, 26; heritage 87–90; Indigenous 61–62, 72, 87–88; local 87–88; politics of 116, 123–129; racial subset of 83; science 89; for transformation of Black/African education 83; Western 12, 24, 322
Koistinen, M. H. 52
Kothari Commission 123
Kropff Causa, L. 3

Lahman, M. K. E. 283
Langford, M. 268
Latin America 96–107; accepted culture 99–100; consciousness 100; criticised/disputed culture 100; culture 99; development programmes in 101; history of education in 102–107; imposed culture 99; monitorial system of education in 106; overview 96–99; postcolonial approaches in cultural studies 99–102; and Spanish pedagogues 103; unity to oppose imperialism 100
Latour, B. 120, 121
Law, J. 116, 120

Lebakeng, T. G. 83, 89
Lee, R. M. 136
Le Fanu, G. 50
Leggo, C. 286
Leung, D. Y. P. 139
Lewis, D. 121, 122
Li, N. 139
life history approach 52
limited cultural pluralism 187
Lincoln, Y. 31, 35
listening: horizontal intergenerational 305–308; mythic-ritual 312–315; social structural 303–305; vertical gender 309–312; vertical gendered 309–312; *see also* Habitus Listening Guide
Listening Guide (Brown and Gilligan) 301
lived experiences 63, 78, 79
lived realities 48, 154, 170, 209
locality 175, 176, 180
local knowledge 87–88
local realities 47–50
local voices 50, 79
logic of productivity 24
looking at looking 267
love 158–160
Lykes, M. B. 267
Lynch, P. 50

Ma, J. L. C. 135
MacKenzie, S. K. 283
mainstream classrooms 51
Malawi 50
majority world: focus groups in 225–226; researching across difference in 224–225; working to strengths of the method 225–226
Majumdar, M. 127–128
male domination, internalisation of 309–312
male honour 309–310
Mariátegui, J. C. 100
marketisation 5, 32
masculinities 248, 271
Mason, M. 147
master narratives 80
material culture 271–272
Maton, K. 118–119
Mbembe, A. 29
McFarlane, C. 8
McKeever, K. 12

Mckenzie, J. 48
meditative 152, 155, 169
meek dictator 124, 127
member check 197
meritocratic 306
Merton, R. 147
messiness 88, 118
metanarratives 23–24
meta-theoretic 118
methodological rigour 221–239
methodology of surrender 152, 155, 157–160, 162, 164; *see also* endarkened feminist epistemology
mianzi ('maintaining face') 135
Mignolo, W. 101
Millennium Development Goals (MDGs) 42, 61
Miller, W. R. 246–247
minority world: focus groups outside 221–239; methodological rigour outside 221–239
misguided rationalism 138
Mitchell, C. 267, 268, 269, 270–272, 282
Mji, G. 49
Mohanty, C. T. 64–65, 73–74
Momsen, J. H. 225, 230
Mooij, J. 127
Moore, R. 117
moral mediation 81
Moses, M. 187
Mosse, D. 121, 122
motherhood 66–67, 72, 306
motivational interviewing 245–247
Mukhopadhyay, S. 50
Muller, J. 117
multi-epistemes 81
multiple positionalities 224
Mundy, K. 61
Muralidharan, K. 125, 127, 128
Murphy, L. 61
Muthukrishna, N. 48
Muzammil, M. 125
My Space 276
mythic-ritual listening 312–315; spiritual poem 313–315; spiritual poem of fate and duty 312–315; *see also* poetic inquiry

Nadiranga 173–174; ethical dilemmas 176–178; informed consent 178–179; language education research in 174–176; right to withdrawal 178–179; Western research ethics 176–178
narrative vignettes 284
national and regional borders 96
National Policy of Education 124
nation states 37, 65, 208–210, 212
Native American: community 320, 323; urban Native American youth 323–326
Nego-feminism 69
neo-liberalism 33; governmentality 23, 30
Nepal 52, 267
network models 248
new imperialism 22
New Zealand 12, 44, 73, 208, 218, 222
Nigeria 66–68
Nkala, N. 52
Nnaemeka, O. 66–67, 68, 73
non-Chinese researchers 134–148; challenges of data interpretation 144–146; Confucian cultures 134–136; Hong Kong context 134–135; implications 146–148; outsider *vs.* insider research 137–138; sensitivities associated with research 136–137; studies 138–144
non-governmental organisations (NGOs) 53–54, 174–175, 321, 326
non-traditional methodology 285
nordomanía (North America materialism) 100
Nordtveit, B. H. 139
Northern hegemony 9
Northern ways 2
novice researchers 2, 10, 198
Nóvoa, A. 103, 105
nudge theory 245, 247
Nuwagaba, E. L. 47
Nyamnjoh, F. B. 80, 82
Nyerere, J. 31

objectivity 163, 200, 207
O'Hanlon, R. 316
'on tap'/'on top'/'on shelf' 55
onto-epistemic groundings 320
Operation Blackboard 124
Ospina, A. 106
othering 23, 73, 223–224, 230–231; of motherhood 66–67; Othered 3
outsider *vs.* insider research 137–138

Ownership, Control, Access, Possession (OCAP) 212
Owusu-Ansah, F. E. 49
Oyewumi, O. 67, 68

Pakistan: children with disabilities and education 52; educational research in 187–201; informed consent (IC) 187–201; recommendations 198–201; research environment in 188–189; tensions and accommodations 192–198
Pakistan Association for Research in Education (PARE) 189
Pang, D. 136
parallax perspectives 11
para-teachers 66, 125, 130
parental aspirations 305–307
Parpart, J. 224
participant-researchers 243–248, 253, 255, 257, 260–262
participatory action research (PAR) 11, 200, 245; see also action research
participatory methodologies 283, 297
participatory observation 321
participatory/other visual approaches 266–269; cinematic texts 271; drawings 267; family photographs 268–269; interpretive processes and visual research 272–274; material culture 271–272; photo-elicitation 268; photo-voice 267; researcher as photographer/visual ethnographer 269–270; video 270–271; visual images within popular culture 272
participatory video 270
particularities 26, 319
pathological personality 86
Patient Protection and Affordable Care Act 213
Pedagogy of Absence, Conflict and Emergence (PACE) 321–323; coloniality in Lisbon, Portugal 328–330; overview 319–323; Rap Kriolu 328–330; Roma 326–328; standardisation of education 326–328; urban Native American youth 323–326
peoplehood 209
people with disabilities: and education 42–56; low- and middle-income countries 48; movement in the UK 45; and poverty 42
periphery 96, 99, 101, 103–106
personal accountability 152–154, 164–166
personal expressiveness 154, 157, 166–167
phenomenological: perspectives 285; philosophers 209
photo-elicitation 268; see also visual methodologies
photographer, researcher as 269–270; see also visual methodologies
photographic participant-observer 270; see also visual methodologies
photo-voice 267; see also visual methodologies
Pijl, S. J. 51
Pillow, W. 117, 118
Pineau, P. 106
Pink, S. 270, 273
Pithouse, K. 267
pluralism 187, 282; of vocabularies 282, 292
poetic inquiry 281–297; collective poetic inquiry 285–288, 296–297; collective poetic performance 293–295; collective poetry-making as analysis 291–293; found poems 288–291; interanimation 283; interillumination 283; poetry as research 283–284; setting the scene 284–285
poetic performance 286–288, 289–291, 293, 294–297
poetry as research 283–284
politics of knowledge 116, 123–129
The Politics of (M)othering: Womanhood, Identity, and Resistance in African Literature (Nnaemeka) 66
polyphonic voices 11
polyvocality/polyvocal: collective poetic inquiry 285–288, 296–297; collective poetic performance as 293–295; collective poetry-making as analysis 291–293; constructing found poems 288–291; in educational research 281–297; poetic performance 286–288, 289–291; poetry as research 283–284; in research

281–283; setting the scene 284–285
popular culture 272
Porsanger, J. 208
Portugal: coloniality in 328–330; communities of Cape Verdean in 319; Portuguese Empire 96; Rap Kriolu 328–330
Portuguese-Brazilian Congresses 105
Posel, D. 29
positionality 69, 74, 121, 145, 222, 238–239; data generation 224; decentre 233–236; directing feminist gender education 71; insider-outsider debate 10; limits of 9; power dimension of 231–233; principles of 70; researcher's 226; statement 152–153
postcolonial: condition 21–22, 29, 36–37; ethics in educational research 31–33; feminists 71; national state 102; research ethics 29, 33–36; studies in Iberian 102–107; theory 21–29; unequal power relationships 34
postcolonialism 21–23, 96–97, 102–103, 107
postnationalist approach to education 319
Potter, R. B. 225
poverty of school culture 84
power: educational biographies in field of 303–305; of the *Habitus Listening Guide* 315–317
power gradient 231–232, 239
Pratt, D. 136
presence of absence 6
pre-service teachers 267, 272
prestige 135–136
primary text 266
privacy 180–182; -deficient environments 181; private spaces 181
problem-based declarative statement 255–256, **257**; *see also* Social Network Interviewing/Interviews (SNI/SNIs)
production texts 266
productive ambiguity 293, 296; *see also* poetic inquiry
productive workers 63
progress 99, 104
Prosser, J. 273

public pedagogy 319
public sphere 307
Punjab: empirical study in 301; family lives in 300–317; interviews were conducted in 303; newly irrigated areas 302; structural inequality in 300–317

quantitative avoidance 207
queer theory 6
Quine, W. V. O. 210
Qureshi, R. 9

racial imaginary 102
racial subset of knowledge 83
rahi aql 37n4
Ralfe, E. 272
Rangpur Dinajpur Rehabilitation Services (RDRS) 174
Rap Kriolu 328–330; contesting coloniality in Lisbon, Portugal 328–330
rap music 320–321, 331
Rashida, S. A. 52
reciprocity 6, 98, 103, 105, 152, 155, 162–163
recognition 117, 155, 194
reconstructive aspect, postcolonial theory 25
Red Pedagogy (Grande) 34
reflexivity 70; displaced 117; as methodological power 117–120; as neutral process 118; and politics of knowledge 115–131; in social research 117, 118; as truth 117
reframing: codes, rules and rituals of educational research practice 7–10; of educational research methods 7; empirical research practice 1
reimagining: research approaches for emancipation 10–12
relational materialism 121; research design 301; worlds 1, 49, 66–68, 70, 72, 74, 301
Renzetti, C. M. 136
representation: of development 123; external reality 120; problematic of 118
reproductive mothers 63
researcher: as broker 120–123; knowledge frames 115;

as photographer/visual ethnographer 269–270; as translator 120–123
research ethics: critique of dominant approaches to 29–31; postcolonial, in education 29; *see also* ethics
Research Methodologies in the 'South' (Halai and Wiliam) 4
research methodology: limitations and challenges 274–275; reaching the public 275–276
research/researching 221, 223; approaches for emancipation 10–12; cinematic texts 271; difference in majority world 224–225; disability and education 42–56; explorations 50–53; as freedom 11; interpretive processes 272–274; material culture 271–272; minority world/majority-world 233; outsider *vs.* insider 137–138; as performance 8; as photographer/visual ethnographer 269–274; poetry as 283–284; polyvocality in 281–283; as responsibility 163; sensitive 49, 119, 136–137; video 270–271; visual 272–274; visual images within popular culture 272
research studies 248–254
resistance 65–66; anticolonial 321; and anti-coloniality 89; to colonialism 82, 97; dominant and colonising knowledges 87; globalised 328; to imperialism 97; and Indigeneity 89; Indigenous anti-colonial framework 90; radical 82
respondent validation 197
returnees 189
Riecken, T. 282
Riggins, S. H. 272
right relationships 152–153, 170
rights-based approach 30–31
rigorous 117, 136, 187, 189, 239
ritual 163–164
Robinson-Pant, A. 119
Robson, C. 44
Rodó, J. E. 100
Rogoff, B. 81
Rollnick, S. 246–247
Roma/Romani 326–328, 333n2; associations and NGOs 326; communities 319–321, 326, 328, 331–332; historical segregation of 326; holocaust 328; International Romani Peoples Day 328; and 'standardisation' of education 326–328; students 326–327
Rose, G. 273
Ruby, J. 271
Rule, P. 47, 52
rural poor 300
rural teachers 267

Sabates, R. 51–52
Sáenz, J. 106
Saenz, T. I. 145
Said, E. 3, 28, 33
Saigal, A. 66
Saldarriaga, O. 106
Samaras, A. P. 291, 292
Sanford, K. 283
Santos, B. 2, 23–28
Sarafina (film) 271
Sarangapani, P. 124
Sass-Kortsak, A. 198
schooling: colonial 31; in England 32; formal mass 61; gender equality in 74; input–output model of 128; Romani children 326–327; in rural Punjab 300–317
Schratz, M. 275
science knowledge 89
second-order engagement 115, 117
Second World War 32
self-consciousness 176
self-deployment 232, 239
self-reflexive conversations 282–283
Sen, A. 27–28, 37n4
sensitive research 49, 119, 136–137
Seshradi, S. 271
setting: classroom 124; colonial 23; cross-cultural 12; cultural 197; home 179–180; Indigenous 34; non-Western 31; Northern 45–46; pedagogic 284–285, 288–289, 293, 296; and PhD research 173–174; postcolonial 13, 21, 23, 34–35, 37; Southern 45–46, 48
settler colonialism 323–324, 326, 332–333
Seventh Native American Generation (SNAG) magazine 324–325, 331–332
sex/gendering of the body 67–68

Shakespeare, T. 53
Sieber, J. E. 136
Sierra L. 48
Sikes, P. 175
Singal, N. 44, 46, 48, 50, 51–52, 119
situated ethics 34–35; *see also* ethics
Smith, A. 272
Smith, J. K. 282
Smith, P. 274
social biographies 173; capital 180, 246, 303, 306; change 260, **260**; contexts 257–258, **258**; data meanings 211; desirability 227, 238; exclusion 3, 301, 328; inequality 300, 312; gaze 118; justice 21–29; locations 244, 258, 304; mobility 174, 176, 180, 306, 309–310, 315–316; mores 136; norms 256, **257**; order 135, 306, 307, 310, 312, 315–316; power 119; reproduction 301; structural listening 303–305
Social Network Interviewing/Interviews (SNI/SNIs): challenges of 261–262; community attitudes and social norms 256, **257**; critique of current behaviour and action 258; developed 248–254, **249**; eight stages in **254**, *254*, 254–261, **256–261**, 256–261; as emancipatory Southern methodological innovation 243–263; emergent influences of 261–262; enlarging networks for change 260, **261**; evaluate social contexts 257–258, **258**; individual/collective agency and change 258–259, **259**; institutions/ideology and change 257–258, **258**; opportunities and challenges of 261–262; opportunities of 261–262; overview 243–245; problem-based declarative statement 255–256, **257**; research studies on 248–254; selecting people to interview 255, **256**; strategies for social/systemic change 260, **260**; struggles/strategies for student success 252–254; theoretical footprint and emergent influences of 245–248; theoretical footprint of 245–248; young fathers 248–251, **249**; youth sexual risk taking 251–252
sociocultural specificities 48
sociogenesis 320, 332–333
sociology of absences 25
sociology of emergences 25
socio-structural scape 301
Sontag, S. 273
South Africa: disabled sexualities in 52; educational research in 265–276; HIV incidence among youth in 251; sex education in 271; visual methodologies in 265–276; youth-related topics of importance and relevance in 248
South Asian feminists 72
Southern experiences: of education 5–7; of knowledge 5–7; of power 5–7
Southern gender theory 63
Southern theory 5, 8
Southern Theory: The Global Dynamics of Knowledge in Social Science (Connell) 60
'South inside the North' 320
Spandagou, I. 50
Sparkes, A. 282
specialised classrooms 45
Spence, J. 269
spiritual Black feminist *see* Black feminist
spiritual identity 88
spirituality 88, 163, 214; Christian 153; in lives of Black women 152, 156
spiritual poem 313–315; of fate and duty 312–315
Spivak, G. 3, 69, 71, 301
Srivastava, M. 51
standardisation of education 326–328
Stanley, B. 136
Stening, B. W. 141, 146
structural inequality 300–317
Stuart, J. 269, 272, 282
Stubbs, S. 54
subaltern 69, 106, 301, 316
sumak kawsay 27
Sundararaman, V. 125, 127, 128
Sustainable Development Goals (SDGs) 42–43
swadeshi 27
Swartz, S. 3, 9, 11, 48, 53

Symbolic capital 246, 252–253
symbolic violence 306, 309
systemic change 260, **260**

tameez (moral behaviour) 306
Tanzania: focus group discussions 222–224; focus grouping for opinions in 226–228; focus groups in majority world 225–226; making the method work to its strengths in 221–239; power dimension of positionality 231–233; researching across difference in majority world 224–225; strengths of the method 237–238; tweaking the method to decentre positionality 233–236; type of data generated 228–231
Tappan, M. B. 80, 81
teacher leadership 138–141
Teenage Tata (Swartz and Bhana) 249
temporality 67
temporary shared positionalities 224
tensions 192–198
texts: cinematic 265, 271, 273, 276; primary 266; production 266
Third World Woman 64–66
Tikly, L. 119
Tomlinson, S. 45
Torres Strait Islanders 210, 212
To Sir with Love (film) 271
Transana software 273
transcendence 117, 118
transcultural knowers 248
transgenderism 141–144
transgressive pedagogies 79
translator 116, 120–123
transnational: communication 107; history 98–99; imaginary 97; tendencies 105; turn 97
transparency 44, 141
triangulation 147, 245
Tribal Critical Race Theory 218
tribal sovereignty 214, 218
Tuck, E. 324
Tuhiwai Smith, L. 5, 11–12, 207, 209
Tygel, A. F. 218

Ubuntu 25, 27
Uganda 49
umma 27
uncomfortable realities 118
Under Western Eyes: Feminist Scholarship and Colonial Discourses (Mohanty) 64
UNESCO 30, 50; Global Monitoring Reports 63; 'Live and Let Live' 272
UNICEF 43
United Nations Convention on the Rights of Persons with Disabilities (UNCRPD) 43
United Nations Declaration on the Rights of Indigenous Peoples (UNDRIP) 212
United States Indigenous Data Sovereignty Network 213
universal ethic 23, 187, 200–201
Unterhalter, E. 61
urban education 325
urban Native American youth 323–326

Vasudevan, L. 282
video 270–271
Vietnam 52
Vissandjee, B. 226–228
visual: approaches 266–269; data 265–267, 270, 273–274; ethnographer 269–270; exhibition 266; images within popular culture 272; methodologies 266–276; research 266, 269, 271–276; senses 68
Visweswaran, K. 118
vocal partners 282
voice-based methods 300
voicelessness 281–283
vulnerability 10, 173, 246

Walker, R. 275
Wallerstein, I. 102
Walter, M. 208–210, 214
Wang, C. 267
Washington consensus 32
Washington Group (WG) on Disability Statistics 51
Weber, D. J. 324
Weber, S. 268, 272
Weinberg, G. 99
Werner, M. 98
Wertsch, J. V. 81
Western ethics 23
Western feminism 66–67
Western humanism 23, 25, 28

Western knowledge 12, 24, 322
Western Marxism 25
Western research ethics 29, 31, 176–178
Wheeler, S. 192
white perspectivity 323
Wiliam, D. 4
Willis, D. 268, 306
Wirz, S. 52
Wong, W. S. S. 136
The World and Africa (Du Bois) 85
World Bank 30, 33
World Congress of Comparative Education Societies 34
World Health Survey 44
World Report on Disability 43, 47, 53
world sense 83, 88

World-system approach 101–102
World War II 328

xenophobia 246, 289
xiao (filial piety) 135

Yang, W. K. 324
Yee, W. C. 179
Yesterday (film) 271
Young, R. 24

Zambia 52
Zhang, M. Y. 141, 146
Zimmermann, B. 98
zone of nonbeing 322
Zuberi, T. 210
Zulueta, L. 107